Trade Union Activists, East and West

Comparisons in multinational companies

GUGLIELMO MEARDI
University of Warwick

Gower

HD
6735.7
.m43
2000

© Guglielmo Meardi 2000

Published by
Gower Publishing Limited
Gower House
Croft Road
Aldershot
Hampshire GU11 3HR
England

Gower
131 Main Street
Burlington , VT 05401-5600
USA

Ashgate website: http://www.ashgate.com

British Library Cataloguing in Publication Data
Meardi, Guglielmo
      Trade union activists, east and west : comparisons in
      multinational companies
      1.Labor unions - Officials and employees - Europe, Western
      2.Labor unions - Officials and employees - Europe, Eastern
      3.Labor unions - Poland 4.Labor unions - Italy 5.Industrial
      relations - Political aspects - Europe, Western
      6.Industrial relations - Political aspects - Europe,
      Eastern
      I.Title
      331.8'8'094

Library of Congress Control Number: 00-134484

ISBN 0 7546 1426 3

Printed in Great Britain by
Antony Rowe Ltd, Chippenham, wiltshire.

Contents

List of Figures and Tables

Figures

Tables

Acknowledgements

I cannot start the acknowledgements with anyone but the co-authors of this book: the many union officers, activists, members, as well as ordinary workers who helped me and took part in formal and informal conversations. While having much more important business of their own, they gave me lots of their time and very often their contributions impressed me with their high sociological quality. Not only this, they often received me with friendship and real hospitality. Whether drinking an *espresso* or a *Żywiec*, whether savouring a *golonka po bawarsku* in Silesia or some *spaghetti alla carbonara* in Tuscany, the moments of informal socialisation with the living body of the unions have remained the best experiences of the research project.

The industrial workers were not, however, the only people I exploited. This book originates in my doctoral dissertation, and I am indebted for their invaluable help to my three instructors: Bianca Beccalli, Michel Wieviorka and Colin Crouch who at different stages and with different styles looked after me. They all gave their careful and precious criticism without reservation.

I worked on this book across four countries, five high schools and a dozen plants. I have not maintained a database of the people who helped me but I would like to acknowledge at least Olivier Cousin, Richard Hyman, David Ost, Marta Petrusewicz, Marino Regini, Vittorio Rieser, Philippe Schmitter and Alain Touraine. Several people have struggled with my macaronic English in order to make it readable: Nicki Hargreaves, Nicky Owtram, Conor Cradden and Gerard Sharpling are the heroes.

The most decisive help was received, however, in Poland. Marcin Frybes treated me as a Pole, a honour I did not expect to ever receive. Grażyna Ulicka and Mirosława Grabowska took care of me as *opiekunki* ('protectors') during my *stages* at the University of Warsaw in 1996 and 1998. Wiesława Kozek and Jolanta Kulpińska kindly invited me to the Congress of the Polish Sociological Association in 1997, as well as to various seminars. I also received useful suggestions from Juliusz Gardawski, Leszek Gilejko, Kazimierz Kloc, Ireneusz Krzemiński, Paweł Kuczyński, Piotr Marciniak and Włodek Pańków.

List of Abbreviations

AFP	Piombino Steelworks
AWS	Solidarity Electoral Action
CFDT	French Democratic Labour Confederation
CGIL	General Italian Confederation of Labour
CGT	General Labour Confederation
CISAL	Italian Confederation of Autonomous Workers' Unions
CISL	Italian Confederation of Worker Unions
CISNAL	Italian Confederation of National Labour Unions (linked to the MSI)
Cobas	Basis Committees
CRZZ	Central Trade Union Council (official unions until 1981)
DS	Left Democrats (mutation of the PDS in 1998)
EMF	European Metalworkers' Federation
ETUC	European Trade Union Confederation
EWC	European Work Council
FAT	Food and Tobacco Federation (associated to the CISL)
FIM	Italian Federation of Metalworkers (associated to the CISL)
FIOM	Federation of Manual and Clerical Metalworkers (associated to the CGIL)
FLAI	Agroindustry Federation (associated to the CGIL)
FLM	Metalworkers' Federation (unitary federation of FIOM, FIM, UILM from 1972 to 1984)
FSM	Low-powered Car Factory
FSO	Warsaw Car Factory
KPN	Confederation of Independent Poland (nationalist party)
KPP	Confederation of the Polish Employers
MNC	Multinational company
MSI	Italian Social Movement (neo-fascist party)
NSZZ	Independent Autonomous Trade Union
OPZZ	All-Polish Coalition of Trade Unions (official unions since 1982)

PCI	Italian Communist Party
PDS	Democratic Party of the Left (heir of the PCI)
PZPR	Polish United Worker Party (Communist)
RLS	Workers' Representatives for Safety
ROP	Movement for the Reconstruction of Poland
RSU	United Trade Union Representatives
Sida	Automotive Union (Fiat company union)
Sin-Cobas	Inter-Industry Trade Union of the Rank and File Committees
SLAI	Inter-Industry Trade Union of Self-organised Workers
SLD	Alliance of the Democratic Left (mutation of the PZPR)
UGL	General Labour Union (mutation of the CISNAL)
UIL	Italian Labour Union
UILM	Italian Union of Metalworkers (associated to the UIL)
UP	Labour Union
UW	Freedom Union

Introduction

Some months after the fall of communism, I had one of my first (at that time still accidental and with the help of a language mediator) conversations with Polish workers. At a certain point one of my interlocutors incidentally said: 'You are in a different situation, you're a capitalist'. What I knew about class consciousness from Marxist readings and sociology textbooks, which I already knew to be barely adequate for the analysis of the Italian situation, was challenged by the involuntary offensiveness of an incidental sentence.

When looking at Polish workers (and later, at Czechs, Slovaks, East Germans, Hungarians, Albanians and Yugoslavs) I was continually surprised by a number of similarities, especially in practical situations, with their Western counterparts, and yet at the same time by their difference from them. This was most striking in the case of the trade unions, traditionally the 'spokespersons' (although not necessarily representative) of the working class. I started to wonder whether union activists from the East and the West managed to communicate. From this curiosity stemmed the research project on which this book is based.

A few years after 1989 I found where I could investigate empirically the nature of the differences between the Eastern and Western trade unions. Two important and authoritative Italian employers (Fiat Auto and Gruppo Lucchini) had taken over big Polish factories and started production there similar to that of their Italian plants. If the differences in trade union consciousness were due to the specificity of the local work settings, once the workplaces were made comparable by multinational capital, these differences would gradually disappear. If, instead, differences endured, this would mean that trade union consciousness does not (or no longer) directly depend on the work situation; the *meaning* the actors gave to the situation would turn out to be more important. This was, in brief, the question with which the research began. Gradually, this research question was further elaborated, both methodologically and theoretically. Starting with the French Danone, further cases were considered, though less deeply, to avoid the bias the Italian ownership. Ultimately, the analysis has been organised around three main, interrelated issues.

The first of these (chapter 3) is a paradoxical parallelism between Italy and Poland in the heritage of the past. Activists' histories indicate that in both countries the formerly clear image of unity of the 'working class', rooted in the work experience, has disintegrated in a similar way. As a consequence, the paradoxical 'constant' between Italy and Poland is precisely the *absence* of constants, the disintegration of models. Poles and Italians are similar not in what they are, but in what they distinguish themselves from: notably, the past experience of class struggle, which at the shopfloor was similar under state socialism and Western capitalism. This holds political significance: the search for class politics in Eastern Europe is misplaced, neglecting that the working class there is not being *constructed* but rather *dismantled*.

The second issue (chapter 4) refers to the differences between Eastern and Western unions. While European integration proceeds, new differences emerge. The East-West distinction acquires new meanings, which sometimes even remind an Italian observer of the divide between Northern and Southern Italy. I shall argue that, against the background of class disintegration, the residual differences between Italy and Poland are currently socially constructed. This is due on the one hand to the mediated nature of global and international experiences, which makes workers into potential competitors, and leaves space to reciprocal stereotypes of rich egoist Westerners and inept, dishonest competitor Easterners. On the other hand, the unique experience of 'transition' the Eastern Europeans have lived through is crucial. In order to account for this experience, the teleological term 'transition' is inadequate, and I shall suggest (following Berger and Luckmann) the substitute 'alternation'. As a testable consequence of this unique experience, the popular view of Eastern European trade unions as conservative obstacles to reform and as inertial legacies of the past is mistaken. Just the opposite, Polish unionists, if compared with their real Western counterparts, are characterised by a high acceptance of change and a modernist, innovative standpoint. The dialogue between Eastern and Western trade unions is, then, made difficult by the different ways activists experience social change: under the form of slow crisis in the West, which induces reactions of resistance; under the form of global alternation in the East, which causes an overvaluation of any radical change. This issue also has political implications: the distinction between East and West, instead of disappearing with political integration, might take on a new meaning. It is not surprising, then, that in the multinational companies analysed, cross-national union cooperation is, to use a euphemism, embryonic.

The third issue (chapter 5) is raised by the consequences of the previous, namely working class fragmentation and the difference between East and West: how to deal with diversity? The international difference among workers in a globalised economy is evidence of a more general rising importance of diversity for the trade unions. Concretely, the inquiry across different plants and unions suggests that trade union activists perceive international differences (like that between Italians and Poles) and other kinds of difference emerging *within* the national working classes (gender, age, ethnicity, employment status...) in similar ways. Both *external* and *internal* forms of differentiation actually raise the same problems of redefining identity and solidarity beyond traditional working-class egalitarianism. The consequences for the trade unions' agenda should be manifold.

This book, then, concerns the transformation of *class consciousness*. The term is old-fashioned, but the issue is remarkable nevertheless. The problem of consciousness was raised initially at the end of the 1950s by many outstanding sociologists as diverse as Dahrendorf, Lipset, Lockwood and Touraine, because sociology still lacked a *link* between structure and action. The issue is not yet closed. To analyse consciousness is not to fall into idealism, and less so into descriptive opinion polls. Schematically, consciousness is something less than ideology, something more than orientations, and something intrinsically linked to action.

Consciousness has been analysed and explained with reference to subjective experience, as a main determinant of the definition of identities and interests. In the current period of transformation, the stress on experience is all the more important: more so than in the past, the boundaries of experience today do not correspond with the boundaries of interests. Experience is the arena of social construction. This piece of research will attempt to show that most differences between trade union activists in the West and in the East are not inherited from the past but are socially constructed. In other words, instead of saying – as do most analysts – that Eastern trade unions are *not yet* like their Western counterparts, we would rather argue that they are *no longer* like that.

Although references are repeatedly made to other Western and Eastern countries, the present inquiry has concentrated on Italy and Poland. The book is about East and West, but not in the sense that it accounts for the whole of the two sides of Europe, but rather, in the sense that it investigates, in a comparative perspective, the *meaning* of the concepts of East and West. This explains why the discussion might be relevant beyond the Italian and Polish borders, and why the term 'Eastern', instead of the more pertinent 'Central-Eastern', is adopted.

The two countries were chosen primarily because it was there that comparable work settings were found. The peculiarity of Italy and Poland also lies, however, in their distinctive comparability. Not only do they share features like religion and level of industrialisation, but more importantly, they have represented, on the two sides of Europe, the same model of unionism: political, competitive and class-based. In other words, the model of *social movement unionism*. This analogy makes the two terms more comparable. Italy is not typical as a capitalist country, and Poland even less so as a communist country. However, if the main hypothesis is that of a basic difference between East and West which lies beyond tradition, these are logically the best cases for a test. In other words, if the union activists analysed here, in spite of the similarity in work situations and in the model of unionism, display significant differences, we can expect even greater differences between the unions in the other countries of Eastern and Western Europe.

A final remark should be made on the comparative perspective. I am Italian, and a Westerner who had never been to the East before the summer of 1989. The risk of a national and cultural bias has been a constant concern all through the research process. I tried to familiarise myself as much as possible with the new reality I was studying. I spent in Poland, altogether, thirty months, repeatedly visited the other Central-Eastern European countries, and went to Albania and former Yugoslavia as an international electoral observer. I also made an effort, in the interaction with the field, to reduce or disguise my Italian identification. The long stays abroad and the connections with non-Italian institutions were very helpful. Sometimes it worked. When I now call my former collaborators Italian union officers for some feedback and updating, they welcome me as 'the Pole'. And in Poland, I occasionally even managed to be treated as a Pole (although in a few occasions with unwanted consequences: after the first aberrant mistake of grammar or pronunciation I was suddenly looked upon as a mentally sick person or, even worse, as a Russian.)

The three main points outlined above will be discussed through an in-depth analysis of the findings, in the 3rd, 4th, and 5th chapters respectively. Before arriving at the empirical study, however, it will be necessary to elaborate the research hypotheses and the theoretical framework (chapter 1), as well as to introduce the field and the methodology (chapter 2). However, the Reader will not find in this book any introductory chapters on Polish and Italian industrial relations. As well as being redundant, this would not have been in keeping with the empirical approach 'from below' adopted here for the understanding of unionism. Therefore, I commend to the Reader instead the already available reference works in the local languages (e.g. Kozek, 1997; Cella and Treu, 1998), or to the reports in English or French (e.g. Florek and Seweryński, 1996; Gąciarz and Pańków, 1997b; Regalia and Regini, 1998).

1 Understanding Trade Union Activists

Rationale of a Research Perspective

This study focuses on the rank-and-file activists of the trade unions of two different countries, Italy and Poland, considered as the heirs of the labour movement. It follows the tradition of interpretative sociology, which is old, authoritative, and even noble if one calls it *verstehende Soziologie*. It uses a method – comparison – which a century and a half ago Auguste Comte considered as *the* method of sociology.

Labour movement, interpretative sociology, comparison... so many pages have been written on these words that any introduction ought to be redundant. However, nowadays, the approach, the method, and the topic of this study require, probably more than ever before, a justification. I shall therefore start with a step-by-step rationale of this research perspective: an interpretative (or understanding) comparison of trade union activists. Subsequently, I shall elaborate the main research questions around which the book is organised and explain in what the adopted approach differs from the available interpretations of post-communist industrial relations. Finally, I shall explain in a historical digression why the experience of Solidarity in Poland is comparable to that of Western trade unions.

Why Understand?

Trade unions, as interest organisations, are usually analysed from economic, institutional, and organisational standpoints. Quantitative studies, investigations of collective bargaining or game-theory analyses may appear more suitable than a qualitative, interpretative approach.

However, trade union action is not only a matter of interests, since interests have, firstly, to be defined, recognised and expressed. To use Przeworski's words (1985, p. 70), class struggle 'is a struggle *about* class before it is a struggle *among* classes'. Offe, Touraine, Melucci, Pizzorno, Tarrow, Cohen, Habermas (and the list might be longer) have all, though differently, stressed the importance of identity for collective action. This was valid at the time of the 'making' of the working class studied by

Edward Thompson and is still valid now. The fact that the 'working class' is becoming, in multinational companies (MNCs), really international, does not automatically imply the expression of international interests. Subjectively, it does not imply a similar, cross-national consciousness. Moreover, historically, the trade unions have defended different sorts of interests: in terms of class, category, 'craft', nationality, gender or race. In this regard important differences among countries have emerged and endure. The complex nature of interests is the first, general rationale for a comprehensive study of the attitudes of trade union activists.

The particular aim of this piece of research is to show the complexity of the interpretative resources (images, identities, representations) used by activists in the construction of their identity and to make sense of their situation. These resources have come, traditionally, from two sets of experiences: work experience and societal experience (sometimes mediated by subculture). Many sociologists have tried to classify models of workers' consciousness on these bases: either the kind of work done or the kind of society lived in.

Nowadays, it seems to be increasingly difficult to classify orientations according to only one set of factors. The experience of workers is one of complexity and change, no longer of unity and clear conflicts; this complexity is constantly contrasted with a memory of a clearer past. By stating this, I do not wish to imply that social reality has objectively become more complex: proving this statement would go well beyond the possibilities of such a modest piece of research.

Memory is always, and necessarily, selective. Social actors are usually prone, if not to the 'reactionary cult of the past' denounced by Marx, then at least to nostalgia. However, between working class consciousness as described by classical sociology and current trade union consciousness there seems to be a qualitative gap. The working class was at the centre of unionism; now, it is somewhere on its fringe. It is impossible to measure change precisely, especially in a qualitative study. What can be observed, however, is the current use of the past as an interpretative resource. This is relevant to the opinions of activists, either as a feeling of nostalgia or as generational fracture or as a perception of decadence or the need for change. Trade union activists construct a past on the idea of unity, and a present on the idea of difference. This feeling of disintegration makes the differences among workers *politically* more important, which contrasts with an economy which is increasingly integrated and globalised. The emergence of different identities in the East and in the West is a notable case where the way the subjective meaning of the past does matter.

The idea of unity gave rise to high levels of solidarity. Whether the acceptance of diversity will also do this is still unknown. Certainly there are currently trends among industrial workers (for instance the vote for extreme-right parties) that suggest a negative answer. However, it has still to be tested whether among rank-and-file members a reconstruction of identity, via the combination of old resources with new issues is taking place.

A higher level of awareness of the logic underlying trade union action can contribute to the understanding of which interests will be represented in which forms.

Why a Comparison?

The choice of an Italy-Poland comparison does not justify itself automatically, even if one is interested in East-West comparative studies. The main rationale for such a comparison is the availability of similar work situations, in the same multinational companies, against the background of two different combative labour movements. These circumstances allow an evaluation of the respective roles of the current work situation and of past identity in the construction of trade union consciousness. Indirectly, such a comparison will contribute to the understanding of the communist past (which for obvious reasons has remained largely unexplored), and of its distinctive legacy in a Europe on the road to unification.

In other words, this choice of cases aims to control one set of experiences (the work setting) and to contrast as much as possible another, societal experiences, including ideological traditions. Italian and Polish union traditions can be opposed: a democratic trade union movement in a communist country contrasted with a predominantly communist trade union movement in a democratic country. At the same time, Italy was during the investigation the European country with the highest level of investment in Poland. Notably, there are at least two cases (Fiat and Lucchini) of large industrial companies having comparable factories in both countries. These are the best places to observe the difference between East and West.

Moreover, there is a general reason for conducting comparative studies in multinational companies. When globalisation becomes an economically relevant phenomenon, sociology should investigate how actors make sense of it. The attitudes towards each other of unions operating in the same companies in different countries could take the form of a stereotyping of the other or, alternatively, that of communication and exchange. A study of only the *interests* at stake would not be able to explain which one of these directions is more plausible.

Why Activists?

The word 'activist', after that of 'militant', is also starting to be seen as archaic, and to have negative connotations. The institutionalisation and, often, bureaucratisation of trade unions has rendered activists superfluous to a large extent. In France, where the crisis of trade unions is particularly deep, Rosanvallon (1988) has suggested the scenario of trade unions not only without militants, but even without members.

However, the study of a country with high union bureaucratisation (Italy)[1] and a country with unions which are relatively weak in private workplaces (Poland) shows that, in spite of all, activists still exist. In fact, workplace unions could not survive without having a more complex relationship with the workforce than simply representation. The construction of union policies cannot be reduced to the representative/represented dialectic: this is why the reality of the trade unions never really conformed to Olson's theory of collective action. Workers' engagement is continuously constructed in the everyday practices of the workshops. It is not the outcome of individual, isolated choices. Moreover, rank-and-file workers maintain an autonomous role; they do not simply 'join' a given, pre-existing association. Without paying attention to the pressures from below it would be difficult to explain the change in political orientations of Solidarity in 1992 in Poland (Kloc, 1993) and the wave of spontaneous strikes in autumn 1994 in Italy. More recently, on the 13th April 1999, the national leadership of FIOM-FIM-UILM was sensationally forced to change its proposal during a national assembly with 5,000 *delegati* in Bologna, because of the rebellion of the rank and file. In Poland, pressures from the rank and file have often challenged the position of the national leader Krzaklewski, with important political consequences. The role of the rank and file seems today no less important than in the 1970s or 1980s. Furthermore, the same job of shop-steward generally in both countries, though not always, implies an availability and a personal engagement which cannot be ascribed to a 'bureaucratic' pattern.

That dictionaries do not yet offer a better substitute for the word 'activist' cannot justify a lack of attention to them. We should therefore speak of the 'transformation' rather than the 'end' of activism. To some extent, union commitment is becoming more 'voluntary' than in the past, because it is no longer due to subculture pressure. Thus it comes closer to other kinds of 'voluntary work'.

Following this perspective, the investigation carried out on the Italian and Polish union activists aimed to test three working hypotheses:

- that in both Italy and Poland the trade unions are experiencing the same crisis involving disintegration of a previously lively working class consciousness;
- that starting from the fall of communism new differences between East and West have been constructed at work and in the trade unions;
- that nowadays every union can be characterised by the way it copes with the central dilemma of how to deal with differences within the workforce.

These three hypotheses open very broad research questions. They will be defined and explained in detail in the next section.

Three Arguments on Trade Union Consciousness

Unity in the Disintegration of Working Class Consciousness

The search for a unitary working class consciousness among trade union activists from different countries is nowadays bound to be in vain. This point was made sufficiently evident by the exploratory phase of research carried out in Polish and Italian Fiat plants (Meardi, 1996). On that occasion, I wanted to check whether, with the decline of ideologies, *in similar working situations, workers' consciousness displayed any 'principle of unity' despite deep historical and cultural differences.* The findings were clear-cut: very deep differences prevailed between the activists of the Italian left-wing FIOM-CGIL and the Polish activists of Solidarity, and both sides were unable to concentrate on work conflict as such.

The immediate sociological problem, then, is to account for such a differentiation, i.e. to define its forms. The hypothesis I suggest is that unity is not realised because the experience of work has largely lost its weight as a factor contributing to the collective identity of industrial workers. In other words, the hypothesis is that a general disintegration is taking place on both sides of Europe; but behind this disintegration there is, paradoxically, a unity in the historical process involving the loss of the centrality of industrial work, in Italy as well as in Poland. This historical process allows differences (and in particular cross-national ones) to become more visible than in the past, when trade union militancy forged the 'meaning' of personal life. The same phenomenon has been noticed in the case of the French CFDT by Tixier (1992): the disappearance of the meta-representations which articulated work experience and class experience allows internal differences to appear.

A definition of the 'experience of work' is imperative here. I do not mean by this term either 'professional experience' or 'employment experience': in these terms, work nowadays is increasing in importance rather than decreasing. I mean, by contrast, the set of relations of production. That is, the relations on the one hand between worker and product, on the other, between the worker and the organiser of his/her work.

We can contrast today's trade unions with the sociological and historical literature on work, class consciousness and unionism in the classic period of industrial society. The chronological definition of this classical period depends on the country and is in any case historically controversial. Generally, it may be seen as coincident with the Fordist period, but this is not a necessary coincidence (it does not occur, evidently, in communist states). In Italy I shall consider in particular the period since the *miracolo economico* until the turmoil of the 1970s. In Poland, the period is almost the same: from the end of Stalinism in 1953 (under totalitarianism there are not the conditions for a labour movement) until the crisis of the 1980s. The periods which I define on the basis of social and political history are basically consistent with the periods of predominance of employment in the industrial sector. According to the International Labour Organisation Statistical Yearbooks, in Italy industrial employment was predominant from 1960 through 1965, and reached its absolute peak of 39,7% in 1971 (in the middle of the long *autunno caldo*). In Poland, it was predominant from 1974 through 1991, with the absolute peak of 38,9% in 1980 (Solidarity upsurge). In both countries industrialisation peaked almost at the same level and at a distance of few years, and coincided with the swan-song of the labour movement. Parallelism in the history of industrialisation is one rationale for an Italy-Poland comparison.

I shall argue here that in industrial society, work relations were a significant element in the construction of identities. Therefore, workers of different countries, despite major differences in national systems and ideological orientations, displayed a comparable level of workers' consciousness. This does not mean that union and worker cultures were equivalent in all factories of the world: workers never really answered to the 1848 appeal for unity by Marx and Engels. Yet insofar as the most structural features of work relations were common, and the awareness of belonging to an industrial society was widespread, there was a core of common *working class consciousness*. I identify the three distinguishing features of that consciousness as:

- a link of collective solidarity;
- the awareness of a conflict between workers and organisers;
- a positive trust in industrial progress.

These three features may be respectively associated with the three broader components Identity, Opposition and Totality of Touraine's analysis of workers' consciousness (Touraine, 1966). More important, all these elements are actually easily identifiable in the oral data we have from the unions in the past. So spoke, for instance, in a long interview Cesare Cosi, militant of the FIOM in the Fiat Mirafiori factory, still in 1981.

> 'I have to say that I don't dislike my job. This also because I reflect on my job, I think how could it be modified, I discuss with the others on what can be changed. What we don't accept is that we must work for the boss. Everybody here in the factory has the feeling that a minority benefits from all the advantages of our efforts. We obviously hope in an autonomous work, in self-management, without a boss, this is the hope of everybody. Not because of money – the point is not that one – rather because we want to decide about ourselves and our future'. (Tatò, 1981, p. 129)

In this short extract all three elements are clear: work identity, opposition to the boss, and a hope in progress. This statement, in 1981, might have been undersigned by any Solidarity member.

A common consciousness fostered a common identity, based on the image of the working class. In this way, what is usually seen as a structural and objective category (the working class) became relevant for workers as a cultural and subjective configuration. In the Italian case (but not only there), it has been noticed that the mass workers became the key point of reference for the union movement in a period when they constituted only a very marginal part of the working class (less than 2%). This point underlines how the interpretative and cultural resources of the unions may turn out to be as important as the structural features of work relations (Accornero, 1992, p. 76).

Working class consciousness must be analytically distinguished from a broader, political class consciousness and from a narrower worker consciousness. The former concentrates on economic development (Totality, in Touraine's jargon) and largely depended upon national features.[2] The latter, worker consciousness, has only a very vague awareness of conflict (Opposition), and is closed to popular culture. This has often been defined as 'proletarian consciousness' or 'proletarian traditionalism' (Lockwood, 1966).

Of course, not every worker displayed the levels of awareness, solidarity or trust implied by the definition of working class consciousness. However, as far as trade union members are concerned, this consciousness was a dominant feature and the rare trade unions that did not display it could hardly be considered part of the union movement. It is here that the common element of experiences – in other respects so different – had to be searched for. We are speaking of a deeper (at the same time lower and higher) level than that of the concrete forms of union action. This consciousness was also present in situations where unions were forbidden, in other forms of conflict (e.g. slow-downs). At the same time, it was an immanent element of representations of society and of politics. At this deeper level, as it will be discussed, among Eastern and Western workers there was a similar perception of Identity, Opposition and Totality.

Now, careers, qualifications, and contracts are less and less standardised, making work identities more individual and less collective (Dubar, 1992). The sociological problem becomes the interpretation of this change. Many authors have analysed the process of individualisation at work. Some interpretations (e.g. Brock, 1994; Valckenburg, 1996; Zoll, 1992; 1996) differ from previous analyses which assume that individualisation is necessarily negative for collective action (e.g. Offe, 1985): it is suggested that the individual might become a resource, at least if a new 'socio-cultural model' (Zoll, 1992) develops. Some analysts go so far as to question the meaning of the private/public distinction as regards social commitment (Ion and Peroni, 1997).

In this context my study asserts the 'disintegration', that is even more than the 'fragmentation', of the experience of work as *a source of collective identity*, and not necessarily the overall decline of work as an important sphere in people's lives. By contrast, a number of new issues linked to work but no longer to the working class (part-time, individual realisation, professional history, equality, discrimination) have become more and more important.[3]

For a long period, the Left hoped that work would foster social integration into the working class. A manifestation of this (well-grounded but too categorical) belief was the quick execution of 'proletarianisation' policies by newly established communist regimes. Nowadays, the process of differentiation and segmentation within the working class and society generally calls for a reformulation of trade union consciousness beyond the role of work. Some unions, like the Italian UIL, have decided to define themselves as *'citizens'* unions'. Others, like Solidarity in Poland, emphasise *human* rights more than *workers'* rights.

The working hypothesis will be that *working class consciousness*, as opposed to just any kind of worker consciousness, has been decomposed. However, ideological expressions can strengthen even after the decline of the workers' movement. Concretely, this means that not only is the effect of the experience of work different in different countries, but also that it is increasingly difficult to isolate this effect in the cultural orientations of workers and union activists. If this hypothesis is true, we should expect, among trade union activists working in similar conditions, a deep variety of discourses on work, and a lack of direct links between the experience of work and union experience.

Workers and trade union activists in major industries are the best field to test the hypothesis of a transformation and disintegration of consciousness. They do not represent the whole of the productive world, but they are the *hard core* of the classic industrial working class. If change is detected *even* among them, the hypothesis of a general change will be proved valid *a fortiori*.

What is the point of making an Italy-Poland comparison on this problem? The usefulness of such a comparison is twofold. On the one hand, it shows that, since disintegration occurs in two such different countries, it is probably misleading to look for the causes of trade unions' difficulties primarily at the national level. This is not a particularly novel approach. For almost twenty years many scholars have been underlining the global character of the trade union crisis (for instance, on the basis of the general drop in unionisation rates during the 1980s). It is not that surprising, therefore, that with the advent of freedom unions in post-communist countries have not found clear and strong patterns to follow.

There is a second, more profound reason, however. An interpretative analysis could show what in different countries is common to the process of disintegration. In this case, neither the points of departure (Polish and Italian trade unions have very different historical patterns and ideological traditions) or the points of arrival (the current developments are largely path-dependent) are common. Instead what is common is the process of disintegration of what has been defined as working class consciousness.

There are, in the discourses of workers committed to the unions, repeated suggestions of the idea of decline, of a break with a previous model. In both Poland and Italy, radical as well as moderate activists display in their discourses a certain unease: a loss of reference point and a fear of fragmentation. If observed from a historical perspective, and if linked to the definition of working class consciousness presented above, this suggests the following hypothesis: *disintegration finds its unity in the breakdown of the image of the working class and the worker movement.* If elements of 'disintegration' were significantly diffused, and sufficiently time-referred (that is, implicitly or explicitly contrasting the present experience with the idea of the past), the hypothesis would be supported. This would mean that current reality is to some extent perceived using similar interpretative resources, inherited from the same pattern of working class consciousness. The historical process would therefore be, at least subjectively, comparable in Italy and Poland.

This hypothesis of a parallel disintegration has a theoretical and practical importance. It explains why 'differences' are today seen by the unions as challenging and menacing, and why dealing with them requires a switch in general orientation, starting with a reformulation of the idea of solidarity (which will be discussed with regard to the third hypothesis).

'Unity in disintegration' denotes that the increasing visibility of national differences does not necessarily stem from an *absolute* increase in cross-national heterogeneity but from a *relative* one. Patterns of action differ primarily because former models no longer work. This is relevant in two separate respects:

1) the contrast with the background of globalisation: the globalisation of capital is quicker than that of labour; subsequently, international differences among unions have not become *deeper*, they have become *concretely important*;

2) the sharp weakening of the experience of work as a determinant of consciousness increases the relative influence of societal differences, even if these have not become stronger or have actually been reduced.

At the same time, individual differences become relevant. Of course, workers were only ever all alike in the iconography of socialist realism. However, individual differences were not relevant for trade union identities, since these were founded on similarity. As union leaders now sometimes acknowledge, for the unions individuality was not a resource but a hindrance.

A New East-West Divide

This piece of research concentrates on a particular type of cross-national difference, that is, the East-West divide. In Italy and Poland unionism in the past embodied the workers' movement in a very ambitious way, although for a shorter period than in other countries. The reference to what I defined as 'working class consciousness' was one of the very few points which these two cases had in common. For the rest, economic systems, and subsequently industrial relations and models of unionism, were deeply different.

After 1989, the thesis of a quick transition from the communist model (portrayed as unitary and coherent) to the 'market and democracy' model (also portrayed as unitary and coherent) prevailed in the analysis of the changes in Eastern European societies. In the case of trade unions, this turned into the hypothesis of a 'convergence through the market'. This hypothesis was explicitly formulated, in a cautious and rigorous way, by Schienstock and Traxler (1993), but is implicit in most analyses.

My previous hypothesis of a parallel disintegration makes things more complicated. As a matter of fact, the current state of evolution confirms that convergence is far from automatic and linear. Something like an invisible iron curtain has endured in many aspects. Social dumping practices justify the fears of a *'Peripherisierung'* of Central and Eastern Europe (Dauderstädt and Meyer-Stamer, 1995). The first nine Eastern European trade unions had to wait six years before being accepted into the European Trade Union Confederation in December 1995, and East-West co-operation is anything but easy. Even in the only case of perfect institutional convergence (German reunification), deep differences remain between Western and Eastern trade unions (Lattard, 1995; Hyman, 1996a), although convergence is taking place with respect to the role of works councils (Frege, 1998).[4] In the case of the steel sector, it has been stated that from Western trade unions 'solidarity with Eastern European steel workers has been notable for its absence' (Bacon and Blyton, 1996, p. 778). In the motor industry, moreover, the historic 'Eurostrike' at Renault in 1997 was limited in a way which has rarely been noticed: while the strike was successful in Belgium, France and Spain, there was no strike at all in the Slovenian plants. In Slovenia, there is no right to strike in solidarity (which is itself an interesting distinguishing mark of that system), but even had there been such a right it is very doubtful that Slovenian workers would have supported their Belgian colleges.

The problem is that beside the disintegration of class consciousness, national models are also likely to lose their coherence. If the findings confirm this hypothesis, this will reveal a first shortcoming of transition theory, making it more difficult to speak of two unionisms in the way that Gilles Martinet (1979) spoke of *sept syndicalismes* almost twenty years ago. Therefore, the process of change should not be interpreted as a shift from one model to another.

The main hypothesis to be tested is that the East-West cleavage remains significant but has changed its meaning. The recent experience of labour movements, in fact, is different. The breakdown of the existing model of unionism was experienced in Poland in a much more abrupt way than in Italy. Self-identity and trust that there was a 'stake' in the action (industrial development) suffered a more serious injury. Maybe even more important, deep bewilderment about the identity of the 'opponent' (no longer the state, not yet the private employers) followed.

The specificity of this evolution stems from a number of different factors. The immediate reason has to be sought in the totalitarian vocation[5] of Eastern European societies. As well as denying any autonomy to the sphere of industrial relations under communist rule, this vocation still binds the concerns of trade unions more tightly to the general societal experience. Secondly, the current pattern of economic development in post-communist countries implies a more abrupt reduction of the role of industrial workers and is associated with an international division of labour in which Eastern Europe has become a low-wage area.

Until the 1980s the industrial working class in Poland had a high-level self-consciousness, in the factory as well as in society (Gardawski, 1996). Polish-American comparative surveys curried out in 1978 revealed a higher self-consciousness among the Polish working class than their counterparts in the United States (Kohn and Słomczyński, 1988). This dramatically changed after 1989. The Italian working class has also ceased to occupy a central position, yet its decline as an economic and political actor was less sudden. In Poland, the crisis was sudden, deep and many-sided (Kulpińska, 1995). Some of its consequences have been noted. From the economic point of view, the degradation of workers' living conditions has been ascribed the fall of productivity and of consumption, the delays in restructuring, and the growth of the informal economy (Amsden, Kochanowicz and Taylor, 1994; Vaughan-Whitehead, 1998). From the political point of view, industrial workers have started to be seen as a potential for non-democratic forces (Ost, 1994). Yet apart from such comments on the 'consequences' of this crisis, little effort has been made to understand its real dimension and nature.

The investigation shows that where the resources of the Eastern European working class, and particularly of trade unions, are not 'reconverted' or evaluated as positive, a 'neo-proletarian' consciousness emerges. This is due not only to a fall in standards of living, which at least in Poland have actually improved in the second half of the 1990s. It may be better explained by the distinctively brusque disintegration of all the elements of working class consciousness.

The idea of a new divide takes into account not only the changes occurring in the East, but also the smaller-scale transformations taking place in the West. It is linked to the general assumption that in a globalized world, space becomes an interpretative resource more effective than in the past when international relations were less relevant. In this framework, the attitudes towards each other Italian and Polish workers employed by the same companies becomes an interesting subject of research: do they follow a stereotyping pattern? Are they characterised by feelings of similarity, or rather of opposition?

One purpose of this research is to show how deep differences can emerge among interests groups dealing with similar situations. Multinational companies seem to be the best field to investigate it. They should be the main actors of the 'transition', transferring Western practices into the East. In fact, there is already strong evidence that they also 'construct' new differences (Jürgens, 1995; Makó and Simonyi, 1995; Makó and Novoszáth, 1996; Tóth, 1996a; Tóth, 1996b; Kloc, 1997; Meardi, 1998). These findings suggest that one ought to be more attentive to the interactions among social actors and seek other, less deterministic ways of understanding their action.

The Centrality of Differentiation for the Trade Union Agenda

The crisis of the work-based pattern should push trade unions to other levels of action (primarily the political one) and to a more encompassing solidarity. This conclusion is all the stronger for having reached from different theoretical standpoints (e.g. Crouch, 1982; Touraine, Dubet and Wieviorka, 1987). However, contemporary reality shows that this shift is far from automatic. A more 'encompassing' solidarity means dealing with two kinds of differences: within the working class and among national working classes. Trans-national differences become an interesting field for evaluating trade unions' attitudes.

The concern that unions develop strategies on international problems like European construction and the international division of labour is shared by many union leaders (e.g. Anderson and Trentin, 1996 or Stainkühler, 1989) as well as by many industrial relations scholars. It is enough to look at the number of titles containing words such as 'globalisation', 'Europeanisation', or 'cross-borders'. Normative statements such as the following have become common:

> If they fail to coordinate their policy, centralise decision-making and merge together to form collective transnational European organisations, Europe's trade unions will be condemned to pursue a policy of adaptation and retreat while competing against one another for scarce resources of jobs. (Visser, 1995, p. 41)

Employee representatives must develop a unified, cross-border strategy towards corporate centres whose operations transcend national boundaries and sites. (Lecher, 1994, p. 260)

Yet union strategy is not merely the object of theoretical deliberations. As a particular form of collective action, unionism cannot elude the identity question. That is, even if theorists or leaders achieved a theoretical solution for union dilemmas, the problem of understanding and interpretation on the ground would remain. And in the case of a gap between the rank and file and their leaders, the 'progressive' orientations of the latter could turn out to be a factor of internal weakness and mistrust rather than a new resource. If it is not subjectively understandable, the imposition of solidarity from above may easily backfire.

Working class solidarity was based not only on shared interests, but also on a common experience, and how it was mainly a group solidarity. In the current situation, a search for new solidarities must take into consideration changes in experience and consciousness.

The hypothesis put forward here is that of the *centrality*, and therefore *unity*, of the differentiation dilemma for the unions. This means that there should be a correlation between attitudes towards internal and cross-national differentiation among the union members of transnational companies.

Why there should be such a correlation? There are two main reasons. First, the problems of differentiation are logically (although not materially) connected. Secondly, the development of solidaristic attitudes across the traditional boundaries of the core working class requires a focus not only on the social relations of production, but also on other experiences. It must take into account the social framework: it would be impossible to simply claim equal salaries world-wide. Furthermore, within national borders, work is not self-sufficient: on the one hand, it is becoming less important for collective identities; on the other, it is to a large extent outside work that people familiarise with differences.

Looking beyond the workshop walls, in essence, should facilitate a reformulation of solidarity in all directions. However, there is a general condition for the applicability of this hypothesis. This is, that there must be some kind of common experience, involving communication.[6] The problem is obviously more complicated for cross-national solidarity, since physical encounters are improbable. Yet in today's world, the possibility of an experience of globalisation certainly exists, although it is usually mediated.[7]

In conditions of late modernity, we live 'in the world' in a different sense from previous eras of history. Everyone still continues to live a local life (...), yet the transformations of place, and the intrusion of distance into local activities, combined with the centrality of mediated experience, radically change what 'the world' actually is. (...) Although everyone lives a local life, phenomenal worlds for the most part are truly global. (Giddens, 1991, p. 187)

Investigating the capacity of trade union members to deal with difference is directly linked to a more general problem, that of the recognition of otherness. If the reconciliation of identity and rationality is a major problem in the globalised world, it seems to need a recognition of otherness. Touraine (1995; 1997) calls this problem the 'emergence of the Subject', and there have already been some attempts to look at the possibility of such a reconciliation of rationality, identity, and recognition in the work situation (Ollivier, 1996). A definition of the subject-worker is offered by Thuderoz (1995) as a combination of cooperative individualism (that is, the association of personal project and ability to weave social links) and experimentation with new 'social plays'.

This problem of the recognition of otherness is linked to other complex questions, first of all, with that of communication, an important field of speculation at the border between philosophy and sociology (Habermas, 1981; Jonas, 1984). In this thesis, the problem of 'Subjectivity' will be a constant concern insofar as the development of the 'Subject' at work seems to be linked to the trade unions' avoidance of an 'egoistic' (in the real sense of the word) professionalism.

As a space for personal projects, professional development, social relations and conflicts, work can be a space for the emergence of Subjectivity. At the same time, such an emergence requires a double emancipation from pure economic rationality and from communities. Subjectivity implies that the individual is not entirely defined by his/her social position (in our case, by the work situation). Becoming critical of one's own social position requires, therefore, a degree of 'exteriority', that is, the capacity to combine different experiences. On this issue of differences and individualisation there are some very optimistic views with regard to the unions and solidarity.

New individualism is the expression of the existential situation of the individual disposing of free will, with therefore the possibility to opt for everyday solidarity and even found new forms of collective action. If a renewal of unionism is to happen, it would start from the new individualists, from union minorities, women, clerical workers, young; it would be manifested in everyday life, that is in private life as well as in the neighbourhood and in the company. It would pass over the boundaries between social groups and also between trade unions as old social movements and the new social movements. Many signs of this movement already exist. (Zoll, 1992, pp. 154-155)

These optimistic views require investigation. It is here that the logical connection between the three hypotheses of my work lies: in the study of the possible reformulation of trade union identities by combining different experiences in the construction of a more encompassing solidarity.

Understanding Post-Communist Industrial Relations

Before shifting to the findings, the theoretical assumptions underlying the research perspective need some explanation. In particular, it is necessary to outline an interpretative approach to the study of Eastern European social actors. Today this part of the world shows how necessary is a sociological contribution to the understanding of political, economic, and legal issues. An approach developed with a view to studying a delicate field such as the post-communist world might then be tested on countries more familiar to Western sociology.

For reasons of clarity, I shall concentrate on only one of the two comparative terms – the Polish one. Eastern European research is here taken to be paradigmatic, but similar issues could be raised with respect to Western Europe. My choice is due to the fact that – as it will be shown – social processes are sharper, and therefore more visible, in the East. They therefore raise wider theoretical issues in a more direct way and prompt a re-examination of sociological categories.

The process of transformation in the post-socialist societies has proved to be much more complex than expected. In the field of industrial relations there is a broad consensus on this point. The research problem is, then, not that of confirming this fact (the complexity and the length of the 'transition' process), but of understanding it in more depth.

No theoretical revolution is attempted. Work relations are very refractory to all-inclusive theories, and not only in Eastern Europe. They are by their nature controversial and heterogeneous. This means that any approach must be open to complexity. This can be done in an unashamedly empirical way. We need more information about work relations, and any source for this might turn out to be useful. My particular focus has, however, turned into a micro-sociological approach, which if further developed might improve our understanding of even very 'macro' phenomena.

Whether consciously or not, we all look at social reality through 'paradigms', that is frameworks which help make sense of our perceptions. The 'paradigms' currently employed in the case of Eastern Europe, and especially of industrial relations, are mainly inherited from the cold-war past and therefore – I shall try to show – are often unsuitable for the end-of-century situation. Although the literature is already large, two general paradigms in the analysis of Eastern European industrial relations can be distinguished as particularly popular: the 'future-centred', or 'teleological', paradigm, and the 'past-centred', or 'path-dependent' one. They do not constitute coherent theoretical approaches, and each has been used in a number of different theories. At a high level of abstraction, they are just general paradigms followed, not always consciously, by the analysts. Both of them have contributed to knowledge and the understanding of the topic, yet both also encounter important obstacles. My aim is not to substitute them with a new kind of truth. It is rather to show how interpretative research, comparative thinking, and finally a good measure of theoretical eclecticism can contribute to the overcoming of some of the problems encountered by these paradigms.

Future-centred Paradigms: Transition and Engineering

The most common example of the teleological way of looking at the post-communist world is represented by the image of 'transition'.

The idea of 'transition' was most popular in the early stages of reform, when Jeffrey Sachs created the images of 'in-only-one-jump' and of shock-therapy (Sachs, 1994). A rare example of the pure transition paradigm is to be found in a book by Leszek Balcerowicz (1995), Polish economist and Finance Minister, in which the word 'transition' is continuously used. By now it has become common sense to state, as the Economist did (22nd November 1997, p.3), that 'the switch from decadent communism to primitive capitalism was *just the first step*' and 'a huge part of the transition is yet to come' (my italics). One jump was not enough. The authors of the most accurate and rigorous hypothesis of a *marktvermittelte Konvergenz* – developed on rational-choice ground – (Schienstock and Traxler, 1993) had to acknowledge after only few years that a divergence was in fact more probable (Thompson and Traxler, 1997).

However, the transition paradigm keeps on operating, consciously or unconsciously, in most analyses. Eastern European reality is constantly in conflict with the end point of transition – an ideal-type of capitalism, supposed to have an unexplained power of attraction. Any discrepancy from that ideal-type is seen as 'abnormality', as something which has to be corrected in order finally to achieve normality.[8]

After the first period, analyses have become more cautious and it has become commonplace to criticise the term 'transition'. However, the paradigm has not been changed: it is simply the case that the 'jump' image has been replaced with a 'catch-up' one. According to the transition paradigm (both the 'extremist' and 'revisionist' versions), the process of social change consists mainly of imitation, the safest way of operating 'the big bound'. As Vaclav Klaus put it very clear, Eastern Europe wanted a capitalist economy just like the West, without wasting time on experiments.

Almost a decade after the beginning of the transformation, the unavoidable result of this way of thinking is deep frustration. It cannot be coincidental that this frustration is greatest in the country most committed to the transition ideal, the Czech Republic.[9] If an ideal-type is taken as 'normality', then reality can do nothing but remain very far from it, and it ends up looking 'pathological'. This can be best seen in analyses of industrial conflict. Rather than a cost that could be reduced but never eliminated, conflict is usually considered a 'social problem' stemming from former 'bad habits' or other usually unexplained diseases (e.g. Gąciarz and Pańków, 1996a; 1996b; Konecki and Kulpińska, 1995). One could ask, however, why, if communist Europe was as they argue characterised by a lack of interest differentiation, should the post-communist mentality be characterised by an orientation to conflict. The same can be said, however, about a number of topics. The slow pace of privatisation is condemned as a perverse resistance of communist élites or of communist-educated workers, but even Mrs Thatcher needed more time to privatise less than the post-communist states are privatising.

One could say more. Eastern Europe might quickly turn out to be more 'advanced' than the West in the way the countries defeated in World War II (Germany, Japan, Italy) grew much quicker than the winners after 1945: they are not 'held up' by the established distributional coalitions which reduce economic dynamism with their slowness, bureaucracy, over-regulation and barriers to entry (Olson, 1982). In many fields, ranging from computer usage to political communication, the post-communist societies have already promptly 'picked up' the latest versions offered by the West. That way, they 'skipped' some developmental stages and 'surpassed' some Western realities characterised by stronger inertia.

In a global world, normality is represented – both statistically and logically, if one considers the current trends – not by the West, but by the disordered Second and Third World. Lepenies (1996) notices how after 1989 the global process of change is deeper in Eastern than in Western Germany, so that the former is definitely more modern than the latter. He refers notably to the processes of industrial restructuring and related unemployment. Moreover, even in the most extreme case of Albania, the financial disaster of early 1997 could be seen, rather than as a local pathology, as a distilled form of a globally emerging 'casino-capitalism', following Carl Schmtitt's idea that it is precisely the exceptional case which has a decisive, explanatory relevance.[10] The Albanians have even been defined as 'postmodern', suddenly identifying themselves with the international community (Negri, 1997). Taking literally the values of this community, 'in a global market [they] consider it obvious that they have the right to offer themselves as a commodity; consequently, [they] use any means available to exercise this right to engage in a nomadic search for jobs that capitalist propaganda promise on the global scene' (p. 14).

After all, Habermas (1990) had already tried to reverse the transition paradigm, stating that it is the West which is 'catching up' with the East as far as democratic ideas and communicative civil society are concerned. Although this statement is probably factually mistaken, it opened at least an alternative conceptual perspective on the East-West link.

The transition paradigm, in its enviable simplicity, is so idealistic that stating a need for empirical assessment is very easy. But there are other approaches centred on the future which are more sophisticated.

I shall consider as an example political 'engineering', which often, although its ideology is often in radical contrast with the 'transition' theory, concurs with it in its teleological posture: the goal is clear and reality is evaluated by comparing it to that goal. Concerned above all with the implementation of a given political recipe, political engineering usually attributes specific roles to the social actors. While the neo-liberal 'transition' theorists are frustrated by the resistance of the 'social material' to the market, the 'actor-centric' political engineers are usually puzzled by their incapacity to transform this resistance into political action.

The best example is perhaps neo-corporatism.[11] Although certainly estimable for its focus on real institutions, it introduces high expectations as to the role of social actors. Especially after the socio-economic crisis of 1990-93, in Eastern Europe the concern with social regulation and with the role of the state has rapidly increased. In Eastern Europe neo-corporatists suggest on the one hand tripartite forms of interest regulation, on the other an active role for the state in constructing the social actors whose participation is required by the same corporatist model (e.g. Burda, 1993). In so doing, they face the dilemma of what comes first, corporatism or appropriately organised social actors. This general theoretical problem with corporatism becomes more complex in the post-communist state. Here evidently neither the state nor social actors are spontaneously committed to corporatism, although they sometimes pursue 'corporatist' practices of one kind or another (Staniszkis, 1991; Tatur, 1995). On many accounts, this dilemma is as insoluble as the problem of the chicken and the egg. The lesson appears to be that, both for employers' associations (e.g. Frieske, 1997; Kozek, 1999) and trade unions (e.g. Reutter, 1996; Frieske, 1998), we need to pay attention to what actually happens in the everyday experience in order to foresee what can follow at the central level.

On the other hand, the discrepancy between Eastern European reality and neo-corporatist models is not abnormal. In Western Europe too corporatist practices in the 1990s are significantly different from the 'classic' ones of the 1970s. Very often what we observe is a kind of weak corporatism between weak social actors, developing precisely in the countries lacking the classic preconditions for the neo-corporatist model, as the Italian case reveals (Regini, 1997). We shall see in more detail in chapter 3 how both the Polish and Italian corporatisms, far from corresponding to the wishes of political actors, seem to be a mix of macro-facades and heterogeneous micro-corporatisms.

Past-centred Paradigms: Path-dependency and Culturalism

The emergence of multiple obstacles to transition theories drove many industrial relations scholars to concentrate on the legacy of the past, sometimes explicitly (e.g. Blanchflower and Freeman, 1994; 1997). Of this types of theory I shall consider path-dependency theory and culturalist analyses. The path-dependency approach (Stark, 1992; Hausner, Jessop and Nielsen, 1995) suggests that the institutional *legacy of the past*, concretised in consolidated routines, affects social reality and precludes a simple and painless 'transition'. Theorists following this paradigm pay more attention to the 'human material' of the institutions than the 'transitologists' usually do. Yet they inevitably fall into making the opposite mistake. Instead of overestimating change, and being frustrated by inertia, they stress the legacies of the past. In so doing, they fail to explain the changes which, nevertheless, occur in both institutions and behaviour. This is not to say that they disregard change, since, on the contrary, they are concerned with precisely this theoretical problem. However, they lack an understanding of innovative change of rupture. We shall see in the interviews that an awareness of a rupture between a 'before' and an 'afterwards' is common among Polish union activists.

In a period defined by many sociologists as one of 'deinstitutionalisation' (Touraine, 1997, pp. 55ff.) and especially in societies differentiating so quickly as Eastern Europe, such a stress on institutionalised patterns of behaviour seems misplaced. For instance, the standpoint of Solidarity in Poland changed considerably more than once between 1988 and 1993, and change started always from below. The same path-dependence theorists, in fact, reach one of their most interesting conclusions while speaking of the complexity, and not of the predictability, of Eastern European institutions (Stark, 1996).

A variation of the legacy approach is offered, in a more Marxist perspective, by Pollert (1999), who distinctively goes back beyond the state-socialist period and stress the role of pre-1939 roots. Here, the attention is paid more to the nature of class arrangements and relations rather than to institutions, leaving more space to agency but still requiring more attention to the pressures from below in order to avoid the determinist risks of historical materialism.

Other analysts are concerned not by the economic and institutional path, but by that of culture, using concepts such as 'socialist habitus' drawing on Bourdieu or 'social capital' drawing on Putnam. In its purest version, this culturalist approach has developed the concept of 'Homo Sovieticus' (Levada, 1993; Zaslavskij, 1995). Accordingly, post-communist workers would look at the new reality through the lens of the old system, expecting from capitalism what socialism promised but failed to deliver (Tischner, 1992). Adamski (1998, p. 47) concludes that since they 'are the only influential social class which has not yet come to terms with the status which the newly-emerging economic system has to offer', blue-collar workers 'can be expected to stimulate enough social and political problems for at least several more governing coalitions'.

In spite of proving to be useful in particular cases, the culturalist views encounter problems of determinism symmetrical to those of the 'transitologists'. It is not explained whether current orientations are inherited from the past or are rather a peculiar reaction to the present. Workers' attitudes are not locked in a past culture, as suggested by some external interpretations (e.g. Kramer, 1995): this point is demonstrated by the rapid change in attitudes towards work and unemployment after 1989 (Kozek, 1994).

In most cases, cultural variables are not considered as an object of study, but rather as a convenient 'emergency' variable intended to account for the 'unexplained residua'. In short, what does not fit the evolutionary paradigm is explained by reference to an obscure and innate cultural diversity manifested by Eastern Europeans. This attitude is very common among Western human resource managers, always ready to see some irrational cultural handicap in Polish workers, even the best qualified (Durand, Le Goff and Tobera, 1997).

The theoretical contradictions between the (generally) economic approach of transition and the culturalist one are striking. The fact that they are often associated reveals the theoretical laziness of many accounts. As a result, workers' attitudes which are in fact shared with the 'developed' capitalist world, are considered specific to Eastern European. When, in December 1998, Polish miners went on strike to defend early retirements, they were criticised for defending Gierek-era privileges, while they actually work longer hours underground than their Western colleagues. Why, then, should we consider a legacy what is actually an aspiration to Western standards? An illustration of this syndrome is provided by Ploszajki, who remarks on the following peculiarity of Polish workers, a 'peculiarity' actually not unfamiliar to most workers of the world (even if with important cross-national variance in its diffusion):

> Some respondents oppose the privatization of their own firm ('because it is special') while at the same time accepting ('naturally') the general principle of privatization ('because it is necessary'). (Ploszajki, 1995, p. 205)

The short discussion I have presented on these approaches does not imply that the paradigms are useless. The future-centred ones give reference points for the analysis of the present: in order to understand disorder, we need after all some representation of order. In the same way, past-centred paradigms furnish very often indispensable *ad hoc* explanations, and remind us that any social actor has an history and a cultural background which cannot be easily dismantled. However, they still fail to provide an explanation of why Eastern European social actors have recently so deeply changed, while remaining very far from the normative models which have been proposed.

Refusing Paradigms? Rational-choice Approaches

If the intellectual paradigms are all thought to be unsuitable, one could attempt to avoid any meta-historical or macro-sociological concern and study just the given situations through an 'agnostic' approach which disregards historical context and political ideals. The best examples of such a way of proceeding are rational choice approaches. While they have strongly influenced the interpretations of post-communist industrial relations, they do not really constitute a 'paradigm' in themselves. Rational action theory is a general mode of looking at social reality, and is not linked to a particular image of post-communist change. By contrast, as a methodological approach, it has been described as 'agnostic'. It is not directly connected to any theoretical 'macro' paradigm, although it has a link with methodological individualism and thereby with the suppositions of neo-classical economics. However, I shall avoid a discussion of its fundament. Rational action theory may also be useful in Eastern Europe in formulating and testing different hypotheses. What is important here is to recall that in the case of transforming societies the general problems of the time-horizon and of information become particularly significant. As has been noted elsewhere, rational-choice approaches (e.g. game theory) 'impute an extraordinary amount of knowledge to emerging political actors who operate in environments characterized by extreme uncertainty and high strategic interdependence' (Kitschelt, 1992, p. 9)

This situation gives a particular slant to the general criticism of rational-choice assumptions:

> Utility maximization has little empirical content without strong auxiliary assumptions on the utility functions and other model ingredients. Because a trained economist can see through a utility maximization, stating auxiliary assumptions is often little different from stating empirical predictions outright, as, say, a sociologist might. In this sense, the utility maximization merely packages the prediction. (Coulisk, 1996, p. 685)

Such criticism can actually be contested on theoretical grounds. Yet it has a particular force when, like in Eastern Europe, the 'assumptions' are not a separate problem, but *the* research problem. Our research problem is understanding the differences in trade union consciousness: this is simultaneously a theoretical and empirical question. As we shall see, not only are the conclusions reached by the trade unions different, but so are their points of reference. The different outcomes are not produced simply by the different contexts; they are also produced by the different way the actors look at the context, that is by the different *rationality* they use. The unbounded rational worker is perhaps a useful concept; the only problem is that he does not exist.

In transforming societies we do not know the preferences of the actors; however, even macro-sociological issues largely depend upon these. As Claus Offe (1994), for instance, states about social policy, before planning solutions we have to see whether we are dealing with *Homo Sovieticus*, *Homo Oeconomicus*, or *Homo Hungaricus*. The assumptions we make about preferences (are they the same as in the West? Are they different? Are they changing?) directly affect the answer to the research question about the nature of transition. Stating as an assumption the answer to the research question would hardly be a scientific way of approaching the problem.

Seeking Interpretative Categories

Overcoming the illusions of paradigms does not require only an empirical assessment. If we do not want to fall into an absolute empiricism, we need to develop theories and concepts with which to define reality. We can then shift from empirical reportage to the definition of sociological research questions. In Eastern Europe, we must first check the actual meaning of the concepts we use.

I shall use three main comprehensive concepts in my analysis of workers' collective action: class, consciousness, and the social construction of reality. They will be used to describe the meaning of Polish and Italian union traditions, and to explain the ways in which they change. The main theoretical sources I shall exploit are also three: Marxist and materialist sociology of work, Touraine's sociology of action, and different branches of phenomenological sociology.

This theoretical eclecticism may seem surprising, but it is in fact neither strange nor new. First, these are categories that are so popular that sociologists can rarely avoid – the problem is that their actual meaning is not always explained. Secondly, there are already sociological works explicitly using, in turn, two of the three references used here. One could mention François Dubet (esp. 1994), who uses both Touraine and the phenomenological tradition; a number of ethnomethodologists such as Willis (1977) who combine a phenomenological orientation with Marxist views; and finally the earlier Touraine himself insofar as he was deeply influenced by Marxism (and often even defined as a neo-Marxist). Yet the Reader will quickly see that here there is not a 'division of labour' among theorists: all the concepts I use are simultaneously influenced by different theoretical sources. Graphically, we can illustrate the interrelationship of theoretical approaches and concepts in a sort of Star of David, as shown in Figure 1.1. (Father Jankowski, Solidarity confessor, would perhaps see it as evidence of a Jewish conspiracy behind the trade unions; the Reader will understand that this is not the meaning of the illustration, and that the Jewish origin of Marx, of the founders of phenomenology Husserl and Schutz, and of one of the closest of Touraine's collaborators, is here absolutely irrelevant.)

Figure 1.1 - Theoretical framework

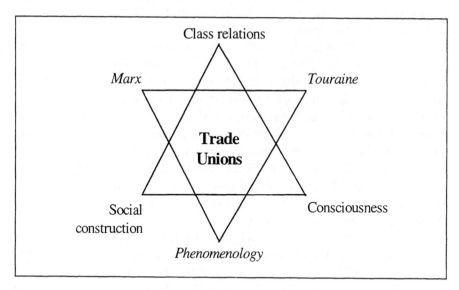

Class

The concept of class is used here mainly in Touraine's sense, which is in turn connected to Marxist and materialist sociology of work. This conception could not be further from the idea of a social stratum, in which the word 'class' is often used.

It may seem strange to make use of Marx in an analysis of trade unionism. Marx (and Marxists') view of trade unions has been since the very beginning ambivalent, as the very title of one of the last orthodox Marxist works shows: *Der Doppelcharakter der Gewerkschaften* (Zoll, 1978). As long as the balance in the *Doppelcharakter* of the unions remains unexplained, one might better speak of the *Doppelcharakter des Marxismus*. Incapable of solving the dilemma of trade unions' ambiguity, Marxists – a notable example being Lenin – often became antipathetic. Historical determinism could not accept that the unions 'defend and represent the workers as they are, and not as they should be' (Cella, 1999, p. 8). In fact, I will not refer specifically to Marx's opinions about trade unions. I will rather – in the spirit of my proposed theoretical eclecticism – make use of some Marxist sociology of work and class analysis, without reference to Marx's political and historical theory.

Marxist and materialist sociology of work have the primary, relevant merit of concentrating on how conflict structures the work situation

(Hyman, 1975; 1989; Edwards and Scullion, 1982; Edwards, 1986; 1992). In opposition to most Eastern European studies, I consider the work situation to be the *primary* situation in which class relationships are constructed. Following Marx, we can understand conflict at work by considering the distinction between labour and labour power. The realisation of labour power considered initially as 'potential' occurs in the factory, outside the limits of the market. It occurs, therefore, through an unavoidable conflict between organisers and workers which has been called 'effort bargaining'. This process is fundamental in any society based on accumulation and on industrial production – that is, in Soviet societies as much as under capitalism. While appreciating this part of Marx's thought, I do not share his opinion that *ownership* relations are the most important aspect of production relations: the reality of state-socialism showed the independence of the latter from the former.

From this perspective, the everyday experience of conflict at work is more important for the construction of class than income distribution. In Mann's words (1973, p. 22), in Marx's analysis 'the [class] break is (...) not financial but rather one of job control'. Although income and profit distribution are fundamental in defining the life chances of different groups, they do not explain why industrial society – more than any other historical phase – has been experienced as a field of struggle between workers and employers, not simply between rich and poor. Moreover, neither does it explain why the aristocracy of labour has usually been on the trade unions' side, while the lower middle class (for instance administrative employees with control tasks) has been on the other. Marxist sociology has no other explanation for the loyalty of employees with control tasks than that of 'contradictory class locations' (Wright, 1976). Their position ceases being contradictory as soon as work conflict is put at the centre of the analysis.

In Przeworski's words, 'class is a name for a relation, not for a collection of individuals' (1985, p. 81). If it is a matter of social *relations*, and not of social *locations*, class cannot be defined by a continuous variable like income. The problem is not so much of counting how many people belong to the working class, but rather of recalling that the working class has been the only class to pose a sustained challenge to rule by social elites. The central role of conflict implies that in a society there can be neither more nor less than two classes. This does not mean, however, that all of society must take part in this conflict, hence a dual class division does not exhaust the social configuration (Marx himself was absolutely aware of this, as he showed in his historical works).

This is not to say that economic issues are unimportant. One should avoid the ideological criticism of economic demands which has been frequent in the Marxist tradition, and strongest in the work of Lenin. The problem here is to see the legitimating structure of demands, the *économies de la justification* to paraphrase Boltanski's terms (Boltanski and Thevenot, 1991). Are economic demands motivated on the basis of relative income differences among social groups, on the basis of workers' needs, or on the basis of surplus re-appropriation? From a materialist standpoint, only the last of these relates to class relationships. In this context it is possible to say that class, rather than a category, is a 'meaning' of action (and here lies the importance of consciousness).

The attention paid by Marxist analysts to production relations suggests an important connection with Touraine's sociology. In fact, Touraine's *La conscience ouvrière* might be considered as an attempt to support this point. The issue of the 'slow-down', the most important class-relationship indicator in both Touraine's and Marxist conceptions, is the area in which the 'overlap' between the two approaches is most striking. Moreover, if slow-down is the link between Marxist sociology of work and the early Touraine, another important topic of materialist analyses, deskilling, seems to me to be a potential link between Marxism and Touraine's recent sociology of work (Touraine, 1996).

This stress on the work situation has been particularly fruitful in the field of international comparisons. In this area it has been shown that job control is uniformly important for workers in Western societies (Mann, 1973, pp. 25-26). Similarities in conflict consciousness at the factory level were found between British and French trade unions, otherwise considered as opposed models of unionism (Beynon, 1975; Price, 1983; Gallie, 1978 and 1983; Rose, 1987). Finally, even the American 'exceptionalism' had to be revisited when the shopfloor demands of trade unions were considered (Jacoby, 1991): in the post-war 'golden age' it was the control of production on the shopfloor which was at stake in labour-management relations in the workplace (Fairris, 1997). I shall show that this is where we can see a sort of 'unity' between Solidarity workers' action and Western workers' action.

The class nature of control issues implies that they already have a political aspect. However, it is not sufficient to identify just any conflict at work in order to speak of classes. If we speak of class and not of group, this is because class conflict has a general social dimension. The general character of class conflict is best revealed by the role of intellectuals in it, but this does not imply that there must be an explicit political conflict on class issues. The overestimation of political ideologies and cleavages is one of the greatest obstacles to the understanding of class relationships. What is important is that the control of industrial production and accumulation must be a central concern in society. This is the reason why, as I shall try to show through my findings, the concept of the working class becomes vacuous when industrial production and development lose their place in society, even though work conflict may remain an important *local* issue. To summarise, I will define social class in industrial society as *social actor involved in a general, social conflict over industrial production and development*.

This issue is assessed by Touraine as follows.

> In the industrial society classes are the actors that manifest social relations of production, that is a mode of management and social appropriation of the machine and of the rationalised instruments of production. In the industrial society class is not a social level, nor an economic condition; it is constructed through a social relationship and this is not analogous to a market relation between seller and buyer of labour power. It lies, as Lukács after Marx defined it, in the social realisation of reason, the contradiction that enters into the natural logic of reason. (Touraine, 1996, p. 98)

Touraine's conception of class was developed via the analysis of workers' consciousness (1966), and later tested in works of general sociology (1977) and on the workers' movement (Touraine, Dubet, and Wieviorka, 1987). The peculiarity of Touraine's thought is the avoidance of the classic dilemma of the distinction between *Klasse an sich* and *Klasse für sich*. His point is almost provocative: 'let it be said here very clearly that *class in itself does not exist*, that there can be no class without consciousness of class' (Touraine, Dubet and Wieviorka, 1987, p. 21). However, this view is not exclusive to Touraine. Mann, notably, writes – albeit from a different perspective – that 'if subjective consciousness is lacking, so too are the objective conditions [of class]' (Mann, 1973, p. 52). This argument brings us to the second sociological concept, that of consciousness. Developing a definition of consciousness analytically independent from action is essential to study the link between the two.

Consciousness

As Giddens notes, 'one of the weakest, or least clarified, aspects of Marx's writings concerns the relationship between class and class consciousness' (1973, p. 92). Lockwood's point is similar: the problem of action is 'the weakest link in the chain of Marxist theory' (Lockwood, 1981). In his early writings, and notably in the criticism of philosophical materialism, Marx was aware of the role of consciousness. If consciousness were not something more than a passive reflection of material circumstances there would be no place for the active role of human beings as creators of social reality. Yet this point has never been adequately developed. In Marx's writings (and later in those by Kautsky or Poulantzas), the shift from *Klasse an sich* to *Klasse für sich* seems relatively unproblematic: through the experience of fighting together, reinforced by some factors such as plant size, the workers should become aware of the general class conflict taking place (Marx, 1847). One and a half centuries after Marx's Manifesto, the question of what makes workers behave as a class is still open.

Hence the problem of consciousness, raised since the late 1950s by sociologists as different as Marshall, Geyer, Lipset, Bendix, Dahrendorf, Lockwood, Wood. Touraine (1966) offers a framework aiming at transcending the dualism between consciousness and structure, and that between consciousness and action (Davis, 1979). Under particular circumstances, workers' consciousness becomes 'class' consciousness. Touraine aims to 'replace a doctrinary conception of class consciousness with a historic and sociological conception, based on concrete observations and leading to reject the idea that class consciousness is the fully developed form of any workers' consciousness, its permanent truth' (Touraine, 1966, p. 119). In Touraine's view, class consciousness is the form of workers' consciousness taken at the central moment of industrial development. It is when industrial work becomes an organisational system at all levels that the private conflict between boss and worker appeals to the whole society and to the general interest.

This orientation moves away from a materialist standpoint. The idea of class consciousness 'rejects any "objective", non social definition of a historical situation. Instead, it places at the centre of the analysis actors' understanding and behaviour' (p. 122). This is the reason why the criticisms of Touraine's 'technological determinism' (e.g. Hyman, 1996b) are not completely convincing. Workers' consciousness is 'the link between "objective" and "subjective" sides of a historical situation, between the conditions and the meaning of agency. It is impossible to speak of workers' consciousness unless we refer to specific human needs at work' (p. 123).

The idea of class as an 'historical actor' or 'acting subject' and the focus on consciousness were present before Touraine in the thought of Lukács (1923/1971). His conception, albeit in a Marxist general framework, was much more idealistic, directly influenced by Hegel. Class consciousness was defined as a conscious sense of the historical role of the class. Lukács himself, however, was aware of the risks of moving away from a materialist standpoint. As a result, from time to time he reaffirms the link with the material nature of consciousness, with a stress (which seems to me somehow forced) on adjectives such as 'practical' or 'concrete'.

> When the worker knows himself as a commodity his knowledge is practical. This is to say, this knowledge brings about an objective cultural change in the object of knowledge. (p. 169)

> [Reification] can be overcome only by constant and constantly renewed efforts to disrupt the reified structure of existence by concretely relating to the concretely manifested contradictions of the total development, by becoming conscious of the immanent meanings of these contradictions for the total development. (p. 197)

These statements are reminiscent of the early writings of Marx (not all of which were known at the time Lukács wrote), in which, as Giddens comments (1973, p. 113), 'consciousness is not the "effect" of human activity in the material world, but constitutes the attribution of meaning which guides conduct, and is inseparable from that conduct'.

The concept of class consciousness seems more useful than other, simpler concepts such as identity or awareness. As defined by Touraine (1966; 1977), consciousness implies the three principles of identity, opposition, and totality (the so-called IOT scheme). Their usefulness lies in the strict connection to the idea of (class) conflict, of a societal stake, and of action. The ideas of identity and awareness, on the other hand, are 'static', and non-dialectical, and they cause a confusion between class and community. Workers' identity is strongest in closed workers' communities, but in these situations class consciousness and action are often weaker, as was clearly shown by Hoggart (1957) and as I shall show in the Piombino case.

Like the concept of class, the concept of consciousness will also be used here in relation to the experience of work: it is rooted in the 'us' and 'them' opposition in the workplace (Lane, 1974). The IOT (Identity-Opposition-Totality) scheme of consciousness developed by Touraine is sometimes recalled as IOTA (by adding Alternative). In fact, the more ideological 'A' was added by other theorists, like Giddens and Mann, under the influence of Mannheim's thought, while for Touraine the idea of an 'alternative' society is not as important for class consciousness as the meaning given to the work situation.[12] By contrast, Touraine makes a distinction between dominant and subordinate levels of normative reference, consistent with Parkin's (1971) point, stating that questions allow grasping the orientations to workers' consciousness when they refer to the actual behaviour, not when they refer to the society altogether (Touraine, 1966, p. 151).

It should be clear from these points that adding the idea of consciousness to the idea of class is not falling into idealism, nor into ideology. It is therefore – even if it represents a substantial theoretical shift – not incompatible with the materialist view of the labour process presented in the previous section. The link between the two concepts remains, however, problematic. Making the relationship between class and consciousness more convincing (a task which was undertaken by Lukács although not in an entirely successful way) will require another theoretical contribution, the third corner of the triangle: the phenomenological idea of the social construction of reality.

The Social Construction of Reality

In order to avoid historicist or idealistic conceptions, we can best define consciousness as the 'sedimentation of experiences and meanings' (Berger and Luckmann, 1967, p. 85). The role of everyday experience in constructing, *making*, social class and social consciousness is underlined in a number of historical and sociological works (e.g. Thompson, 1966; Hoggart, 1957; Katznelson and Zolberg, 1986). I shall limit myself to only a few examples:

> Under capitalism class is an immediate and in some sense a directly experienced historical reality, whereas in pre-capitalist epochs it may merely be an analytical construct. (Hobsbawm, 1984, p. 18)

> Day-to-day experiences at the workplace are likely to be more decisive in shaping a man's views of collective bargaining and strike activity than are the abstract moral precepts of the dominant value system. (Parkin, 1971/1973, p. 94)

> For the most part men visualize the class structure of their society from the vantage points of their own particular milieux, and their perceptions of the larger society will vary according to their experiences of social inequality in the smaller societies in which they live out their daily lives. (Lockwood, 1966, p. 249)

It was by answering Althusser on the issue of the working class that Thompson (1978) suggested the category of 'human experience'. Its aim was to define the imprecise set of situations and emotions constructed by a social class and opposed to their destiny. Much earlier, however, 'experience' had been introduced as one of the fundamental categories of sociology by Simmel (1908). Although it may appear as a purely individual phenomenon, experience is necessarily social (Dubet, 1994). From a social-psychological perspective – on the basis of self-perception theory – the role of everyday experience in building the commitment of union members remains central.

> A sense of shared beliefs about the social and economic aspects of work may be derived from the common experiences of working people, and (...) it is these shared beliefs which serve as the basis for ideological attachment to the union. (Gordon, 1996, p. 248)

Giving some consideration to everyday experience helps the understanding of the *boundaries*, the *timing* and the *forms* of the social construction of class and consciousness. Moreover, it places the worker as a social actor back at the centre of industrial sociology, after a period when the shift in focus from work and workers to economic concerns had transformed the same worker into a passive object *acted* on by macro-level forces (Simpson, 1989). More generally, it allows us to avoid considering the actors – in Garfinkel's words – as 'cultural idiots'. This has substantial consequences. Zoll's recent inquiry on workers' solidarity, for instance, springs from an examination of the experiences in which this is constructed. The decisive factor for creating solidarity – he claims – rather than a definition of interests, is the development of a tie of affection in the everyday practice of work. Therefore workers' solidarity seldom extended beyond the factory gate even when there was an interest in extending it (Zoll, 1992).

The concept of social construction and the centrality of experience allows the link between work conflict and class consciousness to be defined. Class is the highest general meaning given by the workers to work conflict in the effort to raise the level of the struggle. That the relationship goes in the opposite direction (from class to work) seems unlikely. If this were the case, it would be the awareness of an extensive, homogenous community of destiny which prompted struggle in the workplace. The move is from work to class, and not the opposite. Therefore, more important than stratification analysis is the study of social meanings and experiences: the working class declines not because of social differentiation at the macro-level (this can also exist in periods of strong workers' movements), but when work is no longer the arena of clear social conflict.

This argument is consistent with the phenomenological reflection on 'the boundaries of experiences and the experience of boundaries' (Luckmann and Schutz, 1989, Vol.II, pp. 102-106). Understanding the construction of reality through everyday experience has been the purpose of phenomenological sociology since Husserl formulated the idea of the *Lebenswelt*. This theoretical current paid particular attention to the problem of consciousness (see especially: Luckmann and Schutz, 1989, Vol.II, pp. 1-20) and therefore leaves room for Touraine's view.

Phenomenological sociology by its very nature is difficult to define: one could assert that it can only be practised, and never defined. I shall attempt here only to explain the utility of this approach for this piece of research.

According to Schutz, we cannot understand social actors from outside their 'bounded provinces of meaning', that is the sets of experiences which display coherent cognitive styles. The scholar – this is the conclusion which is directly relevant for a methodological approach – cannot understand actors unless they takes part in their everyday life. This point has been the object of extensive criticism for its extreme relativism (e.g. Giddens, 1976), but this is partially answered by another part of Schutz's thought. The object of phenomenological sociology for him is not the inaccessible Other, but rather the idealisations created by the natural way of dealing with reality in order to maintain a 'common world'. More concretely, the objects of inquiry are the everyday interpretative procedures which allow us to give a sense both to our own and others' action. This intellectual project, which has been defined as the 'hermeneutics of social action', was continued separately by the ethnomethodologists and by phenomenological sociologists of knowledge. Both sides searched for a 'third' way between objectivism and subjectivism. Ethnomethodologists stress, among other things, the reflexivity and the interpretative ability of social actors – which has been confirmed in the case of trade union members (Corcuff, 1994) – and the indexicality (the strong reference to experience) of meaning. Both points are particularly important in this study. The sociology of knowledge developed by Berger and Luckmann (1967), in turn, deals directly with the relationship between objective and subjective reality.

Berger and Luckmann maintain a bond with Marx, at least with the early Marx, who wrote in the manuscripts of 1844 that man's consciousness is determined by his social being. In this way the theoretical triangle I drew begins to close itself. On the other hand, the authors of '*The*

Social Construction of Reality' also pay attention to the problem of consciousness, defined as the sedimentation of experiences and meanings (p. 85). Consciousness, they argue, is always intentional – directed towards objects –, never simply existing 'as such' (p. 34). In this way we can avoid the dangers of ideologism while concentrating on trade union consciousness.

Berger and Luckmann place themselves, although they avoid any reference to it in the body of their text, in the historical hermeneutic school, which developed concepts like *Standortsgebundenheit* (situational determination) or *Sitz im Leben* (seat in life) which are consistent with my approach to trade union consciousness. Yet there is a very particular point on which Berger and Luckmann's work offers a still unexploited potential for the interpretation of the post-communist experience. This is their discussion of transformation and of the extreme case of it, which they call 'alternation' but which recalls immediately today's 'transition' in post-communist societies.[13] Of course, 'alternation' is a very extreme case. Yet Berger and Luckmann themselves state that it is only a problem of degree: 'if the processes involved in the extreme case are clarified, those of less extreme cases will be understood more easily' (p. 176). 'Alternation', as a radical form of re-socialisation, resembles primary socialisation, in that it has to radically re-assign reality aaccents. Since it does not start *ex nihilo*, however, it must cope with the problem of dismantling the proceding nomic structure of subjective reality. The basic social conditions for successful alternation are the following (pp. 176-82): the availability of a legitimating apparatus; the ripudiation of all alternative realities; the reinterpretation of the old reality; the mediation of significant others; an effective plausibility structure.

These arguments seem developed at a merely 'micro' level. Yet it is possible to elucidate, through this theory of socialisation, even the most 'macro' among social realities, notably international relations: a good example, in the case of the East-West relations, are the interpretations based on the concept of 'cooptation' and, precisely, 'socialisation' (Levy, 1993).

Let us see how this applies to the case of trade union activists in privatised Polish companies, who experience transition at both the societal and work levels. The problem with transition is that although the goals are relatively clear (economic well-being and democracy), the stages by which they can be reached are not. The overwhelming majority of Eastern European citizens support reforms in opinion surveys, but at the same time they resist their implementation in the everyday life. The entire 'plausibility structure' of workers' lives must be revisited: why make any work effort? Why join the union? Why strike? These usually taken-for-granted questions become compelling. 'Alternation' can be seen as a profound process of reformulation of identities and ideologies, in which there is a risk that very old (e.g. ethnic) interpretations will re-emerge whenever no other 'plausibility structure' is available. Without a concern for the process of re-socialisation, it would be hard to understand the meaning of action in a period of profound change. Berger and Luckmann's work helps this understanding by evincing the role of socialisation stages, of biographical reinterpretation and of 'significant others'. In our case, the 'significant others' are all global actors, from the media to the multinational employer and, if present, foreign trade unions.

Phenomenological sociology helps take the past into consideration without falling into historical determinism. Under the alternation experience, the past is seen differently than under more limited experiences of 'change'.

> To forget completely is notoriously difficult. What is necessary, then, is a radical reinterpretation of the meaning of these past events or persons in one's biography. Since it is relatively easier to invent things that never happened than to forget those that actually did, the individual may fabricate and insert events wherever they are needed to harmonize the remembered with the reinterpreted past. (...) He may be perfectly sincere in such a procedure - subjectively, is not telling lies about the past but bringing it in line with the truth that necessarily, embraces both present and past. (...) Such partial transformations are common in contemporary society in connection with the individual's social mobility and occupational training (...). But these transformations typically fall far short of re-socialization. They build on the basis of primary internalization and generally avoid abrupt discontinuities within the subjective biography of the individual. As a result, they face the problem of maintaining consistency between the earlier and later elements of subjective reality. (...) Broadly speaking, one may say that the procedures involved are of opposite character. In re-socialization the past is reinterpreted to conform to the present reality, with the tendency to retroject into the past various elements that were subjectively unavailable at the time. In secondary socialization the present is interpreted so as to stand in a continuous relationship with the past, with the tendency to minimize such transformations as have actually taken place. (pp. 180-182)

In short, the lesson to be learnt is that transition is a process of reinterpretation and of continuous work on the categories of present and past. The sociologist's task is therefore, less than of reconstructing the actual past (this job can be left to historians), that of observing how the discourse on the past influences the present. Polish trade union activists actually 'work' on their past. They search for continuity either in their relations of opposition (this is usually the case with Solidarity) or in their relations of co-operation (the former official trade unions). 'Alternation' is in both cases so interpreted as to give a coherent subjective sense of one's own action in both past and present. It becomes a pillar of the plausibility structure: 'the world has changed, so X was right then a Y is right now'. The Italy-Poland comparison will show how the experience of alternation influences the way of thinking of trade union activists, affecting for instance trust or attitudes towards innovation.

Interestingly enough, the phenomenological approach was generally banned from state-socialist academic sociology, which first ignored it, then ridiculed it as one can see from the typical Soviet attacks by Roll (1988) or Golenko and Kirsanov (1988), and the later 'rehabilitation' by Rutkovitch (1990). After 1989, it suddenly became fruitful in the interpretation of change. Dessewffy (1992), for instance, criticises from a phenomenological point of view the representation of totalitarianism in cold-war literature. Moreover, through a focus on everyday life and on the individual as the unit of analysis, he makes a first attempt to reconstruct the belief systems of communism and their 'plausibility structures'. He can then attest that these systems and structures make understandable the actual behaviour of actors. Some use of Berger and Luckmann's theory is also made in post-communist industrial relations studies (e.g. Konecki and Kulpińska, 1995).

This quick overview of different theorists should clarify the sense of the double triangle (Figure 1.1). Three concepts are used in order to understand trade unions: class, consciousness and the social construction of reality through experience. The first concept has been defined by starting from Marxism and Touraine's thought; the second one on the basis of Touraine's and phenomenological sociology; the last draws on phenomenological sociology and the early Marx. Concepts and theories are, despite appearances, interconnected. First, 'class' becomes a meaningful concept when it is used to refer to actors *consciously* taking part in a general social conflict. Secondly, consciousness is best defined as a crystallised form of *socially constructed* subjective reality. Finally, in the social construction of the trade unions a central role must be given to the experience of work conflict, a conflict historically capable of having a *class* nature. We can now define trade union class consciousness as the *socially constructed understanding of to the everyday experience of work conflict as a matter of societal relevance*. The components of this consciousness have already been mentioned in the previous chapter. In much simpler words (and unavoidably less precisely) to speak of class conscious workers we do not need to have political revolutionaries; it is sufficient to observe that workers are convinced that any supplementary effort made at work is to the exclusive advantage of the employer, unless workers collectively control (and possibly rule) production.

If class consciousness is fragmented, it does not follow that we cannot study it: we can study precisely its *fragments*, the ruins still present in the consciousness of many activists. Without a reference to the 'class'-level past, as Berger and Luckmann show in their representation of 'alternation', today's discourse would hardly be understandable. Class still lives in some isolated counter-trends of unionism, but above all it still exists as an occasional interpretative resource, which indicates that it was experienced in the past.

A Leap into the Polish Past

Interpreting the Communist Past

The three hypotheses on trade union consciousness involve an assumption: that in the past important parallelisms existed between Italian and Polish workers. I will give no consideration to whether Italian unionism displayed a class character, since the consensus on this point is sufficiently broad. Of course, were 'class' given a different meaning (in particular if it were to mean 'objective social category'), it could be easily demonstrated, as Sylos Labini (1975) did, that the working class in Italy has never existed. However, if 'class' is first of all a meaning of action, then in few other places (one of which is probably Poland) were the unions so concerned by the goal of ruling the factories. What needs to be discussed, by contrast, is whether Solidarity was *something of the kind of the Western labour movement*. This piece of research, which strives to be sociological and not historical, will consider this issue (expecially, in searching for working-class 'remains' in today's Polish trade unions), but only indirectly. It is necessary to refer to the literature and to carry out secondary analysis of existing research.

Comparing Polish strikers with those in the West has been quite an agreeable intellectual exercise for several theorists, as the following extracts suggest.

> How can Giddens seriously believe that the labour process is intrinsic to class relations under capitalism alone, and not to class relations under other systems, such as socialism? Such a proposition implies that the class character

of the proletariat in capitalist society is profoundly different, in some unexplained way, from the character of the socialist proletariat. The Polish workers, to take a notable example, appear to behave as if they are quite unaware of any such difference. (Parkin, 1980, p. 891)

The British miners never managed to rally the same scale of allies as the Polish engineers or miners, and Arthur Scargill never became the world's darling, like Lech Walesa. But the East-West irony in looking at the Polish-British mirror is well worth noting. Polish and British workers in the 1960s, 1970s and 1980s fought for basically the same things, certain short-term protective devices in a world where the bosses were not trusted. The workers' mistrust and militancy were perceived by the government, and the economists of both Britain and Poland as a major obstacle to accumulation. Edward Heath and James Callaghan were politically destroyed by the defensive workers' movement as were Wladyslaw Gomulka and Edward Gierek. But the Thatcher's Tories, working in a parliamentary democratic country, albeit largely helped by the peculiarities of the British constitution, finally succeeded where a whole series of Polish Communist General Secretaries with more or less dictatorial powers had failed, even when deploying the army. The British unions were brought to heel, and their most combative sections shoved off onto the dole. The admiration which a number of frustrated Polish officials of the 1980s had for Mrs Thatcher is understandable. (Therborn, 1995, p. 328)

The issue is delicate, however. Even an attentive sociologist like Giddens fell into contradictory statements:

The state socialist societies (...) have genuinely succeeded in moving towards a classless order, but only at the cost of creating a system of political domination which has altered the character of social exploitation rather than necessarily diminishing it. (Giddens, 1973, p. 294)

The main source for the argument that there is a parallel between Polish and Western working class consciousness is Touraine's analysis of the Solidarity movement (Touraine, Dubet, Wieviorka and Strzelecki, 1983). Just after, in his work on the workers' movement in general, Touraine stated that class consciousness was to be found at its highest level among Silesian workers (Touraine, Dubet and Wieviorka, 1987, p. 36). According to Touraine (1981), communist societies, although engaged in a radically different *mode de développement* when compared to their capitalist counterparts, share with the latter the same '*type sociétal*', that is both belong to the industrial society.

This argument, which allows both *convergence theory* and neo-Darwinian arguments of an innate Slavic backwardness to be avoided, nonetheless requires some elucidation. In fact, the nature of the working class in communist societies is an open issue, not only for sociologists but also for historians. There are a number of sources that confirm the argument that an equivalent working class consciousness exists in both Poland and Italy.

As regards state socialism as a whole, basic similarities with capitalist societies have been claimed by important sociologists like Aron, Bell, Dahrendorf, or Lipset. More particularly with respect to work conflict, parallelisms with capitalist societies were noted among others by Bendix (1956, especially pp. 429ff) and Burawoy and Lukacs (1985), and confirmed by personal accounts from the communist world (e.g. Haraszti, 1977). In fact, since Lenin's times, Soviet organisation of work has borrowed a number of ideas from Western practices, tending to destroy the autonomy of the worker. Others, on the contrary, point out important differences in work organisation (e.g. Beissinger, 1989; Andreff, 1993; Boyer, 1993); or argue that class relations in the Soviet enterprise were completely different from those under capitalism (e.g. Clarke, 1996a). However, their arguments are either orthodox Marxist (giving the decisive role to the ownership of the means of production) or orthodox neo-liberal (giving the decisive role to the market position of the firm). They disregard work conflict as the fundamental field of class relations.[14] Moreover, in-depth case studies (e.g. Rolle, 1995 and 1998) reject Andreff's and Boyer's thesis that in the Soviet social compromise there was no work discipline. The experience of Russian workers was certainly not that they had light work, and even Breznev's era was experienced as a period dominated by growth imperatives. Lane's (1987) analysis confirms the existence of important affinities between Taylorism and the Soviet NOT (*nauchnaya organizatsiya truda* – scientific organisation of work). It also confirms that in the Soviet enterprise too there was pressure on workers to increase their effort.

> A common assumption underlying Soviet thinking (as indeed managerial thinking everywhere) is that the level of effort could and should be increased. (…) The objective of wage policy is to use wages as an incentive for greater effort on the part of the employees and to reward the quality as well as the quantity of labour. At the same time, to avoid inflation, planners have to ensure that wages rise less than productivity. (pp. 116-117)

Labour unrest and slowdowns, indeed, were not alien to state-socialist societies, expecially in periods of social transformation (Beletsevkovsky, 1978; Héthy and Makó, 1974; Arnot, 1981). In a sense, then it is possible to talk of the 'making of an industrial working-class' even for Stalin's

Russia (Strauss, 1997). In conclusion, Burawoy's statement is perhaps the best assessment of this issue:

> The secret of all factory despotism lies in the dependence of material survival upon performance at work. It is this dependence that gives managers their coercive whip. But it can assume different forms. (Burawoy, 1997, p. 81)

The Nature of Solidarity

Poland was the least 'totalitarian' of the Eastern bloc states and therefore the one in which there was the greatest chance that a labour movement would emerge. One could say that work conflict existed everywhere in the Soviet system, but only in Poland (and in other rare situations, like Gorbachev's USSR) could class consciousness develop. In fact, class conflict requires a degree of diversification and dialectics, while under totalitarianism only conflict between individual and system is perceivable: under these circumstances, it is correct to say that the working class dissolved in a '*Gesellschaft der Werktätigen*' (working people's society), as the GDR has been defined (Ernst, Klinger and Timm, 1998). I shall therefore concentrate on a specific comparison of Solidarity with Western working-class action.

Touraine's assessment was the following: 'socialist and capitalist countries (...) to the extent that both belong to industrial society, are both based on the same central class relation between a workforce, with its strength, its skill, its experience and its group solidarity, and, on the other hand, the organisers, the managers, who impose on the workers production rates, working conditions, and a pay structure: who, in short, exploit them' (Touraine, Dubet, Wieviorka and Strzelecki, 1983, p. 41).

According to the Franco-Polish research team, Solidarity as a trade union is not only the company-level organisation of a wider political movement; its trade union action is above all 'class' action.

> In all our research groups, but especially in Katowice and Gdańsk, the activity of the trade union was constantly defined in terms of class struggle, even where these were not the words used by the militants. For the miners, the union's main job was to be 'against the bosses'; at Gdańsk, Marian (...) explained (...): 'I wanted to win the things we'd been fighting for in 1970 – better working conditions, an end to this monotonous work from morning till night followed by the pub (...). I wanted work to be better organised, because they so often gave us deadlines we couldn't meet (...)'.
> The first task of free trade unions had to be to protect the interests of the workers against the employer and to obtain better pay and conditions, as well

as freeing the workers from the arbitrary decisions, incompetence and corruption of their bosses. The miners are acutely conscious of being the productive base of the country: without coal, the economy would crumble; and indeed they are better paid than other groups of workers. But they felt crushed by brutal working methods and conditions, in which their health and their lives were disregarded and put at risk. (p.41)

Hence, the parallelism with the West, while important differences become evident *beyond* the shopfloor.

Such language is identical to that of workers subject to the laws of productivity and profit in the industry of the West. (...) Polish workers complain as do most others that they do not understand their wage-slip, and they see this as proof that they are being robbed, that they are not being paid for the work they have done. They do not criticise the managers of the economy for the same things as workers in a capitalist economy, accusing them of incompetence and corruption rather than blindness to anything other than the profit motive; but as far as their direct masters are concerned, their complaints are the same, bearing on working conditions, pay, and the exercise of authority. (p.41-42)

The authors went on to remark that Solidarity displayed very clearly the two sides of working class consciousness. The positive, offensive side was evident in their constructive orientation and in the deep solidarity of the strongest categories with the weakest (as in the case of the doctors striking for nurses' rights, or of the Gdansk workers who, having just obtained substantial material gains, pursued their protest to extend these gains to workers in the other companies). The second, defensive side was frequently expressed in the need for protection against the worsening of living conditions. The two complementary sides were kept together by an increasing feeling, already noted in Polish surveys, that social gaps were widening (Nowak, 1979). This 'class' character of Solidarity was in any case present in the widespread suspicion of 'experts' (union counsellors) and in the rule allowing only employees to join the union, which, for example, caused the isolation of the student movement.

The coexistence of both sides of class consciousness is confirmed by the account of one of the main Solidarity experts, Jacek Kuroń. As early as 1979, while organising assistance to persecuted workers with the KOR (Committee for Workers' Defence), he remarked that in each workers' concentration two milieus coexisted. The first one included the skilled, stable workers, whose 'affluence' depended on the link to the company. The second one was constituted by the unstable, unskilled workers.

These two cultural sub-groups (unskilled and skilled workers) adopt a very different attitude to strike action. The former easily engage in such action, feeling they have no link to the company, but they meet difficulties in organising, for they have no prestige. For the latter, the opposite is the case. (Kuroń, 1993, pp. 98-99)

A few pages later, Kuroń declares that Lech Wałęsa managed to combine these two groups. Kuroń's political and historical statement corresponds quite well, in sociological terms, to the idea that the workers' movement welds the proletarians with the 'proud workers' or aristocracy of labour.

With respect to Touraine's classic analysis (the role of the social relations of production at work), there are, in fact, other data which make the issue more complex. Most notable is the international comparative surveys on workers' consciousness launched by the Japanese Denki Roren Trade Union Centre for Social Research and carried out in 1984 on electronic plants in eight countries (Japan, Sweden, West Germany, Italy, United Kingdom, Poland, Yugoslavia and Hungary).[15] These surveys showed a gap between Eastern and Western countries, including between Italy and Poland (Table 1.1).

Eastern European workers displayed a much higher affinity with their superiors than their Western counterparts. This point – if we accept respondents' answers as reliable, which is not self-evident in non-democratic countries – would undermine Touraine's analysis, based on the social relations of production. Yet this can be partially explained by the different social hierarchy within socialist firms. In Eastern Europe it was observed (and sometimes still is) that the direct superiors (*brygadziści* in Polish) had less authority than in the West, and that they were treated as fellows by the other workers. Still now, the lowest-level supervisors in Poland are more unionised than the average (Gardawski, 1999, p. 93). Real authority started at the foremen's (*maistrowie*) level, and was mostly held by different boards, such as the party organisation and management. As far as the managers are concerned, the class consciousness of Polish workers seemed to be much closer to that observed in the capitalist world. With regard to workers' collective interest definition, both Italy and Poland emerge as particularly compact.

Table 1.1 gives rise to another consideration with respect to the Polish trade unions, and more generally to the risks of comparative surveys. In 1984, just after the martial law period, the only trade unions admitted to the workplaces were the reconstructed official trade unions (OPZZ). The lack of trust in them among Polish workers is an indicator of the presence of class consciousness rather than the opposite, which the authors of the Denki Roren study seem to believe.

Table 1.1 - Industrial workers and interests' convergence

Do you think that the interests of workers are convergent with those of the following groups? (Yes answers among workers)

	Italy	Poland	Capitalist countries mean	State-socialist countries mean
direct superiors	42.7	63.5	35.5	67.3
managers	14.6	29.7	17.3	49.0
workers	90.4	84.2	71.4	80.4
trade unions in the workplace	73.6	37.2	54.6	54.4

Source: Adapted from Cichomski and Morawski (1988)

Touraine's interpretation aroused some criticism (Goldfarb, 1989; Scott, 1991; Perdue, 1995; Martell and Stammers, 1996). There has been quite a lively debate on 'Who done Solidarity'. Significantly, the greater part of the debate took place abroad. It was as if the 'class' nature of that movement had been embarrassing, though for different reason, in both past and current Polish political systems.

Laba (1991) and Goodwyn (1991) categorically defend the working-class character of Solidarity. Above all, they demonstrate that Solidarity rose in a region (the Baltic Coast) where the long-standing traditions of workers' struggles and organisation (notably, the preference for sit-in strikes comes from the pre-war period) were strongest. Just the opposite, it did not develop in places like Warsaw and Radom where oppositional intellectuals were most active.

Laba recalls some aspects that exhibit a striking parallelism with the Italian situation. An example is the egalitarian demand for flat-rate pay rises (as against percentage increases). This is equivalent of the Italian *aumenti uguali per tutti*, the spontaneous claim of Italian workers during the *autunno caldo*, and of the *punto unico di scala mobile* considered as the most advanced achievement (or the most absurd, according to one's point of view) of the Italian labour movement in the 1970s.

A different argument, although reaches a similar conclusion, is presented by Staniszkis – although she suggests that under state socialism collective representations are more important than social stratification

(Staniszkis, 1989). According to her, Solidarity rejected the state-corporatism model, giving rise to a 'class, rather than corporatist, form of interest representation' (Staniszkis, 1984, p. 40). Solidarity's rejection of branch organisation in favour of a regionally-based structure can be cited as evidence of this point. We might also note that in Italy the local, horizontal structure of the *Camere del Lavoro* is emblematic of the unions' class nature.

In the accounts by Ash (1983), Bakuniak and Nowak (1987), Kennedy (1991), and Bernhard (1992; 1993) the role of workers as a class emerges sharply, but it is not treated as exclusive or 'causal' as it is by Laba. Kennedy, in particular, shows the importance of social alliances for Solidarity. However, it emerges even from his account that the technicians' contribution occurred in a second moment, and rather at the 'margins' of Solidarity, that is in the self-management movement whose class character was much less clear.

A few analysts, finally, have contested the idea that Solidarity is a working class movement, especially by stressing the intellectuals' role (e.g. Kubik, 1994a; Ost, 1990; Pakulski, 1993; Tymowski, 1991; Osa, 1997). Many of their arguments could be reassessed through a discussion of the meaning of class they adopt. In some cases the meaning of these critics goes no further than the incontestable observation that Solidarity was not *only* a trade union. The most elaborate and systematic version of this argument goes further. Kubik suggests that the concept of class should be substituted with the Weberian concept of status (1994a) and develops an alternative, cultural-anthropological explanation (1994b). Interestingly enough, the stress on political and cultural factors brings Kubik (in 1994) to conclude that 'by 1992 Solidarity – this unique social reality – disappeared from the social landscape almost without a trace' (Kubik, 1994a, p. 461). Closer attention to workplaces would probably have avoided such a major mistake: Solidarity remains, in 2000, the most impressive social organisation in Poland. Theoretically more important is to note that Kubik himself acknowledges that things would be different if one used a more culturalist concept of social class, a type of conceptualisation which has actually proved to be useful in dealing with Solidarity (e.g. Rychard, 1988). The unsuitability of orthodox (i.e., focusing on ownership) Marxist theory does not prevent the suitability of a more elaborate concept of class. This is also valid as regards interpretations which speak of civil society rather than of working class (Arato, 1981).

My interpretation, following Touraine's, by no means takes an orthodox class approach. In a word, it places itself halfway between Laba and Kubik's positions. Nobody would seriously argue that Solidarity was *only* a labour movement, least of all Touraine, who spoke of the triple social, national, and democratic nature of Solidarity. After all, his method of 'sociological intervention' is aimed at detecting the 'highest', and not the 'central' meaning of a movement's action. In the case of Solidarity, the presence of other meanings explains why so many people not strictly belonging to the working class, such as administrators, technicians, foremen and even directors, joined the union, albeit in smaller numbers than industrial workers.[16]

My own investigation suggests that the class character of Solidarity was not even its most important component. This seems to be confirmed by the fact that in the region where the Franco-Polish team detected the highest level of class consciousness (Silesia) Solidarity was weak during martial law, unable for instance to engage in underground activity. Moreover, after 1989 many Solidarity activists effortlessly jumped to entrepreneurship or senior management. However, the historical problem of the relative weight of the different components in the Solidarity of the 1980s is here secondary. Touraine's investigation showed that each one of the Solidarity's three elements (social, democratic, and national) was essential. What is important is to state that a class component was *both present and significant*, not that it was the *most important* one.

1980-81 Research Evidence Revisited

> If we are unable to oppose it today, nobody will ever be able to do anything against norms increase, against the violation of safety rules, against the imposition of overtime. (quoted in Wałęsa, 1987, p. 183)

This was the central part of the leaflet distributed at the gates of Gdańsk Lenin Shipyards on the 14th August 1980 to protest against the dismissal of Anna Walentynowicz, founder of the independent trade unions. That day started the strike which gave birth to Solidarity.

One leaflet is not yet evidence. Empirically, the task here is to find evidence consistent with the definition of class employed in this work. Unfortunately, the historical accounts of Solidarity, as it is usual in the history of social movements, very much concentrate on the political level of the events, with little if no interest for the factory level, although this is fundamental for the interpretation of a trade union movement. The most significant example is given by the early and authoritative Holzer's work (Holzer, 1984), which limits itself to the political and organisational dynamics.

It is better to focus neither on the demands of the official unions, since they often hide different meanings (the best example is the issue of self-management, as Touraine among others revealed), nor on textual rhetoric (well analysed by Laba), too much a reflection of the political circumstances. In order to focus attention on the rank-and-file level, and to avoid discontinuity with the evidence that will be presented in the next chapters, I shall concentrate on oral data similar to mine. I shall discuss the four most important sources. The first is Touraine's research itself, whose materials have never been exploited beyond the already extensively quoted book, and on which I carried out a secondary analysis. The other sources are three very little known inquiries carried out by Polish sociologists, stopped by martial law and published only many years later. To finish, I shall also mention two sources of a different methodological nature, which were also published only after 1989: a nation-wide survey and an extensive analysis of Solidarity's written sources.

Three 'Interventions Sociologiques'

Touraine *et al*'s book *Solidarité*, in spite of its truly sociological nature, had an unavoidably newsworthy character, for it was published only a few months after Jaruzelski's coup. In addition, it represented solely the French view (the Polish side of the team did not contribute to the drafting since as well as the Solidarity experiment, martial law also interrupted the Franco-Polish sociological dialogue). I therefore decided to carry out, eighteen years later and with a different historical and geographical perspective, some secondary analysis on those materials.[17]

Touraine's research was principally constituted by six groups of *intervention sociologique*,[18] entirely composed by rank-and-file workers, and organised in six towns in two consecutive phases (June-July and October-November 1981). While examining the fourteen large files of meeting transcripts, I concentrated on the three *interventions* of the first phase, carried out in Warsaw, Gdańsk, and Katowice. The choice is due to the fact that in the summer 1981 Solidarity was still at its highest level of action, while in the autumn it was already concerned with the deepening political crisis. I shall discuss here only the issue of the class nature of Solidarity, but I shall mention the materials on other topics later in the thesis.

The *interventions sociologiques* with Solidarity had an advantage, that of collecting people from different realities, which becomes a disadvantage if one is primarily concerned with work matters. The groups' members came from different work settings, and in Gdańsk and Warsaw none of the interlocutors represented the 'class adversary' in a strict sense (plant directors or foremen). As a consequence, the discussions were rarely about the details of productive issues. The weight of the work conflict is therefore rather underestimated than overestimated, as it would have probably happened if homogenous workers' groups had been analysed. The debate, by contrast, easily reached the higher levels of social movement action. In this regard, it may be said that if there was any 'seduction', it was not of the activists by the researchers but the opposite. Opposition, for instance, was readily expressed in philosophical-cultural terms, and the groups preferred the discussions with political interlocutors to those held with experts, directors or economists. The 'total social movement' nature of Solidarity is constantly manifest in the materials.

However, from time to time work-centred principles come into view. In Warsaw, the guest from the official unions is assailed by the activists' group with such severity that by the end he had to acknowledge himself that '*at the plant level*, unions' activity was actually nothing'. In general, the activists often define themselves on the basis of their plant of origin, showing how their experience was in any case almost totally concentrated on the workplace. The class (and therefore necessarily partial and not total) nature of Solidarity emerges also from the clear distinction between the tasks of the union and those of the work councils: the first must defend the employees; the second, the enterprises altogether. In Gdańsk, it was denied that salary increases were a main preoccupation for the union (this point contrasts with activists' priorities in the 1990s). A strong, typically 'blue-collar' diffidence towards intellectuals appears in the words of some activists: 'the intellectuals are simply lazybones: the normal workers are more combative; these intellectuals, we should simply kick them out'.

The most interesting group from the perspective of class consciousness was the one in Katowice, in Silesia. The analysis must be cautious because the group represented almost exclusively the mining sector (six miners and two mining machine production workers), which is known the world over for its very particular culture. The primary 'working class' feature of the Silesian activists, which is reminiscent of remarks by historians of the working class like Hoggart or Hobsbawm or by sociologists like Parkin, is their active resistance to external ideas and formulations. They instinctively opposed any hypothesis advanced by the researchers, with a strength not encountered in other groups, or even in most of the other social movements studied using the same method. In this way, they confirmed the cultural foundation and separateness of the Silesian working class.

Although the Katowice group, like the others, also manifested the three democratic, national and social orientations, the working-class elements were clearer than elsewhere. A feeling of exploitation was reported to have been the fundamental reason for the first strikes in 1980. The workers claimed control over task definition and the organisation of working time, contested the salary system, and denounced supervisors' behaviour. The class divide also affected representations of welfare and of life-styles.

> In the mines, the technicians were separated from the working people. They had excursions organised separately for them, they had completely different benefits, they received flats in different ways. The miners were annoyed by this situation. [a miner from the Katowice group]

In conclusion, the union was not simply the work-level manifestation of a political struggle. On the contrary, the opposition to the official unions and to the ruling party was expressed in class terms.

> When workers' unions establish themselves, the employers automatically establish their own unions. In my view, at this moment the branch unions represent the employers' union. [a machine production worker from the Katowice group]

> The Polish Unified Workers' Party [the ruling communist party] after 1956 [the year of the bloody repression of Poznań workers] no longer has the right to call itself a workers' party. A party that orders the shooting of workers is not a workers' party. There are more intellectuals than workers in the party now, but a workers' party ought to be made up of workers. We know that it is possible to win everything thanks to the workers. We need to create a workers' mentality by any means. [a miner from the Katowice group]

A Study of the Birth of Solidarity

Leaving Touraine aside, the working-class character of Solidarity on the shop-floor is palpable in the unpublished interview materials of a 1980 inquiry. This was carried out in fifteen plants (among others the *Huta Warszawa* analysed also by this piece of research) by sociologists from Warsaw University but was stopped by the authorities. In 1983 one hundred copies of the research report were printed by the University of Warsaw with the label 'for staff use only' (Bakuniak, Banaszak, Krzemiński and Kruczowska, 1983).[19] Subsequently some shorter accounts were published, again in small numbers, at the very beginning of democratisation (Krzemiński, 1989). An overview of these materials has finally been made available in a recent publication (Krzemiński, 1997).

Although Krzemiński rejects a class analysis in favour of the concept of community, the findings speak for themselves. They reveal that, contrary to the conventional wisdom, Solidarity's earliest demands were not made in reaction to a rise in prices, but only in reaction to the requirement for increased productivity.[20] That is, the demands emerged not from distributive arguments, but from 'class' arguments against exploitation.

> In the Spring and early Summer they implemented the 'salary regulation', which consisted of a major increase in salaries, but also increased productivity, which in fact caused not an increase but a drop in earnings as related to effort. Workers in many plants did not realise the consequences of these changes. In the Summer of 1980 the new pay system and the new production norms became effective. The workers' awakening to this salary fraud occurred at the same time as the rise in prices of meat and the increase of shortages, and the wave of protests exploded all across the country. (Krzemiński, 1997, p. 62)

Interview extracts are even clearer: 'First they gave us an increase, and then they said that we have to increase production by 250 pieces (...). Some bloody increase it is when I have to sweat to get my production up...' (*idem*, p. 64)

Other findings by Krzemiński's team confirm the working class nature of Solidarity. Not only were the unions' typical shop-floor tasks of primary importance – and not limited to salary demands which were rather secondary (Bakuniak, 1983b, pp. 312-313) – but work conflict also played a decisive role. The workers reported:

> 'For years nobody helped us. If someone complained about something, nothing ever happened. A bloke[21] didn't know whether to go to the supervisor on his knees because he was just a worker or what. Now it's somehow better. When he knows that his mates will back him up, a bloke will fight for his rights'. (Kruczkowska, 1983, p. 599)

> 'It has already changed, things are better for us somehow, because now a worker comes to work self-confident, the supervisor doesn't shout so much any more, he doesn't frighten anymore (...). The supervisors can't just do what they like any more. They used to be the lords and masters and they did, didn't they, whatever they wanted and nobody sided with the workers'. (p. 600)

The emergence of Solidarity was then not merely a reaction to a situation of crisis.[22] It was much more rooted in a cultural opposition and in work conflict which had already started to be socially constructed. Krzemiński's team reminds us that, especially in the case of the Huta Warszawa, during the 1970s there had already been work stoppages linked to effort bargaining (Bakuniak, 1983a, p. 70).

Still other typically working-class attitudes are revealed. The major indignation about organisational waste reveals a positive image of industrial production, and is confirmed by some accounts given by the protagonists (e.g. Bujak, 1991). Also stressed is the important role played by manual production workers, even though the common view speaks of the leading role played by the technical elite in Solidarity.

> Our interlocutors show that the most active group in the organisation of the trade union were the production workers, people from the lowest level. Engineers, older workers and white-collar workers were more afraid rather than less. (Krzemiński, 1997, p. 140)

The reference to work conflict was only the first step towards a wider consciousness, which if it is not defined by Krzemiński as class consciousness, certainly was rooted in personal experience.

> The crystallisation of the social tie in the workplace during strike actions in the summer of 1980 was the first concrete sign of the construction of an all-Polish feeling of community. (...) A feeling of community of interests appeared, a feeling that everyone's situation was the same, and against this background developed a representation of those who eventually experienced that similarity. (pp. 77-78)

Other parts of this account are consistent in other ways with the theoretical grounds I have chosen here, revealing a process of social construction of the labour movement. A common definition of the situation, Krzemiński writes, is the condition for mobilisation. This suggestion is confirmed by the fact that the leading workshop was always the toolroom or a comparable workshop, that is the workshop where interactions among workers were most frequent (p. 72). Although their commitment stemmed from the workplace, protagonists were aware that their action affected the whole society. The following interview extract expresses quite well the centrality of the workers' role.

> '[We deal with] anything which concerns workers and people (*człowiek*). This is a very broad concept, because even ensuring the supply on the market

concerns the worker, because the worker is a worker not only when he's at work. When he also exits from the workplace, he still is a worker.' (Bakuniak, 1983b, p. 317)

The difference of the Eastern economic system, with for instance the relevance of the supply problem, did not exclude a feeling of exploitation and of class conflict. It is more correct to say that in state socialist societies a variation of the feeling of exploitation was manifest, which eventually was at least as strong as in the capitalist world. The relevance of the company not only for the economy, but also for broader social organisation, allowed workers to perceive national wealth as *their* product. They subsequently concluded that this wealth was largely expropriated by the ruling élite. Anything that was produced, from buildings to services, was a product of their work, and it belonged to them – since it was either materially produced by them or it was at least paid for with the factory's money. This peculiar form of the perception of exploitation is important for the understanding of workers' reactions during the privatisation of housing and of social services, as the next chapters will show.

'Everybody agreed that actually all the machinery, this factory is simply our property, only, formally speaking it does not meet, let say... this property wasn't really controlled by the employees. It was real property but the right to conduct, to rule this property was usurped by a narrow élite. Workers didn't want to agree with this situation.' (Bakuniak, 1983b, p. 316)

Krzemiński's work not only confirms the appropriateness of a class analysis for 1980-81 Solidarity. It also offers some pointers for the understanding of the following phase of class disintegration, showing how, after Jaruzelski's coup, work was suddenly strongly devalued in workers' eyes, and consequently how identification in the factory and in the working group declined (Krzemiński, 1997, p. 238). Similarly, Staniszkis (1991) detected among the strikers of 1988-89 a new, 'post-modern' mentality. Its main features were a disbelief in progress, an uncertainty about one's identity, and a conception of action as an independent value. All those points correspond to a disintegration of the I-O-T principles of class consciousness. As a consequence, work conflict also started to be expressed in individualistic, non-class forms like absenteeism, lack of discipline, and low quality work (Pańków, 1990; Kubik, 1991).

A Study of the Strikes

Equally important are the findings of another investigation by the Polish Sociological Association in 1980-81 and also unpublished until democratisation (Kulpińska, 1990). In particular, I shall consider the analysis carried out on the strikes in the Warsaw region in the summer of 1980 (Drążkiewicz and Rychard, 1990).

Kulpińska's team, unlike Krzemiński's, explicitly uses a class terminology, and in a way turns it against the socialist state. This might have a rhetorical nature (although published in 1990, the texts date back to the 1980s and were not revisited after 1989), consisting in appropriating the regime's ideology as a justification scheme. This scheme has been followed by many internal opponents of state socialism during the century, the best example being perhaps the Chinese students singing the *Internationale* on Tian An Men Square in 1989. In any case, what is here interesting is the empirical grounding of Kulpińska *et als'* statements.

The Polish sociologists adopt an actor-centred interpretative scheme that recalls Touraine's standpoint. The main task in the analysis of the strikes is then the definition of the conflicting sides. On the strikers' side, are found first of all the direct production workers. The first workshops to go on strike are the production and some auxiliary workshops (like the power shop, the toolroom, maintenance), and the most active are blue-collar workers. The technicians rarely go on strike, and the administrative workers almost never.

More complex is the picture of the 'other side of the barricade'. There are multiple criteria for its identification: the research team investigated who fought the strikers, who was seen by the strikers as 'the other side'(e.g., to whom demands were addressed), and who took part in the negotiations. In this way, the ranks of the adversaries were quite large. At the plant level, they comprised the foremen, the workshop directors, the secretaries and the activists of the plant party organisations. Beyond the plant level, new opponents were met: party officers, local authorities, government authorities. With some exceptions, the official unions also were an enemy (at *Huta Warszawa* for instance they officially condemned the strike). In some cases, at the end of the negotiations the official unions' representatives signed the agreement as part of the same side as the director and the party representatives.

The sociological assessment of this empirical investigation of the strikes in Warsaw reads precisely like support for the 'class' interpretation. The authors note that foremen used to actively solicitate workers to go back to work and to cease the strike.

In the debate on whether foremen are still part of the working class, which exists in the sociology of work and of organisation, the strikes in Warsaw in 1980 offered quite a clear answer. It is notable that the strikers were almost exclusively common workers, that is people devoid of any influence on economic decisions. Against them stood their immediate superiors. The behaviour of lower management, e.g. of the foremen, shows that their role in the system goes beyond the normal organisational functions originating in the requirements of work organisation. They are a sort of outpost of the proprietors of economy, placed on the frontier (or rather at the lower border of the social structure) as representatives of the ruling élite, which defends its power monopoly even at this lowest level. (Drążkiewicz and Rychard, 1990, pp. 14-15)

A Collection of Life-stories

Marek Latoszek with his Gdańsk's colleagues produced quite a different piece of research. They collected in 1981, through an open contest, 201 diaries by people either taking part or closely observing the strikes on the Polish Littoral (especially in the shipyards of Gdańsk, Gdynia and Stettin) in August 1980. They subsequently analysed in depth the 36 most interesting diaries. With this method, which in Poland has a famous precedent and model (Thomas and Znaniecki, 1927), they offered a point of view 'from below' on events that have been widely accounted for 'from above'. As with Krzemiński's and Kulpińska's work, the publication of the results was prohibited after Jaruzelski's 'putsch'. They were printed in an edition of one hundred copies as a methodological study in 1987, and finally published in 1991 (Latoszek, 1991).

Concentrating as it does on a very limited period of time, and above all on a clearly 'exceptional' situation, Latoszek's materials leave less room for speculation on workers' consciousness than the previously mentioned works. In fact, one of the most interesting arguments is about the shift from a 'workers' movement' to a 'social movement' identity, due to exchange with people outside the plants. These people 'beyond the gates', for their part, were in no doubt about the 'leading role' of the workers. Some other points are worth mentioning.

First, Latoszek – along with many others – stresses the role of conflict in the construction of a collective identity: 'the working class goes through an accelerated process of becoming a political subject; its members become conscious of their position, role, and chances, they organise themselves, they start fighting' (p. 292).

The strike initiative, consistent with Krzemiński's account and with the argument on the basically 'worker' nature of Solidarity, came from the workers subject to the heaviest work conditions in the big factories.

> The strike started from workshops such as the hull-shop and the toolroom, where the work conditions were the heaviest; by contrast, the engine workshops were considered a sort of workers' aristocracy. (p. 296)

Yet the most important point is the presence of a work conflict with the lower hierarchy: 'the attempts made by directors and foremen to organise work during the strike met the immediate counteraction of the strikers' (p. 297).

Surveys and Text Analyses

Besides Touraine's, Krzemiński's, and Kulpińska's research, there has been other precious, although methodologically different, sociological research on the early Solidarity. Two works in particular allow a general theoretical discussion. The first one is a nation-wide survey carried out on an all-Polish representative sample in 1981, once again censored by the regime and published only recently (Adamski, 1996). Its conclusions conflict with the hypothesis of the class nature of Solidarity: the author suggests that the most important divide in Poland was not between interest groups, but between society and power. However, the survey was not concerned with work-related matters, with the exception of the question: 'which are the most important problems to be solved in the company?'. Answering to this question, Solidarity members mentioned, in order (p. 23):

1. tools, raw materials, energy, work organisation (21.9%)
2. economic reform (10.4%)
3. salaries (10.4%)
4. participation in the management (7.5%)
5. work conditions, security and hygiene (7.2%)
6. social conditions (6%)
7. modernisation (5.1%)
8. bad relations (4.9%)
9. work discipline and productivity (3.1%)
10. others (23.5%).

The only indication the survey gives (and which will be important in Chapter 4), is that in 1981 financial issues were not expressed as a central concern by Solidarity members. From such data, however, it is impossible to infer anything about the class or non-class orientations of Solidarity. The situation is the same with other surveys carried out on Solidarity members in 1980-81 by the union's research centre (Kurczewski, 1981; Radźko, 1981). It is worth noting, nevertheless, that in these surveys 62% of Solidarity members in Mazovia (Warsaw region) and 74% in Katowice defined themselves as belonging to the working class (Kurczewski, 1981).

The second sociological interpretation is based on an extensive analysis of Solidarity publications at the local and national level, reinforced by a personal observation of the events (Kowalski, 1990). A first version was published in 1988 by Warsaw University in only one hundred exemplars. A 'publication' in the real sense of the word had to wait until 1990.

From the point of view of sociological theory, Kowalski's analysis is the most elaborate among those mentioned here. Unfortunately, Kowalski does not include in the analysis workplace bulletins. As a result, the political and cultural issues are pushed in the foreground, while the problems at work receive less attention than in any other of the mentioned analyses. However, at a certain point the issue of 'who done Solidarity' is considered. In this regard, Kowalski's sources, even though indirectly, show that the workers used (also) class arguments in the defence of their decisional power in the union.

'Without the intellectuals, I wouldn't manage anything in the *Huta*... But the decisions should be taken by the workers. They are more numerous. They have a stronger pressure force, and in spite of all they are the most responsible people. They don't sit behind single desks'. [from *Głos Wolny*, bulletin of the first Solidarity Congress] (Kowalski, 1990, p. 111)

'In many conversations I had with workers from big industrial factories in various regions of Poland, they repeated that the creative intellectuals and the white-collar workers should have the function of counsellors and experts, and not of decision-makers (...) [because] the workers *as a class* are more decided (...); after the dolorous experiences of '56, '70, '76, and '80, the Polish working class has no longer doubts on the nature of power in Poland, whose non-working class nature is evident'. [from *Jedność*, bulletin of Western Pomerania Solidarity] (*ibidem*)

However, neither Adamski nor Kowalski are in a position, through their data, to clarify Solidarity's role at work. Oral-sources-based research has been more useful, although this also was not concentrated on the work situation. The next chapters, through the analysis of the union discourse in the 1990s, will try, joining a historical perspective with the sociological one, to add some points to this still open issue.

A provisory conclusion is possible. The relative unpopularity of the class concept as regards Solidarity, especially among Polish scholars is understandable on the basis of their opposition to the communist system. It has emerged that the Polish members of Touraine's team in 1981 initially expressed some scepticism towards the vocabulary of French sociology, which was much too 'Marxist' in their eyes (Frybes and Kuczyński, 1994). This kind of cultural resistance, because of its sociologically ideological nature, was naturally more prevalent among researchers than among workers. The fact that, despite the cultural resistance of the analysts, so many indicators of class consciousness appear in the findings of Krzemiński's team, should be treated as strengthening the evidence.

Notes

1   In Italy union bureaucratisation exploded during the 1970s, achieving at the end of the decade one of the highest formal bureaucratisation rates in the Western world, with an officer for every 700 members (Biagioni, Palmieri and Pipan, 1980).

2   The distinction between political orientations and social consciousness is at the basis of Touraine's criticism of classic studies on workers' consciousness: '... these so-called empirical studies generally reach the conclusion that working-class consciousness is weak. And indeed if no distinction is made between class consciousness and consciousness of the historical mission of the proletariat organised politically in trade unions or, more simply, between class consciousness and political will, it is possible to conclude that class consciousness is far from widespread. However, this is really only saying that the working class is not revolutionary, which is a quite different assertion' (Touraine, Dubet and Wieviorka, 1987, p. 32).

3   It was impossible, for me, directly to investigate the role of work during the golden era of the workers' movement. For want of empirical foundation, the theoretical references have to be mentioned. The role of the experience of work in constructing social consciousness has been shown by Touraine (1966). Later, while studying Solidarity, Touraine noticed that the main thing that Polish and Western union activists had in common was the experience of work relations (Touraine, Dubet, Wieviorka and Strzelecki, 1983). In different ways and from different theoretical standpoints, the weight of the experience of work is stressed by most Marxists (one could mention Marx himself) and materialist analyses of work conflict (Edwards, 1986). The particular significance of the experience of work for worker solidarity (one of the features of working class consciousness) has been described by Zoll (1992): only that daily experience, and not the mere sharing of interests helps to build such a strong, everyday link between workers. The centrality of work helps to understand why worker solidarity has always been a *group* solidarity, rarely concerned with the enfranchisement of categories outside the working people (women, peasants,

minorities, the unemployed). Other authors agree on the traditional centrality of the experience of work for the construction of identities, although they doubt the 'unity' of such experience. For instance, Sainseaulieu (1977, pp. 412-413) argued for the existence of a link between collective action and cultural learning experience at work. More precisely, cultural learning in the work setting involved a habit of sociability, and the latter involved, in turn, the development of collective action.

4   In the German case, social psychological studies also confirm relevance of the East-West cleavage (Piontkowski, Öhlschlegel-Hanbrock and Hölker, 1997). Other studies, specifically on trade union members, conclude that the structure of choice-making is basically the same in the East and West Germany (in other words, there is no anthropological difference between Eastern and Western workers), but their behaviour and frames of reference are different (Frege, 1996). Sociologists may be dissatisfied by these studies because of their lack of explanation. One can suggest that this 'constant relevance' is the 'algebraical' result of a trend of convergence and a new trend of divergence. My study will try to explore this hypothesis.

5   I use for Poland after 1956 the term 'totalitarian vocation' instead of 'totalitarianism'. If we can speak of worker movements for some periods of the history of some communist countries, it is because they were not, at that time, definitely totalitarian. Speaking of social movements in a totalitarian country would be oxymoric.

6   During a study on the disabled at work (Meardi, 1993), I noted the importance of equal-basis experiences and of communication for the development of attitudes of solidarity towards the disabled. These experiences could well have occurred outside work, for instance at school.

7   An example is the one of the Renault factories in Belgium and France in February 1997. Here, the management *contemporaneously* announced the shut-down of the Vilwoord plant and the redundancy of 3,000 workers in French plants. The coverage of this by the press and political actors produced a 'domino effect'. It is not by chance that it gave rise to the first 'Eurostrike'.

8   In 1997 a Polish journalist opened an interview with me with the question: 'what differentiates the Polish trade unions from the normal ones, like the Italian?' (*Gazeta Wyborcza*, 24.9.97). The shortcoming of this way of thinking – evident to an Italian not used to seeing his country defined as normal – lies in neglecting the actual Western reality, subordinated to a mythic image of normality.

9   It seems even less coincidental that the countries which implemented Sachs' receipts of liberalisation and privatisation most quickly and literally (Albania and Russia), are also the less successful, whereas the slowest one (China) is doing very well (whatever we think of its political regime).

10   Tonino Perna, a sociologist of the economy working in the field in Albania, formulated the opinion in Spring 1997 that Berisha's country was anticipating global trends (Perna, 1997). At that time it may have appeared to be a provocative idea, but much less after the global financial turmoil of the following months (Perna, 1998). A similar point, but from the different theoretical perspective of 'demodernisation', is made in another sociological study of Albania (Romano, 1997), according to which the same general processes which occur in the West also occur in that country, but in a purer and wider way. The case of the country of the eagles will be mentioned again in the text as an extreme, pure case of a totalitarian past followed by an abrupt transition.

11   I call neo-corporatism what Philippe Schmitter calls corporatism *tout court*, the distinction being necessary when dealing with the Italian case where corporatism has particular historical connotations. I recall here for the sake of clarity the classic

definition by Schmitter: 'corporatism can be defined as a system of interest representation in which the constituent units are organized into a limited number of singular, compulsory, noncompetitive, hierarchically ordered and functionally differentiated categories, recognized or licensed (if not created) by the state and granted a deliberate representational monopoly within their respective categories in exchange for observing certain controls on their selection of leaders and articulation of demands and supports' (Schmitter, 1974, pp. 93-94).

12 Recently, some authors have even argued that the 'A' element precludes, instead of contributing to, class consciousness. Accordingly, class consciousness would develop only when labour gives up any illusions about changing capitalism and devotes its efforts to getting a better deal within it (Hattam, 1993). Seen in this way, business unionism would not conflict with class consciousness.

13 This part of Berger's and Luckmann's thought allows to reject Szakolczai's (1996) opinion that phenomenological sociology would be unsuitable in a period of deep change.

14 From a less orthodox Marxist standpoint it is possible to state that the Soviet system was a 'sub-group' within the societal type of capitalism (Chavance, 1995). Three arguments support this statement. Under state socialism, as well as under capitalism, firstly production was mediated by monetary exchange and a wage-labour system; secondly, co-ordination was achieved through both hierarchies and markets; finally, the division of labour was co-ordinated in despotic forms within the enterprise (technical division of labour) and through exchange within society (social division of labour).

15 The research was repeated in 1994-96, offering a unique comparison over time (Consoli, Ishikawa, Makó and Martin, 1998). In both phases the surveys concentrated on the electric and electronic machine industry.

16 A 1981 survey (Adamski, 1996), although it almost certainly overestimates the overall Solidarity figures, gives some indication on the social composition of the union. Solidarity was joined by 86.7% of the skilled workers from heavy industry, 74.1% of the skilled workers from light industry, 73.5% of foremen, 69% of technicians, 51.7% of administrative employees, 51.7% of high-level administrators. Unfortunately, Adamski merges the categories 'unskilled workers' and 'agriculture dependent manual workers', so that the overall figure for both groups (55.4%) is absolutely meaningless. In this regard it must be recalled, however, that for political rather than organisational reasons in the communist states unskilled industrial workers were officially not numerous.

17 I am extremely grateful to the authors of that investigation for the unlimited access to the research materials.

18 On the method of 'sociological intervention', see Touraine (1981) and Dubet and Wieviorka (1996).

19 This version is also used as a source, though with different theoretical goals, by Kubik (1994a).

20 Holzer's historical account is consistent with this point (Holzer, 1984, p. 89).

21 The interviewee uses the term (popular in Polish) *człowiek*, that is 'human being'. It has a strong moral and, in this theoretical perspective, 'subjective' connotation. English lacks a precise equivalent.

22 The functionalist approach has been applied to Eastern Europe starting with Parsons and finishing with many *ex-post* analyses of the breakdown of the Soviet Union. It seems however the least suitable approach to the understanding of Solidarity. Even if

many analysts do not agree with the class interpretation, to my knowledge nobody has dared to explain that movement as a simple reaction to a crisis or to some system disfunction. By contrast, both class- and Weber-like analyses agree on a much more deeply rooted subjectivity.

2 Interviewing Trade Union Activists

The research questions outlined in the first chapter have been dealt with a specific approach and on a specific field, which will be presented in this chapter. Many research tools have been used: interviews with managers and with union leaders; analysis of union documentation and publications; observation of the plants and some participant observation in unions' meetings and demonstrations. However, the principal method utilised has been the unstructured interview with union activists from specific companies. In this chapter, I shall first present the six factories chosen for the inquiry. Then, I shall discuss the advantages and disadvantages of the method. Finally, the comparative perspective will be presented.

The Field of Inquiry

The Choice of Cases

Originally, the inquiry concentrated on a two-by-two case comparison. The cases considered were the Fiat car factories in Turin and in Southern Poland, with a particular emphasis on the assembly line workshops, and the Lucchini Group steelworks in Piombino and Warsaw.

The main criterion in the selection of the cases, trade unions, and people, was 'theoretical relevance' as defined by 'grounded theory' (Glaser and Strauss, 1967, p. 49). Accordingly, the actual research strategy has been adapted in the course of the inquiry. Four main changes took place.

In the case of the Fiat factories, the investigation became a secondary two-by-two comparison since two plants in each country were considered (Mirafiori and Rivalta in Italy, Bielsko-Biała and Tychy in Poland). In the framework of a 'disintegration' hypothesis, it seemed useful to investigate not only the extent to which one can speak of 'national patterns', but also of 'company patterns' in industrial relations. The idea that firms' behaviour affects work relations more than states' behaviour is becoming increasingly widespread (see for instance Katz, 1993; Marginson *et al.*, 1988; Müller and Purcell, 1992), and should therefore be tested. The Fiat case, even if not representative, strongly suggests that in industrial relations there has indeed recently been a strong tendency to focus on the enterprise (Crouch, 1993; Kochan, Locke and Piore, 1995). Nevertheless, firm-level strategy and culture, albeit very important factors, are not the sole determinants: divergence also occurs nowadays *within* companies across different plants (MacDuffie and Pil, 1997). The differences found between the Tychy and the Bielsko-Biała plants, as well as between Rivalta and Mirafiori, are almost as striking as the cross-national differences. The case of Turin is the most telling. The Rivalta and Mirafiori plants are only about ten km from each other. Moreover, the workforce is demographically homogeneous. Today production is different (it is more quality-oriented in Rivalta than in Mirafiori), but this is a recent development which is a *consequence* of the plants' differences and not a *cause* of them. Therefore, the analysis of these cases offers good arguments for the assumption that union action is *socially constructed* in the micro-sociological experience of work more than it is *socially determined* by some order of 'macro' factors. The six plants of Fiat and the Lucchini group have remained the principal case studies, and their main characteristics are given in Table 2.1.

Besides dividing the Fiat case into a two-by-two comparison, a second change in the research strategy was the addition of a number of control cases to assess the representativeness of the findings. The main risk of bias is the nationality of ownership asset of the plants studied: Fiat and Lucchini are foreign employers for the Poles, and 'national' for the Italians, therefore they may be differently perceived. Moreover, it is commonly believed that Italian companies have a distinctive management style that strongly affects work relations. In fact, there are good grounds to consider Fiat Auto and Lucchini Group as typical cases of a paternalistic and anti-unions family capitalism, which characterises Italy making of it a difficult term for comparison. In his popular book on the diversity of capitalisms Michel Albert could even write about Italy: 'the Italian economic model, dominated by family capitalism, by state weakness, by an enormous deficit of public finances and by an amazing vitality of SMEs, can be compared with no other model, exept maybe the one of Chinese diaspora' (Albert, 1991, p. 24). However, the pressures of globalisation and the scale of their activities are gradually forcing these companies to adopt more mainstream management styles. In the case of Fiat this change became evident with the Agnelli and Romiti succession in the mid 1990s and might be completed by the agreement with General Motors in 2000, but had in fact already started few years earlier with the re-orientation of production towards quality and the organisational project *Fabbrica Integrata*.

In order to assess this issue, a non-Italian case (the French Danone company, and in particular the plants in Casale Cremasco, Warsaw and Bieruń Stary) was added, in which a smaller number of interviews helped to assess the 'disturbance effect' of the nationality of capital. Danone is not a secondary case. It is the leading group in food production in Italy, and its presence in Eastern Europe (besides Poland it also has plants in Russia, Czech Republic, Hungary, and Bulgaria) is consolidated and often dominant not only in retailing but also in production.

Table 2.1 - Plants and trade unions

Plant	Approximate workforce at the time of the investigation	Trade unions present and approximate membership (*object of investigation)
Fiat Rivalta	7,000	FIOM (16%)* FIM (5%)* UILM (5%)* Fismic (12%) Sin-Cobas (<1%) UGL (<1%)
Fiat Mirafiori	29,000	FIOM (14%)* FIM (5%) UILM (7%) Fismic (16%) Sin-Cobas (2%)* UGL (2%) CISAL (<1%)
Fiat Bielsko-Biała	6,000	Solidarity (25%)* Metalowcy (15%) Solidarity 80 (3%) Sierpień 80 (1%) Engineers & Technicians' T.U. (1%)
Fiat Tychy	6,000	Sierpień 80 (30%)* Metalowcy (16%)* Popiełuszko (8%)* Federacja (3%)* Engineers & Technicians' T.U. (1%)
Lucchini Piombino	2,500	FIOM (50%)* FIM (10%) UILM (15%) SLAI-Cobas (5%)*
Lucchini Warsaw	2,500	Solidarity (65%)* Hutnicy (10%)*

Thirdly, the very diverse and changing Polish situation required a broader look. Therefore a more superficial collection of information on trade union activity (but also a few open interviews) was carried out in a number of other firms in different sectors and having different capital assets. These observations were not made on a comparative basis, as no comparable situations could be found in Italy. The rationale lies in the need to gather more information about an emerging (and therefore still little known) national system like the Polish one: for this reason, the generalisation of the findings is more delicate in Poland than in Italy. This does not mean that Fiat and Lucchini represent (or anticipate the developments of) the Italian system. Nevertheless, their great significance is universally acknowledged in that all the national actors consider them (especially Fiat) reference-points.[1] In Poland, it was convenient also to consider other companies: the Ursus tractor plants in Warsaw and Lublin (state-owned), the Daewoo car factory in Warsaw, and a few industrial companies in Płock in Central Poland (Petrochemia Płock, New Holland, Cotex).

A final, smaller 'deviation' from the original plan occurred in Piombino. One of the main current transformations of industry is externalisation or 'outsourcing', that is the contracting out of some activities previously integrated in industrial concerns. This process is taking place in all six plants. In Turin it has already become a topic for research and political debate, especially during the successful '*bisarche*' (trucks) strike of 1996 and the contracting out of internal transport to the multinational company TNT in 1998. Its effects are most striking in the Piombino steelworks, and for this reason I also interviewed some union activists from a contractor firm (Siderco). The rationale was a need to understand the process of 'dualisation' arising *within* the plants in order to conceptualise better the 'dualisation' *among* plants.

The supplementary cases (Danone, Daewoo, Ursus, Petrochemia Płock, New Holland) are described in a specific section of chapter 4; here, I shall present the six 'main' plants.

An Alternative Classification

This would seem to be an appropriate point at which to classify the plants described in the research. If the internal history and social environment of the plants rather than their external characteristics (location, property assets etc.) are considered, it is possible to classify the six companies used in this research according to their 'crystallised' type of union consciousness (Table 2.2). The different types depend on the different sets of experiences significant for the trade unions: work relations, political struggle, and local community.

This classification is far from exhaustive in its account of the features of trade union activity. There are, of course, internal differences within the plants, and other inter-plant similarities and parallelisms in some respects. Nevertheless, this 'alternative' typology based on the plant histories, with their sets of experiences and belief-systems, is no less significant than a national or company-based typology (a Poland-Italy distinction or a Lucchini-Fiat one). Therefore, I shall give here a preliminary explanation of these 'consciousness types', which will be useful in the next sections and chapters.

Table 2.2 – Plant consciousness typology

Type of consciousness	*Italy*	*Poland*
class/politics oriented	Fiat Mirafiori	Huta Lucchini-Warszawa
class/work relations oriented	Fiat Rivalta	Fiat Tychy
community/labour-market oriented	Lucchini Piombino	Fiat Bielsko-Biała

Trade unions, as has been pointed out by a number of scholars including Marx, operate in two different areas. The first is the labour market, with its employment opportunities. In this area unions aim to reduce competition among workers in order to achieve better conditions. This side of union action, which was best formulated by the Webbs in England, is a pure case of instrumental collectivism. Moreover, it has often been found to demonstrate discriminatory attitudes towards some segments of the workforce (e.g. women, foreigners, or the less educated...). Therefore it develops best in stable communities, where both economic structure and the social composition of the population are under tighter control.

The other side of trade union action develops *within* the workplace, and it deals with work conflict as defined in the previous chapter. This is the side that has to do with 'class', and with an alternative view of how industrial production should be. It is necessarily collectivist, but also intrinsically concerned with the individual needs of the man (and potentially of the woman) at work. A further distinction can, however, be made: the working class, as the bearer of a positive idea of industry and of an alternative view of its organisation, always has a general political relevance, but only in some situations does it undertake political action in the strictest sense.

The limited scope of this inquiry is to analyse the transformation of union consciousness in a period of universally acknowledged decline of the labour movement. In this context, it should be checked whether a tradition of 'class' consciousness and political involvement does matter in the present.

Why are the six plants distinguished in this way? Each one must be described in more detail.

Fiat Mirafiori

In 1998 (before the agreement with General Motors of March 2000) Fiat was the seventh largest car producer in the world, and had, as a holding, a turn-over of Lit. 88,621 billion and a workforce of 220,549 people worldwide (*Relazione Semestrale degli Amministratori*, 1st Semester 1999). The Mirafiori plant in Turin, built in 1939 on Mussolini's prompting to be the biggest factory in the world, has in the past employed up to 52,500 people.[2] Together with the other Fiat factory in Turin, the *Lingotto*, it bestowed on Turin the character of a 'company-town', and it became the object of several sociological studies (Bagnasco, 1986 and 1990; Bottighieri and Ceri, 1987; Barbano, 1992). Mirafiori was a momentous example of the Taylorist conception of industrial organisation; that is, of the kind of industrial organisation considered by leading French sociologists of work (Friedmann and Touraine) as the most suitable situation for the development of class conflict and class consciousness. Moreover, at Fiat for a long time industrial relations have been a strategically vital area: unlike in most other similar companies, they have been dealt with by managers at the very top of the hierarchy.

In the 1950s, industrial relations at Fiat were managed in an extremely unilateral way. In particular, the left-wing union FIOM was firmly isolated and combated.[3] The massive flow of unskilled workers from Southern Italy which had its peak at the beginning of the 1960s was followed by a difficult process of integration between the new 'proletarian' mass and the local skilled workforce. This eventually resulted, in 1969, in the so-called *autunno caldo* ('hot autumn'), a very turbulent period of workers' action. During and after the *autunno caldo*, the labour movement managed to attain a real 'counter-power' in the workshops, and rarely if ever have job control issues become so important. The unions, and notably the CGIL militants, had at that time an almost epic vision of workers' managerial capacities (Manghi, 1987).[4]

Because of its size and location, as well as the history of the Turin working class rooted in Gramsci's *consigli*, Mirafiori was not just any work setting. It was also a political symbol. In the 1970s, it was frequently said that 'governments are made in Rome, but unmade in Mirafiori'. Even now, when economic or social issues are in the headlines, Italian journalists go to the Mirafiori gates to ask the opinion of the 'Italian Worker'. As a consequence, the experience of the Mirafiori metalworker was two-edged. They experienced both a situation of conflict in the workplace and a situation of political centrality. Since the 1960s Mirafiori has been the favourite hunting ground for extra-parliamentary left-wing groups, including the terrorist organisations which emerged from the disintegration of the *autunno caldo*.[5] October 1980, with the defeat of the Mirafiori trade unions after a 35-day strike, is seen in Italy as the end of the long Italian *anni caldi*.[6]

Nowadays, Mirafiori employs 'only' 29,000 workers (including the 2,000 'sold' to TNT in 1998). In the 1990s there was a new process of rationalisation at Fiat which has yet to be concluded: two plants in Northern Italy (Desio and Chivasso) were closed and both Rivalta and Mirafiori underwent further cut-back. The most important reduction at Mirafiori, in 1994, gave birth to a resurgence of union conflict, for the first time also involving white-collar employees, previously almost by definition loyal towards the employer and hostile to the unions. As a consequence, the workforce is today quite old (the average age being around 48) and the education level has remained very low (not more than five years for half of the manual workers).

Change was not only quantitative, however. In the 1980s production was substantially automated (Becchi Collidà and Negrelli, 1986; Santielli, 1987; Lerner 1988; Locke and Negrelli, 1989; Locke, 1992), and in the 1990s the 'Japanese' concepts of lean production and total quality were introduced (Bonazzi, 1993, 1994, 1997 and 1998; Cerruti and Rieser, 1991; Rieser, 1992 and 1996; Cosi, 1993; Carrieri, 1993; Pessa and Sartirano, 1993; Camuffo and Volpato, 1995; Camuffo and Micelli, 1998). Management claimed to be shifting towards more participatory Human Resource Management approaches, but the effects of the implementation of this change[7] are not always obvious in the older sites, although they are impressive in the new green-field plant in Melfi, in Southern Italy (Rieser, 1997; Pero, 1998). All the new joint committees (working time, training, equal opportunities, job mobility...) between 1996 and 1999 have had only a role of communication, with the only exception of a negotiated agreement on part-time.

Trade unions are now much weaker than in the past, especially in the largest and once influential body plant where the FIOM now organises only 9.7% of workers. *Cobas* is present and active as well as the 'traditional' FIOM, FIM and UILM. As in the other Italian Fiat plants, there is a company-based union, the Fismic, the heir of the so-called 'yellow union' SIDA, created by Fiat in the 1950s. Today Fismic is also present in other factories (more or less linked to the Fiat group) and though promoting participation rejects any charge of collaboration. However, since it is traditionally considered extraneous to the labour movement, it will not be an object of this study. The same can be said about the last two, very small, unions active at Fiat: the autonomous CISAL and the right-wing UGL.[8]

In conclusion, the Mirafiori plant represents a suitable case for investigating the transformation of a working class undergoing both change at work and a political decline. Because of its complexity, political involvement and de-unionisation, it might be caricatured as 'the French pattern'.

Fiat Rivalta

The Rivalta factory, located a few kilometres South of Turin, is younger and smaller than Mirafiori: it was established in 1967 and today employs 7,000 workers (peak employment having been 15,000). As a consequence, Rivalta does not have the symbolic significance of Mirafiori. Trade unions have concentrated much more on work conflict, and have been less affected by the loss of political centrality. This does not, however, mean that political commitment was weaker: in fact, the PCI and CGIL were more influential than in Mirafiori. For example, Cobas, which is very active in Mirafiori, is absent in Rivalta. However, the local communist subculture has been very pragmatic and has clearly distinguished political issues from work issues. Moreover, unlike the usual 'Latin' model, the union was perceived as having priority over the party. Speaking on this point, the workers interviewed in my inquiry reported that the PCI was the transmission belt for the union, and not the opposite. The enduring vitality of this union subculture is visible in the magazine published by the local FIOM, '*Spray*', which does not have an equivalent in Mirafiori or in any other plant in this study.

Sociographically, the workforce of Rivalta and Mirafiori are homogenous, and have even been mixed to an extent in the last years as a result of internal mobility. Given its expansion in the 1970s, the period of massive women's entrance in the Italian labour market, Rivalta has been traditionally more feminised, but today the differences are reduced: 25% of women in Rivalta and 20% in Mirafiori.

Currently the trade unions (especially FIOM) are stronger than in Mirafiori.[9] Moreover, the unions still exert active influence and control over work matters, and have developed a proper approach of 'participation through conflict' (see as an illustration: Pessa and Sartirano, 1993). During the implementation of the Lancia K assembly line, almost daily stoppages forced the directors to accept suggestions by the unions. This case could therefore be represented as a kind of 'German' *Konfliktpartnerschaft*, presenting both workers' institutionalised sub-cultures and *Mitbestimmung* practices.

Lusid Piombino

The Lucchini steelworks (earlier AFP, today officially 'Lusid') in Piombino have a completely different history. The small town of Piombino (50,000 inhabitants) has since prehistory been linked to iron ore deposits. The steel industry developed early (compared to the Italian industrial development more generally) and rapidly at the end of the XIX Century. In 1905, 70% of the active population worked in heavy industry. The strong local trade unions attained improvements in working conditions and contractual terms (e.g. the 8-hour working day, housing subsidies, job safety regulations...) earlier than in the rest of the country (Carignoni, Luchetti and Poli, 1985; Favilli, 1974; Banconi, 1970; Cresti and Orefice, 1990). Under the fascist regime, however, the biggest steelworks 'AFP' (*Acciaierie e Ferriere di Piombino*), then belonging to the ILVA holding, developed differently from the global steel industry. 'Taylorist' organisation principles, which had been introduced in the United States in the 1920s, did not find any implementation in AFP. More distinctively, the majority of the workforce was engaged in directly productive tasks, and discipline was achieved through a kind of 'military control' (Amatori, 1992).

Towards the end of World War II the Piombino steelworks, together with the harbour and a large part of the town, were destroyed by the retreating German Army. The plants were readily and spontaneously reconstructed by the population, and taken under their control by mass organisations (Left parties, trade unions and anti-Fascist resistance groups). This event, still alive in the memory of the inhabitants of Piombino, is emblematic of the symbiosis between the town and the steelworks. The ILVA industrial group, including the Piombino plant, was subsequently nationalised. For a long time the governance of AFP, and to some extent all of the town, remained a political issue. This involved the City Council – after 1945 dominated by the PCI, then the PDS –, national government, and the trade unions. Piombino was for a long time an area of full employment, where the recruitment was tightly controlled by the trade unions.

Because of the industrial structure, there was also a typically male dominated economy. In 1981 the employment rate was 98% for men aged 30-54, and 32% for women of the same age; moreover, 51% of men, and only 12% of women, worked in industry (CLES, 1988). Even more significant than the employment data is the fact that a timid attempt made by the AFP unions in the 1980s to employ a group of women in production failed miserably. 23 women out of 25 resigned or moved to the offices after a few months, and as acknowledged by union leaders themselves this happened because of the 'male' culture dominating the workshops. Neither the unions nor the employer have ever dared to repeat the experiment.

At the political level, the Piombino workers' community took the form of a communist subculture, deeply rooted in the factories (Favilli and Tognarini, 1994). After 1946 electoral support for the PCI was massive, never below 50% until its dissolution (1991). The PCI had a virtual monopoly of workers' representation, since the extreme-left parties scored below the national average (Comune di Piombino, 1987). This hegemony also the cultural level: almost all the literature on Piombino reflects that culture.

This strongly integrated and uniform steelworkers' community started to be seriously undermined during the 1980s. The crisis of the steel sector, which in Europe between 1975 and 1992 lost 52% of its workers and saw the virtual closure of entire districts, also affected Piombino. The number of workers employed in the various steelworks dropped from about 15,000 in the early 1980s to less than 5,000 in the mid-1990s. AFP has been continuously declining, from 8,000 in the early 1980s to 2,500 in 1997 (when the interviews were collected) and 2,100 in 1998. Most important, the plant was privatised (like the majority of the Italian steel sector in the period) and taken over at the end of 1992 by the Lucchini group. This is a family-owned holding with an 80-year history in steel production, and a turn-over in 1997 of Lit. 3,000 billion. It is based in Brescia in Northern Italy and oriented to high-quality steel and export. AFP is the largest plant in the group and the only one with an integral production cycle, since Lucchini has traditionally concentrated on scrap-based mini-mills. Lucchini (who was president of the Italian employers' confederation in the 1980s) is well known for a determined opposition against trade unions' involvement in management decisions. This characteristic was very clear in the style adopted by Lucchini to introduce organisational change in the 1980s, a style very different from the 'participatory' one of other Italian (private or state-owned) companies of the steel sector (De Luca, 1992).

Privatisation provoked a long conflict, with a 38-day strike and the suspension of production (which is a serious occurrence in a plant with blast-furnaces). The trade unions aimed to keep all the guarantees they had in the state sector, and possibly to avoid privatisation altogether. The strike was unsuccessful and 600 workers (among whom were a large number of union activists) were made redundant. However, the state-inherited pay system was maintained. Thanks to massive state subsides and a working time reduction (to 28 hours a week) through the *contratti di solidarietà* (job-security agreements) all workers either moved to early retirement, or re-entered the factory after a few years.

In 1995 (during a boom in the steel sector) 500 young workers were recruited but with new, much worse terms of employment, provoking a deep generational conflict.[10] In 1997-98, a new restructuring involved the redundancy of another 350 workers and revealed the weak position of the formerly very strong unions, whose resistance was unsuccessful. In summer 1998 there was a modest recovery, with the satisfactory negotiation of a modernisation plan, but this proved to be illusory. In the autumn the conflict exploded again leading (for the first time since the war) to the closure of the plant for two weeks, something which was perceived by the unions as a lock-out.

Industrial relations, then, have taken a variable course, but have remained better than in the other Lucchini-owned steelworks in Piombino, *La Magona d'Italia* (until the latter was sold to the French Usinor in 1999). In Piombino the trade unions were for many years considered very strong. As mentioned, they were characterised by the dominance of the PCI: in the mid-1970s about 70% of the AFP workers were members of the PCI, whose plant branch in turn had a dominating influence on the trade union. Since the 1980s the role of the PCI, and then the PDS, has rapidly declined, and today neither the DS nor *Rifondazione Comunista* have a plant branch. Nevertheless the trade unions maintain a very high membership (80%), although the historic FIOM hegemony has been undermined by the rise of *Cobas*.[11] In spite of the high membership, in the ballot on the restructuring agreement of February 1998 there was a surprising 49.4% against, which suggest widespread discontent with union representation.

The Lucchini plant thus represents a typical case of a besieged industrial workers' community. The ecological issues are emblematic; these currently oppose large segments of the workforce to the town population, which no longer depends on the factory and has therefore stopped passively enduring the pollution. Interestingly enough, the agreement on reclaimation reached at the end of 1998, after a long conflict, between company and local authorities was not signed by the trade unions because work problems were not solved in parallel.[12]

The main concern of the unions, tied to local political power, has always been the control of employment. The rapid increase of unemployment (17% in 1997) and the differentiation of demand and supply on the local labour market is the main source of problems for them. The 'local' factor is important for unions' identity, as shown by the fears of transfers of production to other plants in the Lucchini Group. This case could be labelled 'Belgian'.

Huta Lucchini Warszawa

The recent history of the Warsaw Lucchini steelworks (*Huta Lucchini-Warszawa*) displays some striking similarities with the Piombino case. First of all, the number of workers employed declined from almost 10,000 in the 1980s to about 4,600 at the moment of privatisation and below 2,000 at the end of the 1990s, and as a result the average age is high (46-47 years). Although the decline was more rapid and paradoxically less disputed in Warsaw, the numerical similarity with Piombino is strong, and representative of what has been happening in the steel industry in Europe in the last 20 years. A more notable parallel is the privatisation process. Both companies were privatised in 1992, after a long history of state and political management. In both companies the privatisation process was accompanied by important conflicts with very long strikes (immediately in Piombino, two years later in Warsaw). In both cases, these conflicts represented decisive turning points in workplace industrial relations. Historically, *Huta Warszawa* even more than the Piombino steelworks was a realm of workers' aristocracy, and salaries were by far the highest in the capital for the industrial sector. Party membership was also relatively high. From a productive point of view, both companies are today oriented to the high-quality-steel market segment, but only Piombino has an integral production cycle, including blast-furnaces and cokery.

In spite of these similarities, the meaning of workers' action in Warsaw was significantly different than in Piombino. *Huta Warszawa* was the leading plant in the emergence of Solidarity in the capital: the first to go on strike in solidarity with Gdańsk workers, and the most 'militant' during the whole 1980-81 period (Drążkiewicz and Rychard, 1990). The Warsaw population still remembers the striking *Huta Warszawa* workers marching to the centre screaming '*chodźcie z nami*' ('come with us'). In 1990, the local trade union played a leading role in the *Siec*, the inter-factory net which almost alone and independently from the national Solidarity opposed Balcerowicz's 'shock therapy' (Ruszkowski, 1991; Gilejko, 1993). In the early 1990s, the *Huta* workforce was called 'the army of the President', because of its support for Lech Wałęsa.

In 1992, 99% of the *Huta* workforce actually accepted company privatisation in a ballot and the plant became the first steel company in Eastern Europe. The situation in the state-sector looked dark, and two years earlier the unions themselves had been compelled to reduce salaries by 30%.[13] When Lucchini eventually took over the steelworks, he promised large income increases ('at Italian levels within ten years', the workers say they were told, while in 1992 their income was about eight times lower than in Italy). The large-scale reduction of the workforce did not meet particular resistance. This occurred not only because the Warsaw labour market displays a continuous supply shortage, but also because, contrary to the 'homo sovieticus' theory, many workers were willing to exploit the opportunities opened up by the transformation process.

The two-month occupation strike of 1994 was mainly motivated by the total lack of investment and salary increases up to that point. This was due at least in part to intricate legal problems with the property assets of the company which dragged on for two and a half year (the land still resulted to have been the army firing range of the Czarist army since 1840). Other reasons for the conflict were cuts in spending on spares (according to the workers, machines were held together by strings), increases in accidents, excessive overtime, and the violation of union agreements by the company (Gilejko, Gieorgica and Ruszkowski, 1997). The strike took a very adversarial form, was not without anti-Italian feeling (in a demonstration the strikers threw pots of macaroni at the Italian embassy), and also gained the attention of the media abroad. The Polish media initially displayed some sympathy towards the national pride of the strikers. However, this suddenly turned into hostility when the class nature of the strike became evident with the proposal to restart production under the workers' control.

Finding a solution to the conflict required the mediation of important politicians, a bishop, and the secretary of the European Trade Union Confederation. Eventually a compromise was found, and an elaborate participation system, with a bipartite management board, was designed and implemented. Within two years salaries had become the highest in the Polish steel industry, and modernisation had started at least in some workshops. Discontent remained about ownership: workers were not given shares, as happened with companies privatised later on. Like at Fiat, this issue has remained a constant trade union claim to the government and an important obstacle towards orderly industrial relations.

The *Huta Lucchini* now resembled the reformed Eastern German steelworks, rather than the other, still state-owned, Polish ones (Von Hirschhausen, 1996; Hardy *et al.*, 1996). After a few years, however, a feeling of disappointment started to emerge among the unions, and all the more so among the workers, with the participation system implemented in the plant. Employer-union relations took different forms according to the level and the issue, ranging from conflict to alliance. For instance, the two sides combined vis-à-vis the government to obtain higher subsidies for the plant within the steel-sector restructuring plan.

At the same time, the plant Solidarity returned to a political commitment they had left outside the factory since the early 1990s. The leader of the union in *Huta Lucchini-Warszawa* is also an influential politician in Warsaw AWS (the party created by Solidarity in 1996), who after the electoral victory in 1997 met the premier on a regular basis, before finally being elected president of the regional organisation of Solidarity. Solidarity of the *Huta Lucchini-Warszawa* also plays a leading role in the developing national industry-wide bargaining, and even in the writing of the steel industry restructuring plan with the government and the European Union. Not only Solidarity, but also the post-communist *Hutnicy* (*Związek Zawodowy Hutników*, linked to the all-Polish *Metalowcy* and OPZZ), have been directly involved in recent electoral campaigns, especially in local elections. However, both *Hutnicy* and Solidarity endeavour to keep work and political matters separate, managing in this way to keep good reciprocal relations. The cooperation between *Hutnicy* and Solidarity and the similarities revealed by the interviews suggest that the activists of the two unions can be treated as a single group in many respects (the strike of 1994 was conducted jointly by the two unions).

Today about 2/3 of the *Huta* workers are members of Solidarity and about 1/10 are in *Hutnicy* (although there are doubts as to the reliability of *Hutnicy* figures). In the early 1990s, Solidarity 80[14] was also active, organising around a former Solidarity leader, Seweryn Jaworski, known for his religious convictions (he always carried a large crucifix). Solidarity 80 dissolved after having refused to take part in collective bargaining with the new employer, revealing the unsuitability, in this plant, of a union action not linked to work matters.

The factors of political centrality together with the traditional attention to work-related matters explain the class-political orientation of the *Huta* unions, which are far from the communitarian and labour-market-oriented attitudes of their counterparts in Piombino.

Fiat Tychy

No other Western company has been present in the communist world like Fiat. The first production programmes in the USSR date from 1931, in Yugoslavia 1954, and in Romania 1977. In 1970 the enormous factory of Togliattigrad – about five times bigger than Mirafiori was in 1939 – was opened in the USSR. In Poland, Polski Fiat was already producing cars in 1934. In 1948 the first agreement with the People's Republic of Poland for the production of Fiat cars in the FSO (*Fabryka Samochodów Osobowych*) plant in Warsaw caused the irate reaction of the US administration (Castronovo, 1999, p. 843). In 1965 a new contract with FSO, and in 1971 the first agreement with FSM (*Fabryka Samochodów Małolitrażowych*) were signed. The latter foresaw the production of the 126p model in Bielsko-Biała and the construction of a new factory in Tychy. In 1987, Fiat became the first Western manufacturer to concentrate the entire production of a new model (the *Cinquecento*) in an East European country – at FSM. Nevertheless, all these factories working under Fiat licence remained typical socialist factories, where, for instance, in the case of a labour shortage the army was called to the workshops for help.

FSM, which owned the factories in Tychy and Bielsko-Biała, was taken over by Fiat in 1992, one of the very first cases of an important privatisation with foreign capital. Fiat is still the most important foreign investor in Poland – and also the first 'Polish' exporter. It has been noted that human resources management at Fiat is strongly centralised, following an 'ethnocentric' pattern. Given the high mobility of managers, one might say that the interlocutors of the Polish and Italian trade unions are *physically* the same.

The Tychy body plant employs about 7,000 people and produces the *Cinquecento* and *Seicento* models for the global market. It was built in the 1970s to produce the Polish Fiat 126. The workforce was carefully chosen from among the best graduates of technical and engineering schools, as the factory was intended to become the cream of Polish industry. Tychy workers, with an average age of around 37, are still much younger than their colleagues in Turin. Along with the factory, residential areas were built for the employees, strengthening their link to the workplace. The plant is located in the industrial and mining district of Upper Silesia. The city, which today has 200,000 habitants, was built from nothing in the post-war period and is defined by Polish sociologists as an archetypal socialist town (Szczepański, 1993).

Tychy workers and unions, who in 1990 had designed a privatisation plan giving a majority stake to the workforce, did not welcome the new investor. The negotiation of the take-over occurred in Warsaw, without consultation with the local unions, with the exception of two leaders. A two-month occupation strike stopped the factory in the summer of 1992 and marked the further development of workplace industrial relations (Gąciarz and Pańków, 1996b; 1997a). The industrial action was organised by the small radical trade union Solidarity 80, and, after the first few days, was opposed by the main trade unions Solidarity and *Metalowcy*. It should be noted that at the time of the strike Fiat was not yet the official owner of the plants, so that the unions lacked an opposing management side. The strike took on a national relevance but the most important political forces and the mass media were hostile to it. Finally, the intervention of the police put an end to the industrial action without any of the workers' demands being met. The experience of the strike, in spite of its failure, crystallised a militant identity, and 2,000 out of 2,800 members left Solidarity to join Solidarity 80. Surveys carried out in the town at that time confirm the considerable solidarity of the population with the strikers: 60% considered that the workers were right, and only 18% thought the opposite (CBOS, 1992).

After privatisation most workshops (especially the assembly line and the painting workshop) underwent a substantial modernisation. Work organisation was redesigned and an enormous increase of productivity followed. Fiat waited until 1996 before implementing the 'Japanese' organisation already launched in the Italian and Brazilian factories. The management thought that a period of clear distinction of roles would extirpate the former 'socialist' participation and Solidarity self-government.[15] At the same time, in 1996, real salaries started slowly to increase above the inflation rate. Among the most important changes introduced in the first period of restructuring are (Gąciarz and Pańków, 1997a):

- the weakening of the Polish executives' position;
- the weakening and the numerical reduction of technicians in R & D;
- a massive move from indirect to direct production jobs, and increased internal mobility and working time flexibility;
- the recruitment of young workers less qualified than the old workforce;
- an impressive drive for workers' retraining (3,000 workers were involved in training between 1992 and 1993, and hundreds visited the Italian plants), which according to the workers had much ideological and little technical content.

Another important change was the widening of salary differentials (the ratio between the pay of a workshop director and that of a manual worker increased from 3 to 7 times).

The strike of 1992 left as a legacy agitated and adversarial workplace industrial relations, with numerous conflicts not only between employer and unions but also among and within unions. A long sequence of splits has occurred. Today ten different trade unions are present in the Polish Fiat factories,[16] and in Tychy Solidarity no longer exists, the residual militants having created in 1997 *Solidarność-Catholic Trade Union Father Popiełuszko*.[17] The disappearance of an institution like Solidarity reveals what drastic changes can be produced by the entry of foreign capital.

The attitude of the employer to the unions is well revealed by the company bulletin, *Wiadomości*, which for instance in 1996 charged the unions of being manipulated by competitors like Daewoo or Opel. The attitudes of most unions towards the employer are equally, if not more, hostile; moreover, the unions also tend to be antagonistic towards each other.

A certain improvement in industrial relations occurred only in 1998, when a complete collective agreement for Fiat Auto Poland was finally signed. To improve the situation the company even organised training for union representatives and implemented a more formal system of communication. At the same time, however, fears emerged about the worsening employment situation (due to increased competition in the Polish automotive market) and about the wide process of outsourcing.

Altogether the unions organise over 50% of the workforce. Dominant are the radical unions and especially *Sierpień 80*. The only 'moderate' union is the post-communist *Metalowcy*, which in 1996 was even accused of being a sort of 'yellow union' although in other situations it collaborates with the other organisations.

Tychy workers are embedded in one of the largest industrial districts of Europe, and display typical working class features. In 1981 Touraine found among Silesian workers the highest level of class consciousness. Insofar as Tychy trade unions concentrate today on work conflict much more than on political issues, they display some parallelism with the Rivalta situation in Italy.

Fiat Bielsko-Biała

The other Fiat plant, in Bielsko-Biała, is older and slightly larger than Tychy. The general management of Fiat Auto Poland is situated here. The workshops (both body and engine production) are more old-fashioned and have not undergone the same modernisation as those in Tychy. Bielsko-Biała is located not far from Tychy, but is in fact outside Silesia, in a small mountain district on the border with the Czech Republic. The workforce is socially and culturally much more homogenous than in Tychy, and is very concerned with the problem of the economic future of the region. In 1998 the town of Bielsko-Biała revealed a strong localism by mobilising against the administrative reform which erased Bielko-Biała voievodship (district) and attached it to Upper Silesia.

In the Fiat plant unions are moderate and weak: the unionisation rate is around 40% with Solidarity and *Metalowcy* being the strongest organisations. The radical unions *Sierpień 80* and Solidarity 80 here have only a few dozen members. Solidarity 80 here has explicit right-wing orientations, similar to those of *Popiełuszko* in Tychy (although this is not the case everywhere in Poland). During the summer of 1998 it was directly engaged in the demonstrations in defence of the 'Pope's Cross' in Auschwitz,[18] and the local leader is also an activist of the nationalist party KPN.

Bielsko workers did not take part in the 1992 conflict which blocked the Tychy plant for two months, and many of them even participated in a company-led demonstration against the strikers in Tychy (although the interviews reveal that their participation was anything but voluntary). After privatisation in 1992, in Bielsko – as well as in Tychy – only one short strike was called, in September 1994.[19] The weakness of union organisation leaves the field open to other, individual and not class-based, forms of conflict like of sabotage. It is an old finding of academic industrial relations that forms of conflict are largely interchangeable, the trade union channel being only one of them (Knowles, 1952; Ingham, 1974). In Bielsko, the typical forms of class action are hardly visible. Solidarity, and to a slightly lesser extent *Metalowcy*, are instead very involved in politics, and tightly linked to external political activity. The features of a closed community, not particularly involved in class action, make this plant somewhat similar to the Lucchini one in Piombino.

In 1998, due to increasing competition on the Polish market and to the planned cessation of production of the old model 126p, the Bielsko workforce started to look excessive. 600 temporary contracts were not confirmed, and 650 workers were temporarily reassigned to Tychy. In 2000, redundancy for further 525 people was planned. The fear of unemployment instantly induced a wage restraint and an alliance among different unions. The workers and the unions started to suspect that Fiat might leave in Poland only the assembly lines, following the example of most other auto producers.[20] Bielsko plant, with its engine production and its old models, is structurally in a worse situation than Tychy. However, rather than with the market union leaders associate these difficulties with to the situation of the local community: the problems, they argue, originate in the loss of autonomy by Bielsko voievodship.

It would be too difficult to compare the Polish plants with a national model as was done with the Italian plants. This is because, as the next chapter will show, Eastern European situations display, together with important parallelisms, also distinctive deviations.

The Collection of Interviews

The first of the 91 interviews with Fiat and Lucchini workers was carried out in Bielsko-Biała in April 1995; the last one in October 1998 in Mirafiori (the further 21 interviews in the supplementary case-studies were collected between September 1997 and February 1999). They were carried out under different conditions, something which must be taken into account while evaluating the findings. As always in qualitative research, much incidental information has been extremely useful. It would be impossible to assess workers' assertions about their economic situation without having visited their flats and having travelled in their cars. An unexpected but inestimable source of information on Italian-Polish relations within the factories proved to be informal contacts with a number of interpreters working or having worked in the plants. Moreover, as Mehan's cognitive ethnology suggests, relations to the field must become an integral part of the findings.

Only the first interviews in the Fiat plants and some interviews in the *Huta Lucchini* were carried out in the workplaces. The Fiat management's withdrawal of permission for access to the plants[21] at first appeared to be a drawback, but it revealed itself to be paradoxically positive at least with the most radical unions. In workers' eyes, it neutralised the suspicion consequent upon the employer's involvement in the investigation. Some Polish workers even revealed that they would be afraid of meeting a researcher in the workplace, dreading being labelled as 'political militants'. Secondly, carrying out interviews outside the trade union offices in the plant made it easier to express any criticism of the union itself.[22]

Eventually, interviews were carried out in the plants, in trade union or political parties' offices outside the plants, and in pubs or cafeterias (especially in Poland). It is not necessary to resort to social psychology to understand that a talk in a pub takes a different form from one held in an office. It is even easier to understand that while interviewing three workers in sequence in one afternoon in a pub, the social obligation of drinking a beer with each one somewhat affects the quality of interviewer's questions, at least during the third conversation. In few cases interviews were not carried out individually, but with two or three people at the same time. This increased spontaneity and talkativeness but probably created some 'social pressure interference' on certain topics.[23] Nevertheless, the 'soft' treatment of the data, attentive to the internal coherence of the talks more than to pseudo-quantitative schematic comparisons among interviews, should be sufficient to prevent significant distortions. In such an open investigation, variety is preferable to uniformity, even if natural scientific methodological criteria risk being violated. Moreover, the interviews were integrated by other instruments: analysis of union materials, moments of participant observation in meetings and demonstrations, interviews with company executives.

Different unions treated the researcher in different ways. It is very significant that when Fiat had already refused access to the factory, the *Metalowcy* accompanied me inside without any formality. By contrast *Sierpień 80* and *Popiełuszko* officers from the same plant told that if *they* had asked for permission to invite me, this would have guaranteed that I would never be allowed to approach the factory. It is also interesting that the *Metalowcy* offices in all plants (Bielsko-Biała and Warsaw, to a lesser extent Tychy) are very quiet and ordered while in those of the other unions there is a continuous movement of people. Finally, very significant is that the most 'militant' or communitarian unions, in both Italy and Poland, were much more open to finding people willing to be interviewed. In this ranking, the unions of *Huta Warszawa* occupy the last position, just after the UILM in Turin, while the Piombino unions, *Cobas*, and *Sierpień 80* were the most co-operative.

The research question was to understand how people look at their own activity at work and in the union. This is however too abstract a question to be asked. Since directive, particular questions had to be avoided, the only possibility was to give a 'structure of talk' to follow. There were two options: the historical one or the everyday life one. The first consisted in asking people about their history at work and in the union. Trade union activists are quite confident with historic narrative, and this is the easiest way to get autonomously developing talks. The second option implied asking them to recount what they actually did every day. This could be more interesting for studies of pure sociology of work, of everyday life, and of organisation. Since the working hypotheses required an understanding of past experience and of political culture, the first option was chosen. However, several workers quickly abandoned a narrative structure in order to concentrate on other sorts of discourse, and coherently with the non-directive assumption this was accepted even when they 'got off the point'.

The Interpretation of the Interviews

The analysis of the interviews has followed several general epistemological principles, but not a predetermined iterative procedure such as content analysis (Berelson, 1952), proposition analysis (Ghiglione and Blanchet, 1991), or opposition relations analysis (Raymond, 1968; Lévi-Strauss, 1964). While these procedures are important in socio-psychological studies, and valuable in recalling the need to respect the singular coherence of the interviews against over-confident cross-interview treatments like thematic analysis, it would, in a sociological comparative study, be sterile to limit the study to them. In fact, they lose their usefulness when a very low number of interviews is exceeded, just as a statistical model loses its usefulness by introducing too many variables. Moreover, one can seriously doubt – on the basis of the considerations made in the first chapter on qualitative methodology – whether these procedures can ever achieve a 'unique' objective interpretation. Meaning analysis is rather inexhaustible and necessarily polemical.

The first principle was to follow a 'constant comparative method' as expressed by grounded theory (Glaser and Strauss, 1967): during the collection of the interviews the findings were continuously re-examined and compared, searching for similarities and contrasts and trying to make sense of them. The second was to investigate the taken-for-granted, which became more evident thanks to the constant comparison. Different things were taken for granted in different places, and this required a deeper understanding. In this way the 'belief universes'[24] were reconstructed and questioned. Thirdly, a progressive proposition coding, first open and then gradually axial, integrated, and theory-oriented, was undertaken. The process is gradual in order to respect the substantive categories of the actors and their internal coherence, in a way inspired by grounded theory and exemplified by Demazière and Dubar (1997). It was maintained that interviews display *words* and not *facts*, and therefore can be understood only in their coherence. Only after a sufficient codification could a systematic comparison and in some cases a typology be proposed, following empirical procedures of typology (Grémy and Le Moan, 1977). Uncoded interviews, all the more so if in two languages, are too heterogeneous for a comparison.

Of this long process only the last phase (the final comparison of already coded interviews) will be described in this text, which has an empirical-sociological nature and not a methodological, psycho-sociological or epistemological vocation. However, I will repeatedly give examples of the way the concepts are built, and of how theoretical categories are linked to the 'substantial' ones (proper to the actors). This methodological choice requires some elucidation.

Understanding by Interviewing

The Usefulness and Shortcomings of the Qualitative Approach

From their beginnings, industrial relations studies have taken a number of different approaches, ranging from historical accounts to econometrics, with a lot of space given over to theoretical discussion. Over time, however, the role played by institutional agencies in the demand for research in this field seems to have promoted quantitative analysis more than other methodologies.

Quantitative methods of research in these subjects have indeed made enormous progresse. One problem, however, is that in a changing society the meaning of the indicators employed in statistical analysis must be periodically verified. In the example of strike action, it has been noted

(Bordogna, 1995, pp. 171-172) that the expansion of the service industry makes the use of conventional indicators for the measurement of conflict misleading. When change becomes rapid and profound like in Eastern Europe after 1989, extreme caution in using quantitative data (from official statistics as well as from surveys) becomes obligatory. Staying with the example of strike action, the unofficial habit of paying salary for strike hours (widespread until the law on collective disputes of 1991, but persisting in many cases in the following years) invalidates any quantitative analysis of industrial conflict in Poland.

There is another, general rationale for qualitative research on trade unionism. The meaning of unionism goes beyond the borders of the workplace and of the economic relationship between employers and employees. The asymmetry of work relations includes the fact that on one side they directly affect not only economic interests but also human life. And since human life retains a degree of complexity which can not be reduced to straightforward and measurable variables, we depend partially upon 'field' accounts to understand this aspect of the phenomenon.

Certainly, the shortcomings of qualitative methods are virtually as numerous as those of quantitative methods. Their criteria of validity and reliability are controversial, and sometimes researchers seem to be doing nothing more than 'aping' scientific methods.

Nevertheless, these techniques have a particular value. In this section, I shall attempt to show the usefulness of qualitative methods for theoretical development and for a better understanding of unionism. I do not, however, claim for them the validity of scientific method. The human personality of the researcher being a constitutive part of qualitative methods, and human personality being unstandardised, qualitative methods can only approach the scientific model, never reaching it. In reality, one could also be sceptical as to whether quantitative methods in the social sciences proceed on a scientific model. However, their less directly 'human' nature and their use of identifiable and standardised indicators and methods possibly bring them closer to it.

In short, I shall argue that quantitative and qualitative methods, in this as well as in other fields of research, are complementary rather than in competition, keeping in mind that on methodological issues 'the retreat into paradigms effectively stultifies debate and hampers progress' (Hammerslay, 1992, p. 182).

The first part of the section will develop these arguments in the following way. First, I shall present a short review of qualitative research which has produced useful results in the field of work and unionism. Second, I shall consider the particular method (unstructured interviews) chosen for this inquiry. Finally, I shall discuss some of the open issues in qualitative analysis for example criteria of validity and the treatment of data.

The Tradition of Qualitative Studies of Trade Unions

If a pragmatic position is taken in the debate between methodological approaches, one should begin the defence of a given methodology by showing its achievements. Does this methodology offer findings that cannot be obtained otherwise? Or, at least, does it offer them at a lower cost than do 'concurrent' methods?

The answer to these questions is not so easy as might appear. In fact, it is sometimes difficult to ascribe the paternity of findings in social sciences to a unique approach. Sociologists working with statistical tools are often led, in their treatment of quantitative data, by assumptions obtained from secondary literature based on fieldwork, or by their personal familiarity with the topic. Any data treatment is to some extent 'qualitative': ethnomethodologists have shown very effectively how even natural scientists are inevitably guided by notions and practices rooted in 'common sense'.

Even if the border between methodological approaches is not clear-cut, it is possible to cite some examples of pieces of research conducted with qualitative tools (either exclusively or in combination with quantitative methods) that have undoubtedly contributed to our understanding of unions.

Among the general studies, one can cite Touraine's *Mouvement ouvrier* (1987), which, applying the qualitative method of 'sociological intervention', proclaimed the end of the workers' movement at a moment when this idea had not yet been accepted by most French sociologists and intellectuals. A good example of integration of quantitative and qualitative methods is Gallie's comparison of British and French workers (1978), in which semi-structured interviews are used to make better sense of surveys. In Germany, attitudes to work have been the object of qualitative research projects conducted by Rainer Zoll (1992). His findings, mainly based on interview data, form the basis of a rich theoretical discussion.

In Italy, the best analysis of the labour movement of the early 1970s is probably that of Pizzorno's team (Pizzorno, Regalia, Regini and Reyneri, 1978), which was based on some case studies and devoted a lot of space to oral sources. Even if the authors viewed the latter feature as a limitation, one can easily detect the crucial contribution of this kind of source in Pizzorno's analysis. Much more recently, an inquiry on the Melfi Fiat plants was carried out on the basis of fifty semi-structured interviews, and the authors themselves acknowledged the superiority of this method when compared to studies based on questionnaires which they also had carried out (Di Siena and Rieser, 1996). Far away from Italy, the same conclusion is reached by an important study on General Motors workers in the US (Milkman, 1997).

There are other qualitative traditions dealing with topics that, even if slightly different from the sociology of trade unionism, are connected with the same field. One of these is ethnographic work studies (Edwards, 1992; Bélanger, Edwards and Haiven, 1994a). Notably, and dealing with a problem similar to that of the current enquiry there is the work of Burawoy, and in particular his comparison of American and Hungarian factories (Burawoy and Lukacs, 1985; Burawoy, 1997). The conclusions of that comparison (the equivalence of the two situations, and even the superiority of the Hungarian organisation of work in some regards) have revealed themselves to be in large part wrong. This example stresses therefore the prudence one must use when using circumstantial and personal observation, and the importance of a continuous questioning of the starting hypothesis. Despite all these limits, however, Burawoy's work had an important theoretical impact, notably in introducing the concept of 'regimes of production'. The attention paid to theory is one of the most important features of qualitative approaches, and one which distinguishes them from journalism and anecdotal accounts. As Mitchell (1983) put it, in the case of qualitative research the issue should be couched in terms of the generalisability of cases to *theoretical* propositions rather than to *populations* or universes.

Another qualitative research tradition is oral history (Passerini, 1988), which found important applications precisely with respect to Turin working class (Passerini, 1984). Oral history uses in depth interviews in order to reconstruct particular moments of labour history. The positioning of such 'labour studies' between history and sociology is difficult to define. Nevertheless, sociologists have contributed with their own work to this tradition (e.g. Stepan-Norris and Zeitlin, 1996) as well as having explicitly appreciated it (e.g. Della Porta, 1992; Yow, 1994). More generally, one can recall the Chicago School, which made exemplary use of autobiographies and life-stories starting from the classic study by Thomas and Znaniecki (1927).

If we shift to Eastern Europe, a region where profound changes have taken place and many 'grey areas' persist, the need for qualitative studies increases. Surveys have become very popular here, but are often inadequate. The fact that they are at times still conducted on the phone, even though a significant part of the population does not own one, reveals the cultural and social distance that researchers have to cross before becoming familiar with their new subject. It is not surprising, therefore, that

Western scholars usually have no better explanation for survey results on Eastern union members than the 'social schizophrenia' of Eastern Europeans (Blenchflower and Freeman, 1994, p. 11). By contrast, in Poland in the 1980s life-story interviews with Solidarity activists and members of the ruling elite showed an irreducible moral divide (Misztal and Wasilewski, 1986). These findings predicted the failure of Jaruzelski's normalisation rather more accurately than surveys carried out at the same time, which showed a demand for order and a trust in the army (Adamski, Jasiewicz and Rychard, 1986). As far as workers' opinions are concerned, the author of the only systematic surveys on Polish industrial workers, Juliusz Gardawski, himself admitted:

> On the basis of qualitative studies carried out in the years 1991-94 at the same time as the questionnaire surveys, we could suggest that the problem of ideological attitudes cannot be satisfactorily examined by way of standardised interviews. (...) In order to obtain suitable information, it would be necessary to hold a relaxed conversation, conducive to retrospection, to identify and revive some latent states. (Gardawski, 1996, p. 93)

The arguments about the utility of qualitative methods in research on industrial workers are particularly authoritative when they come from authors of quantitative analyses, like Gardawski, Rieser, and before them Blackburn and Mann (1975). They are all the stronger if one is concerned only with a specific segment like the union activists, because given the smaller size and the more elaborate consciousness the need for representativeness is reduced while that for interpretation is accentuated.

Qualitative research on post-communist countries has already proved its adequacy. Touraine's method of 'sociological intervention' allowed an understanding 'from within' of Russian trade unions (Berelowitch and Wieviorka, 1993; 1996). These studies showed early on that the apparently lively independent miners' movement was declining and that, by contrast, the former official unions were succeeding in a process of reconvertion. The same method was used to analyse unionists and employers from Central Eastern European countries (Frybes, 1993; 1995). In the case of Polish industrial workers, occasional studies based on autobiographies have made a significant contribution in undermining the widespread stereotype of Eastern European workers as a passive group, and in revealing the importance of their personal choices and projects (Latoszek, 1994).

Textbooks on methodology usually state that qualitative methods should be reserved for the exploratory phase of research, and that later on the intuitions of qualitative research should be 'tested' by quantitative analysis. Yet qualitative research may also 'test' hypotheses, whether by a choice of critical cases or through Popper's 'falsificationalism'. My experience, for instance, led me to conclude that a question used in a well-known survey on Fiat workers (Accornero, Carmignani and Magna, 1985) as the determinant variable for constructing a typology, did not, in fact, have a link with the attitudes that this typology aimed to explain.[25]

The Interview and the Unions

I shall consider here a particular qualitative tool, the unstructured interview, which is similar to the 'non-directive' interview introduced by Rogers (1945) into psychotherapy and the social sciences.[26] This method has met with considerable success, especially among sociologists with a liking for interactionism or committed to feminism (e.g. Oakeley, 1981), but also among constructivists (e.g. Bourdieu, 1996). It is the type of interviewing most concerned to avoid arbitrary suggestions and interference by the interviewer.

The interview is not simply a way of collecting data. It is also, and especially, a particular social interaction with its own features. This characteristic has given rise to an unresolved criticism of interviewing as a method in the social sciences. Yet interviews, in spite of such well-founded criticism, have not disappeared from social research. I shall argue here that this has occurred, at least in the field of labour studies, because the limitations of the interview are at the same time a hardly substitutable resource.

> [The interview] is irreplaceable to have access to undoubtedly interesting information, but it remains an unacceptable methodology from the point of view of the scientific ideal. (Blanchet, 1987, p. 85)

It would be extremely naïve to treat interview answers as passive filters towards reality. Interview responses must not be seen as true or false, but only as displays of perspectives and moral forms. Therefore, this method is clearly unsuited to researching most kinds of behaviour or organisational phenomena. It becomes functional only when the aim is to understand cognitive frames of references and motivational processes. More particularly, as regards unionism, it can say little about internal organisational dynamics, and the accounts of historical facts can be artificial. Yet it can reveal the cultural and symbolic orientations of individuals, as well as the links between individuals and collective identities. It may at least partially open the 'black box' which, in statistical analysis, transforms social variables into social attitudes.

This method seems particularly profitable in the field of trade union studies because of some particular features of the subject. The features of the interview as a social situation vary according to different factors, but especially in relation to the topic and the relative status of the interviewee and the interviewer. It is intrinsic to the social role of the activist to be ready to give his/her own opinions. To be a union activist in a private company, furthermore, implies some degree of willingness to resist authority. When the interviewer is relatively young, clearly not very rich, and sympathetic (not to be confused with flattering), the risk of the interview becoming directive is reduced even further. My experience shows that union activists are very sensitive to any unintended attempts by the interviewer to dominate the interview (e.g. by summarising disordered answers). More generally, it has been stated that:

> In any event, the interview displays some strong analogies with usual trade union activities (union meetings, in which dossiers are assessed or activities are evaluated, leaflets drafting, union training sessions...). Thereby, union actors' cognitive-discursive work does not appear as an artifice created by the sociologist; rather, it is rooted in everyday experience. (Corcuff, 1991, p. 519)

On this point, interview-based comparative studies require some 'trick' in order to make sure that this power relationship remains the same in all the cases considered. All the external features (such as the environment in which the interview takes place) have to be controlled, although "it is virtually impossible to 'standardise' procedures in order to get similar results from different interviews" (Della Porta, 1992, p. 184). Yet the problem of power relationships acquires a particular importance in cross-national studies in which the nationality of the interviewer might give rise to systematic distortions. When the researcher comes from an economically more powerful country (and what is more, from the country of the employer), the power position of the researcher is apparently reinforced. For this reason, as already noted by Hoggart (1957), workers may remain evasive when faced with an interlocutor enquiring into the popular milieu and recognised as a member of another social class. In fact, the opposite is frequently the case. Interviewees facing a foreigner has a knowledge advantage: they can assume that the interviewer has little familiarity with the field, and that consequently almost everything can be told.

The 'tricks' to avoid national biases change according to the specific situation. In any case the familiarity of the researcher with the country they study seems to play a major role. A knowledge of the local language allows the heavy interference of an interpreter to be avoided. If they show some familiarity (*unique adequacy*, in Garfinkel's words) and links with the country, the risk of being treated as a kind of naïve tourist are reduced. On the other hand, the researcher interviewing in his/her own country should avoid too close an investigation with interviewees (for example, by stressing the international character of the inquiry or his/her own links with other countries). In this way, a major limitation of the social sciences may be partially overcome: the researcher might achieve a degree of the 'exteriority' demanded by the scientific model, and at the same time a degree of the familiarity required by the nature of social reality.

As already remarked, the 'unstructured' character of the interview should not mean researcher's passivity. Indeed, it has been observed that 'the passivity of the interviewer can create an extremely powerful constraint on the interviewee to talk' (Silverman, 1993, p. 96). This involves a rather 'humanistic' approach which is difficult to standardise since it exists only as an embedded feature in the unique interviewer-interviewee relationship. Its main features are attention, help in synthesising, intellectual support, and trust. This also involves 'listening skills'.

> There can be little doubt that the commitment to explicating the subject's interpretation of social reality is a (one might even say *the*) *sine qua non* of qualitative research. (Bryman, 1988, p. 72)

What is important is to leave interviewees free to speak about the topics *they* consider relevant for the subject of the interview. Precise questions which are theoretically relevant may be included, but should come at the end of the interview in order not to undermine its non-directive nature and not to trigger a question-answer relationship. The same point is even more valid for the collection of personal data.

The 'Validity' of Qualitative Methods

Although we have seen that qualitative methods allow access to union members' views and orientations, their scientific validity remains an open problem.

The answers given by qualitative methodologists have ranged between two extremes. Some of them reject, in an extremist way, altogether the issues of reliability and validity, and with this any scientific model. Others have replied by developing their own lists of validity criteria (e.g. Mucchielli, 1991). Most of these criteria have been criticised (see, for instance, a critical review in Silverman, 1993), and they often reveal a defensive attitude on the part of their proponents.

I shall not discuss criteria such as internal acceptation, external acceptation, or triangulation, whose weaknesses have been already shown by Silverman. More useful, even if they can also be defined as departing from a truly scientific model, are the criteria of saturation and coherence.

Saturation is the phenomenon that appears when the data one is collecting are no longer new. That is, a qualitative inquiry on n members reaches saturation when the interview of $n + 1$ member does not give any supplementary information relevant to the research questions. Since a statistically representative sample may hardly be attained in qualitative research, (and, given the goals of this methodology, it is not necessary), saturation would substitute for it: 'when saturation is achieved, it confers a very sound basis for generalisation' (Bertaux, 1980, p. 208). This 'criterion' is, however, far from irrefutable. Firstly, it depends on a subjective evaluation of the 'novelty' of the information. Secondly, statistically the fact that the $n + 1$ interview repeats the features of previous interviews by no means precludes the possibility that $n + 2$ will be completely new. I prefer, therefore, a 'softer' version of this criterion: a qualitative study reaches saturation when a deep *familiarity* with the population is achieved, such that any new information can easily be understood and related to individual particularities without changing the way in which the group is represented.

Internal coherence as a validity criterion is a logical construction. Qualitative analysis is 'coherent' when, in short, it makes coherent sense of the data, a sense which is understandable to (although not necessarily shared by) other researchers. It assumes that once the researcher has succeeded in apprehending the point of view of the actor he is studying, this can be understood by anybody (assuming that the presentation of the findings is clear). This is, rather than a true criterion of validity for qualitative research, a core feature of interpretative sociology. For instance, Weber's ideal types are useful for sociology not because they are empirically 'valid', but because they are a coherent representation of behaviours and orientations.

Other methodologists, rather than speaking of 'validity criteria', prefer to talk of general orientations or strategies like analytical induction (Robinson, 1951) or grounded theory (Glaser and Strauss, 1967). The former implies that the researcher has to redefine the hypothesis and return to the field any time a single case inconsistent with the hypothesis appears. This seems to encounter problems similar to those met by the criterion of saturation. The latter strategy is indeed a general sociological strategy, not exclusive to qualitative research. Its main feature is to 'mesh' theorising and data collection, so that the hypotheses are continuously redefined.

From this very incomplete discussion what emerges is a certain confusion about the actual validity of qualitative studies. This is likely to be the result of the confusion about the aims of qualitative research.

No 'criteria' will could grant qualitative methods a scientific nature. Nevertheless, these methods hold an irreplaceable role in that they offer access to some kind of information and, more generally, to common sense. This common sense is relative to each group ('indexical', in the jargon of ethnomethodologists) and makes sense of its expressions, orientations and, sometimes, its behaviour.

I shall be considering the case of interviews with union activists. By analysing how people talk, direct access is gained to a cultural universe and its normative assumptions. The accounts are not reality; yet they are a part of the world they describe (Garfinkel, 1967). In particular, interviews give us access to the repertoire of narratives that we use in producing accounts (Gilbert and Mulkay, 1983).

In other words, reality is always viewed from a particular perspective; hence our accounts *represent* reality, but they do not *reproduce* it (Hammersley, 1992, pp. 50-51). If we study collective actors, we must investigate not only 'facts' but also representations; and it is here that qualitative methods come into their own.

This argument has been discussed widely in the case of interviews with workers who clearly do not always tell the truth (Weller, 1994). A first outcome of this consideration is that the existence of inconsistencies between the views expressed in interviews and actual action suggests that the assumption of coherence between rationality, representation and the logic of action which underpins much industrial sociology needs to be revised. What is more, however, is that it is possible to reconcile subjective accounts and sociological studies.

A reference to Goffman's work is very helpful here. Goffman developed a theory of identity that took into consideration the breakdown of individual coherence (Ogien, 1987). By distinguishing the notions of *Self* and of *Face*, he showed that individual existence is the expression not of an essence, but of a 'face work' (Goffman, 1967). The Self is embedded in a multitude of territories, and the territorialisation of the subject removes the question of essence. It is the concrete ability to unify reality and to transform the scene in a coherent way which seems to make up the actor.

The construction of Self during the interview is consequently not a lie, but the fragile but real result of a coherence (the face work). This coherence is visible in what the interviewee *knows*. This set of knowledge, skills, and references (the *Lebenswelt* of phenomenological sociology) allows then actor's multiple positions, which vary according to contexts and situations, not to break down. Drawing on this point we can say that more important than the statements (which may be true or false) are the frames of reference (which are necessarily meaningful). Analysing actor's identity means then for the sociologist analysing the 'political wisdom', taken not in an objective sense but in an endogenous one (Pharo, 1985). The internal relations of narratives are more important than their relations to the 'objective' reality.

> Interviews (like other narratives) display cultural particulars - which are all the more powerful, given the connections which members make between them. (Silverman, 1993, p. 114)

Concretely, in the case of trade unionism interviews are not objective accounts of workplace industrial relations. However, they reveal the cultural resources and orientations used by the actors. Since these are collective resources, and the language they use is necessarily 'social', even a non-representative sample can unveil the group culture. In other words, while it is obviously possible that the opinions of a qualitative sample do not represent the opinions of the larger group, it is hardly imaginable that language, references, styles, and ways of arguing are not shared by the other members. This would be to imply that social actors (in our case union activists) do not understand each other when they meet, which is evidently false. As regards workers' culture it has been actually stated that:

> Conversation, dialogue, oral account are a part of a system of cultural exchange, enriched by variations which link the word to the cultural models typical of every social group. Consequently, the communicative structure that feeds talk is, sociologically, a totality in which one must notice, with the semantic fields, the correlations which link these fields to wider areas of experience. (Crespi, 1997, pp. 12-13)

Another problem of qualitative methods concerns the choice of the cases and, in interview-based research, the interviewees. Is it possible to choose cases in a way that allows for some generalisation? First of all, as already argued, the kind of generalisation allowed by case-studies and qualitative research is a theoretical, not a statistical one (Mitchell, 1983). That said, in the field of ethnographic studies of work five ways to generalise the findings of case studies have been proposed (Edwards, 1992):

a) the discovery of hidden forms of behaviour (which is as such a general-value finding);
b) the identification of critical cases;
c) the exploration of causal mechanisms linking phenomena;
d) the explanation of variations (especially of deviant cases);
e) the understanding of the nature and the sources of variation.

One could certainly question the validity of some of these proposals. The fifth is tautological, while the third and the fourth stress the depth of the findings rather than their generalizability. The first one is valuable, but applies only to a limited set of findings. The second one, the identification of critical cases, seems, however, a very important way of proceeding, especially in comparative research. In this respect qualitative methods may be more rigorous than quantitative studies, since they reproduce the high level of complexity of societies that is often concealed by quantitative studies, which reduce cases to a limited set of numerical indicators.[27] In cross-national comparative studies, moreover, the issue of generalisability can partially be faced by choosing more than one case per country.

> Choosing a matched set of workplaces is an especially useful technique for comparative analysis. It is a good way of eliminating several confounding variables in a qualitative study, as long as the researcher is careful to acknowledge what can easily be controlled and what cannot. The two-by-two (or three-by-three) comparison is especially versatile. The movement beyond a single set allows for a much greater ability for generalise, yet the small number also allows for the intensity of ethnographic investigation. (Bélanger, Edwards, Haiven, 1994b, p. 277)

As regards the selection of the interviewees, random sampling is usually impracticable. Choice thus depends on the relevance of individual experience, or on the expressive capacities and interest in the research (Della Porta, 1992, p. 182). Certainly, diversity is as important in these methods as representativeness is in surveys: the main social types (e.g. generations, genders, professions) must be represented in the sample. In the case of union activists, moreover, the problem of representativeness might be partially faced by the assumption (arbitrary but realistic) that workers willing to talk to the researcher are *intrinsically* representative of union commitment. Indeed, such a willingness is not always immediate (interviewing is not a part of union activity), therefore the quality of the sample will depend, once again, on the bargaining abilities of the researcher.

The Treatment of Qualitative Data

Besides the problems of validity, there are further difficulties concerning how qualitative data are treated, analysed and interpreted. What can we infer from the jungle of qualitative data?

A first problem is how to systematise and present the number of interviews. The usual way this is done has been strongly criticised.

There is a tendency towards an anecdotal approach to the use of 'data' in relation to conclusions or explanations in qualitative research. Brief conversations, snippets from unstructured interviews, or examples of a particular activity are used to provide evidence for a particular contention. There are grounds for disquiet in that the representativeness or generality of these fragments is rarely addressed. (Bryman, 1988, p. 77)

Silverman (1993, pp. 110-114) presents two strategies to overcome the dangers of subjectivity and partiality: tabulating many cases and investigating deviant cases. Della Porta (1992, pp. 184-185), in turn, suggests two possible solutions: analysing interviews with the help of quantitative methods and publishing the interviews as they are recorded. Yet she immediately asserts that both seem too radical. In this regard, as in that of validity criteria, those with ambitions to reach scientific standards are probably deluded: interpretative analysis can hardly be schematised on a grid. Instead, it is possible to argue for a systematic and reliable presentation of the data. The inevitably subjective presentation (qualitative methods are altogether subjective insofar as the researcher becomes a part of the process of data collection) should be organised by issue and topic, so that all the relevant statements about relevant points are taken into consideration. Secondly, the data (in this case, the interview recordings and transcriptions) must be available for secondary analysis. That said, the strategies suggested by Della Porta can partially be applied: including the full transcript of a few interviews can illustrate both the methods and the coherence of the findings, and statistics can be used, with discretion, to synthesise and organise the data.

The problem of reliability raises another important point. Since the way data are collected can bias the findings so profoundly, there is a strong need, even stronger than in quantitative studies, to detail the relevant context of the enquiry. It becomes all but useless, therefore, to recall Merton's appeal to include in publications

a detailed account of the ways in which qualitative analyses actually developed. Only when a considerable body of such reports are available will it be possible to codify methods of qualitative analysis with something of the clarity with which quantitative methods have been articulated... This codification is devoutly to be desired both for the collection and the analysis of qualitative sociological data. (1966, p. 444)

This reflexive work is important for more than methodological reasons. All the phases involved in access to the field reveal much information which must become an integral part of the piece of research (as Mehan's cognitive ethnology suggests). From my experience, I can state that the way unions receive the researcher is a fairly good indicator of the type of union. Such 'marginal' observations achieve sometimes an unexpected degree of scientific validity. For instance, the fact of having been received – as an Italian researcher – very warmly by activists of the unions which are considered the most nationalist and anti-Italian falsifies the theory which views xenophobia as a main feature of today's Polish unions.

Methodological Integration

This section is not intended to be a mystical defence of qualitative studies. I have argued that their suitability is limited by research aims and topics. Trade unions are complex phenomena, and while quantitative methods can successfully portray some aspects of their 'macro' behaviour, things change if one is interested in the deeper orientations of their members, even if one would not go as far as one attentive analyst of working class consciousness.

> Qualitative techniques alone, among sociological research methods, are capable of uncovering the relationship between attitudes and actions that is class consciousness. (...) It is difficult to see how the shortcomings of social surveys, as a means of studying class consciousness, can be overcome (...). It is not that qualitative research of the kind here advocated *complements* surveys in this field. Rather, such research provides a more suitable *alternative* to the large-scale survey. (Marshall, 1983, pp. 290-91)

Marshall's dismissal of quantitative methods is not fully justified. A moderate view would be that there is a need for an integration of methods in sociological research. Statistical analysis requires some degree of familiarity with the data: there is something 'qualitative' also in the choice of statistical tests. At the same time it has been observed, with some irony: 'by our pragmatic view, qualitative research does imply a commitment to field activities. It does not imply a commitment to innumeracy' (Kirk and Miller, 1986, p. 10).

This piece of research, consequently, will not disregard the opportunity for a quantitative treatment of the data. At the same time, references to surveys will integrate qualitative studies in order to offer a cross-temporal and multinational picture of the topic. One of the aims of this project is to allow, through qualitative research, a better understanding of surveys.

Understanding by Comparing

Every year a couple of comparative books on industrial relations and on trade unions are published. Among these works, there are studies which manage to 'put in order' international chaos according to a set of clear hypotheses. A well-known example is Clegg's analysis of six countries, based on the forms of collective bargaining (1976). Much more common, unfortunately, are simple juxtapositions of national monographs. These are often valuable sources of information, but they compare the 'whole' to the 'whole' without building either an analytical grid or an explanatory framework.

This is the classic problem of comparison, about which there are two basic and opposed viewpoints. The first stresses the irreducible complexity of every national case and therefore the impossibility of term-to-term comparison, especially in East-West comparisons: 'First understand, and then, but only then, compare' (Bate and Child, 1987, p. 33). On the other side, since the beginnings of sociological thought the contribution offered by comparisons to the understanding of the same singular cases has been emphasised. Durkheim's declaration in the first page of *Suicide* '*on n'explique qu'en comparant*' was maybe too categorical, but it undeniably inspired much of the ensuing sociological elaboration.

Are East and West too different? Sure, but only comparisons can tell us the actual depth of these differences. Precisely the difference among the cases allows to distinguish the unity of a sociological problem, in this case the way in which trade union activists relate to the work situation and to history. Certainly, the discussion of the findings will have to take into consideration the complexity of international comparisons. Among the factors which differ, the external (national situations) will have to be distinguished from the internal (differences related to the workplaces, which even if similar are not totally equivalent). Although complicating our task, the complexity of international comparisons has the value of connecting sociological analysis to other approaches and fields like history, political science, and ethnology (Casassus-Montero, 1989).

Rationale for Comparison

What I present is not a comparison of 'whole' national systems. Instead, it is a selection of a particular, comparable field (similar working situations in two different countries) and a particular issue (trade union consciousness). This was an attempt, if an imperfect one, to investigate the influence of a set of variables in a way inspired by laboratory practices in the natural sciences.

Italy and Poland make useful subjects for an inquiry into the role of the East-West cleavage in the transformation of trade union consciousness. In the not so remote past, trade unionism in both countries embodied to a very high degree the characteristics of a social movement. Yet opposed political traditions (as previously mentioned, a democratic trade union movement in a communist country contrasted with a predominantly communist trade union movement in a democratic country). The loss of the social-movement perspective involves a detachment from the old models. The question must be whether subsequent trends are convergent, at least when the features of the work situation clearly converge. The choice of comparable working situations within the same multinational companies attempts to provide a 'critical case' where differences are easier to detect.

The comparison makes possible a discussion of all three hypotheses formulated in the previous section. It should show the permanence of deep differences, a long side the presence of a common nostalgia for the past. The findings should also confirm that the East-West cleavage explain differences both objectively and subjectively. By becoming an interpretative resource used by actors, the East-West distinction reinforces the cleavage itself. Finally, it should become clear that differences between Italy and Poland are made stronger by a new interplay between life-sphere experience and the experience of work. Subsequently, it can be observed whether attitudes towards differences in the life-sphere are in any way connected with cross-national attitudes.

There are several approaches to comparison in the study of trade unionism. Maurice (1989) distinguishes three broad approaches: functionalist, cross-cultural and societal. The last assumes that actors are socially constructed within their relations to society, and pays attention to multiple, interactive causality in the micro-macro interplay. This is the approach I shall follow here.

The choice of national cases is quickly explained. Poland is, among post-communist countries, that with by far the strongest worker movement. Italy is, among Western countries, the only one with a legacy of a communist-oriented worker movement and a degree of economic integration with Poland allowing the choice of comparable industrial cases. These are countries where the *forms* of unionism were similar: in both cases competitive, ideological, combative, weakly institutionalised and with a visible social movement vocation. One can point to similarities in the experience of works councils (Poland 1956, Italy 1968), in their egalitarian orientations, in their links with intellectuals since the 1970s, and above all in strike behaviour. Today, union density is in both countries between 30 and 40%. One feature of union structure which is very telling with respects to union orientations (especially their level of centralisation and their strategies) is the presence of strike funds (Crouch, 1982), and neither Italian nor Polish unions have ever had them. The comparison between these two countries is therefore easier than between, for instance, the United States and Czechoslovakia or between Austria and Hungary.

Poland is not representative of the East: it was the least totalitarian country in the Soviet bloc. Neither is Italy representative of the West. In fact, it has even been argued that:

> In domestic political polemics Italy has often been described as the Western country with the highest proportion of elements of real socialism. It is a country, therefore, that may constitute (even though scarcely aware of it) an important 'reference society' for the European post-communist countries inasmuch as it illustrates how the state and market can collaborate against both tradition and modernity. (Grancelli, 1995, pp. 3-4)

However, if one is interested in testing the hypothesis that the meaningfulness of the East-West divide has endured, albeit that the content of that meaning has changed, these two 'close' cases are very suitable for validation purposes. Further, the 'visible' social movement past allows a more rigorous testing of the hypothesis of a disintegration of the social movement consciousness.

There are, moreover, secondary features (religion, industrial development, party systems, low institutionalisation, recent adoption of liberal economic policies...) which make these two cases even more comparable.

Within these two national cases, I have studied two industrial situations which lend themselves to the testing of the hypotheses: the Fiat plants (of Turin in Italy, of Tychy and Bielsko-Biała in Poland) and the Lucchini steelworks in Piombino and Warsaw. Moreover, a few 'control' cases are also considered.

Are Poland and Italy Comparable Overall?

Comparisons exhaust their usefulness when the terms are too different. This does not seem to be the case with industrial relations in Eastern and Western Europe. Books on post-communist industrial relations are constantly concerned with the issue of 'convergence' with the West. In multinational companies, human resource management tends (or at least claims to tend) to uniform policies. There should be, therefore, no reason for these cases to be incomparable. The situation of Eastern Europe is certainly peculiar, but this is, rather than an obstacle to the comparison, the real reason for interest in such a comparison.

The problem of the Polish past has been delt with in the previous chapter. If we shift to the particular field chosen for research (Fiat and Lucchini factories), the comparability of past experience is more striking, primarily because of the similarity of the 'opposing actor'.

The Polish FSM factories in Tychy and Bielsko-Biała have produced cars under Fiat licence since the 1970s, long before being taken over in 1992. Even if they remained absolutely typical Soviet-type factories, the closeness of the opponent had surprising consequences. In 1980, trade unions from Turin started a program of 'twinning' with another Polish factory working under Fiat licence (FSO in Warsaw). This twinning was indeed an asymmetrical relationship, and Italian trade unionists (as I discovered from my personal interviews with the protagonists) sometimes found speaking about 'workers' matters' problematic, because the Poles were concerned with 'higher' issues. Yet it gave rise to strong solidarity and to a recognition of mutual interest. Moreover, in the accounts of Jaruzelski's coup-d'état (13 December 1981), the most generous to the regime among Italian newspapers was not *l'Unità* (organ of the PCI) but the Agnelli-owned *la Stampa*. It was on Fiat invitation that Jaruzelski made in 1987 his first official visit in Western Europe.

In the case of the Lucchini steelworks, both factories studied were state-owned until 1992. The management of the Piombino plants (and of the whole town, considering that all mayors since 1945 were communist, and then PDS) displayed striking similarities with state-socialist practices. This point is important in recalling that the opposition of clear-cut models (West=market vs. East=state) is often misleading.

One final problem is how to generalise to the national level from observations made at the plant level. A first procedure is to choose a three-by-three comparison (six factories belonging to two companies), which allows a better generalisability than the analysis of singular cases. Moreover, a third comparative case study, although less deeply analysed, was carried out in the Danone plants. Even if the food industry is quite different from that of manufacturing, this case allows us to test the influence of the 'ownership asset' variable. Having also in Italy a foreign-capital owned company, it may be investigated whether the divergence of Polish activists as compared with Italians at Fiat and Lucchini is due to the 'foreign' character of the employer. It must be remembered that, according to World Bank data (cited in Jarosz, 1996, p. 10), in Eastern European private companies research has been possible in only 3-5% of cases (which seems less than under communist rule).

On the Polish side, which is less well-known than the Italian one, other theoretically relevant control 'cases' have been observed: the choice has striven to include 'extreme' cases, theoretically relevant for the validation of hypotheses *a fortiori*. A second procedure is to link the fieldwork to a review of the secondary literature and of national-level survey data (which also allows some cross-time comparison).

Common Sense and Social Science

One last question can be asked: in the final analysis, are qualitative methods a part of the social sciences, or are they instead simply common sense? Certainly, qualitative methods strongly reduce the epistemological fracture between scientists and lay actors. In the field of unionism this epistemological fracture is almost closed: union actors use a number of interpretative resources borrowed from the social sciences, so that a process of exchange between the social knowledge of scientists and actors is instituted (Corcuff, 1991). Reducing the epistemological fracture is not a limit but, conversely, a merit. It unveils two major social facts: the interpretative and cognitive capacities of social actors, and the embedded nature of the social sciences. Besides, even famous sociologists nowadays agree that:

> there is no clear dividing line between informed sociological reflection carried on by lay actors and similar endeavours on the part of specialists. I do not want to deny that there *are* dividing lines, but they are inevitably furry, and social scientists have no absolute monopoly either upon innovative theories or upon empirical investigations of what they study. (Giddens, 1984, p. xxiii)

This study is not an inquiry into the actual 'opinions' of trade union members: if this were the case, the method would be different and the sample statistically representative. This study is rather interested in the way actors build their identity and account for their activity. The resources used to 'communicate' identity and choices must be, to a certain extent, 'collective', 'social', 'indexical': this is why even a non-representative sample can offer valuable results.

According to the methodological orientation sketched in this section, the actors should become the real analysts. It is implicit in interpretative sociology that actors are able to make sense of their situation: they are not just 'cultural idiots', condemned to repeat orientations imposed by some kind of superstructure.

Which kind of knowledge, then, can be added by a sociologist, if members are already able to understand and describe? Just a collection of common accounts?

Even if this work were a simple collection of common accounts, this would not be totally useless, given the still very unequal access to expression in modern societies. However, the real contribution a sociologist can make lies in comparative reflection. Having some degree of exteriority, and more time for theoretical reflection, they can compare the accounts with information which actors usually do not have at their disposal. Of particular relevance, in the current case, are historical knowledge of the past of unionism and the cross-national comparison. Cross-national comparison allows us to question a number of supposedly 'self-evident', 'natural' facts; it makes easier what Wright Mills called the 'sociological imagination'.

The analysis of the findings, I shall keep in consideration the research questions and the theoretical framework presented in the first chapter. Only theory, and not statistical inference, can make the generalisation of a very limited case-study to the understanding of national cases less than entirely arbitrary.

Notes

1   On Fiat as a kind of anomalous seismograph of the Italian situation, good points are made by Giugni (1987), Accornero (1988), and Berta (1993). The Lucchini factories are more rarely in the headlines, although the personality of Luigi Lucchini (former president of the Italian employers' association) draws some attention.

2   On the history of Mirafiori, the best recent reconstructions are Berta (1998a), Bonazzi (1991), Olmo (1997). On the history of Fiat more generally, see among others Revelli (1989), Berta (1993), Volpato (1996), Gianotti (1999), Musso (1999), and the monumental '*Fiat 1899-1999. Un secolo di storia italiana*' by Castronovo (1999). The relevance of Fiat for the Italian labour movement also explains the attention of non-Italian scholars (e.g. Freyssinet, 1979; Sabel, 1982; Rollier, 1986; Golden, 1990; Mehl, 1993).

3   The period is recounted in detail by the protagonists (Garavini and Pugno, 1975). For an historical analysis see Berta (1998b).

4   On the *autunno caldo* and the '70s in the Fiat plants the collections of interview materials with union militants are particularly useful for this research and allow a degree of cross-time comparison (Aglieta, Bianchi and Merli Brandini, 1970; Totò, 1981; Polo, 1989). Useful sources are also the accounts from discussion and focus-groups (Briante, Oddone and Re, 1977; Girardi, 1980). In the analysis of this material the specific ideological and political framework must be held in due consideration. An example of the careful attention given by the unions to the control of production at Fiat is available in a research on the engine plant of Mirafiori organised by the plant unions (Bronzino, Germanetto and Guidi, 1974).

5   On the relationship between the labour movement and terrorism, with references to the Turin case, see Wieviorka (1988).

6   The importance of this event is confirmed by the large amount of literature on it (among others: Baldissera, 1988; Bonazzi, 1984; Perotti and Revelli, 1987; Manghi, 1987; Galli and Pertegato, 1994).

7   Which could not be stronger if one limits oneself to the analysis of two books of interviews with Fiat managers published just before and just after this change (Degiacomi, 1987; Annibaldi, 1994).

8   In 1997 the RSU (*Rappresentanze Sindacali Unitarie*, Unitary Union Representatives) elections at Mirafiori (without considering the central offices) gave the following results: FIOM 33.5%, Fismic 20.5%, UILM 17.6%, FIM 16.7%, Cobas 5.6%, UGL 5.2%, CISAL 0.9%.

9 In 1997 the RSU elections in the body plant and the presses shop gave the following results: FIOM 44.3%, Fismic 21.8%, FIM 15.3%, UILM 14%, CISAL 2.7%, UGL 1.2%, Cobas 0.8%.

10 First of all, the newly employed do not receive 300,000 L. per month of '*emolumento siderurgico*', obtained in 1989 by the state-sector steelworkers. In total, the wage gap between a young and an old worker *in the same position* at Lusid may reach the 700-800,000 L. per month. In addition, job security is much lower for the young employees due to the specific *contratti di formazione e lavoro* (contracts of training and work).

11 The 1997 RSU elections gave the following results among manual workers: FIOM 40.2%, FIM 23.7%, UILM 19.5%, Cobas 16.6%. The Cobas started for the first time and originated from a FIOM split. For the first time in history FIOM lost its absolute majority.

12 The unions as organisations, however, in 1998 showed notable courage by demanding the cokery displacement.

13 Hartch and Co., the Canadian consultants that drew up a plan for the steel industry for the first Solidarity government, had recommended the closure of *Huta Warszawa*.

14 *Solidarność 80* was founded in 1989, in opposition to the Round Table negotiations, by Marian Jurczyk, the Solidarity leader in Stettin and Wałęsa's adversary. The union, even if never exceeding 200,000 members, quickly gained importance between 1991 and 1993, leading many protests in strategic companies, especially in Southern Poland (e.g. many Silesian mines and the Cracow steelworks 'Huta im. T. Sendzimira'). After that period, however, the union was broken up by internal rivalries and splits. Jurczyk created the '*National* Solidarity 80' and was elected mayor of Szczecin in 1998. Today, some factions side with the extreme right, whereas others support the left-wing party Labour Union.

15 I infer this rationale from conversations with Fiat top managers I had in 1995 and 1996. A supplementary reason was the lack of preparation of the foremen.

16 They are: three variations of the former official unions – Metalworkers (*Metalowcy*), Solidarity, Solidarity 80 (radical split of Solidarity in 1990), August 80 (*Sierpień 80*, a radical split from Solidarity 80 in 1993), Popiełuszko (radical, right-wing split from Solidarity in 1997), Workers' Federation of the Tychy Fiat Plant (*Federacja*, a radical split from Sierpień 80 in the assembly line workshop in Tychy in 1997), and two unions of engineers and technicians. The Polish law on trade unions is an incentive to unions' fragmentation (ten people in a plant are sufficient to create a union, and each union is given separately a number of rights) and there are companies with as many as seventeen different unions. Nevertheless, such a sequence of splits in Solidarity as in Tychy is unique.

17 The *Popiełuszko* union was created in 1992 by Seweryn Jaworski, the Solidarity (and then Solidarity 80) leader in the *Huta Warszawa*, but at the national level is today almost non-existent. It is characterised by extremist nationalist and Catholic orientations. In the Tychy case, it is close to right-wing organisations, although its birth in the Fiat plant seems largely due to local antagonisms with Solidarity of the Bielsko-Biała plant.

18 From summer 1998 through May 1999 small groups of traditionalist Catholics and nationalists demonstrated in Auschwitz (10km away from the Fiat plant in Tychy) against the removal of a cross from the area of the concentration camp. The demonstration, which was of an openly anti-Semitic character, was led by Kazimierz Świtoń, one of the founders of the free trade unions of the '70s (*Wolne Związki Zawodowe*).

19 This element confirms that today, especially in Eastern Europe, strike hours statistics are a very misleading indicator of work conflict.

20 The concentration of engine production together with the 'dispersion' of body construction allows the producers to achieve better economies of scale, tighter links to the market outlets, and the avoidance of tariffs.

21 To my knowledge – having spoken with union activists, sociologists, and journalists – I was the first and last observer allowed to visit the Fiat plants of Bialsko-Biała and Tychy. In 1998 the possibility of a new permission was suggested under the condition of limiting the inquiry to certain trade unions, which was obviously unacceptable.

22 Revealing, and paradoxical, are the remarks of a researcher who found herself in the opposite situation. Ruth Milkman, in the course of a similar inquiry on a General Motors factory, received the collaboration of the company and the unions: 'For some potential informants – most of all, rank-and-file workers – the very fact that we had legitimacy with management and union rendered us eminently untrustworthy. In the intensely political world of the factory, academic researchers were an entirely unknown quantity and could only be understood as serving someone else's immediate interests' (Milkman, 1997, p. 192).

23 Again, the remarks of Ruth Milkman also make sense in the light of my own experience: '[interviews with more than one person] turned out to be among the best interviews, since they developed a group dynamic in which my presence often became marginal (...). I came to feel that these interviews constituted the most valuable data I was able to obtain' (Milkman, 1997, pp. 198-9).

24 Belief universes have not to do only with the imaginary in a strict sense. They can be more rigorously defined as 'sets of statements linked to the key-categories of talks and taken for true considering elementary logical analyses' (Martin, 1987).

25 The question was: 'What do you think of collaboration between workers and employers?' Three answers were possible: 'It is necessary because it is convenient for everybody'; 'It is possible but it must be negotiated'; 'It is impossible because workers and employers have opposite interests'. In my interviews, the attitudes were inversely correlated with these answers, because of a kind of self-censorship among the most radical activists. The excessive significance given by Accornero's team to this question may be explained, perhaps, by the fact that the inquiry was commissioned by the PCI.

26 Rogers' advice is very useful; all the same I shall speak of 'unstructured' interviews rather than of 'non-directive' interviews because the passivity of the interviewer which is necessary in the latter case must be avoided in the former.

27 Indeed the choice of the cases is highly biased by the process of 'bargaining' for access (data are, however, always bargained, even in quantitative studies). Very often, when researchers are sincere, we read statements like this: 'The choice of workplaces reflected three criteria: product characteristics, workplace size, and probability of obtaining access; often only the latter was a critical determinant' (Frenkel, 1994, p. 245).

3 Deconstructing Class Consciousness: the Paradoxical Parallelism of East and West

Discussing the idea of class consciousness disintegration exposes several risks: overstylisation of the past, nostalgic class iconography, ideologism, lack of historical perspective.

This chapter is an attempt to avoid these risks, while holding that a rupture with the class paradigm is a central point for understanding today's unionism. First, not the past itself, but its subjective representations are considered. Second, class is not given an evaluative meaning (either positive or negative): it is merely treated as a system of references which activists effectively use about the past, but not about the present. Third, consciousness is not an ideology, but rather a complex construct of principles (identity, opposition and totality): each will be analysed separately before seeing how they are interrelated. Fourth, the analysis will try to be dynamic rather than static by treating disintegration as a process: special attention will be paid to time references and to the discursive structures constructing the idea of turn.

Identity

A Plurality of References

Trade union activists define themselves in different ways, and often only implicitly. Among the three I-O-T principles, identity displays the strongest variation, and consequently is the most difficult to interpret. A first distinction should be made between *individual* and *collective* identity. However, this point will be more extensively treated in the 5th chapter, in relation to the subjectivation problem. Here, I shall consider only collective identity. The kind of collective identity defined as 'individual' means that the distinctiveness of the union – as a collectivity – is seen to be in its care for the individual.

Because of the high variation, the progressive proposition coding could not reduce the number of identity forms below eleven. They are presented in Table 3.1 for the different plant cases. Each interview could be assigned more than one identity reference (multiple identities), and in a very few cases no clear identity reference was detected. Therefore the sum of the cases does not coincide with the total of observations. However, in such small samples, much more important than frequency is the way in which a reference is present. Language is a social and not an individual attribute, therefore it must be understood and put in context rather than counted.

This qualitative-empirical evaluation, parallel to the quantitative one, is shown in the table in the following graphical way. In bold characters will be shown the references which strongly structure the interviews, and which are coherent with the other interviews of the group even if not explicitly present in all of them. In non-bold characters are presented the cases which appear either in a non-dominant way, or in interviews which for some individual reasons deviate from the local pattern. Negative frequencies mean that a particular identity is explicitly rejected by the interviewee.

The identity references of Table 3.1 require a definition and some illustrative examples.

Political identity refers to an ideological and/or party system cognitive framework: Left, Right, majority, opposition, etc. It often emerges in politicised trade unions like the Italian and Polish ones. However, it becomes central – that is, it organises discourse – only in particular situations and organisations. The cases where political identities acquire an importance comparable to work identities are the extreme-right *Popiełuszko* in Tychy and the left-wing FIOM in Turin, more in Mirafiori than in Rivalta. In the *Metalowcy* case political identity is neither strong nor clear. However, in a union displaying no other value references, left-wing and anti-clerical orientations are the only bases for common identity, and are therefore *relatively* dominant. More important is that, with the exception of *Cobas*, political identity is almost exclusive to elderly activists.

> I already knew about the union in Apulia [before migrating to Turin], because the greatest trade unionist of all time, Giuseppe Di Vittorio [the post-war CGIL leader], was born amongst us. (...) During the struggles of 1969 I saw older workers weeping, and I asked them why. They told me that it was not because they didn't want to strike, but because after so many years of being pushed around they were once again able to go on strike, they could remember the struggles of the 1940s. Then I began to ask a lot of questions, so as to

Table 3.1 - Identity principles

	political	historical	weak	pride	moral	cultural	work	class	community	national	individual
Fiat Bielsko Solidarność N: 9	-	6	8	-	2	2	3	3	2	1	-
		-1					-1	-1			
Fiat Tychy Sierpień 80 +Federacja N: 14	-	-	9	4	2	-	7	8	-	1	4
							-2	-1		-1	
Fiat Tychy Popiełuszko N: 2	2	-	-	-	-	-	1	1	-	1	-
Fiat Tychy Metalowcy N: 3	1	-	1	-	-	1	1	-2	-	-	1
Huta Lucchini Solidarność +Hutnicy N: 11	1	3	3	-	1	-	4	3	-	1	2
							-3	-2			
Fiat Mirafiori Fiom N: 9	3	4	2	1	1	2	5	8	1	-	1
							-2				
Fiat Mirafiori Cobas N: 6	1	1	2	2	2	-	-	3	1	-	5
	-1	-1						-3	-1		
Fiat Rivalta Fiom N: 8	2	-	1	2	-	-	4	-1	-	-	3
Fiat Rivalta Fim+Uilm N: 10	-	-	2	2	-	-	-1	-3	-	-	5
Lusid Piombino Fiom+Cobas N: 16	4	-	6	2	-	1	8	2	6	-	1
							-2	-2	-1		
Siderco Piomb. Fiom+Fim N: 3	1	-	1	-	-	-	-	1	-	-	-

understand what the factory was like before. I became interested in the history of the union and of the PCI. [mf6][1]

Political identity is usually signalled by a fear of political betrayal.

I'd really like the Right to govern the country, I'd really like it. But if Solidarity eventually only shares the governmental offices, then Solidarity will lose: people have expectations linked to the electoral promises. [tp1]

Similar to political identity is the *historical* one, which in addition creates a break between past and present. It is characteristic of Solidarity, a union considered by some observers to be a sort of myth (e.g. Frybes and Michel, 1996). The activists of this union, unlike all of the others, strongly prefer a historical structure for their narrative. In Italy, historical identity is frequent amongst the Mirafiori FIOM activists.

I started union activity at the beginning of the emergence of the union, that is in 1980. Then the name Solidarity came out (...). The union, as it operated, was a spontaneous revolt, linked to workers' dissatisfaction, afterwards the intellectuals joined the movement. It was a social movement. What were we dealing with? With everything and anything (...) It was dangerous, a lot of anonymous party members were infiltrated (...). It lasted until the 13 December 1981. I was at the historic congress in Gdańsk and on the road they arrested us. (...) Now I have resigned from standing for the delegates' election because I don't like as it is now. [bs1]

In order to get advances it was necessary to be a party member, there wasn't any alternative, so I joined it. Most people in the party were there for personal interest. In 1980 we spontaneously and en masse moved to Solidarity and quit the party, with the exception of a few zealot leftover. We did it because we were fed up with that way of lying. We were Solidarity supporters, supporters of democracy, of a democracy we still didn't know. [hs7]

We went on strike when the dictators took over in Chile, because Chile wasn't far away; it was close to us because even in Italy at that time something similar was happening, a *coup d'état* by stealth... So we sounded an alarm for the country and for the union. I don't regret it, we did well because we kept democracy alive in this country, because democracy is not something guaranteed on paper but something that must be won day after day, inside the workplace as well as outside. [mf4]

However, this model of identity is less and less fruitful for union action. As sociological studies on memory have shown (e.g. Candau, 1998), memory cannot now act as a foundation for collective identities:

memory has become personal, flexible and opportunistic, and the 'holistic' rhetoric of history is regarded with increasing scepticism. As a young Polish Danone worker told me, few things leave Warsaw youth so indifferent as Solidarity's historical rhetoric.[2]

In many cases identity is formulated on an indistinct weak-strong axis: we are weak, poor, mistreated... This stress on poverty (*weakness-based* identity) is the 'proletarian side' of class consciousness, which, however, if not associated with a positive working class identity, remains at a defensive stage. Birgit Mahnkopf (1985) calls it *Arbeiterkultur* as distinct from the *Arbeiterbewegungskultur*. As a rhetorical resource the stress on weakness appears here and there in all unions, but it is not only a matter of rhetoric: actually, in the most radical Italian union, the *Cobas*, the proletarian elements are rare. The most extreme, and 'politically incorrect', expression is the frequent Polish sentence 'we are white niggers'. The 'poor' image is a fundamental reference in the Polish Fiat factories.

> The worker is completely poor, he does ordinary, physical work, and for this work he gets some money, but this money is not enough to survive, only to vegetate. Everybody just lives in order to live, it's a dead end. It is not a problem of strength or will or character, he has children and he has to live. Not everybody goes and lies down on the railway track, but it is true, there are such cases, I personally know some cases of people who were that worn down. [bs7]

> He [the employer] thinks and he creates, while we achieve nothing, we just wait for the moment to act but are unprepared. It is as if the employer has the union surrounded on every side, we are in the middle, and the employer can strike whenever and wherever he chooses, and he will always win. We have neither lawyers, nor money. The employer can screw us however he likes. [bs5]

> At a certain moment the elderly workers arrive at the point that they resign spontaneously because they can't afford to perform the job, their nerves can't resist. There are periods during the year when the number of suicides amongst Fiat workers grows. Nobody talks about it too much, but there are periods, like last year there were maybe four cases. People on the way out read the death notices at the gates, cases of 30-40 year old guys, these are not old people, they are young, but this is the effect of the job, of the stress and insecurity. [tz1]

An opposite, *strength-based* kind of identity, consisting in a proud feeling of force and of a positive role, appears more rarely but is consistent among the radical unions of the Tychy plant (*Sierpień 80* and its split

Federacja) and in FIOM in Rivalta. Such a positive self-definition is clearly linked to the experience of conflict, and to some extent has a rhetorical nature.

The *cultural* and *moral* identities, if appearing alone, are the furthest away from working class consciousness, and they appear especially in workers' communities. Indeed, workers' subculture played a decisive role in the development of unionism, as shown by Thompson (1963). Cultural and moral identity principles are useful resources for collective action (especially during crisis periods), but displace the focus from work conflict as the main field of class struggle. This is the case in the Bielsko plant, where one frequently hears expressions of the kind: '*I am a Pole*' [bs9], '*I was brought up with Catholic values*' [bs3], '*all of my family was in the opposition, it has always been conservative, these are our family traditions*' [bs5], '*I chose Solidarity because it was the most trustworthy union, the most patriotic, consisting of people ready to make sacrifices*' [bs9]. Rare expressions of these non-work identities were detected in the other Polish plants and in Piombino, but strong references to external 'values' also appear in the radical Cobas. In Solidarity, the fieldwork detected a few cases of enduring 'ethics of Solidarity'[3] among activists who presented themselves as a sort of 'conscience' of the trade union. They recall that union goals of justice were of a moral more than of a material nature, and are disappointed by those who do not remember it.

> It was us who saved the factory, we cut our salaries (...). We cut our salaries by 35%, we took an unpaid holiday for two weeks, for the sake of saving this plant, because here maybe not everybody remembers what could have happened, very simply, the shutdown of this factory. Just looking at the human side, people with my qualifications, or electricians, or others, wouldn't have any problem finding a job here, but what about the people who do the real steelworking jobs, casters, millers (...)
> They say it was better, but I ask who for? Even chatting in the workshop, a guy who's going to retire says that it was better, I say what was better? He could go on holiday, but can't he go now? Don't you remember, I said, after all you're older than me, that when there were 250 of us in the workshop there were only two places for four people each, and who went? Only that *nomenklatura* and those secretaries, the same people, sometimes twice a year, the others didn't go at all. The coupons for the car, who got them? [hs6]

The *national* mode of self-definition appears only in Poland – where the employer is a foreigner – but much more rarely than one might expect according to the extensive literature on ethno-nationalism in Eastern

Europe. It is dominant only in the singular *Popiełuszko* union (but off the record), occasional and never central in the other unions.

> But the Italians have forgotten that the Pole is able to mobilise, there will come a time when we will mobilise like in '56, in the '70s, in '80, and it will be tragic for the Italians, tragic for this factory and for the Italians. It's not like I foresee it, I'm not a prophet. Only it just comes from knowing what's happened that sometime it must happen. We're not talking about a revolution, but someday we'll square things up on all these things. We'll punish what did the government and what did those who have got the big factories and those who burgled this country. Not only me, the majority says that. [ta7]

The *communitarian* identity is present in Bielsko-Biała, especially in the form of self-distinction from the Silesian workers of Tychy.

> It's difficult to agree with them, they are Silesians. They have quite a different mentality, and here there are the mountain people, with an extremely different mentality, like it would be difficult to agree with somebody who lives on the Mazurian Lakes, he has different customs. Similarly, they have different traditions: in the family only the man works, the woman stays at home because it has always been like that in Silesia, here among us it has always been different. [bs6]

However, it is in Piombino where the communitarian identity is the strongest. This is consistent with the typology proposed in the previous section. The fact that this occurrence is associated not with class identity, but rather with its rejection, is absolutely consistent with Touraine's view (Touraine, Dubet and Wieviorka, 1987, pp. 3-7). By contrast, it differs from Kerr and Siegel's (1954) classical idea that union action is the strongest in the 'isolated masses' of homogenous workers' communities. Shorter and Tilly (1974) had already fruitfully contested that idea by showing how French work conflict was rooted instead in urban, socially complex contexts. Communities are indeed a resource for collective action, but only for defensive action, for they do not facilitate the development of 'class' action. The history of the *Acciaierie e Ferriere Piombino* is a supplementary example.

> It's three generations that we're in the factory, my grandfather, my father and me, one town, one combative plant. [pf10]

> I entered the factory in '73, I was 18. I already knew the factory because I had done the steelwork specialisation at school, here in Piombino, it ensured you a job in the factory and since there was the myth of the sure job you put aside

other things in order to go into the factory. Once inside, a thing you noticed at that time and which impressed you a lot was that of having many elders in the factory who basically oriented you in your choices, with the trade unions as well as with politics and also with the job. And there was certainly a very good relationship with the young workers, they really tried to teach them. [pf4]

Today, there remains of this identity above all a deep nostalgia for the times when all the jobs 'remained in Piombino and did not move to Brescia'.

The Link to Work and Class

We can now shift to one of the most relevant sources of self-definition for the working class: *work* identity, including producer pride, skills, and the position in the organisation of work. Without any positive producer identity, class consciousness would hardly emerge.

The Italian worker is valuable. If you view things this way, the worker is worth a great deal, more than double the wages he gets... We are not stupid. I don't believe that the Italian worker, from the professional engineer to the lowest-ranked labourer, is an idiot, if we are managing to sell all these cars, which everybody considers fantastic, if we are even breaking into the American market. [mf3]

In its purest form, work identity implies the exclusion of non-manual workers. The presence of this argument among Solidarity activists confirms the interpretation of that movement as a workers' movement and is relevant for the workers vs. intellectuals debate mentioned in the previous chapter.

People who are in the UW [Union of Freedom, the liberal party formed by famous former dissidents and Solidarity experts] proposed a post-Solidarity alliance: I ask myself whether they were actually in Solidarity or were only advisors, aiming to escape earlier, because (...) they eventually did escape, Balcerowicz [UW president and at the time of the interview Finance Minister] is as he is, but what did he do in Solidarity? He's a professor and he's a theoretician, he's in the Union and what does he remember about workers' issues? He can't remember. [hs6]

Work identity is still widespread, but not in all situations. Notably, it is absent, apart from isolated cases, in the Bielsko-Biała and Siderco unions, as well as in the *Popiełuszko, Metalowcy,* FIM and UILM unions of the Fiat factories. Moreover, in most cases where work identity was detected, some 'counter-trends' were also present, with interviewees explicitly rejecting a work-related identity. Two examples of this escaping from work follow:

> Definitely my commitment was linked to the school factor. The climate in Turin before was really heavy, uniformity, it was a Fiat mono-culture, but still Valletta's [the Fiat managing director of the '50s and '60s] Fiat. [mf2]
> I started doing, I don't say that I enjoyed it, that it fulfilled my wants, but I did work. I thought that there would be some chances, but it turned out that there aren't. I'm considering whether I should stay here at all, I have a couple of interests besides, I study at evening school, I have organised my time and once I've finished at the school I don't know, I haven't a flat... or an income, or anything here... there's nothing to count on. [ta6]

Similar but not identical to work identity is *class* identity. According to the conceptual definition drawn in the previous chapter, class *identity* must be carefully distinguished from class *consciousness*, since the former is only an aspect of one of the three I-O-T elements of the latter, which is a more complex construct. Consciousness is a thorough, dialectical definition of one's own field of action, while identity – taken alone – is static and may even be purely ideological. In other words, identity is simply a sort of self-definition: consciousness includes a view of the social context.[4]

Class identity can be defined as a strong sense of class solidarity, where class is viewed as a collectivism not necessarily linked to offensive projects and excluding those who do not take part in collective solidarity. This collectivism is usually unconsciously instrumental, which contrasts with the dominant image of solidarity. Here it is necessary to define the term 'solidarity', quite an equivocal one in sociological thought. It enjoyed great favour until the beginning of the century, when it indicated (for authors like Marx, Durkheim, Tönnies or Michels) the capacity of the members of a collectivity (group, class or society) to act as a unitary subject. The best example is Durkheim's (1893) discussion of organic and mechanical solidarity. Later on the term solidarity almost disappeared, replaced by others such as social integration or consensus. In the last few decades, after the decline of functionalist and systemic approaches, the term 'solidarity' has reappeared in a different light. No longer a system or group attribute, it is now held to be an action motivation, and usually an individual one. No longer a reciprocal link of cohesion, but the motive of an asymmetrical relation where a subject X altruistically helps an object Y, supposedly in a worse situation. While the ideal of the first version was the gang of labourers, the ideal of the second is Mother Teresa of Calcutta.

Rarely has a concept assumed such different meanings, even in a non-paradigmatic science like sociology. Solidarity-cohesion requires, and creates, institutions and organisations; solidarity-altruism by contrast is seen as pure when it develops *outside* organisations. This is relevant for the trade unions, a traditional field of 'solidarity'. Studies on trade unions now only rarely nostalgically concentrate on solidarity-cohesion (e.g. Fantasia, 1988), which has already been criticised by some sociologists in the '70s (e.g. Offe, 1972). Now, much more attention is paid to the second version of solidarity (solidarity-altruism), and to its internal dilemmas (e.g. Zoll, 1992; Bode, 1997).

In this discussion I shall adopt the meaning of solidarity-cohesion and not that of solidarity-altruism. The latter still is conceptually hazy, as it covers completely different phenomena like cooperation and charity, which from a political-sociology point of view do not have any common denominator. Solidarity-cohesion, by contrast, is empirically disappearing but remains conceptually meaningful. It is in this sense, and only in this one, that the worker-solidarity decline can be discussed. The 'new' solidarity must still be defined, and this issue will be dealt with in the last chapter. Incidentally, the problem is made all the more concrete by the name of the trade union 'Solidarity', which is not only an *object* of definition but also an *active* determinant of the concept: the emergence of *Solidarność* eventually also influenced the ideologies of the Western unions.

References to class as a component of identity appear in both countries, although they are not omnipresent and some workers reject them. The endurance of class references in Poland must be stressed with regard to the class nature of the early Solidarity: in all plants, for instance, Solidarity activists report that the employees who created the union and abandoned the party in 1980 were manual workers.

In the interviews, class-identity is deemed present where manifestations of solidarity, collectivism and egalitarianism are formed. Equality-orientation is indeed a necessary component of solidarity, considered as an action system (Pizzorno, 1966).[5] This identity form is the strongest amongst the radical unions of the Tychy plants, and in Mirafiori, where it is characterised by a strong egalitarianism. Cognitively, it is linked to the image of the mass-worker. Because of this origin, it can be associated with sexist attitudes, although this is rare, especially in Italy where the exchanges between the feminist and labour movements have resulted in wide self-censorship (if not a thorough consciousness) in the trade unions.

Class solidarity, you can see it in people's attitudes, in helping a mate with his work when he needs it, in the belief that people must not betray one another (...). In a class society, the great majority of people are those who work, who are aware of their rights, people who do not have much education but who understand who is a friend and who is an enemy. [mf7]

In those unions it has been different, there are people, maybe not among us, but in the other unions in the factory, there are people in careers, aiming to sit at the table regardless of the consequences for other people. It's known that they take bribes, that they make decisions according to the bribes from the Italians, they sign different things which don't correspond to members' wishes, this doesn't matter for them. There was such a discussion once, our guys went to a meeting with the management board, a representative from one of the other unions said to our guys 'let sign, what will it cost you?', my rep says that he won't sign as a matter of honour, and the other one said 'why do you care about people, I don't give a damn about people' [the interviewee uses an untranslatable expletive]. We have it recorded on tape. (...) Krzaklewski [the successor to Wałęsa as Solidarity president and the leader of the AWS party] came here to the factory, they invited him obviously, came with the directors, and how did he come? Podrzycki, our national leader, they sent out patrols to prevent him from entering the factory. Krzaklewski, he came in a *Lancia*. [ta7]

By contrast, in other cases, such as *Metalowcy* or the Rivalta FIM-CISL, there is a definite rejection of class identities, even if in different ways and directions.

In 1992 I was on the union executive and I went on strike for 3 days, I had lots of friends, when I gave up the strike they erected a wall around me, but I didn't care about that and I kept on working, and now it's OK (...), it was horrible but I survived. Now I have friends again, only now I am already different, I used to help everybody, whether from the union or not, now it's changed, life changes, people too. And it's not bad for me, it's all right. [tm3]

I arrived at Fiat in 1987 and I came from 10 years of experience in a small workshop. I must say that the experience was traumatic, so traumatic that for one or two years I looked for other jobs in order to resign from Fiat. I found an enormous lack of humanity when moving from the small to the big. (...) If a post is overloaded with work, they try to unload it, maybe even on a friend, saying to the boss 'that one works less than me'. That is, not only do they try to offload work, sometimes they try to give it to a specific person, this is even more 'yellow'. It's very difficult to find somebody who'll make a move for you, I never saw it (...). Myself, I do it this way, by now I have changed and as a matter of fact I consider myself a robot like the others, even if I still don't accept it that way. Before, I saw people who cared only about themselves, now I'm also becoming like that. If something's wrong, I quarrel, but for me, if it's somebody else's problem, I turn a blind eye, I avoid discussing it with the others, because sometimes people diddle you, it's happened. [ri4]

As already mentioned, class identity is only one of the identity components of class consciousness. 'Weakness' and 'work' identities are also essential. On this point it is important to notice a difference between the Tychy radical unions and the Mirafiori FIOM. In the former case, class, work, and 'weak' identities are strongly related.[6] In the latter, the 'weak' element is almost absent and the 'class' and 'work' ones are related to a lesser degree. Moreover, they are occasionally associated with the 'historic' pattern, and the examples given are generally from the past, mainly the '70s.[7] The fact that the two Mirafiori workers with the strongest class identity are also the only two white-collar workers in the sample, suggests that class identity, left isolated, has an ideological character, in the sense that it is not rooted in experience.

There is a residual form of identity found in the interviews. This is the case of those who underline individual attributes as fundamental to their identity, and for the identity of trade unions as collectivities of *individuals*. They speak of the *man at work*, and sometimes of the *woman at work*, rather than of the worker or, even worse, the working class. This highly complex kind of self-definition was detected in Rivalta, in the Mirafiori Cobas, and to a lesser extent in Tychy.

I have always been independent as an unionist (...) You can have 20 degrees, but if you don't accept the dialogue as they want, you're done for. There, at Fiat people pay the price of being human beings, of saying 'sorry, I am a human being', this is the price one pays at Fiat. [mc3]

This last identity form is particularly relevant with reference to the subjectivation issue. This point will be more deeply discussed in chapter 5.

Opposition

The Unavoidable Conflict

For union activists the image of the adversary is clearer than the image of self. As a result, the propositions about Opposition are less heterogeneous and simpler to code than in the case of Identity (Table 3.2).

Virtually all of the interviewees had a concept of opposition, which means that they see their activity as bound up with conflict. One could take this for granted, since trade unions have traditionally always been in opposition to other actors. However, if one follows the sociological principle of questioning the obvious, one will immediately perceive that this is not self-evident. First, there are substantial differences in the *extent* and in the *ways* activists perceive this opposition. *Metalowcy* almost reject opposition altogether, and Solidarity activists from Bielsko-Biała have only a confused image of it. Secondly, and more important, since the beginnings of capitalism important currents of thought, also present within the trade unions, have argued for the non-conflictual character of work relations. In our interviews, in one way or another, almost all the activists in different national and plant situations perceive that they are engaged in an antagonistic relationship. This is an argument for the materialist thesis of the inevitability of work conflict, which arises primarily between foremen and workers around the issue of control. When the conflict is described precisely in these terms – similar in Italy and Poland –, it takes on a *class* value in the sense illustrated in the first chapter.

> By blaming Fiat, I don't mean the managers, because they are in Corso Marconi [the Fiat head office], they don't know what happens in the factories, but of course it is the fault of the leaders of the Ute [*unità tecnologiche elementari* - basic technological units, introduced by 'Japanisation'], which until a few days ago were called teams. They are the ones who always try to push us to the limit, maybe to make a good impression on their superiors. [mf1]

> Now man has been transformed into such a stupid machine. In the steelworks a saying started going round, 'you don't have to think, you have to do the job'. And this doesn't seem very good to me. For this I don't blame the management, God forbid, I don't blame Lucchini, he doesn't have any idea, but the management maybe yes, because through their substitutes and so on they send here (...). This can be seen first of all with the foremen, definitely, the relations with the foremen are really bad, that is, this happens in my workshop, I don't know about the others. [hs8]

Recently participation, 'concertation' and 'Japanese' production concepts have become increasingly popular, and they all undermine the idea of conflict (e.g. Womack, Jones and Roos, 1990). It is interesting to see how activists view these topics in order to assess the relevance of the opposition principle. Not only is participation rejected by the activists of the most radical unions in the historically adversarial Mirafiori (FIOM and Cobas) – the most emblematic statement here was '*to make participation real, we must be more rigid*' [mf5] – but also within the most 'participative' unions discrepancies with the image drawn by the company

(Fiat Auto, 1997) emerge clearly. Apart from the fact that Fiat's recent experience remains very far from a democratic-participative style (Garibaldo, 1993), and that various levels of participation may be distinguished (Cerruti and Rieser, 1993), it is the idea itself of participation which takes a particular meaning in activists' eyes. The plant where participation is considered most developed is Rivalta. Here, the idea of participation is, however, rooted in a strong opposition feeling, sometimes in contrast to the central trade unions' attitudes.

The participative aspect of FIM is important, it is part of what are, we face problems in a constructive way. As regards the organisation [the external union], it tries to... in any case it pushes us on these matters because it takes it very much into consideration, that is, participation according to them...[hesitation] and according to me, in any case is constructive, that's for sure. But for me the situation should... I mean, there are different situations, not every situation can be approached through participation, which means that participation exists but should also be evaluated in some regards. When it is shaky, conflict remains (...). I already do it, participating in the workshop problems, so that if they ask me to do something *I participate, I don't discuss.* (...) There still are some problems, Fiat would even agree, *but which company wouldn't be interested in participation?*[8] [ri9]

As FIM we're changing, with the discourse of the participative union (...) I absolutely agree, dialogue first, *but sometimes you feel they're making a fool of you.* [ri2]

After 1980, when there was a tremendous disaster in the union and it really broke down, now the union is regaining strength in the factories. Times change, people's mentality, work organisation, *we're forced to participate*, the other unions too, *without removing the struggle which after all is always behind work relations.* We participate because we want to solve workers' problems, and also to get more seriousness from the company side, who should show themselves interested in making people work better and in solving their problems. [ri5]

Participation, this is ruling the factory, establishing production on the basis of the staff, at the workshop level, every morning. It means preventing problems, involvement in ruling, concrete control. [rf8]

This does not imply that participation at Rivalta does not exist. By contrast, it underlines that effective, aware participation from the unions must be rooted in an opposition feeling. Otherwise, participation is nothing other than an ancient, paternalistic practice. The same can be said about reciprocal trust: only if the unions maintain a separate identity, will trust be well placed, 'merited', instead of 'unmerited' (Crouch, 1993, p. 46).

Participation is seen as a continuation of war under different forms, to paraphrase von Clausewitz. In Rivalta, this is a consequence of the 1980 defeat. Similar opinions are expressed by the *Huta Warszawa* activists, quickly disappointed by the participation which began after the 1994 struggle. In Mirafiori, where the feeling of opposition takes a more political and general value, participation is rejected. These findings challenge the assumptions of cooperation as a matter of rational choice based on a recognition of common interests with the employer and a calculation of the possible gains from avoiding conflict. In the view of activists, participation is rather a forced choice, the result of a defeat, or alternatively a way of fighting only on work-related matters disregarding other issues. In fact, participation in Rivalta is associated with ongoing disagreement, and strikes there are more frequent and more successful than in Mirafiori.

In all the plants covered by this study work organisation was recently modified, to a greater or lesser extent, by the introduction of 'Japanese' production principles. Workers' 'participation' indeed increased, and according to some studies the relationship between workers and management also improved, even in the most 'adversarial' Mirafiori (Bonazzi, 1997, p. 1998). However, crystallised attitudes give different meanings to specific measures. The interpretation of the *Fabbrica integrata* by the unions, in Turin as well as in Tychy, is generally negative and precludes its actual implementation. Numerous unionists denounce the fictively participative character of some bilateral committees, and their weakening effect on workers' bargaining power.

> The union made a big shit because now [in case of innovations] for two months you can't intervene on the charges, until the company verifies the problems and arranges it a little bit. But it is precisely in that period that there are the biggest problems, and the union cannot intervene according to the rule. This is sell, the union trampled on its own foots. [ri4]

> Now there are the famous committees, which are meetings, tables, where we arrange little or nothing, we always remain at vague discourses. This is not a committee, when there were the workshop delegates, the area delegates, there was more power. Now on the contrary it's as we were imprisoned, for instance if I go to raise a problem of my team, they say 'no, this is not included in the *Fabbrica Integrata*, this belongs to the security committee'. And so you have to abandon it, the committees are a real cheat. [mf8]

Table 3.2 - Opposition principles

	generic	class	work	past work	national	history	political	extrawork
Fiat Bielsko	**7**	4	2	3	3	3	1	-
Solidarność	**-4**			-1				
N: 9								
Fiat Tychy	**8**	**9**	**11**	3	**4**	4	1	-
Sierpień 80 + Federacja			-1	-2	-3	-2		
N: 14								
Fiat Tychy	1	2	1	1	1	-	1	-
Popiełuszko								
N: 2								
Fiat Tychy	1	-	1	-	-	-	1	-
Metalowcy	**-2**		**-2**					
N: 3								
Huta Lucchini	5	5	5	3	**6**	3	1	-
Solidarność + Hutnicy	-1	-1			-1			
N: 11								
Fiat Mirafiori	7	5	4	**2**	-	1	3	-
Fiom							-2	
N: 9								
Fiat Mirafiori	5	-	**4**	1	-	-	1	1
Cobas								
N: 6								
Fiat Rivalta	5	2	3	5	-	1	-	3
Fiom	**-4**							
N: 8								
Fiat Rivalta	**5**	1	**6**	-	-	1	-	**2**
Fim+Uilm	-2							
N: 10								
Lusid Piombino	**11**	**2**	**8**	**-2**	-	**-2**	**4**	1
Fiom+Cobas	-2	-1	-1					
N: 16								
Siderco Piomb.	**2**	**1**	**3**	-1	-	-	-	-
Fiom+Fim								
N: 3								

The same critical remark is made in Piombino about the union renouncing its right to immediately intervene on the hot productions.

The aspects of Japanese organisation that increase worker's stress, even if they possibly reduce the physical effort, are easily detected, and described sometimes in class terms.

> At the moment the worker is so tied up with different sheets of paper, that he basically can't manage to check the car, given the amount of forms there are to fill. And this originates at the technicians' level (...). All the technicians' sit down and make nothing: all their role, all the job is passed to the production workers, and they must, willy-nilly, make certain things (...) Formerly there were the gangs [*komórki*], now there are production *teams* [in English], formerly there was the foreman [*mistrz*], now there is the director of the production team... something else is worrying, that they introduced what they call TPN. This means that workers in production and in quality control, are generally responsible for the material they work on. [tz1]

Polish workers trust the employer so little, that they become afraid of 'participating'.

> There are the boxes for mail, so that workers can express their problems,[9] I say 'let's write: why, what, how...'. Somebody said to me 'OK, but if they notice that I have written something, it doesn't matter whether it's positive or not, the important thing is that I wrote something, they can think that I'm complaining...'. Every attempt to integration... for instance in the cabins it was too warm and people wanted different clothes, shorts. But it was impossible to express it, because they are afraid, and to write something down, this is already unthinkable. [ta1]

Sometimes the refusal becomes radical.

> And they exploit these situations to make fools of the workers, to impose models which are not ours, which are Japanese, like continuous improvement [the *kaizen*, one of the pillars of toyotism], that whorishness, they convince them that they are useful to the productive process, once we were exploited, now we are human resources. [mf8]

The only relevant exceptions to this refusal are the *Metalowcy*, definitely collaborative, and Rivalta FIOM, which as already mentioned has developed an alternative vision of participation. The perplexed opinion of workers and trade unions on the new organisation principles has been confirmed by other studies (Garrahan and Stewart, 1995) and has been explained as a sort of '*proletarische Arbeitshabitus*' (Wittel, 1998).

Employers are actually aware of this problem as can be seen in their preference for 'green-field' sites. My interviews, however, suggest a supplementary explanation. Contesting of new management techniques is not simply a matter of generic, omnipresent and inherited 'habitus'. It is more concretely rooted in the experience of conflict, and therefore affects primarily those unions with an open conflict tradition.

Similar conclusions can be drawn about political-level participation, called 'concertation' or 'corporatism'. At this level too separate identities remain necessary.

> It is vital to actors in bargained corporatist systems that they retain their sense of separate identities, that they continue to rally their 'side' and develop its symbols (...). Were the two sides to lose their sense of conflict and separateness, the whole system would become unnecessary and the representatives would lose their function. (Crouch, 1993, p. 48)

In the plants we note not only that industrial workers maintain a separate identity, but also that they have a rather negative view of 'concertation', especially in Piombino.

> We face a cross-roads, if we go along with concertation, we get into the factory and they will talk to us; if we don't they won't give us that space. It seems to me that we're in danger of being sent away from the factory because we don't want to concertation. [pf10]

This incomplete commitment by the industrial workers suggests that the Italian 'social pacts' of the 1990s, rather than being a resurgence of corporatism (Regalia and Regini, 1997; Regini, 1997), only froze a conflict which was always susceptible to exploding – as it actually frequently does.[10] Indeed, all tripartite agreements since 1993 have been approved by a majority of workers in union referendums. However, especially in the most important of these referendum (the one on pensions reform in 1995), the industrial workers of the large factories voted against the agreements. Their vote was completely disregarded by the confederations (though the left-wing minority initially rejoiced for that massive 'no'). The workers who used to be the central reference of the unions and, in the sense adopted here, constituted the Italian working class *as a social actor*, were treated by union leaderships as just one more minority, less important than retired people. This event is the best proof of the departure from the class pattern by the Italian trade unions.

Similar observations can be made about Polish tripartism, which every year on the most important issue (salary indexation for the state employees) cannot reach an agreement and leaves the government free to take the ultimate decision.[11] From the workers' point of view, these kinds of cooperation with their adversaries are associated with a feeling of decline and social degrading, much more than with a feeling of achievement. And decline, for reasons which rational choice cannot easily explain (the structure of the decision is exactly the same whether the goal is to achieve gains or to avoid losses), may force cooperation at the top level[12] but makes a positive image of cooperation among workers more difficult. To summarise, the picture of concertation emerging from the Italian and Polish industrial plants confirms Crouch's most pessimist scenario: a situation where it is quite possible for national shells of union (and employer) organisations to play an amicable though important game of social reconciliation with each other and with governments while at factory level a membership with which they have little real contact either behaves as it likes or is so oppressed by high unemployment that it cannot do anything at all, pact or no pact (Crouch, 2000).

The relevance of conflict for the trade unions also depends on its frequently 'expressive' character, which is especially important for newly established unions.[13] This point was very well analysed about the Italian *autunno caldo* by Pizzorno's (1978) team, but was also shown by Kulpińska (1993) with regard to the waves of strikes in Poland in 1992-93. My inquiry illustrates it with two eloquent examples in which the usual cost-benefit calculation does not operate. The first is the 1992 strike in the Tychy plant, which although it completely failed, increased the Solidarity 80 (later *Sierpień 80*) membership from 200 to 2,000.

> I personally don't regret that strike, we showed that we're a force. [ta7]

> The strike of '92 wasn't a defeat, actually back then *Sierpień 80* gained members and from that time has basically remained at the same level. [ta1]

The second example is a strike organised by *Cobas* in a Mirafiori workshop although the demands had already been satisfied by the management. The shop steward's tale is eloquent.

> The operative manager, that is the shop foreman, arrived, he says 'listen, in any case we are verifying...', 'I demand two more people' (...), 'It is impossible', 'At one o' clock there is a strike', 'No, no, look, now we'll see...', 'No, I am sorry, now let us do it'. We organise a strike against him, the guy starts praying 'look, now we'll place...', 'We have decided, I have already spoken with the workers, at one o' clock there is a strike'. 'We'll give you the two people!', 'Now stop it, first we strike and then we'll speak about it'. [mc2]

In a way, similar conclusions may be drawn about the employers' side, which is not however a topic for this piece of research. As Kozek (1999) argues, Polish employers mistrust corporatist arrangements because, being a young social formation, are still in search for an identity. For this purpose, they need to mould an 'ethos' of their own, while participation in neo-corporatist structures would 'water it down'.

Only one trade union among those analysed in this study rejected any opposition principle: the post-communist *Metalowcy* from the Tychy plant. This union has apparently made a dramatic change in recent years, developing an orientation which is basically pro-market and pro-Fiat.[14] Their offices are full of typical Western-culture posters. Their leader, moreover, was previously in the Solidarity leadership, which he left because it was too 'old-fashioned'. From a political point of view, it is tempting to speak of a 'reconversion' of this trade union: from socialism to the market. Yet if one observes social relations in the company, a strong continuity in the *cogestion* practices of Soviet-type unionism (Lowit, 1971) comes into view. In spite of the appearance of reconversion, a particularly strong 'path-dependency' is driving change. On the lack of any class principle among the *Metalowcy* in Tychy a statement by one of its leaders is emblematic:

> Workers do not appreciate what the employer does for them. I do, because my wife is herself an entrepreneur. For instance, Fiat gives them overalls, but workers don't give this due consideration. But this is a lot... my wife, she doesn't give overalls to her employees.

The Remains of the 'Class' Opposition

Touraine's focus on opposition as an element in the construction of social movements is a useful approach to the analysis of Eastern European trade unions. In the Russian case, it was discovered that breakdown of the Soviet Union put an end to the miners' movement, which became lame without its opponent (Berelowitch and Wieviorka 1996). The evolution of Solidarity can be interpreted in the same way, although the Polish union was more successful. Its resistance, however, was at the cost of keeping alive the former enemy (in their imagination at least), and of reinterpreting new opposing roles through the old categories. The relevance of opposition first of all explains why a blue-collar-worker-dominated union can endure as an explicitly right-wing organisation. Even more interesting is how the activists of Solidarity and its smaller offshoots manage to create a link between past and present opponents.

The majority of foremen are from the old nomenklatura (…). For me, keeping the old foremen is a waste because they aren't able to manage. The management at the beginning didn't carry out a verification of the foremen and this was a mistake. Incompetence, lack of responsibility… [hs2]
That's only organisational chaos, they don't foresee any alternative… this organisation is communist. It provokes workers' frustration. We need a modern organisation. [hs4]

The current supervision board is composed of those people who were in the PZPR [the Polish communist party], and these are the same people, this is a real gang. These are the guys who stole the most in the factory, I'm not saying all of them, but 50% are people who stole tremendously (…) We went on strike [in the 1980s] against the people who are now managers, foremen, against us, they remember it perfectly well (…). I am still recorded as 'political', that's funny, amazing and funny because the system has changed and I am still recorded as political. The vice-manager told me that. (…) I think that democracy means I have the right to say what I think without anything happening to me. And here there are methods like under communism at the moment you could say there is a regime, if I don't restrain myself tomorrow I could be out of work. [ta7]

These are people who will do anything in order to keep their posts, they don't care about the factory but only about their own jobs. They were called 'red', and the system broke down, now they are capitalists, the former director is a private entrepreneur and rules with the same people as before. We know all his story, who he was under communism. [ta8]

These are the old foremen, who grew up with communism, socialism, in those days they were educated and they maintained a certain attitude. Now they're only foremen and they are not ready to perform this job, they make it only with coercion. (…) These are people who received their offices… as it used to be 'on party lines', their party exploded and now they create this kind of capitalism, in our view this [system] is banditry. [ta1]

This old work opposition is so strong that it is still operative, for instance in the criticism of the so-called '*nomenklatural* privatisation'. The change of the legal identity of the employer (the *ownership form* of the means of production) does not undermine the subjective coherence of the opposition.[15]

The ownership is completely different, now it is completely different, there used to be, let's say, a social ownership of the whole factory. And there is still, let's say, an imaginary somebody who rules here, because this is a big factory, and you don't see the owner every day, because it's a group, some kind of shareholders, so this is not a one-person firm. For this reason it's similar to before, because before the owner was collective too. We know to whom it belongs, but at the same time we don't know it, because this is a group of people, shareholders, owners and so on. The attitude to work hasn't changed, and the organisation hasn't changed so much because of privatisation. People worked before and they work now, what is the difference if it belongs to Frank or to Wojciech? nothing changes, absolutely nothing. [bs7]

By contrast more important are the organisational constraints within the factory, which regardless of the mode of development (communist or capitalist) emerge from a certain industrial logic.

In the previous system there was the so-called socialist economy, but the economy can't be socialist or any thing else, the economy is just the economy. What you produce, you sell – you can't do it any other way. [hs6]

The ability to construct historical coherence is of decisive importance in Poland, but in another form also exists in Italy when changes in work organisation, like in the Fiat factories, deeply modify the former battlefield. Activists in Rivalta and an even greater number in Mirafiori assert that nothing has changed. By doing this, they seriously risk falling into pure ideology, but they manage to keep the union together.

The foregoing extracts raise another important issue, which was touched on in the previous chapter. This is the extent to which we can define Polish trade unions as having been involved in class conflict in the past. If a direct link between current conflict and previous conflict is made so clearly, this suggests that the former experience displayed at least some 'class' elements. Indeed work organisation under real socialism displayed many peculiarities, and workers' descriptions confirm the idea of an 'arhythmic taylorism'.

Under communism it was like that, before 1990 everyone simply pretended he was doing something, he'd look around when some director came from Bielsko, nobody managed to organise the work so that everyone could go on rhythmically and quickly. Somewhere something stopped and we had to pretend, fake or even hide, so that nobody could see that we were standing still. [ta7]

Despite these differences, the protagonists' references to class and work conflict in the past are distinct, even if rarer in comparison to the more 'historic' (and therefore more lucid in memory) political conflicts. In most of the cases, the political and class opponents are associated with a specific image of exploitation.

We carried out the plan as the foreman told us, regardless of whether we had the necessary people or not... unless the shortage of people was so tremendous that we could capture people or produce less. (...) [Now] for us it's better because when there weren't enough people but the foreman wanted to show off people had to work more. And this didn't make any sense. It was impossible to oppose it because what could you say? And we made worse and worse quality cars. Everybody can confirm it, (...) it was insane, when somebody works under constraint it will never be good. [bs8]

The party, always them, ruled the factory, it might have been under different names, whether the management or the plan or whatever, but it was always them. The party secretary didn't have any idea, but it was he who worked out the plan. [hs7]

Under FSM it was like that, the worse the better. The more broken cars, the more failures, the better, because they had the chance to steal. They wrote that the pieces they stole were lacking, the factory guard signed... The ordinary workers actually didn't steal. If the foreman or the director didn't allow it, it was impossible for workers to steal, maybe with foreman's cooperation they could have done it but alone it was hard. [ta7]

There is always such an attitude towards working people from those who are at the top, who rule, who control. And this attitude is at least bad, this can't be changed overnight, the relations are *still* bad. [bs7]

If work relations are *still* bad, this implies that they were bad in communist times: bad work relations are not therefore a distinguishing feature of capitalism, but rather an aspect common to all factories in industrial society. Very revealing, in this regard, is the tale of the abolition of piece-work (a constant feature of work under state-socialism) in Bielsko-Biała, which took place *before* privatisation.

It just happened that before Fiat's entrance the union asked for piece-work to be abolished, yes, it happened before Fiat's entrance. It's good that it happened like that, because I don't know whether we would have managed it later, we can't be sure about that. Some people asked why management agreed to the abolition of piece-work. Afterwards it didn't exist anymore, and nobody could ask for its restoration, because that would be a non sense. We had been fighting for quite a long time for it, so that at least on the assembly line and in the welding shop, we could make up the appropriate plan for the actual quantity of people. [bs8]

It must be noted that the unions most embedded in work and class opposition are also those most directly related to the 1980 social movement experience, as their names reveal ('Solidarity 80', 'August 80'). I recall here that most Polish activists share right-wing political orientations. Therefore, their references to a class opposition can hardly be due to ideology, unlike some Italian activists who repeat trite Marxist formulas. Polish workers have not read about work conflict: they have experienced it.

By contrast, it is not in Catholic Poland, but in the communist-voting Piombino that the presence of class conflict in the past is denied by activists. This has to do with Piombino being a politically regulated, homogeneous community.

> At that time, the experience with the foreman and the shop steward wasn't bad, people were well-intentioned, they discussed things, they talked to each other. It's clear, if there was a decision taken by the foreman the shop-steward intervened, the union was present, somehow the union was present through the shop-steward, who made his comments and said whether something could be done or not, whether there were security conditions, certain things. It was a nice experience because it worked and foremen, shop-stewards, and the union all agreed. [pf12]

> It was much easier, now I realise that it was much easier to participate in union activity when the boss [the interviewee uses the class-related term *padrone*] was the state, because before we always said '*il padrone, il padrone*', but we didn't know what the *padrone* was like, in fact we have met the *padrone* only now. [pf9]

The Piombino unions were particularly strong, controlling recruitment, qualification levels,[16] and work tasks. Control over work was different from that achieved by Fiat workers in the 1970s. It was more pacific and was not so much about the regulation of effort. In order to guarantee high employment and qualification levels, it concentrated on the stoppage of task flexibility (internal mobility).

> In Piombino a watertight system had been created, tasks were fixed for everybody, the young worker reached only the door but he was forbidden to turn the door-handle because this was the task of somebody else. [pf7]
> To give you an example, in my workshop we risked stopping the factory because we refused to push a button which opened the container (...), there was a worker with the exclusive job of pushing that button and nothing else. [pf15]

A last point about the Eastern European past. Interviews reveal how the lack of a developed monetary system did not preclude a feeling of exploitation. Actually, Polish industrial workers repeat that with their productive work they had created all the national wealth, and sometimes give concrete examples in which they were sent to work outside for reasons of social interest. The fact that this wealth was not administered according to their wishes is seen as proof of exploitation, and the current privatisation of that wealth is considered to be a definitive expropriation.

> We built residential districts, the ice-rink, swimming pools and so on, everything has now been taken over either by private entrepreneurs [a pejorative, *prywaciarzy*, is used] or by some kind of City Council, and workers have nothing of it. [ta1]

After examining the different opposition forms (Table 3.2), it can be said that only in the case of the Tychy radical unions is the opponent considered to be the one who organises work in a way conflicting with workers' aspirations. This is the basis for class consciousness, and probably a reaction to the implementation, in the early 1990s, of Taylorist-like work organisation. Particularly significant in this plant is the frequent reference to the abolition of piece-work and to the disadvantages of the assembly line, to which many workers previously doing skilled work were moved.

Class opposition rooted in work conflict is not the only way in which the trade unions express relations of opposition. Table 3.2 indicates a number of other ways in which the opponent is identified.

In many cases, a simpler work opposition appears, which is a criticism of how the employer organises economic activity, but not of the direct, collective relationship between foremen and workers. This often happens in the former official unions of Warsaw, which are engaged in political as well as in work-related issues but lack the Solidarity tradition of 'class' opposition.

> They [the authors of the restructuring plan 'Meta'] are people who don't have any idea about working here. Or they are people who were in production, didn't prove themselves able to work, and moved to Meta, there are such people. [hm3]

In relatively few cases non-economic categories are used. This is the case of nationalism, which is more frequent here than in the case of identity. This difference suggests that nationalism is little more than an emergency resource for Polish workers which is used to account for reality when other categories do not work. Since they cannot, for historical reasons, explicitly use class arguments, nationalism also appears in Tychy where the conflict is nevertheless class-based. In many cases, however, it seems that the nationalist representation of conflict overlaps with the class one.

> They cut the funds for the employees. The only thing they do is a '*Festa Italiana*'. The city council this year put up 900 million for a *festa* organised by the Italians. It seems to me that all around the world if there is a big company in a town, this company offers something, here we see that the opposite is the case (...). They fund disparate things, but nothing for the employees, this year they organised this '*Festa Italiana*' but on a working Saturday, so that workers could not come. [ta1]

> We, in the foreign-owned companies, have bigger costs because we have to maintain the Italian staff, that's why there are bigger operating costs and less money for salaries. [hs2]

> The worker is fearful and performs his job although he knows that it won't work, that it will destroy it, he fears the consequences. If before his vision was broad, now it's narrow like a laser light. The Italian representative, when is there, after he says 'I was misunderstood, I was wrongly translated', he holds back. [hm3]

If nationalism were really the problem, identity (and totality) would also have been defined in that way. More empirically, it can be noted that as an Italian researcher I have been treated not only politely, but even with warmth by the most radical Polish activists. The context of the nationalist statements and the conduct out of the inquiry allow me therefore to reject the thesis, suggested by other researchers (Gąciarz and Pańków, 1997a, p. 97) that the conflict at Fiat Auto Poland is of an ethnic-cultural character. Moreover, in other, non-Italian, foreign-owned Polish plants (Daewoo and Danone) similar, even if weaker, arguments were heard. Fiat is therefore not significantly deviant in this regard.

Sometimes, in Italy as well as in Poland, the opponent is seen through a political lens. This can happen in two different ways: when the responsibility for the workers' situation is identified as lying with the government rather than with the employer, or when the employer is imputed to have a political will. The latter variant appears almost exclusively in the most radical unions (*Popiełuszko*, Cobas), while opposition to the government is also expressed by other unions in Mirafiori and Warsaw. In the Solidarity case, however, the opposition to communism kept alive by the national leadership has been largely abandoned on the shop floor, for instance allowing some OPZZ-Solidarity cooperation at *Huta Warszawa*. Solidarity's opposition to the communists has a moral rather than a political nature: they must be fought because they are 'guilty' rather than because their policies are dangerous. On political issues the adversary, if any, is identified as the liberal Union of Freedom (coalition partner of Solidarity after 1997) more than as the post communist party.

Finally, there are isolated cases where the opponent is identified in different, specific ways: the leisure organisation, the welfare state institutions, the other gender. These rare cases do not undermine the general impression of an opposition which is either generic or class/work related.

Totality

The Ambiguity of Political and Social Struggles

The totality principle is usually defined as what is at 'stake' in taking action, but it cannot be reduced to the mere 'goals' of social actors. It could better be defined as a ground of confrontation implying a certain 'counter project', an alternative idea of how an issue should be treated. For instance, a demand for a salary increase (which seems the simplest form of union action, but is actually the most difficult to analyse) does not display an economic totality principle unless it relies on a general idea, even if embryonic, of how economic relations should be organised. This may be, for instance, according to the idea of basic social rights, or to general moral values, or to an idea of exploitation based on the link between salary and product, or on market arguments, or still otherwise.

On the totality principle variation in the interviews is slightly lower than on opposition and especially identity (Table 3.3).

The definition of the 'confrontation ground' cannot be interpreted in a straightforward manner. This can be seen in cases where action has a *political* stake, very frequent in politicised unions such as the Italian and Polish ones. Interview data offer important information on the actual meaning of propositions. For instance, in the interviews carried out in Piombino in autumn 1997, the topic of the 'welfare state' often appeared spontaneously, and initially seemed an indicator of political involvement. Since the interviewees did not specify what they meant by the welfare state, they were asked what actually did matter in welfare state reform, and the answer was clear-cut: pensions, and more precisely retirement age. The term 'welfare state', newly arrived in the Italian language, was then a euphemistic synonym for 'pension system', and had to be interpreted purely as a social benefits issue rather than as a political one. This is why it is best to distinguish 'political' from 'social' (in the sense of social benefits) goals. Another example of ambiguous political statements comes from Rivalta. The frequent uneasiness of FIOM activists from that plant about the political goals of the trade unions sheds a new light on the 'autonomy' claim of the FIOM Congress which took place at the same time (see FIOM-CGIL 1996). Most observers interpreted this claim as representing a radical left-wing standpoint. However, from the interviewees' words it appears that they refused any political *concertazione* not because they were *left-wing*, but because they were *metalworkers*. Rather than autonomy from political parties, the activists were demanding autonomy from politics, and a return to professional (possibly corporatist) matters. Again, in spite of the language, a political 'totality' is absent.

On the 'political' totality principle it must be noted that, although politics are a recurrent topic during the interviews, political action is widely rejected in those unions which are most engaged in work matters, such as the Rivalta FIOM and Tychy *Sierpień 80*. This point suggests that work conflict has lost its 'general', societal character.

The *economic* 'totality' principle is also very frequent. It could be expected as a constant from trade union activists, since trade unions are considered to be 'interest' associations whose main task is salary negotiation. However, there are situations where economic claims are secondary. In Italy not only are economic issues in many interviews absent or marginal, but some interviewees (especially in Piombino) even deny that salaries are an important concern for the trade unions or for the workers themselves. This finding, in that it contrasts with 'common knowledge', is particularly important.

In Piombino people earn decently, it's not that they don't earn, in addition to the fact that they don't go on holiday, that they're always inside, damn, it's not that... [pf2]

As regards salary, the national contract is favourably viewed, our [new employees] contract can raise some problems, but we're almost all young and one and a half million is enough for us, later on with the professional career that they'll want us to have, and wishing to live on our own, we'll reconsider it. [pf5]

Before [the union] was concerned only with raising salaries, which for me is a very negative thing, it's fruitless, you raise salaries, after that prices increase and nothing changes. [ri4]

Table 3.3 - Totality principles

	politics	economic	coll. barg.	social	work	class	employment	extrawork
Fiat Bielsko Solidarność N: 9	**7**	**6**	4	4	2	1	1	3
	-2		-1	-3				
Fiat Tychy Sierpień 80 + Federacja N: 14	2	**7**	1	1	**4**	1	-	3
	-8		-1					-1
Fiat Tychy Popiełuszko N: 2	**1**	-	-	-	-	-	-	-
Fiat Tychy Metalowcy N: 3	1	**2**	-	**1**	-	-	-	-
	-2							
Huta Lucchini Solidarność +Hutnicy N: 11	**4**	**5**	4	4	**9**	-1	-	-
					-1			
Fiat Mirafiori Fiom N: 9	**3**	3	-1	2	**4**	2	-	-
	-1	-1		-1	-2			
Fiat Mirafiori Cobas N: 6	**2**	2	-	-1	**4**	1	-	-
	-2				-1			
Fiat Rivalta Fiom N: 8	**3**	1	3	2	**5**	1	2	3
	-4	-1						
Fiat Rivalta Fim+Uilm N: 10	1	-1	**4**	2	2	-	1	**4**
	-5			-1				
Lusid Piombino Fiom+Cobas N: 16	**7**	1	1	5	3	1	**8**	-
	-2	**-6**			-2			
Siderco Piomb. Fiom+Fim N: 3	1	**1**	-	1	-	-	**1**	-
	-1							

Such statements could be interpreted as insincere, the interviewees wishing to appear as altruistic in front of the researcher. In any case, the difference between Italian and Polish activists in this regard is so remarkable that it will be examined in greater depth in the next chapter.

In the cases of the most institutionalised and professional trade unions (in Rivalta and Warsaw) the duty of the union is often seen as just *collective bargaining*, that is in the institutional role of negotiating. Working for the union means being in an intermediary position between the workforce and the employer. The procedural goal of participation in decision-making is seen as more important than 'material' ones. This goal, however, requires a relatively long time-horizon; in situations of uncertainty, like in Bielsko-Biała, it betrays a hesitation about more concrete goals.

The *social* goals, already mentioned in the Piombino case, are social benefits not directly linked to the work activity. Social activity was very important for the official unions under real socialism, and this legacy is often seen as an enduring peculiarity of Eastern European unions. The Italy-Poland comparison, however, does not reveal any significant difference in the occurrence of social concerns. An important exception are the post-communist unions, not so much because of their orientations (they also often embrace a market ideology), but because, for organisational reasons, they tend to include retired workers in the company unions. As a consequence, for instance, they claim that retired workers should be entitled to use the company health-care service, which is clearly unacceptable for the employer.

Work and Class: Still the Battlefield?

As in the identity and opposition cases, it is important to distinguish class and work concepts. *Class* totality indicates that activists see their 'mission' as being to take part in a general conflict about the social resources involved in industrial production (even if they are not necessarily clear about who are the actors involved, as is indicated by the Identity and Opposition principles.)

> As regards technologies there have been enormous steps forward, but the technologies offered by science become a possession of whoever owns them, and a company which beforehand employed many workers can now send one third of them home. These technologies should be a possession of the society. [rf2]

In 1980 Fiat found itself in difficulties, not because of any fault on the part of the workers but because Fiat had not carried out its research properly (...). We know very well that when a company makes large investments, this is not to increase the number of jobs but to reduce them, because workers are displaced by technology (...). The task of the company is to make profits, ours is to create jobs. [mf4]

Work totality is a more restricted stake, centred on work organisation. This is, however, a more elaborate concept than a simple criticism or mistrust of employer's choices (work opposition), since it implies an alternative view of the issue. Following the theoretical framework drawn up in the previous chapter, work totality is a necessary component of class consciousness.

One day I pointed out to the foreman that unfortunately we were into supplementary work time, and asked if he would write it down, in the schedule or somewhere. And a mess, as we say, came out, and the director was implicated, he called the team together and pointing at me said that I was quarrelsome. [ta7]

The problem of working conditions originates in the policy of making savings and it's in this framework that they reduce security. This is not a clever policy because afterward come the losses. [hs2]

Work here is not rejected by the unions: it is taken as an objective, something the control of which must be attained. In Solidarity this objective was also present in the past, not only in the thousands of collective agreements signed in varied plants in 1980-81, but also for instance in the frequent statement that Solidarity action at that time *absolutely* did not cause productive losses (the official statistics suggest the opposite).

However, the work control unions managed to exert in the past has been hurt by reorganisation in the labour process as well as in the industrial relations system. In Italy, the creation in 1993 of the *Rappresentanze Sindacali Unitarie* (RSU) in the place of the old works councils democratised and rationalised the bargaining capacity of the unions (although one third of the representatives is not democratically elected, but reserved to the most important organisations). At the workshop level, however, there were collateral effects which ultimately undermined union control on the work process: the number of *delegati* was drastically reduced, and the new *delegati RSU*, being elected by all the workforce in general elections, no longer represent a particular workshop or 'homogenous group'. As a consequence, the workers no longer have their own, visible representative who can be approached with the day-to-day problems of the workshop. The same bewilderment stems from work organisation change.

I remember that we were able to take the initiative with our proposals for the *inquadramento unico* [a common grading system, or 'single status', for all categories of employee - an important issue in the early 1970s] (...), but now we lack a proper grasp of what is going on in the factory, we may have information, but we don't know how to make sense of it. [mf2]

Today the foreman is used to really commanding, he commands without trouble because the workers no longer have specific tasks, you must do whatever they ask you, therefore it's easier for the foreman to command. For us this is a big problem, you don't know any longer when you can say no, you can't refuse any longer, you must do everything. And this conception has prevailed, they imposed it, the union now has accepted it, the people are completely at the foreman's mercy. Beforehand in the workshop before breaching the rules they were very attentive. There were well-established rules, and if there was an exception they came to ask for it as a favour. They said 'this is an exceptional thing, if you might make a certain intervention, please', they came very delicately to ask, knowing that it was an extra. Now they don't, it is an obligation, you must do everything, therefore they don't see the problem. [pf9]

These organisational changes occur against the background of a general decay of work centrality for the unions. Counter-trends against class and work totality appear.

We haven't any influence on production. We make claims only when problems appear, after. We can't regulate anything, why should we? What the point in that? Only once it is written in black and white, will we deal with it. Otherwise it would turn against us. For now, we drudge. [hs4]

The Piombino case must be taken separately – it is necessary to distinguish between 'work' and 'employment'. As already illustrated in the sections on opposition and identity, AFP workers were for a long time involved in the control of tasks and recruitment, and not with production issues as in the Fiat case. The control of recruitment was not limited to obliging the company to employ through the local employment office (*collocamento*), but also had an informal nature, as non-directive interviews reveal. This informal power is now undermined but still existing, as the following extracts from respectively a young and an elderly worker tell.

> In the union... I can tell you frankly what it's like. I was hired with the first groups, and the union had its finger in the pie, because I didn't do it personally, but the fact is that my dad worked, he worked for 35 years in the steelworks, and he had a good relationship with the union. And anyway, he went to find out if they were hiring or not, and how to write the application, and I don't know how I was hired in the steelworks. With the union I felt the duty of joining it at once, because it is a family tradition and because, in one way or another, they were, I believe, those who got me into the steelworks. [pf5]

> The company recruited carefully, picking all these workers with a diploma, new forces, young, new ideas. But these young ones went the wrong way, through management, it would have been better if they hadn't, or at least they should have been led by the union. [pf12]

Finally, there are cases where the goals of the unions are not linked to work (*extrawork* totality). This happens most frequently in Rivalta, where paradoxically the unions have achieved relatively high power at work.

Assessment: The Manifold Meanings of Unionism

To recapitulate, if working class consciousness is to be considered a complex construct requiring (1) a coherence among the three I-O-T components and (2) a link to work, then it rarely appears in the interview materials. The talks show rather a situation of diversity and disconnection. Elements of this construct do appear here and there: the features of the worker movement are well-known to the actors, the Polish ones included. However, there is no coherence in the current experience of work. If anywhere, 'class' is located in the past rather than in the present, or outside work rather than inside. If in the past the unions were embedded in a basic cultural environment which was essentially homogeneous as to the meanings given to work, family, and relations (Carbognin and Paganelli, 1981; Latoszek, 1991), today's reality recounted by the interviewees is different.

At the level of action, the decline of class appears in the tales of individual (no solidarity-based) slow-down practices in contrast with the collective ones of the past. In some interviews, the actors themselves are aware of this decline (demonstrating the overlapping of sociological and common knowledge).

Nevertheless, the most thorough representation of class decline is given by the application of the I-O-T triangle. With its help, we can graphically display the different 'consciousnesses' which emerge from the interviews (Figure 3.1). A wide differentiation takes place. Its forms are more disparate in Poland than in Italy (and in the next chapter we will try to understand why), but in Italy neither any coherent model resists.

Important differences emerge even between Rivalta and Mirafiori, which no institutional or structural variable can explain. As a matter of fact, the literature on Turin Fiat treats this difference as a given rather than as a research problem. Even when they seem to perceive something, analysts overlook the point, like in the case of Locke and Negrelli (Locke and Negrelli, 1989, p. 84). The common explanation given in Turin for the gap between Mirafiori and Rivalta is very little sociological: it gives the decisive role to the different local leaderships. Having met and interviewed the leaders supposed to be the 'explanatory variables', I noted that they do not display any characteristic of 'charismatic leadership'. The interpretative analysis, by contrast, unvails how unionism in the two factories is socially constructed through different references and experiences.

There are unions which are close to consciousness, but they also lack something. Mirafiori Cobas workers lack a class identity, while their FIOM colleagues also lack a coherent vision of their opponent. Rivalta FIOM has an identity narrower than a class one (they display only the 'strong' side), and by contrast the Warsaw unions locate the stake (totality) at too high a level, away from employees' experience. Rivalta FIM, Bielsko Solidarity, *Popiełuszko, Metalowcy*, and the Piombino unions are even further away from class consciousness. Only in the radical unions in Tychy, and to a lesser extent in the above-mentioned Rivalta FIOM, does the triangle approach class consciousness. However, in Tychy there is a complete lack of political interest outside the factory gates: the 'general' character of work conflict is no longer clear.

On the background of differentiation and disintegration, the residual references to the working class can still became occasionally operative, especially in Poland in the moments of organisational change. This is a first finding: in Poland, unlike in other post-totalitarian societies, the working-class tradition can, in some cases, produce workers' strong collective action. However, – and this is the second important finding – these working-class reactions are very unlikely to produce a long-term and widespread class movement: differentiation and contradictions in consciousness are too high. If unions still ever aspire to a role of social movement, they need to develop more subtle identities, which I shall discuss in the last chapter. Rivalta unions and Mirafiori Cobas are already undertaking the first steps in this direction.

The Constants of Disintegration

The previous section revealed a fragmentation in class consciousness which with some rare exceptions takes similar forms in Italy and Poland. Two theoretical problems remain. First, it is necessary to account for the exceptions where a sort of worker movement seems to be still alive (Sierpień 80, Rivalta FIOM, Mirafiori Cobas). Secondly, there is the question of whether this fragmentation is the outcome of a general process occurring in Italy and Poland, or whether it is of an accidental nature. In order to find answers to these problems, it is necessary to look in more depth at the reference points and the arguments used by trade union activists.

In the interviews with workers, many 'taken-for-granted' arguments are recurrent. Some of them, rather than describing a particular reality, express a subjective feeling of distance from class action. They reveal that the activists, even when they declare some sort of class objectives, are pessimist about the likelihood of their being achieved. Among these arguments, six main cross-plant currents ('constants') of disintegration were found. These are ways of constructing value oppositions that reveal a discomfort with the current situation of the union: the positive references concern the past or other situations, the negative reference refers to the present. They are all, directly or indirectly, linked to time, and therefore suggest that class was more relevant in the past than in the present. Their frequencies are presented in Table 3.4 and their meaning will be explained directly.

'*Nostalgia*' is present in a direct past-present contrast about union action: action in the past is remembered as positive in contrast to current activities. It is frequent in Solidarity and in Italy, but is significantly absent in the radical unions operating in the Polish Fiat factories, which are involved in a current, new conflict following the Fiat take-over rather than in the memory of the past. Nostalgia is not an inherent feature of any workers' consciousness: if methodologically accurate qualitative research is in a position to show that, actually, in many cases workers are able to appreciate change (Milkman, 1997; 1998). A radical nostalgia, such as that detected in the interviews, is characteristic of the core of the labour movement at the moment of its disintegration. This is what distinguishes current unionists from the rest of the workforce described by Bonazzi (1998) or other periods of labour history.

Figure 3.1 - Consciousness configurations (I-O-T triangles)

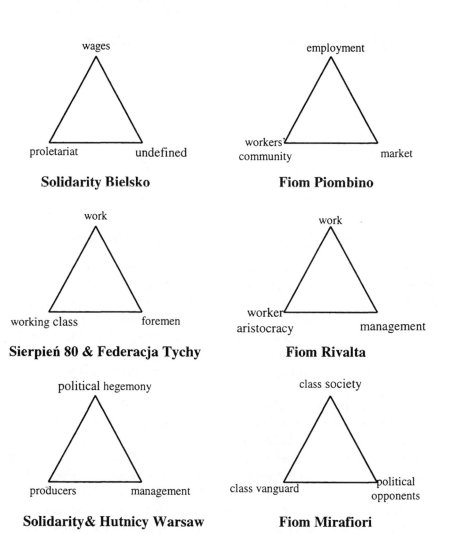

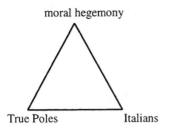

Popiełuszko Tychy

Fim Rivalta

Metalowcy Tychy

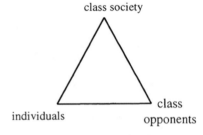

Cobas Mirafiori

'*Withdrawal*' embraces different kinds of 'corporatist' retreat into smaller interest groups than the working class. New narrower social identities and interests are expressed. This pattern has been the rarest among the six 'constants' selected, which shows how union ideology is after all enduring at least as a self-censorship factor. Significantly, however, 'withdrawal' is very strong in Mirafiori, where class discourse is more frequent at an ideological level but workers have negative views of other categories, and especially of state-sector employees who are seen as 'parasites'. In the other Italian Fiat plant, Rivalta, the absence of open 'corporatist' statements seems to be, rather than an indicator of openness, the consequence of a complete, coherent and rather successful focus on workshop issues. Nevertheless, a peculiar 'withdrawal' appears in both Mirafiori and Rivalta in the form of a rivalry among the two plants. To a lesser extent, this happens also between Bielsko-Biała and Tychy.

'*Generation break*' is very important since it is time-related and reveals nostalgia in situations where this is self-censored. Implicitly, it expresses a gap between the current situation, represented by the 'young workers', and the previous one, represented by their senior colleagues. This opposition is central in the Piombino steelworks, a closed community not used to dealing with differences of any kind (of skills, culture, gender or age). It is expressed through reciprocal negative attitudes by young and elderly workers, and is related to the fact that in both countries young workers are less unionised than the average. It is particularly interesting that young workers are charged with working 'too much', rather than 'not enough' as general social stereotypes would suggest. This criticism is directly linked to class decline: young workers are accused of breaking the old, firmly-established slow-down practices.

Similar standpoints were found in the Warsaw steelworks, especially in the *Hutnicy* union. The generation break is also present in Rivalta, in the FIM-CISL, but more in the form of young workers' criticism of the previous generation. This is one of the cases where the elements of disintegration themselves can turn out to be resources for a cultural reformulation of trade union commitment, in a move from class to the individual; this point will be discussed further in chapter 5. In the case of Rivalta FIOM, on the other hand, this disintegration element is rare, probably as a consequence of ideological self-censorship. In fact, the members of the competing FIM say about their FIOM colleagues:[17]

> I see in the FIOM there are always four of them going around, they're always old, I don't see any young people, even those who tried to enter... nothing, if you enter you stay apart, you must obey, you know, this is unacceptable for me, I don't obey anybody. [ri8]

'*Organisation mistrust*' is a very important factor since it contrasts with the traditional compactness of trade unions in comparison with other mass associations (especially political parties, which since their beginnings have been subject to Michels' 'iron low of oligarchy'). It consists of a fear of bureaucratisation, which has been seen as a growing menace in recent times. This current of disintegration takes surprisingly similar forms in Italy and Poland. For instance, in both countries it is expressed via an opposition towards the regional executives of the trade unions, despite strong political and media campaigns supporting regionalism, decentralisation and federalism. A particular case is that of 'split' unions, like *Sierpień 80*, *Popiełuszko*, and *Cobas*. In these 'militant' organisations, involved in strenuous competition with the 'mother' unions, there is strong criticism of the latter (usually seen as undemocratic and/or corrupted), accompanied by some self-justification as regards the speaker's own group. In this case it is particularly difficult to distinguish social attitudes from polemical arguments. Sometimes, however, the criticism of other unions takes the form of a general disappointment with unionism as a whole. It is in these cases that organisational criticism was coded as a disintegration principle.

The fifth current of disintegration is a feeling of *social degrading*, according to which workers today occupy a *lower* and/or *less central* position in society than they did in the past. The best definition is given by a FIM activist: 'the real poor *today* are the workers' [ri1], a definition which associates today's worker with yesterday's poor and thereby creates a discontinuity in time. Although it is widespread in both countries, this feeling takes more definite forms in Poland. This is linked to the peculiarity of the transition experience and not to a real trend in income: Polish workers' income in the last years actually surpassed the levels of the '80s. These points will be more broadly discussed in chapter 4.

Finally, an important point in the case of collective action is a sense of *isolation*, contrasting with the solidarity link typical of class consciousness. This current too takes similar forms in both countries. On both sides, for instance, activists fear that if trade union membership were based on spontaneous declarations, instead of the 'check-off' system, the membership rate would drastically fall.[18]

To conclude, in all plants the activists, through these recurrent taken-for-granted statements, disclose to some extent the disintegration of the labour movement. The only significant exception which remains is that of *Sierpień 80* in Tychy, while Rivalta FIOM does not come out very well from the analysis of disintegration constants (isolation, organisational mistrust, and nostalgia are widespread amongst its activists). Mirafiori Cobas are a relatively simple case. Their class consciousness is in any case incomplete (individual rather than collective identities, and a rather weak link to work), and their optimism can be explained by their recent foundation and their radicalism. This union is profoundly different from the pessimist and defensive Cobas of Piombino,[19] and represents (like Rivalta FIM) new emerging forms of unionism rather than a new edition of the past.

In the 'disintegration constants' analysis it is useful to distinguish between *Sierpień 80* and *Federacja*, which in the other respects are very similar. In fact, the activists of *Federacja* – a new, small split with still the problem of being recognised – are particularly uncertain. Consequently, the disintegration constants (especially the 'isolation' one) appear more frequently for reasons which are probably due to a temporary 'crisis of institutionalisation'. By contrast, in *Sierpień 80* class consciousness endures, and this requires a more detailed explanation.

Sierpień 80 has maintained the principal elements of what is defined as a workers' movement. The working class consciousness is lively, almost

Table 3.4 - Disintegration indicators

	nostalgia	withdrawal	generation	mistrust	degrading	isolation
Fiat Bielsko Solidarność N: 9	6	4	3 / -1	4	3	5
Fiat Tychy Sierpień 80 N: 11	-	1	-1		7	-1
Fiat Tychy Federacja N: 3	-	-	1 / -3	1	-	2
Fiat Tychy Popiełuszko N: 2	-	-	1	-	-	-
Fiat Tychy Metalowcy N: 3	-	-	-	-	3	1
Huta Lucchini Solidarność + Hutnicy N:11	1	2	5	2	3	4
Fiat Mirafiori Fiom N: 9	6	4	2	6	5	5 / -1
Fiat Mirafiori Cobas N: 6	1		3 / -2	3	1	3
Fiat Rivalta Fiom N: 8	4	-	2	3	3	6
Fiat Rivalta Fim+Uilm N: 10	4	1	-	4	4	6
Lusid Piombino Fiom+Cobas N: 16	10	-	11 / -1	5	11	6
Siderco Piombino FIOM + FIM, N: 3	1	-	1	1	1	3

'wild', not yet institutionalised. First of all, it is rooted in the social relations of production and associates both 'proletarian' and 'proud' sides (Touraine, Dubet and Wieviorka, 1987). There is also a mix of typical cultural orientations such as productivity, egalitarianism, moralism, militantism, and, less praiseworthy, some 'machismo' which can be found, in vulgar forms, even in the union bulletin. Moreover, all these elements are very spontaneous and vivacious. It is neither a simple case of the desperate defence of a workers' community (the town of Tychy is not one), nor nostalgia as in Mirafiori FIOM: examples given in workers' talks are very recent. The 'constants of disintegration' are absent, except for social degrading which is here a part of the 'proletarian' side of class consciousness. The only, albeit fundamental, problem is the inability to conceive of a political level of action, and the deep disorientation which arises when the field of the factory is quitted.

The three components of class consciousness are visible in *Sierpień 80* and the *Federacja*: organisation of work is what is at stake, the employer is seen in economic and class terms, and identity is based on both work and poverty.

How is this possible? Their recent history indicates that the intensity of work conflict in the Tychy plant allows actors to keep a form of class consciousness alive, although it is not sufficient to develop a political expression. Fiat assembly lines in Poland and Italy are comparable from the technological point of view, but they are still different with respect to organisation. In Poland, Fiat waited until 1996-97 before introducing 'Japanese' work organisation, believing that a phase of taylorism, however brief, would 'teach workers a lesson' and break the former system of co-management. This implies strong differences between the two national groups in the experience of work, and partially explains the existence in Tychy of an 'industrial niche' for the labour movement. The introduction of taylorism (which occurred at Fiat in the early '90s replacing the previous 'arhythmic taylorism') is particularly important for workers' consciousness: 'class consciousness is nowhere as strong as in the moment of shift, of turn leading from a type of work to another' (Touraine, 1966, p. 118).

What is happening in Poland may be compared to what had happened in Italy about thirty years earlier. At Fiat in Turin the Fordist model and the scientific organisation of work were fully implemented (after partial attempts before World War II) in the '50s and the '60s. The tightening of the hierarchical structure and the deterioration of work conditions caused by that organisational change eventually brought about the turmoil of the '70s (Musso, 1995).

Nowadays, it can be argued that in the turbulence of transition there is a lot of space for local 'countertrends', which can be important but which do not change general trends. So, although Poland is moving towards a post-industrial pattern, there may be reactions which refer back to the worker movement tradition. The worker movement, however, unlike in the previous period is unlikely to emerge as a central social actor. This is confirmed by the Tychy activists' feeling of loneliness. In their case, at the end of the century, a discontinuity between the experience of work and societal experience appears, thus putting into question the sociological idea of the company as *'une affaire de société'* (Sainsaulieu, 1990). Activists are self-confident about work matters, but disoriented about the use of democracy. This leaves some open space for nostalgia for the old regime, even if these activists were the most militant wing of Solidarity in 1980-81. The logical consequence of this bewilderment are nationalist temptations similar to, although weaker than, those of Solidarity and *Popiełuszko*.

For the rest, the analysis presented in this chapter, by showing the incompleteness of the I-O-T schemes and the diffusion of disintegration constants, confirms the hypothesis that Polish and Italian unions are undergoing the same decline in class consciousness. The sort of analysis presented here cannot in itself indicate to what extent the present is 'objectively' different from the past. It shows, however, that activists radically contrast present and past. The turn is significant: from unity to diversity, from offensive to defensive. This turn finds its analogue at the central level. If Fiat factories were once the seismograph of Italian labour, now Italian unions can easily disregard their vote in union referendums. Similarly, Solidarity in the 1980s could hardly have assisted quietly in its disappearance from a factory like FSM Tychy, as it eventually did in the nineties. Even less so could the Solidarity of the 1980s keep friendly relations with FSM management, as its national leader Krzaklewski now does in the 1990s with the new owner Fiat, by regularly taking part in company's promotional events.

The work conflict situation was in the past the basic source of trade union consciousness, but it has lost its meaning. The decline in class consciousness lets differences emerge between unions and factories. This has a paradoxical aspect in a period when globalisation, European integration and the end of ideologies (even of history according to some) should be making industrial relations more uniform around the world: general processes and pressures are the same, but outcomes increasingly different. In this evolution lies the 'paradox' of the Italo-Polish parallelism: the two countries can appear so different precisely because in both the same process is taking place. The unity of industrial society can be found only in tales about the past, when Italian and Polish unions could even cooperate; on current affairs, by contrast, everyone underlines the specificity of their own situation.

In the case of Eastern Europe, this means that the concern of some authors (e.g. Ost, 1995 or Clarke, 1996a) to explain why class politics do not emerge appears misplaced. The problem is that in Eastern European there is *no longer* space for class politics, rather than that there is *not yet* space for it. This is something radically different from arguing that there is no problem with the construction of *interest policies*. There is, but it is not a matter of class.[20]

After having tested this parallelism, the next chapter will deal with the differences which emerge between Polish and Italian trade unions, and test the hypothesis of a dualisation process. Finally, the 5th chapter will be devoted to the consequences and perspectives for the trade unions.

Notes

1   The interviews are coded in the following way. The first letter indicates the plant (b: Bielsko; t: Tychy; h: Huta Warszawa; p: Piombino; r: Rivalta; m: Mirafiori; s: Siderco). The second letter indicates the trade union (s: Solidarity; a: August 80 (*Sierpień 80*); m: *Metalowcy*, including *Hutnicy*; p: Popiełuszko; z: *Federacja*; f: FIOM; i: FIM; u: UILM; c: Cobas). The number indicates the order of observation.

2   There are in fact marginal exceptions of youth movements based on a collective view of history, the most important example being the *Liga Republikańska*. In the workplaces, however, the historical discourse meets little interest.

3   The 'ethics of Solidarity' have been philosophically analysed and popularised by an intellectual close to the movement, Father Józef Tischner (1984; 1992).

4   The best case to use in explaining the difference between identity and consciousness is that of racist groups. Although they usually have a strong and sometimes elaborate identity, they never achieve a coherent consciousness because their logic lies in 'avoiding' social relations (even of conflict) and not in engaging in them. Therefore, they may be better defined as 'antisocial movements' rather than as 'social movements' (Wieviorka, 1995).

5   Pizzorno's definition of solidarity as a system of action is one of the most precise in political sociology. It still refers to a *determined collectivity* (Pizzorno, 1966, p. 254) and therefore matches more with the concept of solidarity-cohesion than with that of solidarity-altruism.

6   5 interviews display all 3 patterns, 4 interviews display 2 of them, and only 3 display one isolated pattern.

7   All four interviews with the work element also display the class one: work is
     included in the class identity rather than being an autonomous principle. 4 out
     of 8 cases with the class element display also the historical one.
8   This extract confirms how on these issues open interview data offer more
     information than closed questions, since the former reveal the actual meaning
     of the words. Open, quiet conversation avoids many of the inconveniences
     stemming from the double system of references used by industrial workers
     (Parkin, 1971), who on explicit, public questions tend to repeat the dominant
     ideas. In this case, the union member firstly repeats the 'dominant' statement,
     but while constructing his own discourse starts revealing personal opinions.
9   These are suggestion boxes, the first step in the introduction of a participative,
     Japanese-like, organisation model. Results were poor in Turin (Bonazzi,
     1998), even worse in Tychy.
10   The concertation system designed by the tripartite agreements of 1992 and
     1993, in spite of important achievements in the moments of deepest crisis, has
     actually never been implemented as a stable 'social pact'. After the very first
     period of Italian political and financial emergency (1992-1994) the system was
     repeatedly disregarded on crucial issues, although at the central level it still
     produced two important agreements on the labour market in 1996 and in 1998.
     To give only the most important examples of the many false steps: in 1994 the
     Berlusconi government did not negotiate the reform of the pension system
     with the unions, provoking one of the widest protest movements in the history
     of the Italian Republic; in 1995 the employers' organisation refused to sign the
     agreement on pension reform achieved by the unions and the Dini
     government; in 1996 the same employers refused to apply the 1993 tripartite
     agreement on the metalworkers' contract, provoking the longest labour dispute
     on a national contract in the history of Italian industrial relations (40 hours of
     national industry-wide strike, not including the numerous local strikes); in
     1997 the Prodi government called for a revision of the pension reform adopted
     only two years earlier as a definitive and stabilising measure; a few months
     later, the same government proposed the reduction of working hours without
     previously consulting the social partners; in 1998, the employers' organisation
     explicitly demanded a revision of the bargaining system created in 1993, and
     the renewal of the metalworkers' contract took place after eight months of
     dispute and 36 hours of national industry-wide strike; in 1999 the government,
     for the fourth time in seven year, proposed a global reform of the pension
     system; in 2000 Confindustria backed, as a way to reform labour law, the
     referendum, that is the very opposite of concertation. If regulation and
     consensus are the distinguishing features of a 'social pact', this is not the case
     with the Italian *concertazione*. For alternative and authoritative views of the
     recent corporatist 'wave' see Grote and Schmitter (1997) and Crouch (1998).
11   In 1999 the OPZZ, that is officially the largest Polish trade union, even
     suspended its participation in the Tripartite Commission. This board was
     charged with being 'unipartite commission', since the main residual

participants (employers, government and Solidarity) are all more or less linked to the AWS, the political party created by Solidarity.

12   This is fundamentally the way Pochet (1998) explains the centralisation of the *'social pacts'* in countries like Italy, Portugal, Spain, Finland, Ireland and Belgium by the prospect of the EMU.

13   Not only for the new unions, however; German union leaders say that a general strike every five years is salutary for the organisation.

14   Interestingly enough, these feelings are returned by Fiat management. During a meeting in Spring 1999, Fiat Italian managers described *Metalowcy* to me as a very serious and effective organisation, unlike all other unions (apart from the Engineers and Technicians' Trade Union).

15   The ownership form is not always a clear concept in Eastern Europe, even for high-level union officers. In 1996 a national officer of *Metalowcy* told me that in Poland there were no private industrial companies. As I asked about Fiat, he explained me that Fiat was a social company, because the ownership was shared among several shareholders. On the sociological issue of post-communist property forms, see above all Stark (1996).

16   Virtually all workers in the AFP are at the 5th or 6th level (the highest in the Italian metalworkers' pay system), while for instance in Fiat almost all are only at the 3rd, and the young workers newly employed by Lucchini Siderurgica, despite better qualifications than their senior colleagues, are only at the 2nd. Of course, work in the automotive sector is generally less skilled than in steel, but the fact that in Piombino *all* workers were at such a high level can be explained only by political factors.

17   Adding heterodefinitions to self-definitions could be seen here as in conflict with phenomenological principles. Nevertheless, it must be noted that the statement mentioned comes from a colleague, and therefore from the same *Lebenswelt*. Phenomenology cannot tell us who is right (the FIOM or the FIM), but helps to reconstruct the cognitive framework of the actors. All points of view give useful information in this regard.

18   In Italy this point became a political issue with the national referendum of 1995 on check-offs, which revealed the mistrust of the majority of the population of the unions as organisations. The logic of decomposition 'isolation' is then linked to some extent to the 'organisation mistrust' one. In Poland, the same process became evident in the summer 1998 in a surprising declaration of the Solidarity president Krzaklewski (1998) against the general efficacy of collective agreements: 'It is unfair, that the unionists with their work lose money, in order to improve the conditions of all workers'. By proposing that agreements would apply only to union members, he contravened Solidarity tradition and admitted that the union was isolated in the workplaces. My inquiry showed that Krzaklewski's idea does not go without support on the shop floor.

19   Piombino and Turin Cobas do not belong to the same group, following the split of 1996 in the *Cobas* movement. In Mirafiori they belong to the

Rifondazione Comunista-backing 'Sin-Cobas'. In Piombino, they are associated with the 'SLAI-Cobas', closer to the extra-parliamentary Left. For our analysis, however, this political difference proved to be of little significance.

20 Some authors, somewhat prematurely, detected an increasing importance of class cleavage in politics in Hungary and Poland after the end of communism (Szelényi, Fodor and Hanley, 1997). However, their findings allow us only to speak of the influence of class on party choice: class issues have become central issues neither in Polish nor in Hungarian political debates. In my terms, this means that there might be an increasing impact of *interests* on politics, but not an appearance of classes as actors. Moreover, these analyses consider only the period until 1994. The Polish elections of 1995 and 1997 seem to contradict their conclusions.

4 The Making of a New European Divide

The Polish 'New Proletariat': Truth and Appearance

The Basic Difference Between Italian and Polish Activists

As we saw in the previous chapter, in both Poland and Italy the elements of crisis, differentiation, and the disintegration of consciousness impede the definition of a unitary model among the trade union activists of Italy and Poland. The classical model of working class consciousness survives only in few, detached elements. Neither have new coherent models yet emerged: the differences *within* the countries are deep. Even within single factories, with the possible exception of the enduringly working-class *Sierpień 80*, confusion, feelings of decline, and incoherence among the three terms of consciousness prevail. It seems, therefore, that a general process of disintegration is occurring, challenging the very idea of trade union 'model'.

Nevertheless, we did not simply find a hotchpotch of disparate references. A comprehensive survey of the elements analysed in detail in the previous chapter reveals that in few respects it is possible to clearly distinguish Polish from Italian reality.

Table 4.1 summarises the data for the two countries regarding the presence (and the rejection) of the various Identity, Opposition and Totality principles in the interviews. Since the sample was not statistically representative, the percentages and the Chi squared test statistic cannot be regarded as referring to the general population of trade union activists. They are used here only for clarity purpose: that is, to set the findings in order and point to problems requiring an explanation. For this reason, the data have been treated according to theoretical, and not inferential, principles. Notably, two measures have governed the account. First, the *Metalowcy* workers from Tychy and the activists from the Siderco company were excluded. The former no longer appear to be heirs of the workers' movement, and are not sufficiently autonomous from the employer; therefore, they lack any *trade union consciousness*, that is, the very object of the comparison.[1] The latter do not have a direct Polish counterpart and cannot be treated in a comparative analysis. The second measure was that of *theoretical* weighting: the frequencies were weighted according to the theoretical distinctions among plant-history types (Table 2.1). This procedure is not concerned with representativeness: the three history types are not equally distributed throughout the industry and even less in the workers' and union members' populations. The point is that the theoretical discussion of Italian-Polish differences did not need to be biased by the theoretical distinction between plants. Therefore, each of the three types has been given the same weight in the construction of the national aggregate, regardless of its number of interviewees. The goal is theoretical, not descriptive: testing whether, *keeping the plant types constant*, there are major differences between Italy and Poland.

Accordingly, the most significant (p<.05) deviations of the Polish findings from the Italian are:

a) a higher frequency of the class principle of opposition;
b) a lower frequency of the employment totality principle;
c) a higher frequency of historical and national identity and opposition principles;
d) the inversion of the weakness and power identity principles, and much higher frequency of economic goals.

Most of these points can be accounted for by *ad hoc* explanations, but a residual, problematic difference remains. Point (*a*) seems to be due to the recent change in work relations in Poland, which, as described in the previous chapter, provokes a 'class opposition' reaction. This does not entail that Poles are developing a thorough, coherent class consciousness. Conversely, the class *totality* principle is almost absent and class *identity* is weaker than class *opposition*. Therefore, class action does not emerge as a positively defined project, but rather, as a form of rejection and resistance. Point (*b*) is due to the peculiar Piombino situation, with its associated high unemployment: the Italian score derives almost entirely from this case. Point (*c*) is almost self-evident, given recent Polish history and the nationality of the employer.

The most striking point, one which might be taken as the central distinguishing factor between Poland and Italy, is the last, (*d*). It seems that the Poles, when compared to the Italians, have a particular feeling of weakness and care about money more than anything else.

Table 4.1 - Summary of the I-O-T principles' configurations

identity	politics	work	class	power	weak	history	culture	moral	comm.	nation	indiv.
Yes: PL	7.2	39.9	38.9	8.3	57.5**	31.3	7.4	14.6	7.4	10.9*	14.4
IT	20.9	35.2	28.6	18.2	26.9**	11.1	6.5	6.7	16.9	0.0*	30.2
No: PL	0.0	17.0	11.8	0.0	0.0	3.7	0.0	0.0	0.0	2.1*	0.0
IT	2.2	10.5	18.2	0.0	0.0	2.2	0.0	0.0	4.3	0.0*	0.0

opposition	generic	political	work	class	past work	history	national	extra-work
Yes: PL	59.8	10.9	47.6	52.9**	28.5	28.5*	39.7**	0.0*
IT	68.1	17.2	51.1	20.8**	15.9	5.9*	0.0**	13.6*
No: PL	17.8	9.1	14.2	3.0**	13.9	7.2*	9.3**	0.0
IT	15.3	0.0	2.1	2.1**	4.2	4.2*	0.0**	0.0

totality	politics	work	class	social	economic	coll. barg.	employment	extra-work
Yes: PL	44.3	43.0	8.8	29.0	52.0**	29.0	3.7**	21.1
IT	33.1	37.0	10.6	24.5	16.9**	17.3	22.2**	21.3
No: PL	24.1	3.0	0.0	11.1	0.0**	5.8	0.0	5.8
IT	27.5	10.8	0.0	4.1	16.6**	0.0	0.0	0.0

*difference significant at the p<.05 level (Chi squared test).
**difference significant at the p<.01 level (Chi squared test).

This difference is constant across all factory types and all unions. It has been clearly detected from the very first research steps, taken in Bialsko-Biała and Mirafiori. The problem was not that Polish workers cared about wages; it was that they did not care about anything else. The absence of any positively defined principle of action and the deep sense of impotence were striking. Solidarity activists defined themselves almost solely by reference to their privations: poverty, effort, lack of rights, socio-political weakness. 'The workers will always lose', the Bielsko activists kept repeating. While taking into account the frequent forms of workers' unrest in the first half of the 1990s in Poland (rare traditional strikes after 1992, but numerous hunger strikes, highway marches, occupations, desperate strikes...), it seemed that the Polish unions had fallen from the level of social movement to something resembling a proletarian revolt. This withdrawal did not signify a return to the past: Polish activists actually seemed, in many aspects, more 'up-to-date' than the Italians, and notably, they questioned their old certainties and references. The withdrawal was a 'social' one: they felt like the 'new proletarians'. Industrial workers, the former pillars of the nation and the victors over communism, were suddenly deprived of their standard of living but above all, of their role within politics, within the economy, and within the plants.

The progression of the inquiry suggested that this representation ought to be reappraised. In Tychy and in Warsaw the unions displayed some positive, albeit disparate, references, and at the same time the general evolution of Polish society contradicted the most pessimistic forecasts of proletarianisation. However, the differences between the identities of Italian and Polish trade unions persist across the plants, as does the peculiar priority given in Poland to economic issues. Moreover, the different types of consciousness take more odd forms in Poland than in Italy, as is shown in Figure 3.1.

The feeling of weakness is revealed not only by the identity references; the descriptions of the employer as almost omnipotent also confirm it. Occasionally, the representations even recall those of the master by the slave rather than those of the employer by the employee: 'the employer has changed, he is very well organised, we have to learn from him, we have to love the employer, we have to respect what he does.' [bs5]

The justifications of unions' claims, in turn, regardless of their concrete content, usually unveil 'proletarian' motives. An example of this is that of working time. In both countries, the unions propose a reduction, and are *definitely* against overtime. In both countries, activists admit that overtime is, for the unions, the most difficult matter to control, and in both countries the number of overtime hours is very high. However, the justification for the same formal claim is very different, not only because the working week for metalworkers is 38.5 hours in Italy and 42 hours in Poland. In Italy the concern is for unemployment and equality: the unions prefer hiring to overtime, and do not accept that some plants should work overtime while others are turning to the *cassa integrazione* (wage guarantee fund for temporary lay-offs). In Poland, the motive for working time reduction is the defence of the human body against exploitation and effort. In other words, it is a 'proletarian' demand, which in its arguments recalls the struggle for the 48-hours week undertaken by the workers' movement a century before. The representations of work which lie behind the same demand are radically different. Similar considerations emerge from different tales about working life. In both countries, for instance, it was reported that people go to work with a fever for fear of reprisals. However, while in Italy this is described as a scandal ('that we should have come to this'), in Poland the same fact is reported as a natural, almost necessary evil, in a fatalistic way.

Similarly, Polish 'economicism' – registered in other post-communist countries[2] – also pervades interviews, and not just in single statements. The Polish economic demands are not important as such: the main task of unions has always, and everywhere, been bound up with wages. Even the heroic strikes of the Summer of 1980 was provoked by a rise in the price of sausages. At that time, however, as Marciniak's (1990) analysis of strikers' claims reveals, these demands were tightly related to political and moral issues. Now, by contrast, salary demands are worth of note because they are isolated, and not supported by other positive references or justification structures (skill, politics or whatever else). Moreover, they are central to the structure of discourse. Many interviews in Poland display a characteristic form of discourse which is almost totally absent in Italy: the discourse built around money counting. Interviewees are able to speak at length on comparing prices and calculating living costs to demonstrate the inadequacy of their salaries. Not only do they claim more money; they also ascribe any other problem, at work as well as outside, to the financial question and to the inadequacy of wages: 'the general problem with security and hygiene at work is that there is no money, there is no money, these four words, and with this every problem is closed.' [hs8]

Interestingly enough, for management, this wage-oriented unionism is not unpleasant. On the contrary, a Fiat manager confessed to me that this is precisely the good side of the Polish unions: they speak only about the important thing (money) and do not waste time interfering with management on other issues. And to contrast this situation with the Italian one, he gave the example of a strike in the 1970s at the Termoli plant, which was called because in the canteen the plum stones were too big. In 1996, the management actually exploited this economicism, pushing the unions to sign an agreement which dismantled the company's social fund (jointly administrered with the unions) to directly distribute the money to the workers in the form of holiday benefits. From a collective bargaining perspective, however, the concentration on a unique issue makes agreements more difficult, and this is what actually happens at Fiat Auto Poland.

In Italy, by contrast, wages are secondary not simply because the activists do not speak at length about them, but when they do, they tend to use 'euphemisms' like 'recognition'.[3] This might be explained by some kind of cultural difference.[4] However, the cultural factor can only explain why Italians 'conceal' economic interests or resist market ideology. It does not account for the occasional active rejection of economic demands (in Piombino a few interviewees spontaneously declared that 'wages do not matter, the national agreement is enough') or even less, the *behaviour* of some of them. Like the single mother of two children (aged above ten, hence no longer requiring continuous care), interviewed in Mirafiori, who has never worked overtime because 'it makes no sense to work more hours to earn more money' [mf9].

A Proletarian Identity at the End of the XX Century?

It is now necessary to give a definition of this 'proletarian' element which apparently accounts for the most remarkable Polish traits. The term 'proletarian' is not used here with the Marxian meaning. The reference points are, rather, the history of working class origins (Thompson, 1963) and of the lowest strata of the working class (Hoggart, 1957), or that sociology able to distinguish different aspects and different groups within the working class (e.g. Lockwood, 1966; Linhart, 1978; Dubost, 1979; Dubois, 1981; Mahnkopf, 1985).

The word 'proletarian', as distinct from 'worker', recalls all the *negative* sides of the working class: their weakness on the labour market, poverty, feelings of inferiority, their lack of organisation and absence of projects. A sociological definition should, however, put in order the constituting elements of the concept. Here, Touraine's sociology can be a useful starting point. In his study of workers' consciousness he described 'proletarian' identity as follows.

> The consciousness of opposition, when isolated from the other constitutive elements of workers' consciousness, may be called proletarian consciousness. It is with a dangerous confusion that this proletarian consciousness is seen as the revival of workers' action. Since it is a negative consciousness of the society, a consciousness of exclusion, it cannot constitute an orientating system for workers' action (...) The principle of opposition degenerates into proletarian consciousness only when it is isolated from the other constitutive elements of workers' consciousness, and expecially from the consciousness of the industrial society. (Touraine, 1966, pp. 321-323)

This point already accounts for the relative strength of oppositional feelings (especially of 'class') among the Poles. Touraine suggests that typical of the 'proletarian consciousness' forms of conflict are slow-down and, to an even greater extent, sabotage. In Bielsko-Biała, the most 'proletarian' of the plants analysed, cases of sabotage were reported by the interviewees, and in Tychy even cases of violence (like the destruction of managers' cars).

In a later work, Touraine identifies several features of a 'proletarian consciousness' which only when joined to the 'proud worker consciousness' might give rise to the workers' movement (Touraine, Dubet, and Wieviorka, 1987). These features are: (1) political heteronomy, which Marx (1852) ascribed to the *Lumpenproletariat*; (2) mobilisation through occasional revolts; (3) 'economicism'. These features are present in Poland, although Solidarity's autonomy/heteronomy in politics remains an open issue. Solidarity is autonomously present on the political scene, but questions may be asked about whether this political presence still takes place in the framework of workers' representation. According to Ost (1996), for instance, non-workers in Poland have regularly succeeded in organising, and even 'colonising', workers' movements. From my inquiry, occasional revolts emerge as the preferred mobilisation patterns of Polish workers (they often recall the heroic, but defeated, revolts of 1956, 1970, 1976), and their 'economicism' is undeniable. To those three features, I would explicitly add fatalism, lack of hope, and the appeal to the generic defence of the 'human being' (*człowiek*), which is recurrent among the Polish activists, while the defence of the 'worker' persists only in *Sierpień 80*.

Nowadays, in any case, it is impossible to define simply as 'proletarian', like the labourers of the industrial revolution, workers who, in spite of everything, experience quite a different reality from that of their colleagues a century before. This is why it is necessary to speak of '*neo-proletarian*'. Touraine's team already applied this concept to the workers at the bottom of the French work hierarchy. According to Touraine the '*new proletariat*' departed from the workers' movement on three important points: it rejects industrial culture; it turns itself towards the state; it becomes politically heteronomous (Touraine, Dubet and Wieviorka, 1987, pp. 206-207).

The Polish case is different from that of the French unskilled workers analysed by Touraine, but does not contradict these three points. Polish workers are less involved in rivalry at work, being, for instance, much less concerned with the increasingly important issue of 'quality' in production. They are politically heteronomous, although they pretend the opposite. By contrast, they are so state-oriented as Touraine's new proletariat. The 'new' character of Polish 'proletarians' lies in their rupture with the past, rather than in a re-orientation to politics (which takes place however at the central level).

The argument about a subjective 'neo-proletarian' model for Polish workers is not in conflict with the idea of disintegration floated in the previous chapter. Actually, it has even been argued (Balibar and Wallerstein, 1988) that a deep differentiation is one of the characterising elements of 'proletarianised' individuals.

The Inadequacy of Structural Explanations

Two alternative explanations might be suggested in order to explain the Italo-Polish contrast. What has been called 'neo-proletarian' might be the simple, and provisional, outcome of a different standard of living or of a lower stage in the institutionalisation of industrial relations.

Both explanations contain one indisputably true element: in Poland the material conditions of workforce reproduction, to use Marx's jargon, are worse than in Italy, and the industrial relations system was recently reconstructed after a 50-year break. As mentioned in chapter 1, the 'material' variables become determining if one follows a version of Maslow's (1954) needs-scale theory: relatively poor workers will concentrate on primary, physical needs until their standard of living increases sufficiently to allow more ambitious goals (social, self-actualisation etc.).[5]

This kind of explanation meets with a number of difficulties. First, it is diametrically opposed to the conclusions of classic sociological research, which has found strong 'pecuniary' orientations precisely among 'affluent' workers (Goldthorpe, Lockwood, Bechhofer and Platt, 1969). Second, this interpretation is totally a-historical. It neglects previous experiences, forgetting that Polish workers, in the very recent past, reached a high level of consciousness that is still visible, if fragmented, in occasional moral, cultural and political references. As argued by Hirschman (1982), the relation between private, concrete interest and commitment to public goals is not linear, but rather, is 'shifting', or indeed discontinuous. Third, although a comparison of standards of living needs care,[6] in recent years the real income of Polish workers has started to increase,[7] and at both Fiat and Lucchini, wages are well above the national average.[8] Fourth, an explanation *à-la*-Maslow remains at a very 'nominal' level: it does not search implicit meanings. Economic demands are actually not so rudimentary.

> Isolated economic demands are not the expression of a rational economic calculation; rather, they demonstrate workers' incapacity to influence the policies and functioning of the company. They are not therefore the most elementary kind of behaviour, but the most complex. (Touraine, 1966, p. 24)

The interviews collected in the Fiat and Lucchini plants confirm that pay can assume different meanings.

> ...maybe not financially, but concerning the atmosphere, personal relationships were different and this is what made work more interesting, and brought satisfaction with that work. And now we don't have satisfaction either from pay or from work. [ta7]

Not only the material *economic* demands, but also the material conditions at work should be treated very carefully. Work conditions do not have an inherent, autonomous meaning prior to workers' interpretation. Moreover, even a quick, superficial visit to the plants – which I made in 1996 – unveils a very differentiated reality within the Polish factories. In Tychy, for instance, the press shop uses old-fashioned machines built in the 1970s in East Germany; the welding department works around the 'Robogate', symbol of the 1980s high-automation phase in Fiat history; the paint shop exploits the best technologies of the 1990s. And yet there is no direct link between technology and workers' consciousness: the two are mediated by organisation and by history. Therefore, the apparent backwardness of Polish workers cannot be explained by the more rude and backward working conditions. Actually, the darkest images of work come from the most modern workshop of the Tychy factory, the paint shop, which a Fiat executive presented to me as 'probably' the most modern in Europe.

> In the paint shop it is horrible, I work in maintenance and it's something... it is the most modern workshop, it is considered a labour camp. [ta1]

As regards industrial relations institutionalisation, the main point borne out by this perspective is the lack of trust in Polish plants. On this view, Poland and Italy would be different for the same reason which explains the difference between Britain and Scandinavia (Ingham, 1974). The institutional approach proved to be suitable in Eastern Europe, as an increasing number of analyses show (e.g. Hausner, Jessop and Nielsen, 1995; Poznański, 1996; Hirszowicz and Mailer, 1996; Delorme, 1996; Flanagan, 1998; Pickels and Smith, 1998; Frege and Tóth, 1999). Indeed, bargaining in Poland is often turbulent and the starting claims of the two counterparts are usually more distant than in the West. The history of institutionalisation may be seen as decisive for the actual content of the rules: only after institutionalisation do formal precepts acquire shared meaning. In particular, industrial relations are seen as largely dependent on reciprocal *trust*, which in turn is seen as laboriously constructed through institutionalisation and experience (Fox, 1974). According to this approach, the fear and uneasiness shown by the Poles is due to their as yet insufficient familiarity with the industrial relations system established between 1991 and 1996, and still in some aspects unachieved.[9]

The institutional approach meets two problems, respectively inherent and contingent. The first question is whether institutionalisation can still be treated as an important and positive process in a period that seems, rather, one of 'de-institutionalisation'. In the economic sphere, the history of capitalism is not one of a gradual, unbroken building of trust; the relationship between time and trust is not linear, and recent trends might even suggest that it could be represented by an inverted U-curve. The second problem is specific to the Italo-Polish comparison. The Italian system is itself considered as typically lacking in institutionalisation. On some issues, like the very important one of strike regulation, Polish industrial relations are much more 'institutionalised' than Italy.[10] Notably, Fiat's century-long history seems one of *mistrust*-institutionalisation rather than the opposite. So speaks, for instance, an activist of the moderate FIM from the 'participative' plant of Rivalta.

> For example, now Romiti [Fiat president at the time of the interview] is under investigation and the *cassa integrazione* [temporary lay-off] has started, as a blackmail to the government, to the town of Turin. 'I put 600 people in *cassa*, the trial finishes? 300 people in *cassa*; they attack Fiat? If things are not arranged, we'll stop the factories.' I say, they have got their orders, but they hide them till the right moment, and then they bring them out and they squeeze people, they make the production, and then again, the *cassa*. So, with this system they put the state into crisis, which has to fork out for the *cassa integrazione*. According to what my colleagues were saying, just today one of them makes the *cassa*, we are in a bad situation, and he made the remark 'eh, they investigate Romiti and they make the *cassa integrazione*'. It seems bloody nonsense, but it may be that something influences, at some moment... If Fiat gets a cold, it sends the cold to everything around, and the whole economy closes down. [ri7]

The findings of this research confirm a low level of trust in both countries. In the Polish case the form of this mistrust is sometimes striking. However, it is impossible to measure and compare trust levels precisely. An interesting example of Polish mistrust comes from the Tychy plant. Here, the trade unions refused even to consider documents relating to the Fiat financial situations presented by the company. These documents have been prepared by one of the 'Big Six' (later 'Big Five'), the multinational auditing companies which have become fundamental 'institutions' of modern capitalism. According to the activists, the auditor had certainly been corrupted by Fiat management. Similarly, *Popiełuszko* activists see as a scandal the fact that AWS, the Solidarity political party, is advised by the same company (another one of the 'Big Six') which was advising Fiat at the time of the FSM take-over. Nevertheless, the interpretation of this mistrust for capitalist institutions is not automatic. Does this really mean that Poles are 'backward'? Or rather that, conversely, they already express,

albeit imperfectly, a new conflict, typical of the period of transition from
the industrial to the post-industrial society, between financial capitalism
and the productive economy, between global networks and local physical
entities excluded from those networks?

The Reciprocal Attitudes

Italians and Poles in the Mirror

Before proceeding to sociological speculations about differences between
Italy and Poland, it is important to listen to the protagonists. The majority
of the interviewees who speak about their counterparts describe them in
negative terms. These feelings also emerge off the record: the Poles tell
jokes about the Italians, the Turinese make offensive gestures at Polish
workers visiting Mirafiori behind their backs. A positive image of foreign
colleagues is very rare in Italy, where the attention paid to foreign
situations is altogether weaker. To summarise, in Poland, out of 39
interviewees, 9 (of whom 6 were from the *Sierpień 80* union) display a
positive image of the Italian workers and trade unions, and 12 a negative
one. In Italy, out of 49[11] interviews I found 2 positive references to the
Poles and 11 negative.

A short methodological remark should be made. The more positive
attitudes recorded in Poland might be due to restraint on the part of Polish
interviewees speaking to an Italian. However, following the
recommendations of reflexive sociology (Rebughini, 1998), measures ware
taken throughout the research process in order to reduce this possible
disturbance factor, and especially the interviewer's identification with
Italy. The measures ranged from telling jokes about the Italians, which
Poles do appreciate very much, to underlining cooperation with French and
European institutions and the absence of any link with Italian
organisations, and to evincing familiarity with Polish life. I also recall that
the interviews were carried out in Polish. Similarly, in Italy national
identification was limited by remarking on French and European links and
the long periods of work and study spent abroad, including Poland: some
unionists after some time even started calling me 'the Pole'.

Since the data do not come from questionnaires but from long, in-
depth and non-directive interviews, the results seem methodologically
satisfactory. The restraint is limited to short introductory statements of the
kind 'I have nothing against the Italians as a whole, but...', which recall
the statement well-known to the sociologists of racism 'I am not racist,

but...'. In fact, the Poles felt no compunction about using nationalist and anti-Italian arguments whenever they wanted, expecially when talking about management. Table 4.1, as well as the figures given above on the reciprocal views, show that in Poland nationalist references and negative images of foreign counterparts are more frequent than in Italy. In the next sections, this will be used as evidence of the significance of their willingness to cooperate with the Italians: if they do not feel ashamed of openly criticising the Italians, why should the statements about international union cooperation (an issue less strongly subject to moral codification) be due to social pressure?

The weight and the meaning of the representations are manifold. Qualitatively, Polish disfavour is stronger than the Italian, especially when it combines with other opposition feelings. This is all the more significant, taking into account that according to surveys, Poles' attitudes towards the Italians are very positive: in 1991 Italians ranked third (after US and France) among 22 nationalities for 'friendship towards Poland' (Jasińska-Kania, 1992). Only extensive quotations can account for interviewees' representations. The first basis for disfavour is a sort of rivalry in work identities. At Fiat, this is rooted in the often negative experience of work reorganisation in 1991-1993, when about 500 Italian workers came to Poland to 'teach' the Poles to produce the *Cinquecento*.

When Fiat arrived here the gentlemen from Italy had to teach us, and it turned out the other way around, we taught them how one should work. Really, I'm not saying that they were incompetent, in a sense they were competent, but it turned out that we know more than they do. They're able to work in a soporific way, and me if I work I work, I can't do differently, that's the way I was taught, I'm not paid to sit down but to work. And the Italian workers, very good colleagues, they know how to enjoy themselves, but at work... yet we taught them something. [tm3]

I know how the Italians worked. An Italian came to us, there were two cars, the Italians changed eight wheels in eight hours. I don't criticise them, I respect them for that, they did work because they were around the car, but a Pole does it in five minutes, and executes the job as skillfully as they do. [ta7]
The [Polish] worker performs the job accurately. For example they have placed the cars, the same cars, produced in Italy and in Poland, incomparable quality, our productivity is higher. I'm not saying that Italians do badly because I've never been to Italy, but you see it from the details. That way it's possible to see what kind of workers the Poles and Italians are, and it can be seen very clearly. [ta8]

Behind a general producer's pride, many elements are present in these descriptions: the absence of any class opposition principle for the *Metalowcy* unionist (first extract), the envy of the Italians' familiarity with resistance at work (second extract), and a pure rivalry with regard to productivity (all extracts). The first two elements are specific to the Polish situation, the last one by contrast can be found in a perfectly symmetrical form in some Italian interviews. The availability of symmetrical imputations strongly argues for their stereotyped nature.

I felt bitter when the *Cinquecento* was moved to Poland, we were the ones who designed it... Fiat made a mistake: the first cars had to be rectified all the time because Polish workers were incompetent at assembly line work. [mf3]

I have a car made in Poland and I'd rather kill myself, it's horrible, a *Cinquecento*, I still have to find somewhere where water does *not* set inside. They should stop for a while with the factories abroad. I agree, but salaries like ours, instead everything is to the boss's advantage. You pay people 800,000 Lire a month and then you sell the cars horribly dear, so you gain. If I were the boss I'd put factories abroad too. I don't agree with this, there should be some control, otherwise Italy will close down. [ri8]

What today, and for a few years, will keep [jobs] here is quality, because we have a culture which in those countries probably allows only certain things to be produced. But in time, this will be less true and without a true equilibrium, in the true sense of the word... because if they work there for less, it's clear that they will be more competitive than us, and there will be some problem. I don't know, we'll have to give more than the others. This is the point, the other is political stability which disadvantages them a bit. [rf1]

The last two extracts immediately reveal that the Italian feeling of superiority is not self-assured. As a consequence, in many cases Italians, rather than opening a risky discussion about competition at work, prefer to stress Polish poverty and Fiat's unfair exploitation of this poverty. This representation has two components. The first is the representation of Poland as an awful place. This is universal in both Fiat and Lucchini, especially among clerks and executives[12] but among blue-collar workers too.

The only danger with investments abroad is that when there is work up there they might send me... when somebody is undesirable, I'm not speaking of myself, I'm speaking in general, if they don't want to fire him, they have only to say to somebody from Piombino 'you go to Poland'. For me it would be a punishment, it would cost me. [pf10]

Italians in this way see the inferiority of Poles not in production, but in their working and living conditions: the competition is therefore unfair. This discourse is delicate however, and Italian activists do not dwell on it, feeling an understandable uneasiness in the unusual role of the 'privileged'. As a consequence, for many Italians the favoured approach (and the second component of the Italian representation of Polish workers) is to treat as inferior not Polish workers, but their trade unions. These are seen as too weak and as guilty of the unfair competition that stems from their weakness: 'then I hope that the *underdeveloped* countries wake up, that the unions strengthen, that they also start to claim rights in those countries.' [ri4]

Many Poles, in turn, see the Italian trade unions as guilty of a lack of solidarity. In both companies, during important disputes (at Fiat in 1992, at Lucchini in 1994) the Italian trade unions did not intervene. In the first case, the FIM-CISL even supported the employer's side, and in the second, there was an absolute lack of interest and information in the Italian unions.

There were sometimes attempts [to cooperate], but the Italian trade unions are not interested. The problem is the labour market: the worse it is here for us, the better there for them; the less we earn, the more they'll earn there; the more they fire here, for example they cede some parts to Italian companies, the less they'll fire there. After all, this is the labour market. The Italian trade unions are not interested. [ta1]

We attempt to cooperate with the Italian trade unions, but they don't cooperate back, even the two foundries in Piombino don't agree with each other.[13] They don't want us because the European Works Council would decide where to invest, they were afraid in Piombino because of investment in Poland. [hs5]

I was in Piombino for two months last year. Down there the unions are different, they go to the director for dinner and they arrange things. I encountered the unionists that way. I was working in my post, two guys in suits come and a colleague tells me: 'these are our unions'.[14] Here it's different, the unionists are normal people. (...) The way of acting for the unions is different, down there they arrange things at the regional level, here they do it in the workshop, and, if we don't manage there, at the plant level. Down there, Rome decides how many hours Piombino has to strike. They're able to organise wild-cat strikes to stop the whole factory, here we don't do it. Down there, there is an informal fair-play, here we're taught that everything must be written and signed. Down there workers have the feeling that the unions don't help. [hs3]

Not all the Poles, however, have such negative impressions of their Italian counterparts. Unlike in Italy, positive views also exist, notably a not uncommon admiration for, or envy of, the Western unions. This happens especially in *Sierpień 80*, the Polish union which comes closest to class consciousness.

> Down there, the trade unions also operate differently, they take care of the worker, they have a much wider range of action, if something is not O.K. it isn't management which decides, but the worker has an influence on what we do. It happened to somebody that a section of the line stopped, I don't know exactly what was it about, but in any case a component was lacking, it hadn't been distributed, and they halted the line. It emerges that a component is lacking and they say 'it must be here'. And here, if a component is lacking you must go and look for it, you must find it. [ta5]

This envy is linked to a wider visionary representation of the West, which even if rapidly declining after 1989 still operates in the Polish imagination.

> Social welfare is better in France than it is here, even though there was a communist state here. There, they look after every need, even satisfy people's whims (...). Here there are no companies providing housing with the job, in France there are many that do. [bs4]

Both positive and negative views, in any case, converge in the effect of widening the perceived gap between Italy and Poland. Negative stereotypes are the most striking form of this gap, and although the majority of the interviewees do not fall into stereotypes, the overall environment is clearly receptive to them. This situation raises a number of problems on which the sociology of racism might contribute to the sociology of work. Prejudices should be weakened by direct experience, but the comments of the Polish worker transferred to Piombino suggests that this is not a sufficient condition. Work is indeed a situation where status in the company may affect external status, and therefore it has a unique potential for integration. Nevertheless, research on topics like racism at work (Bataille, 1997), gendered jobs (Williams, 1989; Crompton and Sanderson, 1990), or the disabled at work (Meardi, 1993) has revealed how the work setting may reproduce invisible niches where segregation persists. Necessary conditions to make the work situation tend towards integration are the effectively equal status of the different workers and the availability of communication channels. These conditions were not met during the presence of about 500 Italian workers in the Polish Fiat factories in the

The Making of a New European Divide 167

early 1990s. That experience ultimately reinforced reciprocal antagonisms, with the exception of a few workers who had personal common experiences or could communicate. The following extracts illustrate the two opposite situations (distance vs. contact experience).

> I didn't have any contact with the Italian workers, but back then when they were here they weren't held in high repute. First of all how they behaved, and then the conditions created for them by Fiat, for example as regards the flats, they gave them 2-, 3-roomed flats, this was really a lot, equipped, furnished, with TV, washing machine, refrigerator, and even a charwoman, and this made people angry. And they also left these flats in different states. They showed their superiority, I don't know how to define it. That was the main thing, but most people got furious about the money they earned too, at that time we earned 3-4 millions and they earned 30-40, this was a lot, a huge difference. [ta4]

> I met an Italian who was here for two months and it was very pleasant. They were very nice, and he also said, we asked him, he had the same stories in his family, he had a son who studied electronics and a daughter medicine, he said that studying in Italy is very expensive. And so on, about studying here, about studying there... And when they noticed that he talked so much with the Poles they arranged for him to go home early. [ta3]

The issue of ethnic prejudices may take on a particular relevance in Poland, and in Eastern Europe as a whole. Multicultural relations in Polish multinational companies have actually already become a topic for research (e.g. Korporowicz, 1996). More generally, anti-Semitism is widely considered to be a traditional problem of Polish society, and even if in 1980-81 it was absent from Solidarity at the political level, it did endure at the bottom level within the union (Wieviorka, 1984; 1992). Nowadays, the anti-Semitism and xenophobia of the Solidarity organisation in the Ursus tractor factory are well-known, although its importance is often overestimated by the media. Even in the Fiat plants, one of the trade unions (Solidarity 80 from Bielsko-Biała) took part in the 1998 anti-Semitic mobilisation in defence of the Pope's Cross in the Auschwitz camp. However, if Ursus Solidarity is marginal at the national level (and not even representative of the workforce of the firm, as I shall show), the role of Solidarity 80 at Fiat is absolutely minimal. My personal observation of the events in Auschwitz in 1998 did not detect any involvement among workers of neighbouring factories.

During the 1994 strike at *Huta Lucchini-Warszawa* it was possible to hear accusations about the Italians such as 'they don't work, they only exploit others' work', or 'they control the media and, through the *mafia*, the financial markets' (as I gather from personal accounts of local observers). These allegations were used by the Poles, in the past, against Russians and Jews. Their 'recycling' against a very different ethnic group would strongly support the sociological assertion that racism is a problem of the 'racialising' subject and not at all of the 'racialised' object (Wieviorka, 1995). In particular, the element of opposition to modernisation inherent in traditional Polish anti-Semitism seemed to operate against Western investors.

However, these kinds of statements have completely disappeared since then and there is no trace of them left in the interviews. At the same time, surveys of trade union members indicate a rapid decline of xenophobia after democratisation. The quota of union members who considered the Jews as the group with 'most influence on the government' dropped from an astonishing 43.2% in 1990 (32.5% for Solidarity, 46.8% for the OPZZ) to 14.1% in 1993 (Gardawski, Gilejko and Żukowski, 1994, p. 78). According to the same survey, in 1993 a much larger group (37%) saw as 'most influential' foreign capital in general, revealing a rapid reorientation from racial categories in the period of maximal mess to approximately 'class' categories once economic reform had produced its first outcomes. Other surveys (Badora and Starzyński, 1995) confirm that emotional reactions against foreign investors stem from the *lack* of contact with them rather than the opposite.

It seems, therefore, that only in the cases of maximal confusion, isolation and tension (as in the *Huta* during the 1994 strike, or at the beginning of 1990 after the dramatic increase in prices following their liberalisation) does anti-Semitism reappear as an orientation for action. The case of nationalist feelings is different: since the beginning Solidarity has been a national movement at least as much as a social one.[15] A general xenophobia with respect to foreign companies appears in statements like 'they're guests here, but they behave as if they were in their own homes', in which foreign investors are seen through the same lens through which many Germans see the *Gastarbeiter*. Moreover, the Polish media have repeatedly shown more warmth toward the nationalist standpoints of the unions than toward the 'class' ones.[16] It must be recalled, however, that the decline of the workers' movement made nationalist and xenophobic feelings more visible everywhere in Europe (although not necessarily stronger). During the last few years in many Western countries xenophobic parties have significantly increased their popularity among blue-collar workers.[17] Again, as in the case of standard of living and of mistrust, nationalism is not satisfactory as an explanatory factor for Italo-Polish difference.

Transnational Trade Union Action: Rhetoric and Practice

The first informal meeting among European Fiat trade unions including the Poles occurred in May 2000, eight years after privatisation. The Polish and Italian trade unions in the two companies analysed here have no contact with each other. Should they? Analysts of globalisation mostly recommend it. Globalisation threatens labour: this is the usual comment (e.g. Tilly, 1995). Pessimism, when not 'catastrophism', prevails in the descriptions of globalisation from labour's point of view (e.g. Barnet and Cavanagh, 1995; Ross and Trachte, 1990). Only a few Marxists display sufficient faith to persist with the view that 'the worse, the better'(e.g. Howard, 1995): the internationalisation of capital makes the contradictions of capitalism more striking, and so accelerates its downfall. However, as soon as one starts to look at the actual labour movement, the reaction to this threat emerges as a complex issue.

Indeed, the problem is not new. Apart from the political appeals starting with Marx and Engels (1848), trade unions have, since their beginnings, seen with disquietude the internationalisation of the economy. When nation states initially proved to be an insufficient regulatory framework, a need for transnational action emerged. Functionalist sociology developed the thesis of a natural internationalisation of the unions following that of the economy (Haas, 1958), just as the emergence of national markets had forced the unions to centralise at the national level (Commons, 1909). This was not the only functionalist forecast to be proved wrong. On the unionists' side, Charles Levinson, general secretary of the International Metalworkers' Federation, in the 1960s elaborated a proposal for international collective bargaining. According to Levinson, transnational union action had to develop through three phases: organisation of international support for local struggles; coordination of collective bargaining across the different branches of MNC; integrated bargaining with the multinationals' management. Apart from very isolated cases (e.g. the Philips group), nowhere have the unions gone beyond the first phase.

At the European level, the issue became compelling in the 1990s, with the Hoover affair (EIRR 1993). However, even the newly constituted European Works Councils (1994) have not yet proved sufficient as a means for effective transnational action, rarely going beyond routine requests for information (Schulten, 1996; Lecher, 1998), and the European Trade Union Confederation cannot yet be called a union (Gobin, 1997). Union attempts to influence internationalisation remained mainly national-level strategies, and the transnational structures remained a rather formal construct (Due, J., Jensen C.S. and Madsen, J.S. 1995; Turner, 1996). Although one can still find optimistic and voluntarist opinions (e.g. Jacoby, 1996), the development of European industrial relations is not impressive. National systems therefore remain for some authors the only practicable horizon for industrial relations.

> In the absence of realistic possibilities for pushing social re-regulation upwards to the supranational level, its prospects depend on a re-building under the new conditions of national capacities for market correction. (Streeck, 1998, p. 453)

Following the theoretical approach described in the second Chapter, I should add that the problem is not only one of regulation and of interests, but also of identity. As even sympathetic specialists have acknowledged, one limit of the ETUC has been

> the incapacity to promote a workers' transnational identity. Consequently, the various interests and identities which compose the ETUC remain mostly unchanged. In fact, the transnational workers' identity, generated by action, may emerge from opposition to integration rather than from its support. (Hoffman, Lind, and Waddington, 1998, p. 79)

Fieldwork in multinational companies can add something to this scientific/political debate, which is often deadlocked in extreme opposing views. The absence of effective transnational cooperation between Italian and Polish trade unions is certainly not only the fault of the unions, but is also the outcome of the employer's strategy. When in 1996 the Fiat European Works Council was created, the Italian unions actually requested the participation of Polish representatives, but Fiat rejected the demand, arguing that the EWC Directive mentions only European Union countries. Leaving Fiat aside, there are cases (usually green-field plants) where multinational management has made a major, and indeed, successful effort to avoid the overall presence of unions. But this will be dealt with later in the chapter: here I shall discuss the importance of workers' views about the possibility of the emergence of a European-level unionism.

First, we can observe unionists' opinions about globalisation. Direct concern with this issue in Poland seems very weak. Only 5 interviewees out of 39 mention it, almost always (4 cases) in moderately positive terms. In only one case, which is more precisely to do with Europeanisation, is the attitude negative: 'we are inclined to Europe, Europe will embrace us, but what for? So that we work for them.' [tz2]

Italian activists dwell upon globalisation much more frequently, but this may be the outcome of the slightly directive character of the interviews on this point. In fact, towards the end of the conversations, if they had not touched on the issue spontaneously, Italians were asked their opinions about the plants 'abroad', while Poles about the plants 'in Italy', which less directly raises the problem of globalisation. Altogether, throughout the 49 Italian interviews (the Siderco company was excluded as it is not a multinational) there are 36 personal references to this issue. The dominant attitude is opposite to that in Poland: 24 interviews display negative representations, and only 7 positive ones.

> By dint of talking about globalization, people have globalized their brains too. Yet, alas, we really must deal with it. What changed in the company strategy? Once Fiat sent abroad, to Poland, to Russia, to Brazil, the worn out products that no longer did well in Europe and here. Now, instead, with globalisation they produce where it costs them less and we even import those things. We can't stop them because there is the free market, commodities may freely circulate and this is globalisation. [mf8]

> The factories abroad, I disapprove of them, because it's clear that if they take jobs abroad they take them away from Italy. If these were supplementary investments it would be different, but if they take Italian jobs abroad this is not positive for us. Also the investments in Southern Italy are negative, for Turin. The union is trying to do something, but it can't do more than that, because if Fiat decides a thing, it happens. Also because at most the union says 'no, you don't open Melfi, you go on working in the North', [then they answer] 'no? if you don't want Melfi, we'll go to India'. Then it's not worth it, let's take Melfi, at least it's in Italy, they always put an alternative which makes their proposal even worse, then you're forced to accept it, you choose the lesser evil. [rf5]

Usually the opposition to globalisation remains at this level of refusal, without any counter-project. Slightly different is the Cobas case, where the opposition is better elaborated and focuses on specific points like Fiat's monopoly: the activists contest neither internationalisation nor investment abroad, but rather the fact that because of the monopolistic position of Fiat in Italy no foreign investment may arrive in Turin. This version, radical in the Turin political context but ideologically liberal, is a rare example in which the unions have a proposal of their own, which allows them, at least in theory, to avoid the Scylla of negating reality and the Charybdis of passive adaptation.

As a matter of fact, when in March 2000 Fiat announced an agreement with General Motors, the reactions from the unions were strikingly different from those of Italian politicians (Left and Right alike) and the mass media. While the latter almost unanimously expressed an acritical approval, without considering the social and economic implications and without questioning whether there was any need for political intervention, the former fell into the opposite temptation. Although they all wanted to make clear that they knew internationalisation was unavoidable, trade unionists manifested so many suspicions and fears that one wonders whether there was any sort of acceptable internationalisation. Rather than focusing on very real problems such as the socio-economic costs of mergers or the impact on industrial structure of short-term financial choices, they declared their firm opposition to any merger, any sale, any agreement between uneven partners, claiming that 'Fiat management and decisional board must remain in Italy'.[18] In Poland, the opinion of the unions was more balanced, though they also complained for the lack of information (own telephone conversations with union representatives).

A total refusal arises by contrast in some interviews in Piombino, where 5 activists speak of globalisation only in order to deny that this is a relevant problem for the unions. Piombino unions not only do not participate in transnational action, but experience serious problems even in coordinating with the unions from the other Lucchini plants in Italy. Particularly eloquent was the apprehension expressed by Piombino unions in 1994 when Lucchini announced investments in the plant of Servola (near Trieste). Activists feel as if Piombino was the quiet centre of the world, though it is precisely their plant which has suffered the most because of international competition.

> If this country sinks, they don't sink because they can go somewhere else, but they sink in this country. If they have to go somewhere else, in Thailand life is not as good as in Italy (...) The worker of Piombino, I think, is concerned only with the problem of Piombino, he doesn't think that the employer has got strange ideas, he knows that he's got this plant in Poland, but the majority know that that plant is old, therefore it does not disturb Piombino so much, he knows that Piombino is the badge of Lucchini Siderurgica... [pf2]

> Foreign affairs are not a worry, there is the conviction that Piombino will be the leader. What is a worry are relations in the factory. International relationships may help but it seems to me that everybody looks to the own business. For somebody, it's fine like that, the others must solve their problems on their own. I've never talked about Warsaw with anybody. If we produce quality Warsaw won't be in competition with us. [pf8]

> We never talk about the investments abroad, it's a problem we're not used to having, and we still don't talk about it. Also because we've been inside for so

many years that we aren't yet in the mentality of private ownership, after 25-30 years of state ownership we have remained... nationalist. [pf9]

The representations of foreign workers (analysed in the previous section) and of globalisation affect opinions on international union cooperation. Some Polish opinions have already been mentioned. In Italy, it seems that historical internationalism has not withstood either internationalisation or the issue of immigration.

We have even got to the point of putting people in *cassa integrazione* in order to hire immigrants, they try to wear down the union on these issues. (...) Last week I was around Brescia [Northern Italy, the town of origin of Lucchini and his company] and I was scared because I saw so many immigrants at work, and the danger is that we have a row, they take the immigrants and bring them here for one million a month, and it will also be chaos for the union, I have no idea how it will be solved. [pf2]

There is a problem, there is, it's a problem that exists and will bring about a problem for us, I don't know how we can get away from it. I don't believe that it's enough to meet as unions, in any case there are problems of culture, and then in certain countries the unions I don't know how much weight they have. In Poland maybe it's different but in Asia I don't know how much weight the unions have, I think they have little weight, and we can't think of combining, it makes no sense, down there people starve and it's clear... also not letting people starve is good, so if this means an impoverishment for us, we'll pay this cost. [rf1]

The transfers abroad are seen as a cheat, it's right, they happen but... We can't love each other so much, competition is natural. Here, we have hopes for product differentiation, keeping the high-quality ones here. [rf8]

Not all interviewees share such negative views. In particular the first extract quoted above is totally non-representative: this is the only vaguely xenophobic statement I found in hundreds of pages of interview transcriptions. However, all three quotations above come from distinctively politicised (on the Left) activists, and they are therefore particularly meaningful: if politically 'conscious' workers freely express these ideas, their 'common' colleagues are probably even more inclined to national withdrawal. The unionist of the first extract is even personally involved in cooperation programs with the German unions, and is a supporter of a 'Europeanisation' of the union structure. This example shows how wide may be the gap in attitudes between the official level of the union structure and the everyday level of work and employment problems.

The fragility of internationalism is not so surprising if one remembers that historians have repeatedly indicated the limits of the traditional ideological internationalism of the labour movement (e.g. Gallissot, Paris and Weill, 1989; Pasture and Verberckmoes, 1998). With regard to ideological tradition, the Italian and Polish trade unions are different. The Italian labour movement has historically been one of the most internationalist. Not only have the unions guided pacifist demonstrations for decades; in Turin workers rebelled against intervention in World War I, and in Genoa the dockers for a long time refused to unload ships from Franco's Spain or Pinochet's Chile. The Polish workers' movement has a different history in this regard. The national question was a fundamental issue for the emerging trade unions as well as for the socialist movement: precisely on this issue Józef Piłsudski argued with Rosa Luxemburg and created the Polish Socialist Party; Solidarity rediscovered the tradition of the struggle for independence.

At the enterprise level, however, the opinions of Italian and Polish activists about transnational union action do not reflect these traditions. Throughout the interviews, we find in Italy 10 positive and 16 negative views (out of a total of 49 interviews considered), while in Poland 13 express positive views and only 5 negative ones (out of a total of 39 interviews). I have deemed negative not only opinions explicitly against (these are very rare), but also the representations of transnational action as basically useless and costly.

This finding would be difficult to understand if one followed a game-theoretical approach: it is the Italian rather than the Polish side which has an 'interest' in avoiding social dumping. Polish unionists may be attracted by the richer resources of their Italian counterparts (Solidarity benefited from huge international help in the 1980s and in the early 1990s), but this does not seem very important at the company level. More convincing may be a hypothesis focusing on strategy: for the Polish unions, Italian solidarity in the case of a work dispute can be useful because of the higher *visibility* of the latter. By contrast, Polish unions' solidarity with Italy would be almost irrelevant because of their peripheral position.

Neither is the current situation easily understandable from the historical point of view. Italian and Polish unions did not meet the problem of *establishing* contacts: these contacts already existed. During the 1980s the Italian unions were among those Western organisations most active in 'solidarity with Solidarity'. This was particularly true of Fiat. In 1981 Turin unions organised a unique program of exchange with Solidarity from the FSO plant in Warsaw (at that time working under Fiat licence, nowadays taken-over by Daewoo), and maintained their connections after the introduction of martial law. More involved, because of its Christian roots, was clearly CISL; this union experienced something similar to the 'identity of substitution' and the fascination shown by the French CFDT in its engagement on behalf of Solidarity (Frybes, 1997; Chwalba, 1997). Nevertheless, in contrast to the French situation, in Italy the engagement was shared, though less enthusiastically, by the communist-led CGIL, which a few months before the August of Gdansk had resolutely and immediately condemned Soviet intervention in Afghanistan. In September 1980, at the gates of Mirafiori, beside the portraits of Gramsci and Marx strikers' placards said: 'we will do as Gdańsk does'. In 1991-92 the FIM-CISL from Turin organised some courses for unionists from the Bielsko-Biała plant. After that, nothing from the 12 years of exchange has remained. The relationships were too asymmetrical to help the construction of effective union cooperation. Moreover, they took place in a period when (maybe for the last time) it was still easy for the unions to distinguish 'friends' from 'enemies'.

Nowadays, and not only at Fiat and at Lucchini, cooperation between the unions from Eastern and Western Europe is difficult. It was not until December 1995 that the first nine Eastern unions were accepted into the European Trade Union Confederation, locked as they were in the dilemma 'enlargement or deepening'(Seideneck, 1993). In the auto sector there has been some attention from the Western side (e.g. Automotive Department, 1992) but in the steel sector the situation has been very deceptive (Bacon and Blyton, 1996). In general, Western unions (and the social-democratic parties they support) are not enthusiastic about the Eastern enlargement of Europe, and in this way dialectically produce a symmetrical mistrust among the Eastern unions.[19] This is most visible in the cool attitudes of the German and Austrian trade unions (the 'hard-core' of the European social model) on the free movement of Central Eastern European workers (Poprzęcki, 1999).

At the same time, in some Eastern countries, the first forms of 'holy alliances' between governments, employers, and unions in the name of national competitiveness have appeared, similar to those frequent in developing countries. Although the main Polish trade unions declare to be pro-European, the radical right wing of Solidarity, Solidarity 80 and *Sierpień 80* are resolutely anti-European, while the OPZZ upholds a 'quiet, after careful meditation' and 'not before 2007' entry into the EU (Wiaderny, 1999). As a result, what were expected to become potential bases for the internationalisation of labour – the ideal of a social Europe (Hyman, 1996b) or a common ground of similar concerns (Jacoby, 1995) – have not emerged as sufficient driving forces.

At this point, older sociological studies may be more useful in explaining this state: solidarity requires common *experiences*, or, better still, the *Kreuzung sozialer Kreise* (Simmel, 1908). Although the workers of the multinational companies may share a set of *interests* at the global level, they have not yet experienced *social encounters*. This is what I referred to in chapter 1 as the emerging gap between boundaries of interests and the boundaries of experience. The nebulous character of the global experience of union activists explains the weakness of their transnational action, which requires something different from the old internationalism.

From the present inquiry, traditional internationalism even seems to be inversely related to actual international solidarity. In the next chapter I shall discuss the possibility of new solidarities and the role of the trade unions in this context. But first it is necessary to deepen the analysis of Italo-Polish differences.

The Impact of the 'Alternation' Experience in Poland

Polish Backwardness under Investigation

A general problem that lies behind Italy-Poland difference is that of social change. Commonly, Eastern Europe is seen as somehow at a backward stage of social development; yet at the same time, those countries recently went through a radical change not experienced by Western societies. In the interviews the issue of social change often appears, but its analysis is very complex because of the variety of topics, contexts, and references.[20] Table 4.2 attempts to summarise the content of the interviews with regard to various processes of change and the attitude to the past.

From this analysis any image of Polish workers as particularly conservative emerges as misleading. This is however a frequent image, in domestic politics as well as in the international scientific debate (e.g. Kramer, 1995; Adamski, 1998; Winiecki, 1998). Sztompka (1993) even argues that post-communist societies as a whole suffer from 'civilisational incompetence', because of the deep cultural *legacy* inherited both from the distant, pre-modern past and the more recent syndrome of 'fake' modernity imposed by 'real' socialism. Interestingly, according to Sztompka the only agents able to undermine this backwardness are the elites most insulated from the impact of real socialism and most exposed to the influence of the *modern, Western culture*. Obviously, union rank and file are not included within the elites.

Table 4.2 - Attitudes towards selected issues

Issue		Poland (N: 39)	Italy (N: 49)
Modernisation[a]	-positive	16	19
	-negative	7	16
	-negation[b]	0	9
Deindustrialisation	-positive	6	7
	-negative	2	7
Privatisation	-positive	8	4[c]
	-negative	13	10[c]
Regime change	-positive	10	-
	-negative	21	-
	-negation	2	-
Globalisation[a]	-positive	4	7
	-negative	1	24
	-negation	0	5
Unions' internationalisation[a]	-positive	13	10
	-negative	5	16
Past	-positive	10	11
	-negative	7	3

[a] Difference significant at the p<.05 level (Chi squared test).[21]
[b] As negation have been coded the attitude of the kind: 'the problem does not exist/does not matter'.
[c] N: 16 because only the Lucchini case has been considered (Fiat is not a privatised company.)

An authoritative view in this regard is that of the former dissident and Solidarity advisor Adam Michnik (today editor of a leading Polish newspaper, *Gazeta Wyborcza*). Already in the mid-1980s, he saw rank-and-file workers as dangerous 'new radicals' who could hinder political reform. After 1989 his fear grew further as he saw workers as frustrated, attached to social security, and unwilling to accept the costs of a market economy. Basically, he saw them as lazybones: 'to use a metaphor, for them the ideal is an economy where they would earn as much as the Americans, enjoy the same social security of the Swedes, and work as they have always worked in Poland' (Michnik, 1990, pp. 52-53).

The interviews do not support this view, especially when compared with the Italian ones. On none of the issues listed in Table 4.2 are Poles more conservative than their counterparts. On three issues, they are even significantly (p<.05) 'more' modern, in the specific sense of being more open towards current social change.

The problem with Polish activists, if any, is that they are *scarcely* critical about current changes. In fact, the current dominant discourse on modernisation in Eastern Europe is widespread, but inherently incoherent. The problems encountered by the current modernisation cannot be ascribed to the resistance of the 'material', and specifically of the trade unions. Actually, this 'material' is already more 'modern' – employing their own concept of 'modern' based on flexibility, capitalism and innovation – than it is in established modern capitalism. Polish trade unions are requested to become more Western-alike *and* more 'modern', but these two goals are mutually exclusive.

Are Polish Unionists more Conservative than the Italian Ones?

The Poles have a positive view of organisational, economic, and technological change; they do not extol the preceding societal model; they are aware of the inevitability, and even sometimes of the profitability, of deindustrialisation. Change is not an enemy; quite the opposite, it is a positive thing, a field of rivalry with the employer, who is accused of changing too slowly. Already in the 1980s Solidarity had been defined – following Habermas's definition of modernity – as a 'modernisational movement' (Tatur, 1989). After 1989, the Polish trade unions, in most cases, have been promoters of reform and restructuring, not of immobilism (Pańków, 1993; 1999). This has not been a deliberate cultural choice, but the outcome, in some way forced, of the unique, impressive experience of the breakdown of communism. Neither is it a simple acquiescence to the employer, since the unions are often (or at least want to be) one step *ahead* of the management.

> The unions did officially request changes, they are at management's disposal in order to change, but few things have been obtained, there are few cases of change. [hs2]

> It's difficult to compare those modernisation processes [of the 1970s] with now, because now here there is no modernisation. (...) Ecologically this foundry has hugely improved, but basically it shouldn't stay here, between the town and the National Park. [hs7]

> They presented it to us in this way, that this unusual foundry in the 1990s, at the time of Balcerowicz's plan, had to be completely scrapped. Everybody knew it, here on this ground had to arise a residential district, can you figure out, later on some kind of goods airport, and I think that precisely this whole campaign around the steelworks changed people's minds. There was very

heavy pressure to accept any investor without consideration, anybody who had some cash to save this company. [hs8]

Polish scepticism about industry might be regarded as an element of *pre*-industrial culture rather than *post*-industrial. While describing post-communist industrial relations, Frybes (1998, p. 204) underlines that the societies of Central-Eastern Europe, with the possible exception of Bohemia, before the communist experience were deeply traditional societies, with typically rural structures and mentalities. The peasant origins of many workers certainly influence their further cultural development. In the Soviet Union, the hurried transfer of entire populations to industrial work and to the urban space procured the preservation of archaic employment forms (Rolle, 1998). In some Polish companies, like the Huta im. T. Sendzimira in Cracow, unions asked for voluntary redundancy packages to invest in family farms (Hardy *et al.*, 1996). Nonetheless, two or three generations of industrial work and urban life (which is more than in the case of most Fiat workers in Turin[22]) and the experience of a true workers' movement like Solidarity (as discussed above) have not been without effect. Most workers are today aware that the decline of Polish agriculture is even more inevitable than that of big industry. It is therefore hard to define the workers of the big factories of Warsaw and Silesia as pre-industrial.

In fact, a degree of 'conservatism', far from being specific to the Polish unions, has always been a characteristic of unionism (Tannenbaum, 1951). In a way, this is, rather than a 'limit', an intrinsic 'function' of unionism: narrowing the gap between economic time (especially change pace) and social (human) time. In Italy, resistance is actually stronger and more convinced than in Poland. This is not a new finding, as the literature since the 1980s has defined industrial workers as 'immobile'.

> The working class – the factor par excellence for contestation of the existing order of things – seems to have adopted as its principal weapon practices of preservation of the status quo, staticness, rigidity, and *resistance*, while, on the other hand, change, proteiformity, and speed – the grand myths of modernity – have to all intents become the attributes of capital. (Revelli, 1996, p. 114)

Many interviews tend to confirm this image. Statements of the kind 'first of all, the union must defend what we already have' [rf6], never heard in Poland, are recurrent in Italy. Opposition to mobility is strong, references to the past as a framework for action are frequent, an activist even confesses 'I can't stand the story of modernity' [mf7]. 'Conservatism' is sometimes explicitly acknowledged.

The old times have remained impressed in our minds, we know that they belong to the past, but we can't help it. They can't brain-wash you from one day to another, I can't forget what I was doing yesterday, so organisational change is a bit traumatic. [pf9]

On substantive issues the difference is more evident. The *negation* of change is clear in some Italian discourses about political affairs, in which it is denied that the situation has significantly changed in the 1990s (when actually a real shock invested Italian politics).

In Italy, the scheme of parties is quite clear, maybe it has changed *a little bit* in the last three or four years, but I see it as quite clear-cut. Previously they had one set of names, now they have another. Firstly there are those who represent the middle class, the self-employed, the business people; secondly, a set of people who live like blood-suckers; finally those who defend the less well-off classes, some of the small shop-keepers and of the most exploited, those with little ability to confront the people in power. Therefore it's quite clear, maybe there are divisions but substantially the scheme is that one.[23] [mf7]

The same negation of reality appears on the issue of unemployment.

Jobs exist, but they have inculcated this idea that there are no jobs. [mf9]

Industrial work, in Turin and even more in Piombino, is still central. This may be seen when speaking of jobs, of security at work, or of environmental issues, though the Piombino unions as organisations officially requested anti-pollution measures.[24]

A permanent job in the steelworks today is maybe more valuable than before for the young: the possibility to create a family, a future. [pf4]

If we had to work under safe conditions, we wouldn't ever work. (...) It's an environment where one must always work, a lot, more... and besides we don't make pasta, we don't make bread, we make dirty things, we work with steel, there's nothing you can do. You can't get everything in life. We may improve it but... Something may be done but... for instance the cokery is an environment where... but it is necessary, we must find the system to... I don't know which system can they find to eliminate so many... but at the same time it's necessary, the steelworks is a dirty place but it's necessary, otherwise we would close down and we make a seaside resort here in Piombino. [pf11]

Interestingly enough, while the previous extract from *Huta Warszawa* (hs8) considered a deindustrialisation of the area to be possible and realistic, this last Piombino worker treats it as an absurdity.

In Italy, workers value very highly their experience.

> It's clear that this factory, because of the integral cycle, its fixed stock and a number of other things, must make high quality production. This also requires our experience, it's clear that the anticipated retirements have weakened this professional knowledge, it's clear, at all levels, technical, organisational, and of workers. [pf4]

There are also counter-trends, but they are rarer. Women seem more likely to develop alternative discourses on change and industry.

> Since the union represents the social side, it must defend the social side, which means that it must also govern outside. In this moment it must take initiatives, construct things which still don't exist, take care, I don't know, of education, of employment, a more open labour market, not a labour market which only produces problems like Fiat, but also other sorts of jobs, some alternatives because we can't live off cars forever. Sooner or later, the moment will arrive when the car won't be used anymore. The industry always creates problems, there is no warranty, there are serious concerns. [rf6]

The comparison of the privatisation processes in Poland and in Italy is very telling. In Warsaw Polish workers accepted privatisation by 98% in a ballot and tried to condition it. In Piombino the Italians tried, in a long strike, to avoid it and later experienced difficulties while trying to influence it. The only Polish plant where opposition to privatisation is strong is that of Tychy, but this is more about the forms of privatisation than the idea itself. Moreover, Tychy is precisely where – as discussed in the previous chapter – a form of workers' movement is enduring, and opposition to private property was almost natural for the workers' movement.

One could add other examples, even more concrete. Italian unionists accept the traditional idea that social security charges should be calculated on wages (although on specific points they used to demand a disconnection of social assistance from social security). Poles strongly criticise it and are therefore closer to new heterodox approaches on welfare state financing. This must certainly be due to the Eastern European lack of familiarity with fiscal systems. However, here again, this makes the Poles not 'backward' but close to the newest, emerging feelings of the Italian workforce

182 Trade Union Activists, East and West

(especially the non-unionised sector), which is increasingly receptive to anti-tax arguments.

In Poland industry-level bargaining is embryonic, but if we compare it with the Italian trends, it is probably the Italian system which is going in the Polish direction, rather than the opposite. If one accepts the Italian employers' point of view (which is usually considered more modern than the unions'), Poland is more modern in this regard. The Italian employers since 1996 have repeatedly demanded the elimination of industry-level bargaining, or at least the strong reduction of its scope: they dream of a Polish situation.

Permanent training is an important issue more in Warsaw, where workers appreciate re-qualification courses, than in Piombino, where the same are seen as a bothersome intrusion in a well-established life-routine. Italians' rootedness in the past also emerges in old-fashioned demands, for instance the restoration of the *scala mobile* (salary indexation system) which some FIOM activists still saw as a very important request in 1998, when the inflation rate in Italy was around 1.5%.

For the Poles, even less suitable than the 'conservative' definition is that of 'state-dependent' workers (Zaslavskij, 1995). The Poles actually very rarely ask for state protection, unlike the Italians who on a number of issues (environment, retirement, redundancy, industrial policy) involve the state.

It is true that in Poland, from time to time, elements of resistance towards the logic of the market appear. But these are not peculiar to Poland: they all exist, sometimes even in a stronger form, also in Italy, like for instance the dislike of advertising expenditure. Sometimes (much more rarely than one might expect, however) Polish unions indeed threaten to use their *negative* power to block unfavourable measures. However, it is only ideologically that this may be seen as an element of conservatism; otherwise, we should treat in the same way employers' threats to desist from investment in the case of excessive union demands.

Other concrete examples of Polish lack of conservatism refer to everyday employment relations. This is particularly visible in the case of jobs' defence. At Lucchini as well as at Daewoo, the unions accept, and even cooperate in, individual dismissals for disciplinary reasons, which Italian unions in all events try to avoid. As a whole, the Polish unions, though they obviously fight redundancy measures, repeat that they do not want to maintain superfluous jobs – an argument stranger to the Italian unionists. As a matter of fact, at Lucchini Solidarity is actively trying to convince the workforce that redundancy measures are preferable for the future of the company and for the (residual) employees' salaries. Like external mobility, internal mobility[25] is also more willingly accepted by the Polish trade unions (although it was previously almost unknown, at the point that often the appointments were made by the single workshops). The 'market' logic is viewed with strong scepticism in Italy, but it is almost welcome in Poland, where even salary indexation should be subject – for the unions! – to the control of the 'market conditions'. Finally, still referring to the US as a model of modernity, the Polish wage differentials are, with unions' approval, closer to the US standards than to the Italian ones. At Lucchini the wage differentials (the ratio between the lowest and the highest wages for productive workers) are 100/210 in Piombino and 100/400 in Warsaw (for the same professional levels). Surveys comparing Eastern and Western European workers confirm this conclusion: living in a rapidly changing environment, Eastern Europeans are even *excessively* flexible, to the point that their organisational commitment – which requires stability – is undermined (Gallie, Kostova and Kuchai, 1999).

Is it Only a Matter of Acquiescence?

It certainly remains disputable whether this form of openness is linked to a simple 'acquiescence' due to bargaining weakness, and therefore to a simple element of neo-proletarian consciousness described in the previous chapter. In fact, when employers wish for 'modern' and 'flexible' trade unions, they often simply mean 'weak' or 'acquiescent' unions.

The analytical interpretation of the interviews suggests that weakness and openness to change are not the same. Beyond the proletarian factor, an inclination to *openness* rather than *refusal* remains in the Polish unions. This also holds good while controlling for the disturbance effect of the collaboration-opposition category, especially by considering the distinctive case of *Sierpień 80* which is definitely not a 'collaborative' union but is nevertheless open to many aspects of the new economy and the new production systems. *Openness* means here not passive acceptance, but capacity to treat an issue as a field of action and not as an external calamity (in the way as the workers' movement struggled over industrialisation organisation and did not limit itself to breaking machines).

Politically, Polish trade unions are not really docile, as the latest animated debate on the reform of the Labour Code shows. The general acceptance of reforms does not mean acceptance of *any* reform. It is also disputable whether the Polish trade unions are weaker than the Italian ones at the national level. If one gave credence to the Polish mass-media, would rather reach the opposite conclusion. Not only the most conservative media, like *Rzeczpospolita* and *Wprost*, but also the supposedly more 'liberal' ones like *Gazeta Wyborcza* and *Polityka* regularly publish articles with titles like 'Trade Unions' State' (*Gazeta Wyborcza*, 5th February 2000) or 'Trade-unionocracy' (*Polityka*, n. 50, 12th December 1998). If one looks at industrial relations, the picture is indeed much more puzzling: large-scale surveys point at the marginalisation, or even absence, of trade unions in small and medium enterprises (Gardawski, Gąciarz, Mokrzyszewski and Pańków, 1999).

Nevertheless, all the variables (economic, institutional and political) usually used to measure union strength would rather argue for a Polish advantage in comparison to Italy. Notably: economic growth is higher and unemployment (especially in the regions studied here) is lower, though increasing again sharply since 1999; the law of 1991 protects the unions in the firms even more than the Italian *Statuto dei lavoratori* (1970), and in 1989 the employee councils had prerogatives none of the equivalent boards in the West has ever had; the party system could not be more union-friendly, since both Left and Right (and not only the Centre-Left like in Italy until very recently) are linked to the unions (OPZZ and Solidarity respectively). Unionisation rate is similar in both countries. Only collective bargaining coverage is lower, but on the other hand, legal regulation is more inclusive in Poland than in Italy (foreseeing for instance a minimum wage).

In the companies, Polish unions are not really weaker than the Italian ones. At Fiat Auto Poland union membership is higher than in Turin, and at *Huta Lucchini-Warszawa* the control on the company's strategy is, though far from complete, higher than in Piombino where the unions are regularly surprised by the ownership's choices. The *Huta* unions also take part in negotiations for the European Union enlargement, with substantial achievements.

A stronger, more disturbing variable is probably workers' turn-over, which is higher in Poland (especially in Warsaw) than in Italy and might explain why the Poles seem less 'locked into the past'. However, high turn-over itself is an indicator of marketisation and flexibility.

As to unions' quiescence, in the cases of Hungary and Slovenia it has been sharply commented that unions 'immaturity' is very useful for employers and highly functional in terms of market efficiency, for it secures a high level of work integration (Stanojevic, 1999). Stanojevic notes that unions' and companies' 'immature' organisational forms in Slovenia and Hungary manifest some striking similarities with the essential features of the HRM ideology. Even more so, they seem to realise an unreachable ideal of the HRM strategy in the West. This point reveals how ideological HRM can be and how many 'ancient' elements are present in the employers' discourse on modernity. There is insufficient space here to analyse this topic. The only important conclusion here is that the charges of conservatism addressed, from the employers' ideological side, to the postcommunist unions are strikingly inconsistent: these unions are already much less conservative than the Western ones.

Ten years after the breakdown of communism, the image of Polish workers as among 'the most contentious of the world' (Ekiert and Kubik, 1995) must be definitively abandoned. The levels of protest were high only in 1992-93, and even then were low if compared to the fall in real income in the first years of transition, a fall which although difficult to measure was without any doubt dramatic (Vaughan-Whitehead, 1998; Milic-Czerniak, 1998). Moreover, that wave of protest was never really against the reforms:

> it was more common in this period for strikers to frame their demands around statements that they were in favour of reforms and restructuring, but that they wanted these programs to be implemented more quickly, more efficiently or with less corruption. (Timko, 1996, p. 17)

On the basis of this analysis, the extraordinary success met in 1998 by the Polish government program of voluntary redundancy packages for the mining sector, which surprised most observers, not least its authors, is absolutely understandable. Polish workers are not an obstacle in the way of the future: they are, by contrast, open to new challenges, at least when some opportunity is given to them and especially if compared with their Western colleagues.[26] The capability to think in terms of globalisation and de-industrialisation seems inversely related to the rootedness of the national model. In this regard, Italian industrial unionism is probably at an advantage if compared to those of other countries like France, Austria or Germany, more anchored to the idea of a national pattern. But it is less well equipped than the Polish one, which, willy-nilly, has recognised the need to change.

An attentive examination reveals how the accusations of conservatism addressed to the Polish unions are internally contradictory. If one pursues the interpretation, would notice that the accusations stem from the experience of the Polish elites, preoccupied to justify the impressive gains obtained from the current transformation. The idea of Eastern European backwardness produces and perpetuates the subordination to external models. At the same time, after comparing Polish and Italian activists, one wonders what the former still has to learn about the market from the latter.

After the investigation of the dominant views, it is now necessary to come back to the main topic of this thesis, namely the explanation of unionists' views.

A Phenomenological Explanation: The Polish 'Alternation'

Ost and Weinstein (1999), through their fieldwork research on the Polish unions, also noted a surprising support for market ideology. They showed how this cannot be explained either by rational choice approaches (in fact, unionists 'irrationally' support the eventual undermining of workers' and unions' rights) or by institutional ones (in fact, the employee councils work in disparate ways). They argue for an 'ideational' explanation, giving a decisive role to the liberal ideology embraced by the Polish activists. In short, 'unionists came to believe in capitalism simply because it was the enemy of their enemy' (p. 30). Why the Poles think what they think, remains for Ost and Weinstein an open question. I shall use my evidence to propose an explanation of how these ideas have been constructed in the Polish unions. If one concentrates on the workshop level, these ideas are clearly not inherited from the 1980s, when – as I argued in the previous chapters – egalitarianism and class consciousness were very strong.

In the interviews with Polish activists the experience of the so-called 'transition' is recurrent and central not only as a topic but also as a structuring element. Most judgements, on the present as well as on the past, refer to the breakdown of state-socialism and the subsequent changes. For instance, the old system is disqualified because it was condemned to failure (that is, giving a retroactive effect to a later event). Actually, the communist breakdown was not foreseen, or at least it was not expected to happen so rapidly. The activists, however, project their current historic knowledge to the past, while recognising that society did not share this knowledge.

> After martial law came in it was clear that this system had to fall, I even have witnesses that I had said this. I repeated that the economy can't endure, and I wasn't mistaken at all, I got it wrong by only one year, it happened in '89, I thought it would happen in 1990-91. [bs1]

Similarly, the image of the future is built around the necessity of change, which unlike in Italy has a strongly positive meaning. The best example is the demand for Western social security standards: the concrete examples indicate that the actual interest is in the preservation of communist-era benefits (e.g. company housing and holidays, or job security), but the justification discourse focuses rather on the West as an ideal model. The frequent complaint '*unlike in the West*, here young people are hired with temporary contracts' is used instead of '*unlike in former times*, ...' – which is what people probably think, but do not dare to say. By contrast, the Italian justification structure is often centred on the past.

This does not mean that Polish workers are enthusiastic about the way the transition has been effectuated. They are often deceived and sometimes frustrated. Even in a position where very few stable evaluating references are available, they attempt to give a critical opinion on events. The disappointment is stronger with the 'transition' in the workplace and with the new employer. However, the 'transition' is criticised for its actual form but never rejected: it is accepted and defended as a necessary and foundational turning point. Even the most negative opinions, mentioned below, ultimately accept the idea of change.

> We started to talk about an Italian investor, among people appeared some hope of that Western life, known through films, TV. After, this Italian investor arrived and [with him] the brutal reality, brutal was the clash of our expectations with the reality which started to be in force here. I think that it is precisely as [it had occurred] in the West, but we didn't completely realise how the reality might look. There were enormous expectations, aspirations to that whole Western life. By contrast, nobody expected that we had to... such an enormous effort to achieve all that. [hs8]

> That at the national level there is this transformation, we move from are system to another, we would be able to get used to it, if only it weren't on such principles... [ta2]

> In the West, all this changed over a number of years, and basically they built that wealth, that fortune and so on. Here there is a mistake in the transformation, people were simply not ready, at a given moment they were thrown in the abyss. People simply don't know how to behave and everybody wants to save himself in some way on the surface, in order not to sink. [tz2]

Apart from the case of post-communist *Metalowcy*, which requires another historical explanation, only one example has been found (in the radical *Sierpień 80*) of apparent fundamental opposition to the change which occurred in 1989. However, this opposition also seems to be to the *betrayal* of the origins of change rather than to change itself.

> Solidarity fought above all against communism, to make communism fall, to change the system, for instance in the Gdansk docks, so that these docks might be private, to change the system. And now what? The owner has changed,

there is the State Treasury,[27] and all this change of system brought about that the docks close down. So now they have to change the direction of their action, of the struggles, no longer those economic changes, only saving this industry. [ta6]

In most cases, the idea of 'alternation', of a basic need to invert the situation is surprisingly enduring.

We see how the world looks, we are a country as we are, many people travel abroad and so on, and someday we'll arrive at that status of free man, who works, knows why he works, and what can he afford. [tz2]

I shall try to interpret this relatively very wide acceptance of the idea of change in spite of difficult circumstances with the help of Berger and Luckmann's sociology of knowledge, of which the relevant points have been summarised in chapter 2.

The processes of change within Poland and Italy, in society and in the workplaces, recall two types of socialisation described by Berger and Luckmann (1967): respectively, re-socialisation through alternation and secondary socialisation. The first one completely inverts the cognitive framework of the individual, and explicitly 'cuts' with the past. The second one, by contrast, tries to maintain as much continuity as possible with previous experiences, avoiding any drastic mutation and minimising change.

The Features of Alternation

Several features characterise *alternation* as the most radical form of re-socialisation. Post-communist transformation is indeed not as drastic as the purest type of alternation, that of religious conversion. The model of religious conversion may perhaps be applied to the particular case of the post-communist *Metalowcy* leadership, which is, however, not central in the discussion of the transformation of the workers' movement. For the rest of the unions, almost all the elements of Berger and Luckmann's model appear in Poland, only in a slightly modified form. As the authors themselves note, it is only a problem of degree. There are five important characteristics of alternation:

- a legitimating apparatus;
- the repudiation of alternatives;
- the reinterpretation of the old reality;

- the presence of 'significant others';
- a plausibility structure.

The first feature of radical re-socialisation is the need for a legitimating apparatus, capable of justifying the new reality and the stages required to achieve it. In Eastern Europe, an extremely powerful legitimating apparatus is the East-West contrast, which is sometimes exaggerated and almost always diverts attention from the local history and 'path'. Any political or organisational proposal for change is presented with the foreword 'this is how things are in the West'. The advantage of this legitimating apparatus is a cost-reducing readiness to imitate. The limit is that though absolutely convincing on the general idea of change, it is less persuasive on the *stages*. In any event, the idea that to achieve Western standards it is necessary to go through a phase of 'nineteenth century capitalism', in order to follow (hopefully faster) the same stages followed by the West, has become common sense, as the above mentioned extracts and many others suggest.

> I know that people didn't realise the costs implied by this transformation. But nothing is for free, it can't be so that as soon as we change the system we're at once in America, we're far away from America. They spent two hundred years before reaching what they have from this democracy, we had two hundred years of slavery, therefore two hundred years of gap, after the war too they gained and we lost, our rulers sold us exactly, almost fifty years of totalitarianism were wasted. [hs6]

The second element, directly proceeding from the previous one, is the repudiation of alternatives. The political debate in Poland does not take place between proponents and opponents of reforms, but between slightly different interpretations of the West as a model for change. The discussion on economic and social matters approximates a sort of *'pensée unique'* (to use a definition hurriedly conceived about the West but not unsuitable for the East). Indeed, the repudiation of alternative is also the outcome of specific strong economic and political pressures. The influential advisors from the World Bank or the IMF forced many choices, while the governmental decision in 1990 to impose a high tax (the *popiwek*) on wage-increases only in the state sector certainly contributed to 'buy' workers' preference for privatisation. However, the shyness of unions' counterproposals still has to be explained: why was Solidarity able to reject the market-oriented reforms proposed by the Messner government in 1987, but so silent – in spite of democracy – three years later? Maintaining Berger and Luckmann's image of conversion, one might remember that the

190 Trade Union Activists, East and West

converted are always the most dogmatic believers. Even the activists who most strongly denounce the costs of transformation do not propose any real alternative, with the partial and essentially marginal exception of the nationalist *Popiełuszko*.[28]

Additionally, alternation implies the reinterpretation of the old reality and past biography. Polish workers are 'working' deeply on their past, as compared with the Italians who repeat crystallised visions of the old times. The Polish vision of the past, as emerging also from Table 4.2, is much more critical than the Italian one. In the interviews, the higher the self-assurance about the direction of change, the worse the image of the past. Sometimes the reinterpretation even approaches the purest form described by Berger and Luckmann: the 'then I thought, now I know' formula.

> Now times have changed, we should move to more professional [union] work, more competent, because formerly we declared 'we don't like it, so we strike', it was like that at the beginning of the 1980s. And those strikes brought about, among other things, the need to make the production again, unfortunately nobody wanted to talk and only after heavily beating... it was a necessity, and now we must change, we must start to speak on the basis of arguments. [hs6]

The fourth element indicated by Berger and Luckmann is the necessity of 'significant others', with whom the *alternating* subject develops a strongly affective identification. It is not easy to identify the significant others of post-Communist transformation. They are not the Western workers: as we have seen, union East-West cooperation is fragile and full of misunderstandings.[29] Certainly they are not foreign employers, vary rarely beloved, and even less politicians or intellectuals. A 'participating' look suggests instead that the unexpected significant others are Western consumers, and the consumption goods and services they choose. As a matter of fact, the country where alternation was most radical is Albania, where a true disintegration of the previous identity produced almost a shame to be Albanian and, the other side of the coin, violent nationalist feelings. This disintegration is not explained only by the particularly rigid nature of the previous regime: Romania or the Soviet Union were also tyrannical. It is to a large extent the outcome of the very strong role played by the Western media (and especially Italian TV advertising) in the country of the eagles. In no other country has the contrast between the two poles of alternation been so rapid, extreme and palpable. In Poland Western goods, advertised by the media and massively imported in the first months of transition, are known much better than Western work conditions or welfare systems. This is the channel through which the country knows its goals and justifies them.

This brings us to the last point, the plausibility structure, which connects all the previous elements and offers a framework for the everyday common knowledge. Following on from the previous point, the plausibility structure is probably the market considered as a system to calculate the value of goods, services, and – regrettably – people too. Although markets were not unknown in the socialist system, monetary marketisation has been a brusque experience. Money has rapidly substituted a number of other resources which were formerly more important: time, acquaintances, group belonging. Moreover, the experience of marketisation, exalted by the hyperinflation of the first months of transformation, rapidly imposed new parameters for the evaluation of anything in everyday life (Kolarska-Bobińska, 1993). 'Transition' has involved a brusque shift in the arguments used in the public sphere from moral or organisational to economic (monetary) categories. This explains why Polish workers speak for so long about money as compared not only to the relatively rich workers of the West, but also to the poorest strata of Western society. As has already been argued, the market orientation of the Poles does not come from the past: in 1980, on the contrary, the 12th of the 21 Gdańsk postulates claimed even the suppression of 'free prices'. Finally, since the comparison of salaries is the first matter raised by workers in non-directive interviews when speaking about their Italian colleagues, this plausibility structure emerges phenomenologically as a (possibly *the*) structuring element of the East-West divide. 'We are the poor, they are the rich': the shift from a class relationship to monetary categories is achieved.

In conclusion, current union consciousness does not seem anchored in the past; quite the opposite, it is interwoven with the idea of radical change which inverted the reference values. This may explain how the same activists, who in the 1980s used a rhetoric of strength and pride, now adopt a neo-proletarian rhetoric. They see their current position, even when it has not really worsened that much, through the lens of social change, which has transformed the 'pillars' of socialism into old-fashioned, often redundant residues.

It may be noticed that the argument I exposed here uses an extra-work experience (alternation) as an explanatory factor for a differentiation taking place *at work*. Once the experience of work is no longer in a position to assign meaning to social actors, we have to leave the workplace to make sense of it. This point will be important in the fifth chapter on the sources of trade union commitment.

What has been described does not, however, account for the totality of the post-communist experience. The alternation model presented in *The Social Construction of Reality* represents the model for extreme re-socialisation, it tells how Eastern European change *should have been.* However, in the case of complex societies, unlike that of the individuals who are the reference for Berger and Luckmann, it is impossible to cut all the links with the past. A thorough and abrupt discontinuity is not accomplished. The result is the problem of maintaining a minimum of consistency with the remains of the past, which was noted in numerous interview extracts, for instance on the issue of the representation of the opponent. Several problems arise for today's Eastern Europe and for the acceptance of the stages of transformation. Nevertheless, the goals remain indisputable: the investigation of the re-socialisation pattern explains that attitude of Solidarity which has been defined as 'desperately seeking capitalism' by surprised Western scholars (Hardy and Rainnie, 1995).

Returning to the interviews, the drastic form of marketisation in Poland may explain the economicism which I have described above. This economicism, outside the peculiar industrial setting of Tychy, *phenomenologically* pushes the Polish workers away from class faster than the Italian ones. The most consistent aspect is the justification of economic demands, explicitly shifting from class to consumption references.

> The problem is that in this country people earn too little money. These salaries are really not too high if compared to living costs, *I am not saying if compared to the executed work, I am saying to living costs.* [hs6]

The Italian Secondary Socialisation

Although the alternation of Eastern Europe is not ideal-typical, it remains very different from the recent experience of Italian workers. The Italians have managed to subjectively minimise change at both work and political level. A good example is that of the fall of communism.

> Somebody smartly made fun of us, 'poor you, the failure of communism'. But in fact it was a reflection which had already started in the 1970s with Berlinguer.[30] These were not radical changes, they had already been started by Berlinguer. [mf6]

There is no critical revision of the past, but on the contrary self-justification and a preservation of continuity. The present is in turn interpreted in a continuous relationship with the past. Not only does the current political discourse follow the rhetoric of the 1970s, but changes in work organisation are also minimised (this is also true of the employer, who intelligently issues different propaganda than in Poland). In this way Italian activists have safeguarded resources which the Poles have lost, but at the cost of remaining locked into an old model, and of greater difficulties in their relations with the youngest workers. This also explains why the Italian configurations of consciousness (Figure 1 in chapter 3) are less disparate and distant than the Polish ones, although both substantially move away from class consciousness.

Of course, recent Italian change is *objectively* less deep than that in Poland: the political crisis and the economic reforms, though important, did not have the dramatic meaning of the Polish ones. However, what is important here is to state that these experiences of change bring about different *perceptions* of reality, and that it is these perceptions, more than the structural factors themselves, that primarily affected trade union consciousness. This subjective approach may explain why Poles appear in some respects more modern than the Italians. The apparently 'primitive' economicism of the Poles acquires the opposite meaning. There is not a natural trend from material to post-material needs, as suggested by Maslow. Actually, if one observes the changes in collective bargaining as well as in workers' orientations in Italy, salaries are becoming increasingly important. That is, Italians are slowly adapting to a subjective reality already brusquely encountered by the Poles.

Indeed, at the national level as well as in many workplaces Italian trade unions are showing themselves able to cope with current problems. They are taking part in a reform of the welfare state (although a slow and ambiguous one), and in many company agreements they are negotiating flexibility in innovative ways. However, the core of the Italian workers' movement, if compared to the similar 'core' in Poland, makes of the defence of the past its main vocation. Entirely understandable from the subjective point of view, arguably justified from a political one, this attitudes entails a conservative self-definition which weakens the unions. The fact that Italian unionism is more 'open' than others in Western Europe, then, is actually a sort of validation *a fortiori* of the argument of a East-West difference.

The alternation-based explanation of Polish reality which has been drafted above is an alternative to the two 'paradigms' through which the post-communist world is normally seen: that of transition, teleological and centred in the future, and that of legacy and path-dependency, centred in the past. The phenomenological approach used here focuses instead on the current experience of change: it emerges that the actual behaviour of actors is coherent neither with their traditions, nor with the prospective goals of 'transition', but only with the transformation itself. At the same time, Polish workers' behaviour differs from that of their Italian counterparts, who experience secondary socialisation instead of alternation, and are therefore more rooted in the past: 'the reality-base for re-socialisation is the present, for secondary socialisation is the past' (Berger and Luckmann, 1966, p. 182).

The Social Construction of the East-West Divide

Two main elements have emerged from the Italy-Poland comparison: a sort of neo-proletarian identity among the Poles, and a higher degree of resistance to change among the Italians. These two findings are not in conflict: the axis proletarian vs. proud identity is independent from the modernisation vs. conservatism one. Phenomenologically, the two findings are even interconnected: in Poland, self-distancing from the West is at the same time a legitimating apparatus for change and a basis for inferiority feelings. In this last section I shall briefly attempt to discuss whether this difference may become a ground for a broader divergence between the Italian and Polish societies.

The distinction between East and West is apparently a meaningful category for workers. They do not speak of it often, but whenever they do, it is in a self-confident way. In only two interviews, with activists of the militant, working-class *Sierpień 80*, is the distinction denied in the idea that workers in East and West experience common problems. In most cases, the distinction is self-evident, especially for the Poles.

> In the firms with foreign capital we've got Western work and Eastern salary (...). We aspire to arrive at the Western standard of living, but we don't know when. And this is what hurts most. [hs1]

> This happens in Western Germany, in Eastern Germany they have poverty, terrible poverty. Everything depends on the occupation, the American one. Look, one wall divides them and this is heaven and hell. Now they've unified it but it decays anyway. [ta5]

Central-Eastern Europe is commonly represented as moving on the road to integration with the West. Economic integration is indeed growing, and political integration is also progressing even though at a progressively slowing pace. However, it is precisely this convergence which makes the enduring differences more visible and problematic. In this regard, the experience of multinational companies is particularly important: while they contribute to integration in a number of fields (e.g. technology), they may also introduce new differences and consolidate them.

At Fiat Auto Poland working conditions are not that much harder than in the Western plants: although automation is in some positions reduced, the rhythms and the pauses are the same and the environmental conditions are sometimes even better. The distinguishing factor is the different path of work reorganisation: in Poland, traditional Taylorism was strengthened at the same time as it was being dismantled in Italy.

The evidence from other multinational companies operating in the post-communist countries confirms this impression. At Thomson-Polkolor, in the Warsaw suburbs, it has been noted that in human resources management, the system of punishment and reward restores authoritarian traditions which had been abandoned in the Western plants (Durand, Le Goff and Tobera, 1997, p. 144).

At General Motors Hungary, compared with other transplants in Western Europe, there is a less democratic and more management-controlled team concept. In Hungary, team leaders are not elected and controlled by the teams, and there are fewer possibilities to increase job-content and to acquire multi-skilling (Tóth, 1996b). Similar conclusions may be drawn from research carried out on the General Motors plant in Eisenach, in the former GDR (Jürgens, 1995), on Italo-Hungarian joint ventures (Makó and Simonyi, 1995), and on the overall attitudes of multinational companies towards the trade unions in Hungary (Makó and Novoszáth, 1995). Most striking is the case of Suzuki Hungary, where the unions experienced difficulties before managing to organise (Tóth, 1996a). Incidentally, it does not appear coincidental that Hungary is both the Eastern European country which has attracted most foreign investment and that with the least labour-friendly legislation.

In fact, the East-West differences within multinational companies relate not only to work organisation, but also to the management attitude towards unions. In Poland, in the green-field US-owned factories of General Motors (Gliwice), Pepsico (Szczecin) and Levi-Strauss (Płock) the trade unions are still absent (in spite of their repeated efforts to establish themselves). Pepsico management even organised an intensive campaign against the trade unions, charging them with ruining Polish industry. Even more striking is the situation of a Norwegian-based multinational, where a trade union was in the end permitted, but on the condition of remaining detached from Solidarity. This circumstance is symptomatic of the tendency by multinational capital to create work settings not influenced by the national context. This is not an easy goal, however: in the above-mentioned Norwegian company the union, forced to be formally independent, maintains informal links with Solidarity, in a sort of revival of underground activity.[31]

This gap is not without consequences. In the plants I studied, there is a high potential for an interest opposition between Eastern and Western workers. To give an interesting example of how the distinction from the West may be perceived, I shall quote the account of a former Solidarity officer, who was a union advisor during the strike at *Huta Lucchini* in 1994, was later engaged by Lucchini, and currently works in a consulting company.

> During that half year I worked in Piombino for Lucchini, unfortunately, I saw that other side, that other, sadder part of the truth, which later on the Italians did not hide anymore. Lucchini strengthened his own capital, he financially strengthened himself since the moment of the *Huta* take-over. Basically, we sold him Peru. We were Peru and he simply made money and from that moment he started to make serious investments in Italy, he bought Piombino, he bought all the big steelworks. Lucchini was known for being the boss of the employers in Brescia, up to 1992 he had two firms, which counted together less than 3,000 people, such small steelworks. Now the group has about 9,000 people. (Gilejko, Gieorgica and Ruszkowski, 1997, p. 96)

History offers abundant evidence for stating that not only is the market insufficient on its own to prompt integration, but it may also become a cause of divergence. 130 years of a unified Italian national market have not been sufficient to overcome the economic distance between the North and the South, and on the political and cultural level have eventually produced the *Lega Nord*. 8 years of German unification have brought the gap in the unemployment rate between old and new *Bundesländer* from 4.9 to 9.3%,[32] and the PDS electoral score in the latter from 11.1% to 21.6% (in 1990 most observers actually thought that the PDS would have quickly disappeared). Similar fears of centrifugal counter-reactions have been expressed within the European Union, especially concerning monetary convergence, which, on this view, might produce as its complement a social divergence between classes and regions (Alvater and Mahnkopf, 1995). These fears have been up to now only fears, but eastward enlargement might make them real. Although Poland (like most of the post-communist countries aspiring to enter the European Union) signed the European Social Chart already in 1997, the actual social and cultural model currently *in statu nascendi* is quite distinctive.

The political and social construction of the East-West category as a divide in identities and behaviour patterns, encountered in the Polish and Italian plants of the Fiat and Lucchini groups, is not yet representative of broader societal trends. Nevertheless, it calls attention to the problem of dualisation.

A Broader Review of the Polish Unionism

The Choice of 'Critical' Control Cases

It has to be verified whether the observations made about the Fiat and Lucchini cases may be extended to Polish unionism as a whole. In a situation of increasing differentiation and decreasing significance of industrial relations models, any conjecture about a societal pattern is risky. This argument, however, does not allow us to avoid the question: since a societal variable (alternation) has been put at centre of the analysis, the impact of this variable on the rest of the society has to be tested. Several 'national' features have already been mentioned in order to connect case studies and societal frameworks. Nonetheless, an exploratory test was still necessary and therefore the unions of a few other selected cases have been considered, though more superficially. In the plants listed in Table 4.3 conversations were carried out with union officers and activists, along with analysis of union documents and some moments of participant observation.

The first, theoretical aim of enlarging the fieldwork was to answer two questions raised by the previous research:

1) whether the 'neo-proletarian' element is peculiar to Italian transplants (or even only to the two Italian transplants considered), as they display a particularly paternalistic and adversarial management style;[33]

2) whether the 'change-oriented' element is peculiar to the privatised companies, and not representative of the majority of industrial workers still employed in the state sector.

These questions – as a thorough exploration of Polish reality remains beyond our possibilities – may best be confronted by choosing extreme cases, that is those with the least favourable conditions for the confirmation of the hypothesis. Accordingly, two cases are required: on the one hand a foreign- but not Italian-owned company with a reputation of being socially-oriented; on the other, a state-owned company with unions considered to be particularly conservative or even reactionary.

The first case is represented by Danone, a French-owned company particularly present in Eastern Europe and traditionally considered as socialist-supporting. The group founder Antoine Riboud was a friend of François Mitterrand and has been defined as 'progressive' for favouring (in opposition to the French tradition) strong and well-organised trade unions in a counter-power role, which the company needs in order to develop (Guarriello and Jobert, 1992).[34] In addition Danone allows a supplementary comparison with Italian plants to be made, in order to test the weight of the employer's nationality.

Table 4.3 - Supplementary case-studies

Company (production)	Localisation	Workforce	Ownership	Unions present *directly analysed
Danone (Dairying)	Warsaw	300	French	-Solidarity* -Dairying Independent T.U. (OPZZ)
Danone (Dairying)	Bieruń Stary (Silesia)	400	French	-Solidarity* -Shift Workers' T.U.*
Ursus (Tractors)	Warsaw	5,900	State Treasury	-Solidarity* -Metalowcy (OPZZ)* -Popiełuszko -Engineers and Technicians' T.U.
Daewoo (Cars)	Warsaw	9,000	South Korean	-Solidarity* -Metalowcy -Solidarity 80* -Engineers and Technicians' T.U.
Petrochemia Płock (Refinery)	Płock (Mazovia)	7,400	State Treasury	-Solidarity* -Refinery Workers' T.U. (OPZZ) -Solidarity 80* -National Solidarity 80 -Engineers and Technicians' T.U.
Bizon-New Holland (Agriculture Machines)	Płock (Mazovia)	1,200	Italian	-Solidarity* -Metalowcy (OPZZ) -Engineers and Technicians' T.U.
Cotex (Textile)	Płock (Mazovia)	1,200	State	-National Solidarity 80* -Solidarity* -Textile Industry T.U. (OPZZ) -Foremen's T.U.
Galbani-Danone (Dairying)	Casale Cremasco (Lombardy)	300	French	-FLAI-CGIL* -FAT-CISL*

The second extreme case is that of the Ursus tractor factory, in the Warsaw suburbs. This plant is very well known for its historical role (site of the 1976 unrest, which gave rise to the KOR[35]) as well as for its current political character. The local Solidarity organisation, led by a famous extreme-right activist, Zygmunt Wrzodak, has been widely accused of nationalism, anti-Semitism, and even fascism (by the regional Solidarity president Jankowski himself). In a street demonstration in 1995 Ursus workers cried 'communists to the gas', and in 1998 they burnt European

Union flags under the Finance Ministry buildings. In 1997 Solidarity refused to agree to the entry of a foreign investor, a US company among the world leaders in the sector. Today, Ursus is still state-owned and Solidarity demands tractor import to be blocked.

Besides these critical cases, other companies have been observed with a more 'exploratory' purpose. This includes first of all another important multinational company, Daewoo, which took over the FSO car factory in Warsaw. This case is not only parallel to the Fiat one from the productive point of view (automotive sector). It is historically important, since it was a fortress of the works councils in 1956 and also had an important role in 1980. Moreover, FSO Solidarity in the 1980s cooperated intensively with the Turin unions. The importance was also strategic: Daewoo was using Eastern Europe, where it almost became the leading car producer, as a 'Trojan horse' to enter the European common market.

Moreover, in order not to avoid a geographical bias (all the plants considered up to now are based either in Warsaw or in the Katowice voïvodships), the unions of three important enterprises of Płock in Central Poland have been included: Petrochemia Płock, New Holland, and Cotex. Petrochemia Płock is the second biggest Polish company in terms of turnover, and the biggest fuel producer in Central and Eastern Europe. It is theoretically important as a case of a state company not in a ruinous situation, where in addition the unions have played an important role as promoters at restructuring. New Holland (formerly Bizon) produces agricultural machines and was taken over by foreign capital (Fiat group) in 1996; its situation is interesting in comparison to Ursus, given the similarity of production. Cotex, finally, is a state-owned textile factory with 1,200 employees (80% women), theatre of some extremely tough work conflict (four months of occupation) and an interesting case of a women's revolt (the factory was visited during the occupation), which will be discussed in chapter 5. Finally, information has been collected, through the Solidarity foreign department in Gdansk, on a number of other foreign companies.

Danone

The Danone case was analysed through long, unstructured interviews with unionists and other 'qualified observers' from the plants of Warsaw and Bieruń Stary (Silesia), taken over in 1996. In Italy, the Galbani plant in Casale Cremasco (Lombardy), taken over by Danone in 1990, was considered. In addition, information was collected also from the French CGT in Paris.

Danone's 'social' reputation is confirmed, in Italy, by the particularly 'soft' management of layoffs, through the policy of 'out-placing'(Viacelli, 1994). Also in Poland the social package is significantly above the Polish standards, and includes sport facilities and leisure activities. In Poland, industrial relations appear, especially in the plant of Bieruń Stary, much more 'quiet' than at Lucchini or Fiat. In both countries the work environment is exceptionally clean and safe, and although this is certainly due to the specificity of the product (yoghurt and cheese) the unionists notice a considerable improvement from the pre-Danone times.

Nevertheless, it has already been noted by French sociologists that Danone, a plant with a definitely 'ethnocentric' pattern of management, considers that in the East an 'authoritarian' command is indispensable to achieve rapid change (Durand, 1997). In Poland, relations with the unions are, though generally quiet, not without conflicts, especially in Warsaw. It is important to note that the plant of Bieruń Stary was built in 1986 and therefore did not see the 'first' Solidarity and lacks a labour movement tradition. In Italy conflicts are more 'open', and there are short strikes from time to time.

The main difference noted between the two countries is the presence in Poland of a parallel form of plant-level employees' representation, special 'Danone Committees' created by the company. Remarkably, the Poles were told that these Committees are characteristic of Danone everywhere, while neither in France nor in Italy is there anything similar. This is a specifically Eastern European solution, implemented first in the Czech Republic and later in all the other post-communist countries, and are a sort of mixture of French *comités d'entreprise* (which are elected on unions' lists) and German *Betriebsräte*. According to Solidarity activists in Warsaw, the aim of these Committees is to eliminate the unions. Some rivalry emerges also from the account of a Warsaw Committee member who was also interviewed (and interestingly enough had never been interested in union activity before). The management attitude towards these committees is described as much more friendly than that towards the unions and extensive training for the Committees' members is organised and financed by the company. Generally, the unions complain about the lack of information on the 'global' situation of the group. However, management, noting the risks of unions' exclusion, decided in a second time to include in the committee one representative for each union. This is not the case, however, in all Central and Eastern Europe.

Wages are kept beyond the competence of this Committee. This policy apparently contrasts with the Fiat preference for concentrating collective bargaining on wages. Actually, the two lines converge in a unique effect:

pushing the unions to care only about wages, neglecting the other issues. As a matter of fact, the Polish workers and unions appear much more concerned with wages than the Italians, coherently with the hypothesis of a specifically Polish 'economicism'. This happens even in Warsaw, in spite of the fact that salaries there are about 40% higher than those of a twin plant in Lublin taken over by a US investor. In Italy, by contrast, wages, though important, are secondary for the unions if compared with work rhythms.

The other characteristic element of Polish union consciousness – the feeling of weakness – is present. Although more satisfied with employment and industrial relations than their Fiat or Lucchini colleagues (something which is also due to the different economic sector), the Polish activists express palpable feelings of weakness and of having been weakened, in comparison with the past. In particular, they report a general workers' fear of striking (at least in Warsaw) and even of joining a union (in both plants).

No sign of transnational union cooperation was found. This is surprising as Danone was one of the first MNCs to create a EWC and to take the first steps towards European-level collective bargaining and 'has arguably the most advanced of all transnational information and consultation arrangements' (European Work Councils' Bulletin 1997, 10, p. 4). Now, the EWC is even surpassed by a World Group Committee established in Geneva.

In fact, at the time of the investigation (April 1998-February 1999) the EWC did not include Polish employees' representatives, and the only transnational contacts were restricted to a narrow elite. In Italy, members of the EWC were office workers detached from the productive plants. In Poland, the union officer who took part in meetings in Brussels never reported to her organisation or to the employees she represented. On the occasion of the last European meeting only Solidarity was informed, and too late to participate. What is more, Polish representatives told that they would not have had their travel expenses refunded by the employer. They also met the problem of finding a translator in order to understand the invitation and had to contact the regional union offices for this. According to the personnel manager for Central and Eastern Europe (interview on April 2000), however, the situation has later changed and Central and Eastern European unions do actively participate, funded by the company, in the 'World Group Committee'.

In the West, the situation is specular. In Casale, globalisation is condemned in generic terms like in Piombino but not really examined. In

France, according to a CGT officer, there is a widespread fear among the employees about possible transplants in Eastern Europe.

In Poland, the contacts between the two plants of Warsaw and Bieruń Stary, and with the employees of the retailing structure are also very weak and difficult. The company did not want the unions from the two plants to meet before the negotiations of the company collective agreement. In Italy the situation in this respect is better: there is group co-ordination and retail workers are paradoxically more unionised than average. However, in the same village of Casale Cremasco the unions from the two neighbouring plants Danone and Galbani-Danone do not cooperate and meet very rarely.

The non-Italian nature of Danone allows the issue of Polish 'nationalism' to be assessed. In Poland, opposition towards the new investor displays, although less violently, the same nationalist features as at Fiat and Lucchini. In particular arguments like the following are used: 'for them whatever is French is good', 'they don't know Polish law', 'in this country they're guests but they behave as landlords', 'they're incapable of taking decisions without asking Paris'. The same arguments have been found at Fiat, Huta Lucchini, and Daewoo. However, in Italy the same themes also appear, with only secondary rhetorical differences. In particular, exactly the same complaint was reported in Warsaw and in Casale Cremasco about the fact that the French management chooses French machines while the German ones have a much better reputation. In any case, national questions are evidently not the main concern of the unions. In Bieruń Stary this is also proved by past experience: before the Danone take-over (in 1996) there had been a resolute union mobilisation against the previous Polish private investor, who was eventually rejected from the plant while Danone was later accepted in a referendum almost unanimously.

Trends towards fragmentation and dualisation are confirmed by other elements. Everywhere, gaps in employment conditions between 'seniors' and 'juniors', men and women, permanent and seasonal workers, and especially Danone and 'subcontracted' employees are denounced. In this regard, the Danone case does not confirm the hypothesis of the Polish unions as better equipped when facing differentiation. The difficulties are basically similar, and solidarity with the subcontracted employees is even higher in Casale Cremasco where the Danone unions are able to go on strike to defend them. In Bieruń Stary, shift workers (about 100) had to create their own union to defend their particular professional prerogatives. The situation with respect to the gender gap is also complex. Women in Warsaw make up 50% of all employees and the large majority of productive workers; nevertheless, they constitute only 10% of Solidarity (the most active union) membership, and the Solidarity executive is entirely male.[36] However, the leader of the second union is a woman and in Bieruń Stary women even constitute a majority on the Solidarity executive.

As to attitudes towards change and modernisation, Danone by contrast confirms what has been written before on 'alternation'. In Poland the representation of the past by union officers is absolutely negative. In Italy, by contrast, the unions complain, for instance, about the loss of health resorts for thermal treatment. This point also suggests that the peculiarly Eastern European tie to established social packages is largely a myth. Danone management, just like Fiat's and Lucchini's, praises Central and Eastern European 'dynamism' and 'innovations' in contrast with the 'old', 'declining' Western Europe.

Culturally, the Polish unions seem more 'modern' than the Italian ones, but this finding is certainly biased by the rural location of the Italian plant analysed. In Casale Cremasco the debate between CGIL and CISL recalls a 'Don Camillo and Peppone' atmosphere, as if nothing had changed since the post-war period. During a meeting with me, CGIL and CISL activists repeatedly accused each other of 'coming from Novosibirsk' and of 'being catholic fundamentalists'. When a CISL activist started to praise the Pope's social thought, he was interrupted by his CGIL colleague who argued that the victory of capitalism was also the Pope's fault: 'he wakes up now with the problems of capitalism; he should have thought about it before dismantling communism'. In none of the plants I visited throughout Poland have I ever heard a debate of this kind.

One further point is that the attention to and the value placed on training opportunities are higher in Poland than in Italy. This is also true for language training, which confirms that there is not withdrawal into nationalism.

Ursus

Investigating the Ursus trade unions was not easy. In particular it was important to define Solidarity: if even this plant executive, the most violently nationalist in Poland, were found to be relatively open to change, the hypothesis could be strongly demonstrated *a fortiori*. This was not the case. After repeated contacts, the local leader openly refused to talk to me or to organise any meeting with activists with the following justification: 'you are not a Pole and therefore we strongly suspect you of working for foreign intelligence or other anti-Polish interest groups'. This statement is eloquent enough to make any further investigation of the Ursus Solidarity leadership redundant.

Given the strongly centralised and rigid organisation of Ursus Solidarity, access to the shop-stewards and most well-known activists was then impossible. In order to understand Solidarity's feelings of 'siege' it has also to be remembered that the plant Solidarity press-officer (known for his particularly anti-Semitic declarations) was killed under unclear circumstances in 1996. Since then the Solidarity activists have made use of the most conservative traditional Polish martyrology. It was possible, however, to talk with Solidarity rank and file during several street demonstrations in which I carried out participant observation between 1995 and 1998. Some of these conversations were recorded.

The main finding, contrasting with the schematic image given by the Polish media, is of a differentiated range of opinions among the workforce. From the talks (which took place during street demonstrations, and therefore in a social situation strongly favouring the expression of radical discourses) it emerges that Wrzodak's nationalist attitude is not dominant. It concerns only a core of the union in one workshop (the assembly line, strategically important indeed) of the Warsaw plant. The majority of the workers, and seemingly a large proportion of the Solidarity members, support Wrzodak only occasionally and instrumentally, displaying a striking awareness of the logic of 'political exchange'. In this sense, these workers appear, in spite of the reactionary ideas of their representative, as in their own way 'modern'.

By contrast, it was possible to meet officers and activists from the second union, the post-communist *Metalowcy*. The Ursus plant in Warsaw in this regard is completely different from Fiat, Danone, and even the other Ursus plant in Lublin (Eastern Poland). In all these other situations the post-communist unions are seen as more or less 'collaborative'.

In the Ursus plant in Warsaw there has recently been a role exchange. Solidarity (the biggest union with about 3,000 members) has kept a dominant control, repeatedly changing the general directors of the company since 1991 and rejecting several restructuring measures. By 1998 it had imposed a friendly director, who, for instance, supports the union's strikes against the government stating, like in March 1998, that 'between management and unions the goals are the same, only the means are different'. Since then, Solidarity has supported the new restructuring plan, involving massive layoffs and a radical process of outsourcing: the workforce was reduced from 12,000 to 6,000 in the first year, with an objective of 1,200 in the next future. In the plans, only the assembly line (Wrzodak's workshop) should remain. The *Metalowcy* (720 members), instead, have moved to purely 'union' tasks, rejecting political and management concerns. The other two unions (Popiełuszko and Engineers and Technicians' T.U.) are quite marginal.

In 1999, a dispute started between the two unions, with even the threat of a strike by *Metalowcy* against Solidarity. *Metalowcy* has accused the Solidarity-controlled management of dismissing (and 'outsourcing') in the first place the members of the other unions, and of 'saving' their own members. Accordingly, this would explain the recent increase in Solidarity membership and even the 'double membership' of some employees. In addition, *Metalowcy* complains about the social costs of the restructuring plan. These would have been easier to bear, in their opinion, if reorganisation had started four years earlier, but at that time Solidarity opposed it. *Metalowcy* also support the need to finding a foreign strategic investor (which Solidarity resolutely refuses) as a long-term solution.

This complex situation (made even more puzzling by the different case of the Lublin plant, where it is by contrast *Metalowcy* and, surprisingly, Solidarity 80 who support the management) confirms the importance of the experience of conflict for union consciousness. The lack of a shopfloor opponent after 1989 pushed Solidarity, by far the strongest union, into an 'anti-social movement', fighting against imaginary Jews and spies, and eventually into management substitution. Solidarity even created a seemingly profitable co-operative society dealing with Ursus spare parts distribution. By contrast *Metalowcy* was forced to take on the role of the employees' defender. This role was not that familiar for them, as the activists and officers themselves reveal by telling of their uneasiness and nostalgia. In a peculiar way, the 'communist legacies' of both unions were inverted by specific 'alternation' dynamics.

As to the issue of differentiation, in Ursus there are important rivalries between the Warsaw plant and the smaller factory of Lublin, where wages are about 40% lower. The process of outsourcing is starting and is changing the power relations in the company, but until now *Metalowcy* has maintained a unified representation, avoiding dualisation effects.

Daewoo

In the Daewoo factory in Warsaw, formerly FSO working under Fiat licence, it is difficult to evaluate the presence of conflict. FSO was taken over by Daewoo in 1996, after the unions had rejected an offer by General Motors proposing redundancy for 70% of the employees and the preservation of the only assembly line workshop. At the moment of privatisation a (quite generous for the employees) social pact and a collective agreement were signed, stating a 3-year moratorium on layoffs and a 5-year moratorium on strikes (the disparity itself indicates uneven power relations). As a result there has not been *open* conflict until the end of the moratorium in 1999. It should also be remembered that Daewoo (unlike Fiat, although many argue that the Italian company has also benefited from important political help) has received for the transition period conspicuous financial support from the state. This was intended to compensate for the fact that FSO, unlike FSM which was taken over by Fiat, was not deeply indebted: the financial point of departure of the two enterprises was different and this makes a comparison difficult.

In fact, only a year after privatisation conflict about wage increases broke out. In some other plants of the Daewoo group, like in Łódź, conflict has also taken adversarial forms. In Warsaw, although no strike has been called, the unions have organised rallies on various issues, but especially in support of wage demands.

In 1999, after the end of the moratorium, all the plant unions started to express serious preoccupation. This concerned primarily redundancy and outsourcing plans, but not only. The unions unanimously denounced delays in the investment plans, discrimination practices at work, unilateral work time organisation. In the Summer they held a referendum among the workforce, in which 96% of the workers said that Daewoo did not realise the expectations it had created, and 89% said to be ready to take part in industrial action in case of collective dismissals.

The strongest (3,000 members) and most active trade union is Solidarity. In this union there are voices explicitly regretting the choice of the investor, albeit not the idea of privatisation and restructuring. In particular, it is argued that Daewoo is actually surreptitiously reducing the workforce, via outsourcing.

The other three unions, Solidarity 80 (around 800 members), *Metalowcy* (600), and Engineers and Technicians' T.U. (500), are conversely more 'pacific'. This is surprising for Solidarity 80, which emerged from an essentially political split with Solidarity but which in the plant is more moderate. In any case, none of the unions has the adversarial nature of *Sierpień 80* at Fiat. Even Solidarity is not hostile to the employer, as is confirmed by the agreement between the union and Daewoo to publish a company supplement in the weekly union magazine *Tygodnik Solidarność*.

Although it is too early to evaluate the 'intensity' of conflict, it is possible to analyse its subjective forms.

Opposition to the new investor, when it emerges, makes use of nationalist arguments just as in the other foreign-owned companies ('they lay the blame on the translators', 'they don't know Polish laws' etc.). The existence of 'cultural barriers' is denounced, but they are not defined in any way. Opposition, however, never betrays racist feelings, even if in the case of South Koreans this might have happened. This remains valid also for Solidarity 80, though this union makes a stronger use of nationalist rhetoric in the definition of its own identity.

Historical references are used more often than nationalist ones. Just as with the activists from Fiat and Lucchini, the Daewoo unionists from Solidarity and Solidarity 80 construct a continuity between the former and current employer, 'inverting' the labels. The South Koreans are then charged with being 'even more communist' than the previous management: they are 'centralised', 'undemocratic', 'value loyalty above all'. The permanence of the former directors is condemned: 'these are people who cheat but who are loyal, and this is the most important thing for both communists and South Koreans'.

Daewoo is a profitable case for evaluating the chances of transnational union action. Solidarity cooperated closely with the Italian unions until 1990. Today, Solidarity and Solidarity 80 have negative opinions about Western unions, the Italian ones included. There is no cooperation with the official South Korean unions, with whom the company itself organised a meeting. The mistrust towards the latter however seems justified, since the South Korean unions proposed sharing information on 'how to increase productivity'. More significantly, Daewoo managed in 1997 to mobilise the company unions in demonstrations against the entry to Poland of its competitor Hyundai, by threatening layoffs as a reprisal if this happened. This would confirm the worst labour fears about globalisation as, basically, MNC's blackmailing.

The situation is, however, different in the two unions. Solidarity 80, uniquely in Poland, explicitly considers transnational action useless ('we don't have anything to learn from the Italians, we know our adversary pretty well'). Solidarity, by contrast, is actively involved in different international networks, like the International and the European Metalworkers' Federations. Moreover, they have contacts with the Romanian anticommunist Fratia from the Romanian Daewoo plant. They even organised training in Romania, 'like the Dutch previously trained us'.

Two Industrial Companies in Płock

Finally, two companies from a small-sized town, in a region with unemployment at 16%, were analysed. In these cases only Solidarity was considered, as it is by far the strongest union. In both cases Solidarity played an important role in the restructuring process.

At Petrochemia restructuring was carried out between 1994 and 1999. The first plan having been rejected by the unions, the final one was jointly managed by Solidarity. Massive layoffs were avoided, and the workforce reduction was relatively limited (from 9,000 to 7,200). The state gave important temporary help through protectionist measures. Now, Petrochemia, in a promising situation, is starting to search for a foreign investor but 'without hurry' and therefore with relatively high bargaining power. It already is, without foreign capital, the second Polish company (after Telekomunikacja Polska) for investments in 1998 (source: Institute of Economic Sciences, Polish Academy of Sciences). Petrochemia is itself operating a strategic investment by the take-over of CPN, the first company for fuel retailing in Poland; this operation, welcome by the Petrochemia workforce, is by contrast resisted by CPN Solidarity, fearing massive redundancy among CPN employees.

At Bizon restructuring was more complex and painful. The factory was in a desperate situation in 1990: sales had fallen from 1,000 to 300 combine harvesters per year and indebtedness was very high. Proceeding at a feverish pace, however, restructuring took the company to the break-even point, and in 1998 it was taken over by the Fiat-owned New Holland. During the restructuring Solidarity (the biggest union with a membership around 40%) had mostly operated under the form of a works council, returning to the union role after privatisation. Unlike at Petrochemia, group layoffs were unavoidable and the workforce was reduced by about 50%, to the current 1,200. However, some social criteria, and especially individual chances on the labour market, were taken into account. In that way, the oldest employees were safeguarded while the owners of small pieces of land (the typically Polish *chłopo-robotnicy*, i.e. peasant-workers) were dismissed first. Wages also had to be reduced during restructuring, almost to the minimum level, but a degree of equality was maintained: administrators were even deposed for having increased their own salaries. In Spring 1999 the company made further 150 employees redundant, because of a negative situation of the world market in general, and of the Russian crisis in particular. The unions negotiated the forms of the lay-offs without opening a conflict. This was the occasion for the first meetings and exchanges with the Western unions.

Although fragmented, the evidence from the supplementary case-studies allows us to sketch a first picture of Polish unionism, probably better than a larger but more superficial survey would do. In particular, the choice of critical and significant cases allows us to 'reject' or 'not to reject' previously formulated hypotheses as well as counterhypotheses.

Firstly, not only Danone but also the more critical case of Daewoo and to some extent *even* Ursus confirm that fears about xenophobic reactions by the Polish unions are exaggerated. Secondly, elements of a 'neo-proletarian' rhetoric and of 'economicism', as well as divergent trends in human resources management, appear *even* at Danone. Thirdly, again *even* at Danone trade-union transnational action is limited. Finally, the unions positively react to change *even* in state-owned, indebted companies in peripheral areas like Płock.

By contrast, the evidence rejects the representativeness of Fiat and Lucchini on the issue of the intensity of conflict. The comparison with Daewoo and Danone (as well as with Usinor in Piombino) reveals that a distinctly Italian anti-union management style persists, although much less than it is usually believed in Poland. This finding might be biased by the industrial sector and the plants' history (with a militant unionism), as well as by the privatisation timing (Fiat and Lucchini entered the Polish market first and, in a way, 'opened the way' for the later investors). A definitive explanation would however require an equally deep analysis of the employers' side, which remains beyond the scope of this thesis.

Other Processes of Dualisation

The divergence in the social consciousness of Italian and Polish union activists is not the only process of divergence occurring in today's world of labour. Dualism is in any case not a new topic for the sociology and the economics of work (e.g. Berger and Piore 1980). For a better understanding of dualisation, I shall mention four other processes of dualisation different from the East-West one, but equally visible in the companies which have been the subject of this study: the North vs. South Italian dualism (and in a weaker way, the West vs. East Polish one); the North vs. South *global* dualism; the core- vs. subcontractor-companies dualism; the dualisms in the workplace.

The widening of the North-South dualism in Italy is manifest in the Fiat case. Fiat workers in Turin are to a large extent immigrants from the South. In the 1970s, among their first claims was investment in the South, even at the cost of some wage restraint: the construction of the Cassino and Termoli plants in that period is seen by the activists as their success.

> The construction of the Termoli plant was a success for the union, thanks to the movement which argued that things would not go well if too many workers were concentrated in the same place [in Mirafiori]. [mf6]

Twenty years later, the construction of the green-field plant in Melfi (in the Southern region of Basilicata) arrives not as a success, but as a threat to the Turin unions. In the SATA[37] factory in Melfi wages are lower and working conditions considerably worse than in Turin (Cersosimo, 1994; Della Rocca, 1994; Rieser, 1996 and 1997). Fiat has started to take advantage of the bargaining weakness of the workers of other plants. In 1994, for the first time in an open way, Fiat set plants against each other in order to impose night-work in Termoli (Cerruti and Rieser, 1994). As a result, apprehension in the Northern unions is high.

> We swallowed the Melfi model, and we didn't like it for two reasons. First there cannot be first and second class workers, so that they are more exploited than we are (...). Second, also because it was blackmail of us in the North. [mf8]

Moreover, opinions similar to those expressed about the Poles appear about Southern workers and unions.

> We know that production in the South has taken jobs away, and conspicuously so. The factories are more rationalised and work non-stop, even though the exploitation of workers is obvious. The unions, as I've heard, in the plants in the South and in Cassino have little influence, they bargain less, they work overtime also there... they've accepted, let's say, not that they've sold themselves, but almost, let's say, in some way. [ri6]

The distance between developed and developing countries, although much more complex and deep, displays some analogy with that between Northern and Southern Italy. The issue of social clauses in international trade agreements is the most significant aspect of the tendency of Third World unions to detach themselves from the Northern working class: they easily embrace their governments' position that social clauses represent discrimination against the South by the North. Moreover, those vanguards of the Southern proletariat – the immigrants – usually do not experience particular solidarity from the Northern unions (Bataille, 1997).

Fiat also has plants in Turkey, Argentina, Brazil, joint-ventures in Egypt and India, and programs in Mexico, China and Russia. Unlike in the Polish case, the unions from the Italian plants maintain some contact with the Turkish, Argentinean, and especially Brazilian unions. This circumstance suggests that the East-West cleavage, for its ideological roots and geographic proximity (which is a source of friction), maintains a stronger meaning than the North-South one. Research evidence from these plants is too fragmentary to risk a general evaluation. Something more is known about the Fiat plant in Belo Horizonte, Brazil, thanks to an inquiry based mainly on a set of 25 interviews (Pimenta, 1996). This is not an old-fashioned factory: on the contrary, it is commonly mentioned as the best example of the new organisational model *'Fabbrica Integrata'*. The quality reorientation of work organisation in the 1990s was, however, preceded by a massive firing of unionised workers. The management attitude towards the unions directly recalls the Polish situation. In an interview a manager explains: 'At Fiat, the union has no space. This is a place to work, not to do union politics' (Pimenta, 1996, p. 411). The inquiry concluded that Fiat was developing a project of individual incorporation excluding any form of workers' representation. The antagonism between management's 'reactionary conservatism' (p. 413) and an isolated union makes the expression of conflict impossible.

Pimenta depicts in this way an extreme case of the neo-proletarianisation detected in Poland and in Southern Italy. Although contacts between Brazilian and Italian unions have existed since 1990, they are still far from amounting to effective cooperation. This is not, however, only a fault of the unions, since the employer has also intervened to prevent the construction of a 'global experience'. In April 1992, for instance, Fiat executives at the Belem plant prevented visiting Italian union officers from entering the factory to meet local supervisors.

The third form of dualism takes place within single countries, and often within single plants. This is the phenomenon of 'sub-contracting', which often creates a gap between the status of the core-company employees and their 'sub-contracted' colleagues, especially as regards flexibility. This problem, although 'local', may take on a particular relevance at the international level. With regard to the European Work Councils, the risk of segmentation between large companies with EWCs and smaller domestic producers based on national industrial relations traditions has been denounced (Schulten, 1996). The unions are indeed more and more aware of the problem, and of the futility of defending only the workers of the 'primary sector'. In Italy, some unionists went as far as to propose the introduction in the bargaining system of a 'contract of product', which would regulate the employment relations in all workplaces contributing to the production of a given good (e.g. a car), irrespective of their societal assets and geographical positions.

The theme of sub-contracting is very sensitive in all off the plants visited. Management is keen on achieving in this way at least a degree of the labour dualisation which made the success of the Japanese model. Fiat, in particular, seems to be a forerunner of 'strategic outsourcing' in comparison with other car-producers (Pessa, 2000). In Mirafiori, about one thousand internal transport workers were outsourced to the Dutch multinational TNT in 1998; altogether, 2443, about 30% of the workforce, was outsourced in the only body shop in recent years. Although the unions have obtained a guarantee that for a period of four years employment conditions will not worsen, the 'negative' selection of outsourced employees (almost 20% of them are disabled) gives rise to some anxiety.

The place where sub-contracting is more problematic is however Piombino. The most striking aspect is safety at work. In the first five months of 1998 three workers died in three accidents in the Piombino steelworks owned by Lucchini: all of them worked for contractor firms. Given the relevance of the problem, three unionists from the biggest contractor firm working in the Lusid plant have been interviewed. This firm, Siderco, deals with internal transport and maintenance work in the Lusid steelworks. It employs 130 workers, 80 per cent of whom are union members. Among other things, it emerges very high labour turn-over and frequent transfers of property. For these two reasons employees do not receive seniority benefits: after twelve years work they may still be on the lowest point of the metalworkers' wage scale. Flexibility of working time is also very high, and industrial relations are reduced to the minimum. What is however more important for my analysis of trade unionism is the widening distance between these employees and the Lusid ones.

> Then, the [contractor] companies are the weakest links. Also the unions take more care of the big firms than the small ones, and they are disdainful of them, they find other interests (...). The situations are similar, maybe some are a bit better or worse but there is an uncontrolled situation, companies that come and go, workers who enter and leave. If I must be objective, the union doesn't have any real insight into the situation, only a partial one.
> The relationship with the steelworks [Lusid] union is difficult, we meet at the meetings of the local trade union executive, or personally if somebody knows someone else. For me it's different because I grew old inside, and there is also personal friendship, but the new delegates who don't know anybody, how can they have a relationship with the steelworks' delegates, there isn't any co-ordination. It would be very useful. There is no willingness to make it because there is the negative tendency to close themselves into their own shell, they also have other problems. I can understand it, the Lusid delegate has his own problems and tries to solve them. If he doesn't take care of us but does solve his own problems, he cuts a fine figure, never mind, the others will think about the rest. [sf1]

The worse working conditions and industrial relations of these companies recall the dualisation idea. There are indeed analogies between the Siderco company and the Polish ones, like for instance the move of conflict from collective bargaining and workplace relations to the tribunal, as the last resource for defending workers' rights.

In Poland the situation is identical: at Fiat Auto Poland 2,430 workers were being outsourced in 1999-2000 only. Polish unions have up to now managed to control the subcontracting process (called by the Italian management *terziarizzazione*) and maintain an influence on the outsourced companies. This nonetheless causes a certain apprehension.

> Now they say that *tercjaryzacja* [Polish neologism invented by the Italian management to translate *terziarizzazione*] starts. Such a word doesn't exist in any dictionary of the Polish language. Basically it consists of splitting firms into smaller ones. This is a problem for the unions. We believe that they do it in order to avoid paying taxes. [tp1]

In the newly established companies the unions have a hard time. By contrast, in both Italy and Poland, the unions may resist the process of subcontracting at the moment of outsourcing. When a part of the workforce is alienated, the alarm among the employees is such that unionisation jumps instead of dropping. In Tychy, the unions are very engaged on this front.

> They know that by moving, they won't resist so long. They don't change working conditions, they have guaranteed for one year the same conditions as they now have, but after one year something might change. For this reason they are afraid for their future, and they set up a union, at the moment of outsourcing when the new firm is established, the same day the trade union *Sierpień 80* is constituted, there is a group of specialised people. So people trust the union, they don't set up other unions. [ta1]

This tale illustrates the singular ease with which Tychy unions face subcontracting. However, this is not that exceptional: Polish unions altogether seem effective in this regard. At Fiat in Bielsko-Biała as well as at *Huta Lucchini* Solidarity has withstood the same process by organising itself into an 'inter-company' trade union, representing both 'mother' and 'affiliated' employees. The same solution was found at Ursus. In the steel sector, the unions made guarantees for the 'outsourced' employees a central topic in the negotiation of the steel-sector restructuring plan. Strong union control of outsourcing is in place at Petrochemia Płock and at the smaller Rafineria Gdańska. The unions of Daewoo encountered some problems with outsourcing, but in this case the unions also remained united and the workforce of the 'mother' plant backed the workers of the 'peripheral' ones. In the energy sector the situation is more differentiated, with the positive case of the Wrocław power station and the negative one of Cracow (Soufflet, 1998).

In general, in Poland the 'subcontracted' unionists do not display a proletarian rhetoric and pessimism like their counterparts at Siderco (in Piombino) or TNT (in Turin). Their relationships with the 'mother-company' unions are more balanced than in Italy. This situation suggests a hypothesis related to the previous discussion of the impact of alternation. Perhaps precisely because they are not rooted in a given type of employment relations, Polish unions sometimes turn out to be better equipped than the Italian ones when facing changes in employment conditions.

The last form of dualisation is internal to the companies and the plants. It occurs between genders, between professional levels, and between age groups. Sometimes innovations in work organisation increase this differentiation, as has been noted about the 'dualising' effects of the *Fabbrica Integrata* at Fiat (Rieser, 1996). Even an author rather positively disposed towards Fiat's 'Japanese' reorientation remarks that at Mirafiori unskilled workers, in the 1993-95 period, received on average only 2,5 hours of training, whereas their supervisors received 100 (Bonazzi, 1998).

To conclude, the various forms of dualisation among countries and companies suggest that the disarticulation of working-class consciousness (the separation of 'pride' and 'proletarian' consciousness) described by Touraine, Dubet and Wieviorka (1987) could assume a spatial dimension. On the one hand, the preservation in the most developed countries and regions, and in the core-companies, of sophisticated production and stable employment relations might lead workers to a corporatist defence of occupational interests, sometimes masked by ideology. On the other, the transfer of labour-intensive production and the search for lower costs, especially if under foreign control, could favour neo-proletarian consciousness. In this case, trade unionism would have great difficulty in unifying workers. The new conditions require a re-examination of the bases for collective action.

Notes

1   For the same reason, the Italian Fismic and UGL were preliminarily excluded.
2   A similar divergent East-West trend has been observed between the emphasis placed on material needs by ex-GDR workers as compared with the post-material needs of Western German workers (Lattard, 1995).

3   Of course wages are not irrelevant for Italian workers. A survey of Turin workers (not just union activists) indicates that 58.3% of manual workers consider wages an important problem. However, most of them are also concerned by other issues, and only 12.7% may be defined as coherently 'wage-oriented' (Cerruti and Rieser, 1999).

4   As a cultural explanation, the religious variable might be used. Italian restraint on economic issues might be due to the deeply Catholic and anti-Calvinist (in the Weberian sense) Italian culture. Of course, the Polish culture is equally, or more, Catholic, but it was for a long time influenced by Protestantism: between 1569 and the First Partition in 1772 Roman Catholics accounted for barely half of the total population, and the principle of toleration governed inter-religious relations, attracting the persecuted from any religion from any part of Europe. In the second half of the XVI century the Calvinists even constituted one of the most powerful groupings in political life, commanding the allegiance of an estimated 20% of the nobility together with an absolute majority among the lay members of the Senate (Davies, 1981, pp. 159ff). By contrast, Italy has never been religiously pluralist. Moreover, during the partitions in the XIX century and Bismark's *Kulturkampf*, which eventually strengthened the identification Pole=Catholic, the Catholic identity took quite a different form than that in Southern European countries. As Therborn (1995, p. 106) argues, sociologically the Catholic-Protestant divide is probably not theological but a matter of ecclesiastical authority. In this sense, Polish ecclesiastical authority under the Partitions and communism developed in a very particular form. Today, although Poles rank very high in Church attendance (88.2% at least once a month compared to 51.1% in Italy, according to the ISSP 1992), they are 'less' Catholic in their political, economic, and moral judgements: the Church did not procure authority on these issues.

5   I refer here to the '*vulgata*' of Maslow's thought, very popular in psychology, sociology, and marketing. Maslow himself was actually aware, at least in his later writings, that one need had not to be totally fulfilled before the 'next' need became activated: the emergence of a need was then defined as gradual and not as a sudden phenomenon. Similarly, he was aware that 'pay' was not important only at the level of physical needs, but also at other, higher levels.

6   Berger and Piore, in their fundamental study of economic dualism, remark:
Since the quality of human experience varies greatly across the segments into which the society and economy divide, and since it varies critically in ways which are not captured by a single variable like income, life experiences seem virtually incommensurate. Is the self-employed street vendor of Bogotà better or worse off then the industrial worker of the Ford assembly line in Detroit? It is difficult enough to compare the two, let alone decide who is better off. (Berger and Piore, 1980, p. 11)

7   This is the finding of the most accurate analyses of real income indicators (Milic-Czerniak, 1998). The rise in income, however, is shown not only by very dubious statistical data. Precise statistical evaluations of real income are almost impossible in transitional economies because of the drastic change in the basket, of an alteration in the relative value of time and money, and of the weight of the informal sector. A participant observation of Polish standards of living during the last eight years has been more revealing.

8   Actually, the East-West category also affects the identities of very rich Eastern-Europeans. So speaks, for instance, the Croat football star Zvonimir Boban, who plays in Italy for AC Milan: 'If I had been a Western, you would have judged me a

phenomenon. We from the East, instead, carry the label of indolent' (from *Il Corriere della Sera*, 24.2.99).

9   In 1991 important laws on trade unions and on collective disputes were passed; in 1993 the 'pact for the enterprise' was signed and the tripartite commission was created; in 1994 the law on collective bargaining was passed, and in 1996 the new Code of Labour. The social 'partners', and especially the employers, have since repeatedly called for a revision of these regulations, which suggests that the institutionalisation is still incomplete and perhaps unachievable.

10   In Italy strikes in the private sector are not regulated, apart from the article of the Constitution stating the 'right to strike'. In Poland, by contrast, a law of 1991 provides detailed regulation. Only, when compared to reality this appears to be an 'over-regulation', and it generally remains a dead letter. This suggests that today's problem is not a lack of institutional regulation.

11   The three interviews from the Siderco company have not been considered, as they do not have a direct Polish counterpart.

12   I shall not analyse the opinions of the higher hierarchical levels because I hold only a very limited knowledge of them, and, above all, the topic of this research is a sociology of the trade unions and of the working class. However, indirect information (through for instance former interpreters) and occasional conversations suggest that Italian executives successfully developed a representation of the Poles as basically 'different', which psychologically justifies a treatment distinct from that reserved for Italian employees.

13   There is some truth in this assertion. The trade unions from Lusid (ex-Ilva) and from the Magona D'Italia (which was also owned by Lucchini, but has always been private) have different orientations (Magona is traditionally more radical) and are sometimes antagonistic. However, solidarity usually prevails among the two plants.

14   This tale, after having visited the union offices in the Piombino plant, sounds strange but not unrealistic: FIOM delegates never wear ties, but the FIM ones do. The paradox lies in the fact that it is at *Huta Warszawa* that full-time union officers always wear ties. This tale is in any case meaningful as to the Polish representation of the Italian unions.

15   Indeed, nationalist arguments are more easily exploited against nationalities with which the Poles were used to having difficult relations. Interesting are the workers' tales, for instance, from a German company which has recently been an object of research.
'Once the team went out for a cigarette, and the German foreman started screaming at them around the canteen: "smoking is forbidden, smoking is forbidden!". Then a guy said to him "what's this, Auschwitz?". The German immediately shut up'. (...) 'People here are scared, you know how Germans treated the Poles (...) We say Auschwitz because the foreman walks around the workshop and continuously repeats "*nicht spazieren, nicht diskutieren, Arbeit, Arbeit!*", like in a camp'. (Marcinowski, 1998, p. 98)

16   During the strike at Huta Lucchini in 1994 the media rapidly shifted from sympathy to hostility when the unions suggested continuing production under workers' control. In the Fiat case as well, the media are usually hostile to workers' arguments but sensitive to nationalist ones. The use of nationalist arguments against Fiat is surprising in the liberal, Western-oriented press, like for instance in the article '*Polska Fiata*' ('Fiat's Poland') in the right-wing, liberal magazine *Wprost* (n.2, 1995).

17   In particular, the *Lega Nord* in Northern Italy (1996 parliamentary elections), the FPÖ in Austria (1995 and 1999 parliamentary elections), and the *Front National* in France (1995 presidential elections) have become the first party among industrial workers.

18   See document of the Executive Committee of the 5th League FIOM (the local union of Mirafiori and Rivalta) on the 13th March 2000. See also the declarations of FIOM national secretary Sabattini and regional secretary Cremaschi on *Il Manifesto*, 14.3.00 and 15.3.00.

19   However, the ETUC did not oppose European Union enlargement eastward, unlike the French FO and CGT who in the 1980s opposed the enlargement to Spain and Greece. Also the US unions opposed the NAFTA agreement, but this is a different case from the EU, as it did not include any political or social integration; by contrast, after the NAFTA implementation forms of ad hoc cooperation between US and Mexican unions developed, especially in the border region thanks to that *Kreuzung sozialer Kreise* which I shall indicate as a determinant factor. In the same way, interesting cases of international union cooperation have developed in the border regions between Germany and Poland or the Czech Republic (Friedrich Ebert Stiftung, 1999).

20   The analysis of these data must be undertaken extremely cautiously since they have an epistemological status even lower than those presented in Table 4.1. While Table 4.1, and all of chapter 3, analysed *references* and therefore respected the coherence of each interview and were not strongly influenced by differences of narrative, Table 4.2 and this section will carry out a more risky *thematic* analysis. Themes, or issues, may vary, and change meaning, across the interviews for very different reasons. A supplementary difficulty is that of distinguishing *positive* and *negative* attitudes on issues such as privatisation or globalisation. An attitudes analysis becomes meaningful only if it analytically distinguishes between the openness/rejection and the radicalism/moderation axes. An attempt in this direction has been made throughout the coding of interviews. Reports have been considered positive where there is an acceptance that a particular problem has to be dealt with and where it is seen as a possible area for union action, including those cases where this is associated with a radically critical view of the same.

21   The significance level would be much higher, but misleading, if the 'no information' interviews were included in the Chi squared test.

22   The peak in Fiat's recruiting of Southern-Italian immigrants occurred in 1961-63 with 22,000 arrivals. The massive migration to Turin from the South was the subject of a classic piece of research (Fofi, 1964/1975). Also Piombino, not because of immigration but because of its geographic position, has close relations with rural society. The rural element therefore cannot be a distinguishing factor between Italy and Poland.

23   The interviewee is clearly referring respectively to: the PLI (Italian Liberal Party) and the PRI (Italian Republican Party); the DC (Christian Democracy); the PCI (Italian Communist Party). None of these parties exists anymore, but for the interviewee nothing has changed. The blood-suckers are corrupted public employees and criminal organisations.

24   At the official level there are no differences between the Warsaw and Piombino unions on the environmental issue, as both have resolutely demanded non-polluting production. In Warsaw the problem had in the past opposed the plant to the district, which in November 1991 even demanded the closing of the steelworks. However, it was basically resolved, especially by closing the Martens furnaces, with the decisive contribution of the trade unions (which at that time had a decisive role in the joint-

venture company). In Piombino the problem is more complicated because of the blast-furnaces and the cokery, and it is still not definitely solved although an important agreement on restructuring and reclamation was signed by company and local authorities in 1998.

25   The control of internal mobility, although in itself is not the fundamental aspect of the work conflict, is extremely important for developing collective action.

26   The Polish miners indeed occasionally organise protest demonstrations, especially when the government's promises are not maintained. These protests are, however, usually rational and much more pacific than those which accompanied similar changes in Western Europe in the 1980s (especially in England, the model country of Polish liberal reformers).

27   Following the 1990 Law on Privatisation of State-Owned Enterprises, a large number of enterprises have been transformed into joint-stock, 100% Treasury-owned companies, as a first step (commercialisation) towards privatisation.

28   Another explanation of the Polish 'market utopia' and repudiation of alternatives has been suggested by Maurice Glasman (1994) drawing on Karl Polanyi's *The Great Transformation* (1944). According to Glasman, in Poland after 1989 a kind of 'market utopia' sprang up as a reaction to decades of oppressive state paternalism, just as happened in England in the early XIX Century as a reaction to the social paternalism of the Speenhamland scale welfare policy. However, Polanyi's scheme fails when it predicts a collective social reaction against the market (which has not taken place in Eastern Europe). Moreover, as it has been remarked by Kowalik (1994), Glasman's point is too evolutionary and constructivist, and misses the complexity of the process when he contrasts the 'stagnant paternalism' of pre-1989 Poland with the 'libertarian atomisation' of post-1989 even more simplistically than the 'transition' theorists do.

29   Ost and Weinstein (1999) argue that a role has been played by the experience of many Poles working as *Gastarbeiter* in the West. Through this specific experience, they would have learnt that working outside union protection (and even against unions' advise) is profitable. In my interviews, however, I have found no evidence of this factor, although a few interviewees told of having worked abroad.

30   PCI general secretary (1972-1984), author of the so-called breach (*strappo*) from the Soviet Union in 1981 (after Jaruzelski's 'auto-golpe').

31   This does not mean that multinational capital is distinctly 'nasty' with the trade unions. Extensive research suggests that local private capital may be even more hostile to the trade unions (Gardawski, Gąciarz, Mokrzyszewski and Pańków, 1999), and similar indications come from other postcommunist countries.

32   In 1991 the unemployment rate was 5.5 in the West and 10.4 in the East, in 1998 respectively 9.4 and 18.7 (Source: Deutsche Bundesbank).

33   In Piombino the suspicion of a typically Italian adversarial management is strongly supported by the events at *Magona* in 1998-99. This steelworks, which under Lucchini saw a permanent conflict between unions and management, was sold to the French Usinor in 1999. Immediately the situation improved and according to the unions bargaining and information are now excellent.

34   Another French-based multinational company, Thomson, has been viewed in Poland as a particularly positive case (Durand and Le Goff, 1996; Durand, 1997). Moreover, at Thomson in Italy there have been protests against production transfers to Poland. Durand and Le Goff's account itself, though generally benevolent toward the management, raises some interesting doubts: workers complain about norms and

stress; the management system has remained basically authoritarian (unlike the Western plants); salary and professional differentials have considerably increased.

35   The *Komitet Obrony Robotników* (Workers' Defence Committee), founded by a number of intellectuals and dissidents like Jacek Kuroń and Jan Józef Lipski, initiated the workers-intellectuals dialogue which proved so important for Solidarity four years later. In Italy, the 1976 events in Ursus and Radom pushed Enrico Berlinguer, PCI general secretary, to explicitly condemn, for the first time, the Polish communist authorities. On the 1976-1980 period at Ursus see Żbikowska and van Kooten (1990).

36   In Warsaw there are about 240 workers; the Independent Union of the Milk Industry has about 80 members, Solidarity (which formerly had 120 members) only 40, ¾ of whom are male technicians.

37   Just as the foreign transplants of Fiat do not directly belong to Fiat Auto (but for instance in Poland to Fiat Auto Poland), also the Melfi plant has different corporate structure and belongs to a distinct company, SATA. This solution facilitates the differentiation of human resources management. The most extreme case is the Turkish one, where the factories belong to Fiat, but the personnel to a Turkish company. In this way, in 1998 it was very easy for Fiat to refuse any responsibility when the Italian unions protested at the massive firing of unionised workers in the Turkish factory.

5 The Challenge of Difference

The Transformation of Trade Union Commitment

The End of Activism?

This chapter will discuss how the activists see the differentiation which is occurring at work and was described in the previous two chapters. This issue directly affects the problems of solidarity and the motives for political participation. It is therefore necessary to describe initially the situation of union commitment. In fact, the investigation in the plants has revealed that trade union activism still exists, but major changes have occurred.

During the inquiry, only rank-and-file workers were interviewed, full-time unionists being excluded. The majority of the sample (58 out of 91) did carry on trade union functions (mainly as shop-floor delegates), but this never implied more than a few hours a week of paid union work. While non-unionised workers and the most radical unions often make insinuations about the abusing of this 'union' time, the reality subjectively recounted by the interviewees was obviously very different. They evinced the personal costs (in terms of time and of loss of career chances) involved in union activity. Since the interviews were always carried out for free and during workers' free time, it may be assumed that at least some voluntary commitment endures.

To some extent, trade union activism has always also been a channel for social promotion which was an alternative to a work career. Within the automobile factories this was already showed in the late 1940s by Chinoy's in-depth study in the United States (Chinoy, 1955). However, today workers report, in Italy as well as in Poland, that the office of delegate has lost much of its attractiveness, to the point that sometimes the unions have trouble finding enough candidates. Although professionalism has increased in the unions of both East and West, the figure of the activist – and of its most institutionalised form of the delegate or shop steward – emerges as complex and involved in a mix of social relations with the workforce that cannot be reduced to the representative-represented pattern. The reality of trade union activity I encountered in the plants strongly differs from the bureaucratic one of trade union local offices which in Italy has been splendidly described by Manghi (1996). The continuous movement of people, the continuous discussion about everyday work problems, the self-distancing from the trade union central organisation, the maintenance of 'identity incentives' indicate a still lively reality. Most workers still identify the trade union as being the shop-stewards and activists.[1] The simple fact that unions' membership is highly variable among workshops indicates the importance of the rank and file activists' local role. In Poland, the activists report that people re-joined Solidarity in 1989 only in those workshops where union activity was visible, regardless of national-level political questions.

The constant tension, in both countries, between workplace representatives and central trade unions confirms the existence of an autonomous role at the rank-and-file level. In this regard, the trade union cannot be reduced to 'an organisation of trade unionists' (Ciafaloni, 1994). In some cases the opposite might even be said: union activism may become similar to other forms of voluntary work, and unionists may play the role of *'entrepreneurs altruistes'* (Bode, 1997). The Italian trade unions' claims to have at their disposal 300,000 voluntary unionists besides the 20,000 full-time officers (De Sanctis, 1996) are probably exaggerated. Nonetheless, there is even less evidence for the opposite statement, i.e. that voluntary activists have disappeared. In both Italy and Poland trade union commitment resists much better than political party commitment, which instead has certainly dropped dramatically. All interviewees agree on this point, and one from Turin comments: 'the party can survive without us, in the factory on the contrary without us the union would disappear' [mc6].

If trade union activists cannot be associated with the 'professionals' of the unions, neither can they any longer be assimilated with the workforce. The 91 interviewees who are the subject of this study are not representative of the employees of the six plants not only because they do not constitute a representative sample in statistical terms. Much more, this is due to the patent discontinuity between workers and unions, which was at best evinced by the frequent feeling of isolation and loneliness among the activists described in chapter 3. This breach between the workers and the trade unions is among the components of working class decomposition, but only when it is connected to the other 'constants of disintegration'. That is, only when it is linked to a wider social and historical process (bureaucratisation, gap between generations, nostalgia...). As such, the feelings of isolation and disappointment with the behaviour of the rank and file are not a novelty. They are sociologically immanent in any social organisation which is not perfectly egalitarian. In Italy, these feelings among unionists were already described in the early 1980s by Ida Regalia

(1984), and in Poland they can be easily detected in the materials of Touraine's 1981 inquiry on Solidarity (Touraine, Dubet, Wieviorka and Strzelecki, 1983).

Nonetheless, some changes are taking place. The profile of the activist is less clear than in the past, and not only the *iconography* of the past. In Poland change is made macroscopic by the political turning point of 1989: the decision to become a union activist no longer has the meaning of a life-choice, as it did during the period of clandestine activity.

> I joined the union when it officially didn't exist, when it was illegal. We paid the fees and it worked, and at that time among people it was interesting. Because simply joining the union took place under specific conditions. First, three weeks of environmental interview, during which the candidate introduced himself, what he thought, that he did not create threats for the organisation. [bs2]

More generally, and not only in Poland, the traditional figure of the 'militant' appears old-fashioned, apart from the case of the particularly nostalgic Mirafiori FIOM. Most interviewees themselves avoid idyllic or epic representations of their own commitment, aware that those images are today backfiring in the relations with the employer as well as with employees. As a matter of fact, sociology is increasingly critical of the concept of the 'militant'(which in English has never been popular, as it was in Italian and French): 'the image of the militant, as well as of the crusader, inspires diffidence rather than admiration' (Touraine, 1997, p. 73).

The field evidence allows us to say more than this. The classic theories of political participation should be revisited in the case of today's unionism. They usually distinguish three concentric circles of participants: sympathisers, members, and militants.[2] In the case of unionism this has never corresponded to reality in countries having some kind of 'closed shop' clause or, for any other reason, an institutionally-founded very high union density. Nevertheless, for decades it has represented a suitable description of the unions in Latin countries. Typically, the unions at Fiat Mirafiori have always preferred securing larger support for mobilisation purposes to increasing unionisation, which has always remained much below the national average.

Nowadays, not only, as we shall see in more detail, has the central circle of 'militants' changed its nature, often reducing in its size, but the two other circles have inverted their size and are no longer concentric (Figure 5.1).

Figure 5.1 - Models of union participation

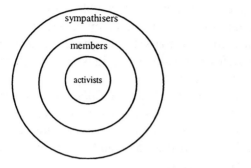
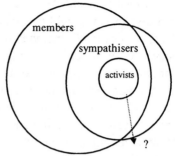

classic view of political participation   today's trade unions

Today, as is acknowledged by the unionists themselves, it is entirely possible to join a union without really supporting its action. This is confirmed by the fact that in opinion polls the orientations of union members do not significantly differ from those of the larger workers' population (e.g. Marini, 1997). In the plants included in this study, the clearest example is given by the referenda organised at Lusid in Piombino on which many union members voted against the unions' proposals. This point makes the issue of union democracy more delicate than ever before, as one can see from the current debate (see for instance Fraser, 1998). In this regard, as in many others mentioned in the previous chapter, Poland is not behind but is rather a vanguard. For instance, in 1998 right-wing members of the ruling coalition proposed that workers should be given the right to expel the unions from their workplaces by majority ballot.[3] This initiative is interesting not for its content, impudently anti-worker and anti-union, but because it is evidence of the critical relationship between democracy and unionism. Union density has clearly become unreliable as an indicator of trade union strength. Necessary instead is a careful analysis of the changing *meanings* of trade union commitment, which will be attempted in this chapter.

A supplementary point is the position of the 'activists'. One might also suggest, with regard to Figure 5.1, that the inner circle of activists is moving across the borders of the members and the sympathisers (as shown by the arrow). In fact, one interviewee (ta6) had *not* joined the union, and a few others did it only after a first period of 'independent' activism. Among the new, radical unions (Cobas, *Sierpień 80* and others) membership clearly does not correspond to union strength: many workers support the unions though they do not join them, or even though they are members of other unions. In the other unions, the activists are often in sharp divergence with the organisation. The transformation of union membership is sometimes extreme. At Ursus there are even cases of 'double membership'. In Italy, in some public companies workers change union several times a year, in a sort of 'membership cards free market'. All these phenomena argue for a process of union *deinstitutionalisation*, in spite of all the simultaneous phenomena of bureaucratisation.

In many unions, especially in the most radical like *Cobas* but not only there, a criticism of the idea of delegation is expressed in even more precise terms. This criticism at the same time emerges from a wider crisis of representative democracy and of its institutions, and on an emerging search for *subjectivity*, as I shall show below.

Among the plants there are important differences in the form of union commitment. First, an *institutional* factor distinguishes the Polish from the Italian delegates. Whereas the Italian RSU are elected by the whole workforce (unionised and non-unionised), the Polish delegates are elected only by the union members. Nevertheless, in both countries collective bargaining, and even more everyday shopfloor industrial relations, is in the hands of plant unions, not of external officers.

Moreover, there are differences in the 'intensity' of union activism. The best ground on which to evaluate these differences is not the subjective discourses given in the interviews, but the experience of access to the fieldwork. While some unions (especially Cobas, Piombino FIOM, and *Sierpień 80*) were very co-operative and easily found a number of people to speak with, the case was different particularly with the unions from Rivalta (with the possible exception of FIM) and Warsaw, where the 'activists' were somehow more 'hidden'. Warsaw Solidarity is in this regard an extreme example. Although no other company was devoted so much time as the *Huta Lucchini-Warszawa*, it proved very difficult to find a quantitatively and qualitatively sufficient sample to interview. This difficulty was partly due to the scarcity of free time among Warsaw workers, because of the almost universal possession of second jobs and the times of transport in the Polish capital. But this was only one side of the coin. The plant union leadership, albeit personally very cooperative, heavily interfered in the access to the lower level of the unions. The interviewees were mostly selected according to their closeness to the leadership's views, and the approach to other people was discouraged. Moreover, the first interviews took place in the presence of an union officer, who often intervened (this also happened with the Popiełuszko union in Tychy). These elements raise the issue of tensions with the rank and file experienced by unions undertaking a participative or a political engagement, like the Rivalta and Warsaw ones. One of the interviewees from the Huta expresses it in the most straightforward way.

> By contrast, as regards the top of our union, that is the *prezydium*, I think that there is some misunderstanding, that is myself I don't really know what should I think. But our terribly low wages result from negotiations between the unions and the employer, and often I question precisely this, why that little. Some people argue that this is definitely not that little, I don't know where this comes from, whether from the understanding of the difficult situation by the unions... Because I wouldn't like to suspect that there is some kind of unwillingness, I think that somehow the employers come nearer to our unions, and this leads to the moderate demands on wages. [hs8]

The End of Work?

Besides the thesis of the end of activism, another recent stream of thought draws pessimistic conclusions with regard to the trade unions. The idea that work has lost its power as a social integrator and as a source for identities has been developed either on philosophical grounds (e.g. Méda, 1995) or on economic ones (e.g. Rifkin, 1995), or even on both at the same time (e.g. Boissonnat, 1995). Sociology has had a hard time in finding its place in this debate. The fieldwork carried out in the Italian and Polish workplaces, however, suggests that sociological research, through an open access to workers' points of view, might contribute by assessing and possibly correcting unilateral theoretical statements.

The older activists remember when engagement in the factory was central if compared to the rest of social life. In heavily industrialised areas like Turin and Silesia, union activity was predominant in comparison with political and cultural involvement. In Turin, the party was the 'transmission belt' of the union, and the University turned around the factory, not the opposite. In Silesia, if compared to the other Polish regions, the focus of Solidarity in 1980-81 was on union action rather than on political or national engagement (Touraine, Wieviorka, Dubet and Strzelecki, 1983). Nowadays, Tychy union activists remember with some nostalgia the time when Solidarity cared about people at work.

The work experience has changed namely in its 'collective' and socialising nature. At Mirafiori, until the 1970s the 'density' of workers was even excessive, to the point of creating security problems. Nowadays, many work posts are so distant among each other, that the communication among workers is impossible. At the Lucchini steelworks in Piombino, the elderly workers remember the times when they had lunch in specific rooms (*refettoi*) in each workshop, and how this was important for the socialisation of the teams. Now, they all have lunch in the canteen, which has certainly been a material improvement but has dissolved the homogeneous worker groups into a two-thousands-employees mass.

Nowadays, the framework of a worker's choice to engage him or herself in the union is more complex, and seems to have lost its 'centre' in the workplace. However, getting rid of the current complexity by simply concluding that work has lost any meaning would be an attestation of intellectual laziness. If the problem were reduced to the alternative 'either the end of work or the endurance of work', the evidence rather supports the latter hypothesis. In this sense, a qualitative micro-sociological study like mine (in any case not representative as it concentrates on the 'hard core' of industrial work) basically confirms the macro-sociological results according to which not that much has changed in the role of work in modern Western societies (Crouch, 1999). Therefore, the idea of the 'end of work' is useful if it induces the investigation of the new, complex and multisided interplay between life spheres; it is by contrast sterile if aims at justifying the lack of interest in work. What does matter, therefore, is not the 'end' of work but its changing, differentiated and individualised meanings.

Especially, but not only, in the still working-class based unions of the *Sierpień 80* type, free time is represented as basically 'empty' time: 'after work, the best thing is to go to bed, to rest, the day after to work again' [ta6]. The activists of this union see any sort of problem as the consequence of the work situation: 'and these problems at work flow over into the home setting' [ta2]. What is more, is that also in the other unions, where work has lost much of its meaning for union consciousness, the rejection of work as a value is extremely rare: in only three interviews (out of ninety one) is work represented as marginal or as simply something from which to escape. We are not entering a kind of Greek *polis* where people, finally free from work, are concerned only by culture and leisure. Life-sphere experiences outside the workplace, although often mentioned and sometimes important, rarely affect the social reality of the trade unions: usually, an invisible barrier still isolates the unions from the world outside.

> I have some very good friends among the colleagues – we go out, we have fun, but we ignore all the problems (...). I meet the others outside work, but we avoid speaking about work. It is as if one said: OK, we're friends, but don't touch work because we think in different ways. We don't raise the serious problems because they might affect the friendships. [ri4]

Another point on the enduring role of the experience of work emerges with a particular distinctness, although it would require more accurate analysis. The influence of the media, which according to common post-modern and post-industrial views should have replaced class position in opinion 'making', appears to be secondary. Only one case of an activist motivated in the first place by mass-media information has been encountered. Interestingly enough, this is the case of an extreme-left-wing supporter of Mirafiori Cobas.

> Then, this choice of Cobas was almost for... I approached these ideas while listening to Bertinotti[4] on TV, I say, damn, in this world of useless people where FIOM, where the unionist takes a coffee with the personnel director, at least this one is saying, as Nanni Moretti[5] says, 'something left-wing'. [mc3]

The other interviewees either do not mention the media, or do it only in order to criticise it. Not only explicit, but also implicit or unconscious references seem rare, although this would require a more systematic test. Generally, the workers display a very suspicious, if not hostile, attitude towards the media. They show in this way the remains of a cultural 'otherness' as well as the subjective capacity to take points of view alternative to the dominant ones. Whether this cultural 'otherness' eventually perpetuates a cultural subordination, in the way the 'otherness' of working-class children reinforces their social disadvantage at school (Willis, 1977), is an open question for further research.

The Indefinite Borders of Working Time

On the issue of the role of work in activists' lives more can be said by analysing their use and representation of time.

Here, a distinction should be made between working hours and working years. As to the working life, in Italy there is indeed a major shift of workers' attention from work to extra-work: the issue of pensions has become in recent years of fundamental importance. Many older unionists regret that while in the past the goal of the workers was to 'change the workplace', today it is to 'escape the workplace as soon as possible'. In this sense they realised Gorz's (1988) ideas of liberation *from* work instead of *at* work. In Poland the issue of pensions has gained the headlines only very recently. It has been of great importance only in the case of the steelworkers and (especially) of the miners, who in December 1998 and in May 1999 mobilised to defend their right to early retirement. In the interviews carried out in Poland the topic of pensions is almost totally absent. Although pensions reform was being discussed in Poland in recent years, this was never to become an issue for mass protest movements like the one that, on the same question, provoked Berlusconi's downfall in autumn 1994.[6]

The issue of working time on the day- or week-base is different. In both countries the unions, although not very forcefully, have been claiming in the last years a reduction of working time at the national level. The shop-floor experience is however much more complex.

First, in all the plants, whether in Italy or in Poland, overtime work was widespread, at least until the slump in the steel sector and of Fiat Auto Poland in 1998-99. Moreover, it is basically outside the control of the unions, although in Italy a frequent and incisive form of industrial action is precisely the overtime ban. 42% of Turin manual workers doing overtime say that it is under unilateral management control (Cerruti and Rieser, 1999). For this reason, the meaning of a legal reduction of working time is for the rank-and-file activists puzzling. In both Italy and Poland there are legal or contractual limits to overtime work (in both countries 150 hours per year, with exceptions for specific sectors and activities), and a central claim by the employers is to raise them. However, the concrete realities display important differences: in the Italian contractor companies and in the Polish plants overtime work seems to have become completely out of control, with peaks of 50 hours in a month. Altogether, the overtime average in the Tychy plant in 1997 was 108 hours during the year. This figure, however, hides important variations among workshops, positions and seasons. To give a term of comparison, at the same time Turin metalworkers put in an average 72 hours of overtime.

An even more important issue is that of second jobs. These are unfortunately, like the whole sphere of informal economy, a much too neglected topic of economic sociology. In Italy a worthy exception to the overall scientific indifference is the work done by Gallino (1982 and 1985). The quota of employees having a second job in Italy in the early 1980s was estimated to be *at least* 15%. However, more important than their inevitably speculative estimations are some remarks by Gallino's team on the *meaning* of second jobs. Having a second job is normally resisted by the unions, and subsequently the bi-occupied are commonly seen as a sort of class traitors. Accordingly, the relationship between bi-occupied and unions should be uneasy. In fact, it was discovered that, in the Turin area, the bi-occupied were *more* likely to join unions and parties than average. Although Gallino's sample was almost certainly biased,[7] the finding maintains its importance and its sociological interpretation is interesting.

This group of bi-occupied is endowed (has endowed itself) with high self-entrepreneurial capacities, which means that it is able to organise in a particularly efficient and effective way its own resources. Which resources? First, time, as it is documented also in the chapter on the family, but also the information necessary to achieve objectives (...). It is simply a kind of complex weaving between actor and system, between individual and collective strategies. It is a lay approach, modern and not traditional, to party membership and the political system. It is not at all coincidental that this behaviour is realised in a larger proportion by the young bi-occupied. (Milanaccio, 1982, pp. 322-3)

This interpretation, courageous at the time it was written, finds today some corroboration from the Polish case, and particularly from the Warsaw one. Here, second jobs are basically conventional among industrial workers. This may explain how they can survive with their salaries and Warsaw costs of living, but this is not the issue here. Rather what is interesting is the fact that many union activists and members also have a second job, and that this supplementary experience may actually reinforce workers' awareness and commitment.

I do extra work in different firms, private and not. The relations between employers and employees are a jungle, absolutely a jungle. If the boss has got work, then the employees come to work, if he hasn't, 'well, stay at home'. [hs6]

The conception of trade union commitment described by Gallino and Milanaccio in the 1980s, and by the Polish activists in the 1990s, suggests that the interference of experiences may be a resource for union commitment and solidarity in a new, 'subjective' way, as I shall define it below. This type of bi-occupied commitment is different from that noticed in Piombino, where, in spite of high unemployment, second jobs are also frequent (60% altogether according to union officers, but including minor countryside jobs). In this case the support for some union claims on pensions or on working hours is purely instrumental. The issue of retirement age is notable.

In the factory there are workers with second jobs, and normally these are the most angry [workers], because those close to the age of retirement who have second jobs hope to take their pension and make the second job full-time. [pf1]

Besides, the amount of working time (including both overtime and second jobs) in Warsaw has consequences that reinforce the dualisation and neo-proletarisation trends described in the previous chapter.

> In my case, in the last month I worked Saturdays or Sundays six times, that is 48 hours, this month I already have 42 hours, we worked both Saturday and Sunday last week, but there isn't any other way to earn extra money. We must earn extra money, because... A man [*człowiek*] who has two jobs, after eight hours here should take a rest, because we know that this is not a light work. From here he runs to the second job, there again he doesn't relax, in fact there is a private boss and again he must be careful. Basically the guy works about 12 hours, with the transport times probably 13, and early in the morning again comes to work. I think that this is why some accidents happen. But you can't keep a family any other way. [hs8]

In this situation of diffuse overtime and second jobs, working time reduction is an uneasy claim. Most workers are more concerned by wages, especially in Poland but also in Italy as reveal surveys on Turin workers (Abburrà and Marcenaro, 1986; Cerruti and Rieser, 1999). Actually, at both Lucchini (in 1993) and Fiat (in 1994) there were cases of general working time reduction in order to maintain the employment levels through the so-called 'solidarity contracts'.[8] In fact, these cases are the outcome much more of a communitarian self-defence against redundancy than of a predisposition to working time reduction. This explains why of the two kinds of 'solidarity contracts' (job-security contracts) foreseen by the Italian legislation only the 'defensive' ones (working time reduction to avoid redundancy) have found application. By contrast, the 'offensive' ones (working time reduction to create new jobs) have remained a dead letter. Today, the 35-hours week is a political demand of the leftwing party *Rifondazione Comunista* that trade unions see with diffidence if not with hostility.

In Poland, working time reduction was paradoxically more an issue in the past than today. The free Saturdays were one of the most important claims (and temporary successes) of Solidarity in 1980, and the workers still remember now that there was a continuity between the claim of 'free Saturdays' and the claim of a 'free Poland'. Today, the Parliament is probably going to guarantee free Saturdays by the law (this was one of the Solidarity electoral promises in the elections of 1997), but in private companies Saturday overtime is common place.

When Polish workers demand a reduction of working time, this happens mainly for 'humanitarian' reasons, that is in order to protect the workers from over-effort. Therefore, more than a reduction of the working week, Polish Fiat workers want rest pauses to be lengthened. But not only this: Polish workers have their mind also on the distribution of working time across the year. Notably they contest the concentration of overtime in the summer, when the Polish climate allows a better use of free time as well as a number of second jobs (but obviously also less energetic costs for the company). In general, in Poland there is a more 'proletarian' attitude towards working time and towards the demand of working time reduction. In Italy, by contrast, this issue is starting to assume a meaning of solidarity with the unemployed.

Besides the Polish and the Italian 'dominant' ones, there is still another way to conceive working time, which is quantitatively marginal but of high social importance. This is the attitude of female workers, whose role in trade union renewal will be analysed below. Notably, female workers are much more sensitive towards a flexible reduction of working time. Their demand for part-time work is typical. In the case of the Italian metalworkers the possibility is foreseen only for up to 2% of the workforce and with the exclusion of assembly line workers (in fact in 1996 only 1.2% of metalworkers worked part-time).

Egalitarianism and Solidarity

The Slow Decline of Italian Egalitarianism

Any trade union, and more generally any organisation aiming at a political regulation of economic relations, must have a conception of social 'justice'. The predominant conception in the worker movement, and especially in the Italian and the Polish ones, was the so-called working-class solidarity. This was analysed in chapter 3 while discussing the meaning of class identity. It is now necessary to examine its meaning as a motive for trade union commitment.

Attention to imagery and mobilisation strategies is important in order to avoid simplistic structuralist explanations: as a matter of fact, historians (e.g. Hobsbawm, 1987) have often pointed out that it is hard to imagine where a 'golden age' of 'organic' solidarity ever actually existed. In Italy, a particularly deep egalitarianism was considered by Accornero (1992) as simultaneously the main resource for the worker movement of the 1970s and the reason for its defeat in the 1980s. According to this view, egalitarianism was functional in a heterogeneous productive world where, in the absence of a strong hard-core workforce, the only unifying image was the figure of the 'mass worker' (*operaio massa*). However, in the long run egalitarianism became a burden for the many categories.

In the 1970s, the Italian renewal of unionism from below was based on a strong egalitarianism. At the beginning, this contrasted with the previous crafts-dominated unionism, but eventually welded with it. That egalitarianism had a strong meaning: it was the 'indicator of a rejection by ordinary workers of the hierarchical system of qualifications, based on the criterion of a professionalism which with the modern organisation of work they will never achieve' (Regini, 1981, p. 99). Egalitarianism contested work organisation in the factory. Yet, when the unions around 1980 lost their control of work organisation, egalitarianism also inevitably lost its mobilising power (Baccaro and Locke, 1998).

Nevertheless it did not disappear. Today, in big factories like Fiat and Lusid, the old egalitarianism is enduring. This is not completely surprising, since the egalitarianism of the 1970s was centred precisely on the figure of the metalworker: it is therefore not strange that it endures in its cradle. However, only the older and more ideological activists defend without hesitation this egalitarianism.

> I don't like the quality circles they constituted. The quality, we all make it together. All the workers without distinction, when something goes the wrong way they are the first to signal it. They [the management] have taken some people who are in the quality circle, and they give them a prize once or twice a year. These four, five people get a coffee, but the other fifty who have worked together? I go on saying that this is unfair, if there is a coffee to drink, that coffee should be divided, a drop each, and it should be given to everybody because everybody has contributed to that thing. [mf1]

Apart from this union hardcore, however, egalitarianism starts to be seen as problematic. Many interviewees notice that, with the new work organisation systems and in the situation of union weakness, workers' traditional solidarity has become uneasy. Moreover, the unions must face strong trends to differentiation. Sometimes the egalitarian barricade resists, like when in 1994 the Piemonte Region tried to hire two hundred young workers with lower wages, but was stopped by the unions. A Turin activist mentions that case, and his comment reveals the uneasiness and the fears of the unions.

> For instance here in Piemonte they wanted to hire 200 young unemployed with a lower wage and less holidays. In that case there was a rebellion not only of that category but of all the categories, to say that the laws are equal, and eventually the union didn't sign that agreement. *This is a moment of solidarity,*

if one signed an agreement like that, then there could be the risk that in all other companies... *The risks of differences must be avoided, because later nobody manages to control them, the union neither.* [mf6]

Equally challenging for the unions are the recent pension reforms, which differentiate between manual and non-manual workers, and furthermore between 'particularly fatiguing'(*particolarmente usuranti*) and 'not particularly fatiguing' jobs. The simple fact that the government has needed six years (from 1993 to 1999) to elaborate the *lavori particolarmente usuranti* list reveals the political delicacy of the issue. On this point the unions must take difficult and painful decisions, establishing differences among workers while their calling is to defend everybody indistinctly. The activists are fully aware of these dilemmas.

On fatiguing jobs there will be those who are permanently enraged, because in my opinion not all jobs within the steelworks are fatiguing. I can't think this because I am a driver of special lorries, I work on different shifts. I consider it a fatiguing job, but only up to a certain point because working in the blast-furnace where it's hot and you have the flames in front of you and cold air at the back, that job is more fatiguing than mine. The administrative employee, who has not even a computer in front of him, this is not fatiguing in comparison with my job, and then everybody has his own specificity. (...) I am absolutely convinced that my job is not fatiguing in comparison with the miner's. Consequently, we have to make a scale, and it will be very complicated and those who are not on scale will be permanently enraged. For the union getting involved in this matter will be difficult. [pf2]

The problem is not only the one of making choices. It is also one of different conceptions of solidarity. The rigid defence of equal treatment in a situation of subjective diversity in fact may hide, behind a solidarity discourse, an egoistic defence against unfair competition from weaker categories. Interestingly enough, in Piombino the inferior employment conditions reserved to the youngest employees are accepted by the people directly concerned, and strongly objected to by their older colleagues.

The Brusque Dismissal of Polish Egalitarianism

The Polish union movement of Solidarity of 1980-81 was, like the Italian one, very egalitarian, as illustrated by Laba's (1991) analysis. At that time, Lech Wałęsa kept on saying that 'everybody has one stomach'. However, in the 1980s, during Solidarity's underground activity, most activists started to shift to a more 'meritocratic' attitude, while at the same time liberal economic ideas started to gain some ground. In 1989-90, during the 'market shock', the trade unions still tried to defend the minimal real incomes and the basic benefits (especially the seniority ones), but with respect to wage collective bargaining they gradually accepted a deeper differentiation (Czujka, 1998).

In the 1990s, surveys show enduring egalitarian views among workers as well as in the Polish population as a whole (Gardawski, 1996; Zaborowski, 1995). In the political debate, the complaint that Poles are too egalitarian and in this way hinder the development of the market economy is recurrent. However, those attestations of egalitarianism are probably less a real orientation than the reaction to a brusque differentiation of standards of living. Still very equal ten years ago, the Polish social landscape saw a sort of earthquake in the 1990s, becoming in a very short period more unequal than most Western societies, including Italy (which is already one of the least equal Western societies). Wage differentials have changed radically, becoming typical of developing countries.[9]

In fact, the inquiry among the trade unions reveals that the Polish activists are more likely than the Italian to favour pay differentials. This takes two basic forms: a stress on the value of skills, or a simple refusal of solidarity and an explicitly egoistic standpoint. The two following extracts illustrate these alternative patterns.

> The people who want to develop professionally are not sufficiently considered. It's just not worth [developing], because we haven't yet elaborated, whether the employer or the union, a pay system capable of rewarding those who want to improve their qualifications. [hs6]
>
> I am not concerned by what happens in the other factories, not even in the other automotive factories, only my factory is important to me because it's here that I get the money. [bs2]

The difference between the two countries is particularly striking on the question of regional differences. Both countries have strong, historically rooted regional discontinuities in economic structure: the North-South one in Italy, the centre-periphery and West-East in Poland. However, the unions deal with these discontinuities in different ways. In Italy, since the 1970s, the Italian unions categorically, although recently with increasing difficulty, defend the principle of equal pay levels for the whole country. They refuse any return to the '*gabbie salariali*' (wage cages), the system which until the 1960s differentiated wages across the regions. By contrast, in Poland, although in 1980-81 Solidarity fought for equal wages countrywide, today pay differentials of 40% and more exist among regions, and the unions accept them. Some human envy notwithstanding, at Danone the unions from Bieruń Stary came to terms with the fact that their Warsaw colleagues should earn 20% more than them for the same jobs. And their argument is surprising for unionists: in Warsaw salaries must be higher not so much because the costs of living are higher, but because *the labour market* is different in the capital. Very rarely can a similar level of acceptance and awareness of market rules be found among the unions of any country.[10]

In their concrete behaviour the Polish unions sometimes seem to have definitely abandoned working-class egalitarianism. Not only is industry-level bargaining still embryonic, but plant-level unions are very jealous of local information. Unlike in Italy, often they refuse to give the researcher data on local conditions with the following sort of argument: 'if the unions from other companies noticed that we have better conditions, our situation with the employer would worsen'. Facing the recession of 1998, the union leadership of the Huta Lucchini not only does not think of a sort of *'contratti di solidarità'*, like thoses implemented in Piombino. They even actively support the redundancy solution (though with some social protection), in order to permit salary increases for those who remain in the factory.

Behind the general discourses of the unions there also is a 'structural' difference between Italy and Poland. The Polish union membership is on average better qualified than the Italian one. The best example is that of maintenance workers, usually more skilled than average. Even passing over the extreme case of Polish Danone (where in Warsaw Solidarity represents almost only highly qualified technicians, and in Bieruń Stary the qualified shift workers have successfully established their own union), the Fiat factories present two diametrically opposite situations. In Poland maintenance workers are usually the core of the unions, while in Italy they are the most sceptical about the unions, as a FIOM activist reports.

> Maintenance work allows you to understand the relationship between the skilled workers, who feel themselves a bit more secure, and the line-workers who work at the press and can do only this. You see it from the relationship the maintenance workers have with the union, there is an attitude of real indifference towards the union. [rf4]

This might be partially due to the less advanced organisational level of the Polish unions, still based on workers' 'aristocracy'. Also the former Polish official unions were composed mainly of the higher strata of the enterprise hierarchies. But Solidarity in 1980-81 represented above all the ordinary workers, according to the accounts and inquiries examined in detail in chapter 2. Highly skilled workers and technicians did indeed mobilise too (Kennedy, 1991), but their role was visible in the self-managing factories' network (the *Siec*) more than in the union. The current situation is therefore not a legacy of communist times, but a recent evolution.

Towards a New Idea of 'Solidarity'?

The collapse of traditional mass production, the increase of women's labour market participation, and the destructive impact of the mass-media on communities 'unmake' the working class. As a consequence, 'workforce heterogeneity now approximates the heterogeneity of the broader society' (Cohen and Rogers, 1994, p. 141). This is not, despite appearances, a simple macro-sociological statement. As the word 'unmaking' suggests, it is a complex process, starting from the neighbourhood and ending with culture. Along the way, old solidarities and above all socialisation practices are undermined. Can new solidarities appear? The presence of common interests across different groups seems unlikely to be able to replace class consciousness in building collective action. Cohen and Rogers argue that new solidarities will be linked to citizenship, to the elaboration of comprehensive views. The issue is 'decolonizing the life world', creating arenas of discussion outside the formal political system and not mediated by money and power: 'pursuing discussion in the context of enduring differences among participants would incline parties to be more reflective' (Cohen and Rogers, 1994, p. 155). It is not imperative to accept the idea of citizenship as the solution for acknowledging that the problem does indeed lie in the 'decolonisation' of the *Lebenswelt* and in the creation of arenas of communication, a new public sphere in Habermas' terms.

As already argued during the analysis of class identity (chapter 3), the term 'solidarity' has two distinct meanings, referring respectively to the idea of 'cohesion' and that of 'altruism'. Nowadays, the attention is shifting from the former meaning to the latter one. The problem is that while the first is sufficiently clear, the second is still nebulous.

In the words of its advocates (e.g. Zoll, 1992), the 'new' solidarity should join collective rights with attention to individual circumstances. This 'magic' combination is not that easily defined in concrete terms, but analytically it is important to stress that both motives of social justice and recognition of diversity are necessary. In a piece of research on the mentally disabled at work (Meardi, 1993), I remarked that these two elements, that I then called 'altruism' and 'tolerance', were not at all correlated. On the contrary, there was an inverse correlation albeit weak.

However, only a combination of both attitudes had positive effects on the social integration of the disabled persons.

How does this translate into union policies? These are many fields in which the theoretical problem of a 'new solidarity' is a very concrete problem in everyday union activity: women's work, youth employment, work relations in small companies, atypical jobs, cultural and ethnic differences, disabled and other weak groups in the labour market. The case of international solidarity, which I dealt with briefly in the previous chapter, is illustrative. On this issue union leaders themselves speak of a 'new solidarity'. This would be based on both individual and collective rights with the goal of social development, in contrast to the 'old solidarity' consisting in a monopoly of representation directed at avoiding external competition. This orientation, accordingly, should guide international action.

> If, for instance, it is impossible to prevent a factory being moved from Italy to Hungary or to Slovakia, it is however possible to claim for the Hungarian or Slovak workers the same rights of organisation, strike, and union membership, as the Italian workers. (Anderson and Trentin, 1996, p. 60)

The implementation of such union policies, however, requires not only some political imagination on the side of union leaderships. Much more, it is a problem of cultural change in the 'body' of the unions. Otherwise, as the already mentioned case of the Italian *contratti di solidarietà* (but also the Renault Eurostrike of 1997, as I argued in chapter 1) has clearly shown, the 'new solidarity' will be realised only when it overlaps with the classic, defensive and collectivist, workers' mechanical solidarity.

In fact, the union activists who perceive the need for such a cultural advance, remark that the trade unions are relatively late.

> The union can do it, the Church has done it therefore the union can too. The Church has done a lot of work recently on immigration and the margins of society. It's what they call solidarity. The union too has worked on it, but should do more. [mf6]

Among the unions considered, the FIM-CISL of Turin is maybe the most engaged on this front. However, its activists underline that this cultural change does not go without difficulties and dilemmas.

> The union went away from the problems of the factory. Previously it emphasised the factory, now it emphasises general problems, deals with many different problems. For instance formerly it was absurd to propose in the

collective agreement the idea of special leave for the mothers of drug addicts, and now there is this. This is a very positive thing, because formerly this was a deficiency of the union in my eyes. (...) Now it is dealing with social problems, only it is doing it too much. Too much attention to problems like the 740 [Italian income declaration for fiscal purposes], the tax system, the pensions... God forbid, it's OK, there must also be these things, but they must also care about work, be present in the workplace, and I see that there is a deficiency on this. [ri4]

Internal and External Differences

The disintegration of class consciousness, described extensively in chapter 3, lets the diversity of the workers appear and become meaningful. The unions face then, phenomenologically, a new subjective reality. Not only is there an objective differentiation of the workforce; this also takes a particular, and worrying, meaning once it is no longer observed through the lens of working class consciousness.

The problems are manifold. Certainly there have always been, at work, differences between men and women, old and young, skilled and unskilled, locals and immigrants. Working class consciousness, however, quite effectively – although often with effects of segregation – combined all these different situations into a stable compromise behind a unifying image, putting specific people in specific places when it was necessary (this is notably the case with women).[11] Today this cannot be done in that way. The higher justification (the struggle for worker-controlled production, economy and society) is no longer believable: it is no longer clear, as specifically described in chapter 3, who are the workers, who are their exploiters, and what they are fighting for.

As already mentioned about egalitarianism, in this new subjective reality the Poles seem sometimes better equipped than the Italians. Two examples are employees' subcontracting and status differentiation. On the former, in the previous chapter it was shown with various examples that the Polish unions are less terrified by outsourcing, and that with a very pragmatic attitude they try to come to terms with it by organising, for instance, inter-company unions.

The second example is more complex. The employment relationship is a very regulated and institutionalised one. Unions – which are with the state the main actor of this regulation – remain very sceptical about any modification of the established rules: in most situations the unions have resisted part-time working, out-working, and any atypical regulation (for instance for young employees, or for 'quasi-subordinated jobs'). The Italian unions are a good example of this attitude. The Polish ones, without falling into an indulgent acceptance of the employers' rhetoric on 'flexibility', are more open on this point. They have very recently experienced a deep transformation of employment regulation (the new Labour Code was passed in 1996) and this prevents them seeing these regulations as immutable. As a result, for instance, they accept the use of 'non-dependent work contracts' (*umowy zlecenia*) with an easiness unknown in the Italian unions, rigidly against the equivalent *prestazioni coordinate e continuative* but absolutely unable to resist them and, what is more, to represent employees working under these conditions. This does not mean that the Italian unions are inert on this front. In fact, the CGIL in 1998 even created a union for atypical workers, called quite generically 'New Work Ideneities'. But at its inauguration in Milan were present only full-time waged union officers. In this framework, the sociologist Sergio Bologna points to the permanence of simulacrum-rules protecting the unions rather than the workers as a worse risk than deregulation itself (Bologna and Fumagalli, 1997). In different words, Supiot (1999) affirms that it is advisable to prevent a gulf from forming between employees protected under contract and persons working under other kinds of arrangements that afford less protection.

Until now 'internal' diversity has been considered. This piece of research has also tried to analyse another difference, the international, or 'external', one. The idea that there might be a connection between these two forms of differentiation will be dealt with in the next section. Following the discussion presented up to now, however, there is at least a logical connection between the two problems. A cross-national unionism would be, by its nature, highly 'encompassing'. It should then necessarily face a number of differences and go beyond mechanical solidarity (Hyman, 1999). On this issue, again, the evidence presented in the previous chapters shows that the Poles are not necessarily worse equipped than their richer, and traditionally internationalist, Italian counterparts.

From Class to the Subject?

The Two Sides of Class

The third research hypothesis presented in chapter 1 suggested a link between the ways the trade unions face different types of differentiation. In particular, among the union members of transnational companies, a correlation between attitudes towards internal and cross-national differentiation was expected. In other words, there should have been a sort of 'summation effect' in the attitudes of trade unionists. For instance, activists already open towards generational differences were expected to be more likely also to develop positive attitudes towards foreign workers.

Unlike the two previous ones, the findings do not directly confirm the third hypothesis. This is true in particular as regards female activists and young activists. Although more sensitive to gender and generation differences, these activists are by no means more open towards other groups. This finding is all the stronger as it confirms other surveys on young union members (Arte, 1993). Moreover, there is no link between union commitment and other forms of social engagement: sometimes, these forms of public participation appear as conflicting rather than convergent.

> Where I am there is a lady who occupies herself with aid to drug addicts, another one is involved in voluntary work at the Cottolengo [a famous institute for handicapped people], another one dedicates her time to a kennel, she asked me whether I want to adopt a dog. These people are very disinterested as regards the union, they don't even want to speak of the union any longer, they're fed up, they prefer to engage outside, they're deceived. [mc6]

This situation requires a close examination. The connection between attitudes towards the different differentiation lines, although it does not exist at the *individual* level, might take place at the *social* level. This would be explainable: the individual activists concerned with a particular category are too engaged on that issue to be, for the present, also open on other fronts. However, their particular activity accustoms their union to communication between different groups. Therefore, the identity of their group, if not their personal identity, will be more 'encompassing'.

In this 'revisited' form, the hypothesis seems confirmed by the data. The unions most open towards their foreign counterparts are the FIM-CISL in Rivalta, the Cobas in Mirafiori and *Sierpień 80* in Tychy, followed by Rivalta FIOM. These unions have given much space to women or to youth, included self-organisation. By contrast, the most 'closed' is Piombino FIOM, locked in an old male worker community and in trouble with the emerging cleavages among countries, plants, employment status and even between plant and town.

The class model of the union movement was characterised not only by a strong egalitarianism or by meta-historical ideals. Although these orientations remained fundamental mobilisation resources, as I discussed in chapter 1 working class consciousness was also rooted in an opposition at work; in other words, in the subjective capacity of the workers to reject domination and to affirm their autonomy, whether in limited defensive ways like the slow-down or in offensive organised ways like unionism.

On the one hand class *dominated* the individuals by assimilating them to a collectivity and subordinating them to an ambitious project. This side of class unionism still appears in unionists' tales.

> I didn't have any political idea, I joined the union only like that, to do something, because I was young, I was 24. I didn't have any experience in the union as such, but the only thing I could share was that united in the struggle, in the strikes, starting from that ideology, in any case united it is possible to win the battles against the boss. [mf9]

An extreme case of 'non-subjective' unionism are the rank-and-file members of the former official unions (while the leaders often display very studied and conscious personal projects).

> Formerly there was only one union, I was there and up to now I'm there. I have always been an ordinary member, I've never been in the union board, I don't want to. I profited from the union only a couple of times, I have no privileges. [tm1]

On the other side, however, class was the expression of an individual irreducible aspiration to *autonomy* and *subjectivity*. This distinction of the two sides of class – political subordination and human subjectivity – is so important that recently Alain Touraine, by stressing the second one, ended up rejecting the concept of class itself. This rejection seems redundant (and may even backfire due to the risk of idealising such a concrete movement) if the distinction between a *subjective* idea of class and the vulgar Marxist one is made clear, as I tried to do in chapter 2. However, Touraine's assessment is worth a mention because of the importance of the distinction.

> The workers' movement did not simply demand better working conditions and conditions of employment, or even the right to negotiate and sign collective agreements. It called for the defence of the worker-subject against rationalization. It did not reject rationalization itself, but it did refuse to allow it to be identified with the interests of the employer. From the end of the nineteenth century onwards, talk of social justice became a way of stressing the need to reconcile the two principles of modernity, namely rationalization and the 'dignity' of the workers. (Touraine, 1995, p. 238)

> According to Marxists, the class-consciousness that exists for itself is not equivalent to a working class that has achieved self-consciousness ; it is equivalent to the interpretation, by revolutionary intellectuals, of a working-class situation which signals the contradictions of capitalism and of their necessary and possible transcendence. When I describe the labour movement

as a social movement rather than as class consciousness, I do so in order to avoid any confusion with Marxist thought. I am referring to a collective actor whose primary goal is the defence of the subject and the struggle for the rights and dignity of the workers. That is why revolutionary thought so often speaks of the proletariat, or in other words defines workers in terms of what they do not have: property. Historians and sociologists of working-class action like myself have demonstrated on the contrary that the workers' movement was the creation of skilled workers who were defending labour and its autonomy, that their action was positive rather than negative and that they were inventing a different world rather than merely criticizing capitalism and scientific management. A *social movement* is at once a social conflict and a cultural project. (...) There can be no social movement unless trade union action has the positive goal of giving workers greater autonomy and, more specifically, unless it fights the brutal assertion of Taylorist employers that 'You are not being paid to think' (pp. 239-240).

The 'positive' side of class was present in the Italian and the Polish traditions. Laba (1991) among others has described the rich cultural production of Solidarity. In everyday activity, Touraine's investigation indicated a strong orientation towards individual autonomy in personal behaviour and even in a 'pedagogical' attitude. In my secondary analysis I found examples like the following story.

A worker comes and says that something happened and that we must do something. Then, we ask him what he has done to arrange it. Did he go to see the foreman, if the problem concerned production? I think that it is better, because this man (*człowiek*) will gradually get used to claiming the things he is entitled to, and this will make work easier to him in the future. [a Gdańsk activist]

If one distinguishes the communitarian and defensive side of class from the offensive and subjective one, it is maybe possible to understand why in some plants, like Piombino or Bielsko, the class discourse has become sterile or even counterproductive, while in other (like Rivalta or Tychy) it still encourages autonomous activity. The distinction between these two legacies of the same patrimony pushes research attention towards the conditions of the emergence of the Subject at work and in the unions.

The Emergence of the Subject at Work...

The interviewees often express a subjective reaction *against* the work situation, though not always as many concentrate on political, ideological or technical discourses. Subjectivity, following a growing sociological stream (Thuderoz, 1995; Ollivier, 1996; Pirdas, 1997; Chauchat and Durand-Delvigne, 1999; Touraine, 1995) may be defined as: 'the only place where the combination of instrumentality and identity, of technical and symbolic, [that] is the project of general life, the desire not to reduce existence to a kaleidoscopic experience, to an erratic series of reactions to stimuli from the social environment' (Touraine, 1997, pp. 28-29).

As 'subjective' were defined reactions that are not limited to condemnation, but also contain a positive willingness to have an impact on the *status quo*. This mainly occurs in two forms: explicitly, with the tale about the interviewee's own activity, or implicitly, through the criticism of a widespread passive attitude. The general feature of the subjective attitude is the elaboration of a personal project at work. This goes beyond another, more primary form of subjective reaction to the work situation, that is all the ways in which the workers try to control effort by slow-down practices or the creation of 'productive games' and 'events' in order to give their job at least some of interest.

Subjective attitudes in the unions are not new. They were already present in the past, although often covered by the very 'high' aims of the trade unions. In Solidarity this sometimes took particular forms due to the specific way the communist system repressed the autonomy of the worker and his or her career aspirations.

> I had had a vocational education. Later while at work I finished high school, by the way I generally like improving myself, therefore I took a number of supplementary qualifications, such as carrier mechanic, general welder, that is I'm able to serve both electrically and by flue. In the 1970s I started with basic courses, I have a number of these supplementary qualifications, electrician's qualifications, maybe in the workshop there is nobody at my level. It was just the first job, because in fact I wasn't registered in Warsaw. I live five km from Warsaw, and I was not allowed to work in Warsaw because the job centre in my municipality gave jobs perhaps in Nowy Dwór, in Legionowo, that is absolutely not on the road. The only company which enrolled people without the mediation of the job centres was the *Huta*, everybody regardless of their education level. Many people started working here for this reason. [hs6]

Nowadays, subjectivity is explicitly expressed with reference either to a personal professional track, or to the interviewee's desire to have an autonomous standpoint on production matters. The first pattern helps to clarify the difference between subjectivity and flexibility. If subjectivity asks for change and conflicts with passive routines, it also implies respect for a personal project and path, for a professional identity and an autonomous life, and limits to internal mobility. In the second pattern of subjectivity the stress is no longer on the *worker* but on the human being.

> The foreman doesn't like such people, the foremen say directly what they want. They eliminate such people, I was for instance degraded, because I shouted a bit. You see too many mistakes, they don't need such people, the best are those who do what they are told. This is the difference. They consider the workers' point of view very little. A couple of times I heard 'if you don't like it you can leave', or 'what do you know about it?'. I was actually the youngest worker but this doesn't mean that I can't see, that I can't be better. It was a foreman who said this. The majority of people remark on it, then there is a group of people who never say anything because they prefer remaining still to... They put up with me sometimes, I say what I think, sometimes this is not good, sometimes it is a disadvantage for me. [ta4]

The frequent willingness to have a personal influence on productive matters in Tychy and in Warsaw obliges us to criticise the common view of post-communist workers as passive. In fact, the reality of work organisation under state socialism *promoted* the search for worker autonomy, as suggested by other recent research on work organisation in Poland.

> It may be argued that people's professional consciousness could, in spite of all, develop in a general demotivating context even more than in the Western countries in the Taylorist period. The unusually irregular production rhythms in Eastern Europe allowed interactions, bargains and arrangements at work, which have today become an indispensable element of flexible production. (Le Goff, 1997, p. 309)

Most frequently, however, self-definition as a subject at work takes the weaker form of a criticism of others' passive attitudes. The affirmation of self and of personal aspirations is then indirect and implicit.

> I notice, however, that every worker in every work station, everybody creates their own routine, if management moves him and gives him another task, it creates a trauma for him. 'I'm in an uncomfortable place, all dirty, but don't try to move me', because he's created his own routine. It becomes very difficult to make people see that there might be a better work situation, the fork-lift trucker will request to remain a fork-lift trucker, the storage worker a storage worker, who works on a dirty and ugly mission will want to stay there, and you disturb him if you give him another job. Everybody makes a niche for themselves, tries to save themselves in their own job, in their own security and also in their own time. We have an assembly line, there are desks, they make their own production, one at 6 o'clock in the morning, bum, bum, bum, at

10.30 has already finished, but you can't tell him to work more slowly. No, you would bewilder him. [rf3]

Some people do not know what they are entitled to, simply somebody came, said 'you must do this', and they have been making it now for ten years. [ta5] People are oppressed to the point of vegetating, really. The worker comes to work, finishes the job, goes back home, at home again has work, and not everybody has time. [ta11]

...and Possibly Even in the Unions!

The main problem that arises for the unions is whether subjectivity at work may become a resource for them or not. In fact, trade unions have generally resisted any change in work organisation going in the direction of the worker's individual involvement in productive activity. In this regard, they feared, not without reason, that these practices would undermine the traditional bases of union power in the workplace. In other words, locked in the 'communitarian' side of union activity they ended up renouncing the 'subjective' one. They very rarely managed to develop an alternative view of organisational change compatible with worker's autonomy and collective rights.

More generally, 'individualisation' has often been viewed with scepticism or even fear by the unions. The emergence of individual preferences is then perceived as an incentive for 'free-riders'. Nevertheless, millions of unskilled or semiskilled jobs, especially in industry, still do not offer a real 'individual' alternative to collective action for social promotion. Therefore, at least in these sectors, individualisation might actually combine with collective action in new forms of solidarity.

In Thuderoz's (1995) definition, subjectivity at work as 'cooperative individualism' joins the two sides of class: personal project and social relations. In-depth interviews offer a good ground to test whether this association is purely speculative (and wishful), or whether there is a common potential ground for the emergence of the Subject behind both work involvement and social commitment.

Concretely, the interviews which displayed a strong and explicit affirmation of individual autonomy, and in which the 'I' form was more frequent than the collective or impersonal tenses have been considered as containing subjective attitudes. The quantitative distribution of subjective attitudes in the two contexts (at work and in the union) shows a very strong correlation of the two sides, almost identical in Italy and Poland (Table 5.1). This might however be only an apparent correlation, due to a rhetorical rather than objective association: the interviewees who develop a strongly subjective discourse on one issue tend to follow similar arguments in other domains. It is therefore more appropriate to take a more in-depth look at the possible link between personal projects at work and in the unions.

Table 5.1 - Distribution of the subjective attitudes

Italy		in the trade union			
		Expressed	Rejected	No inform.	Total
	Expressed	9	0	6	15
at work	Rejected	1	0	4	5
	No inform.	6	0	26	32
	Total	16	0	36	52
Poland		in the trade union			
		Expressed	Rejected	No inform.	Total
	Expressed	8	0	4	12
at work	Rejected	1	0	1	2
	No inform.	2	2	21	25
	Total	11	2	26	39
Total		in the trade union			
		Expressed	Rejected	No inform.	Total
	Expressed	17	0	10	27
at work	Rejected	2	0	5	7
	No inform.	8	2	47	57
	Total	27	2	62	91

One of the most interesting points to emerge from the interviews is the possibility among young workers of moving from a personal project at work to a personal project in the union. In this choice the determining variable is the impact between personal expectations and the reality of a big industry. Work in the factory, in spite of fanfares about the valorisation of the human factor, still offers the opportunity for personal development only to a minority of workers. However, the choice these young workers is not only the outcome of relative failure, and the search for an alternative channel of social advancement. The interviewees seem to have gone through a more complex process involving the development of feelings of opposition, the resistance of an affirmative idea of self, and a will to communicate.

You get to think that in the future you might make a further small step, then you give the most you can, even if you're only on the line. You engage yourself in order to get a better position, for instance there are line assistants who stand in during the twenty minutes [of pause]. I want to be a shift-substitute, or a maintenance or repair worker, where it's more quiet. Until 1990 everything was quiet, then the protests about the canteen started. Then the problems started. The boss said something, promised something, but he didn't keep to it. I tried to do as he said, but I felt humiliated. I made my first protest after three years and since that moment I've understood that I'm not worth so much. I gave everything and I always said yes, OK, but after in fact nothing improved, I remained on the line. [ri1]

I entered with a lot of expectations, many of them wrong. I thought that the company, being a big company, would organise some training, that there would be more chance to get on, also because I have a vocational training as an engine-mechanic, I need two years to get my diploma. During the first two years I kept asking the foreman whether it was possible, but he always said no. At Fiat I see a number of young employees who have diplomas but who are not taken into consideration, they look more at personal ties (...). I tried a bit at the beginning to see whether I had any chance of working on the company side, but I was deceived, and then I was proposed for activity in the union and I accepted because at the personal level it was also an experience, also of information. [ri5]

Apart from these paths followed by the youngest workers, in several cases the activists show a strong interest in the personal aspects and in the affirmation of self. In this context the 'technical' side of union activity acquires a higher connotation of skill development and personal improvement.

Attention to the individual also involves a shift in daily union action: from general regulation to the evaluation and defence of individuals.

And we must take into consideration workers' age, that a worker can make it in a certain post, another one may have problems because it is known that they have for instance different manual skills, this is not considered [by the management], he must work and that's all. [tz2]

In the Cobas case at Mirafiori, particularly influenced by New Left culture, this attention to personal cases becomes very important. In their tales, the highest level of union activity is intervention in cases where it is not the worker's exploitation but human subjection which matters.

This is something which personally I dislike even more than work, that is seeing the foreman daring to say certain things to the workers. If they see that a woman is weak, they allow themselves to say things which might be denounced. [mc6]

There is a story of a girl at Fiat, which if she is not confirmed [at the end of the temporary contract] we should write a book about, about the things she had to endure. To put it simply, the girl had the misfortune to have her father die, and her mother had heart disease. When she went to ask for unpaid leave and said 'my mother has heart disease, I have to bring her to a cardiologist', a supervisor answered saying 'now that we've finished with your father do we start with your mother?'. The story is so long, really a book should be written, if the girl is not confirmed in June we'll put out everything. When this girl told us in detail what she'd suffered... they even said to her that when she went out during the night, and she went to hospital to visit her father, they said that she went to prostitute herself. She suffered so many troubles that it was shocking listening to her, after all such a naive girl who comes to tell such a story, 22 years old, not even a member of the union. [mc2]

The subjective attitude to trade union commitment implies, besides the aim of autonomy at work, also an aim of autonomy *from* the union as an organisation. This element characterises new forms of political participation not only in the trade unions. Ion (1997) speaks in this regard of *'engagement distancié'*, in which the individual invests him- or herself in the organisation, without however delegating the duty of thinking in his or her place. On the same lines, Wieviorka (1998) argues that today engagement must authorise disengagement, and permanently combine with it. In this sense, the criticism of the organisation described in chapter three as a component of the disintegration of class consciousness may become a natural feature of relationship to the union by the new members.

When the boundaries of the unions become imprecise both collectively (because it is difficult to count members, sympathisers and activists) and individually (because it is unclear *to what extent* people are committed) the separation between the experience of work and life-sphere experience must be revisited. The problem is no longer that of the end of work, but that of an interplay: concern with work and concern with other domains are not mutually exclusive, and can even be reciprocally reinforcing in an everyday practical construction (Voß, 1994). In this way, cross-work identities, previously considered as a nuisance for the unity of the unions, may bring new resources to union commitment. The most relevant cases are women and the young. Women are here probably the most important forerunners of change in trade union commitment: the female union committees created in many Italian plants in the 1970s constituted for the first time a complete break with the traditions of working class organisation (Beccalli, 1984). Today, an important autonomous women's committee encountered during the inquiry is that of the FIOM women at

Rivalta. The importance of female participation is so important that will be treated in more detail in the next section.

The second case is that of the young. A vanguard in this regard is Rivalta FIM, which created a lively committee of young workers. But also in Piombino, in the FIOM, there were some attempts in this direction. The demands of young workers are all but silent.

> But it would be enough to have something, to organise, as I proposed during the last meeting, a meeting *only* for the young, even outside working time. We might explain that, possibly using terminology which is not too political, so to say a bit easy, explain what the union would like to introduce in order to achieve an agreement with the company. This might be a step closer to the young. [pf5]

Particularly interesting is the case of the young FIOM Siderco activist [sf2] who started his activity in the union explicitly in order to defend young employees, who had worse employment conditions than their senior colleagues. He was motivated by a feeling of discrimination, that is he entered the union as a young person, and not as a worker, just like the female activists who engaged themselves as women rather than as workers.

At a time when non-work-based identities are becoming important for the unions, these organisations should start taking care of cultural variables. In a post-industrial society cultural (in a broad sense) movements are expected to become more important than class- or interest- based ones. In Italy, as a matter of fact, there is an increasing differentiation of associative behaviour, no longer depending on consolidated 'interests' (Iref, 1997). Poland is however not 'backward': apart from a few strike waves in 1992 and 1993, the main social mobilisations and public debates after 1989 took place on issues such as abortion, regionalism, violence, State-Church or Polish-Jewish relations. In the tense presidential campaign of 1995 (the elections with the highest turn-out since 1989) social and work issues were almost absent and did not differentiate the two candidates Kwaśniewski and Wałęsa, while the issues of the evaluation of past history and of civic rights were at the centre of the attention.

There is no place in this book for a comparison of different social movements. What by contrast can be confirmed is that for the unions it becomes difficult to remain indifferent towards non-work issues, whether the ecological problems of Piombino, the regional autonomy of Bielsko-Biała or intercultural relations with a foreign employer.

. Even the apparently old-fashioned Polish national identity becomes a matter of reflection. In spite of the rhetoric on globalisation, as European-level social movements wait to emerge the national level remains the main field for political participation. A pragmatic understanding of this simple fact might allow the unions to avoid the choice between the Scylla of nationalist withdrawal and the Charybdis of rhetorical internationalism. More generally, the failure of the communist regimes in Central Europe is also the failure of the imposition of a monolithic system on one of the most complex regions of Europe. In this way, the experience of Solidarity recalls by its nature that cultural diversity should be taken into account by the labour movement.

Not only this. The Polish activists, from time to time, still make use of a typical rhetoric, inherited from the experience of Solidarity in the 1980s, which was already mentioned in chapter 1. Notably, they talk of the defence of the *human being* (*człowiek*) against any form of domination. There is in this a potential for the further development of subjective orientations. It is not coincidental, probably, that the Polish unions devote a relatively large amount of time to dealing with individual needs.

Another feature of the 'subjective' side of the unions is the importance of communication. This has always been an indispensable resource for union organisation in the workplace, but nowadays it has a more complex meaning and role. It is not only aimed at organising and mobilising: it is necessary to construct a single reality from different experiences. For subjectivity in political participation communication is even more important than for subjectivity at work. The availability of communication is a fundamental variable in the integration of marginal groups at work, and it still constitutes the main problem for trade union transnational action, as shown in the previous chapter. This point maintains its importance at the international level: as argued by Hyman (1999), international solidarity requires the reconstitution of unions as discursive organisations which would serve more as networks than as hierarchies. While the technical job of unionist is elevated to the level of a personal vocation, with the emergence of subjectivity communication is elevated to the level of dialogue.

At the end of this description, it is possible to suggest an image of a 'subjective' pattern of union commitment more precise than theories of the 'Subject'. It is still impossible to state whether this pattern will eventually impose itself, but it can be declared that it is at least *possible*, as it was met in almost a third of the interviewed activists. This pattern, open towards differentiation following the fragmentation of the working class, includes the following attitudes:

- the presence of a personal, autonomous project;
- the reference to the individual more than to the 'social';

- the affirmation of autonomy from the organisation;
- openness towards non-work based identities, and to cultural factors;
- the conception of communication as dialogue.

The sociological task now becomes to analyse the conditions for the emergence of this attitude. In order to make the first steps on this probably long research path, I shall devote some space to the most interesting case in this regard: that of women activists.

The Decisive Divide: The Unions and Gender

Female Union Commitment

This piece of research, by choosing as case studies six plants of traditional big industry, the theatre of the traditional workers' movement, unfortunately shares one of the main limits of most work sociology: gender bias. The sociology of work has always tended to concentrate on mainly male big industry, and contemporary academic industrial relations research still focuses on regimes that cover mainly male manual workers (Rubery and Fagan, 1995). Thus, women make up only 9 out of 91 interviewees (3 in Poland and 6 in Italy), and they all come from Fiat (where women are more than 20% of the manual workforce) as the steelworks are absolutely single sex.

However, the presence of women acquires a central importance in the light of the discussion developed until now. Not only do macro-sociological studies today converge in considering gender differences as important as the traditional 'class' ones (e.g. Crouch, 1999). Gender difference is also, for its general and basic human nature, in a way 'antecedent' to any conception of difference.

> Isn't the other sex, for everyone, the closest face of the *stranger*? Is it therefore politically crucial to know how sexual difference is recognised or, by contrast, denied. Because the way we think of the *other* in general depends on the way we think of the other sex. (Agacinski, 1998, p.12)

There is not here the space to exhaustively discuss the complex issue of the relations between unions and women. In any case, the history of these relations has been at least uneasy (Cockburn, 1991). Traditionally underrepresented in the industrial workforce (that is the image of the working class) and in the unions, especially at the higher hierarchical levels, women have not had an easy time in the unions. Fantasia (1988) describes how many married women committed to the unions reported feeling guilty about the time they spent away from their children. The workers' movement, which with its policies contributed to the enduring discrimination against women, coherently although rarely consciously also resisted the advancement of women in its own ranks.

Poland is no exception. Few working women (unlike numerous intellectual women) played a leading role in Solidarity in 1980-81, although, after all, the historical strike at the Lenin Shipyards in Gdańsk of August 1980 started with the firing of a woman, Anna Walentynowicz, who was among the leaders of the clandestine free trade unions. Women were as unionised as men (Radźko, 1981), but at the first Solidarity Congress in 1981 they were only 7% of the delegates and among the 82 members of the national commission there was only one woman (Tobiasz, 1999). One of the protagonists of that movement, Jacek Kuroń, in his memoirs recalls as typical the case of a factory where the almost entirely female workforce passively followed an entirely male strike committee (Kuroń, 1993). After the introduction of martial law, women became essential in the underground activity: four women were at the very top of regional clandestine structures, and the most important and circulating clandestine periodical, the weekly *Tygodnik Mazowsze*, was edited by a women-only board. However, women's role has remained unheralded and dismissed (Long, 1996) deserving the definition of 'national secret' (Penn, 1994). After 1989, most of these top-level female activists quitted public commitment and in any case the overwhelming majority was neither feminist nor sensitive to gender difference (Reading, 1992). The authoritarian experience, if 'hid' to an extent *class* demands, even more occulted the *gender* ones.

Democratisation neither was women-friendly. The first Solidarity's Women's Department was rapidly dissolved in 1990 because of its opposition to abortion prohibition. Solidarity still declares to have 45% of women among its members, but recent national-level surveys (CBOS, 1999) indicate that union density in Poland is 24% for men and only 14% for women. Women are heavily underrepresented in Solidarity: at the X National Congress in 1998, there were only 38 women among the 343 delegates (11.1%). Their number goes down as one goes up the bureaucratic ladder, from 18.5% in the regional executive boards down to zero in the national presidium in 1998 (Tobiasz, 1999). AWS, the political expression of Solidarity, promotes a 'family-friendly' wage system based on the most traditional 'male-breadwinner' model.

In Italy, union density is comparable among genders and the unions have indeed, thanks to their distictive egualitarianism, supported several women's demands. As organisations, however, they remain highly gender unequal and little concerned with gender difference (Beccalli, 1984; Beccalli and Meardi, 2000).

Interviews show, in Italy as well as in Poland, that the old diffidence of the unions towards women endures in some male activists.

The employer knows all too well that every strike fails, he says 'strike 3-4 days, and in any case you'll succumb because you go home and *the wife* will tell you 'give me the money for the rent, gas, electricity'. [bs5]

I have also been a member of the *cassintegrati* committee. In those meetings those were mainly women [workers' wives]. There were incredible fractures, they urged us to go back to the factory, to keep our heads down, because they couldn't afford to go on until the end of the month... [pf2]

Male activists see women as the weak link in the chain, as responsible for defeats. A new feature is that they sometimes see them as responsible for recent threats to workers' established practices.

Then there was the terrible contract [of 1974], I remember we made 200 hours of strike and even more, in order to give women parity. Now, I don't have anything personal against them, but they have become quite flexible, they come here at 4 o'clock in the morning. [mf8]

Recently in the unions the role of women has been regarded in a more positive way, and women have started to find new opportunities (Cunnison and Stageman, 1995; Colgan and Ledwith, 2000). Particularly macroscopic are the changes in the United States, where unionism was characterised for a long time by a particularly strong discriminatory attitude towards women but more recently 'strategies for renewal have often been influenced by modes of action, forms of organisation, mechanisms of representation and communication and types of discourse that were originally developed with women wage earners in mind' (Howell and Mahon, 1996, p. 500). In the North-American public-sector unions, the increasing presence of women has been seen as a factor enabling the intersection of urban life politics, gender relations, and the private and public sector labour movements (Johnson, 1995). On a more general basis, women's, and feminists', action is considered by Touraine (1995; 1997) as most favourable for the development of new cultural, 'subjective' social movements.

The interviews with female activists, especially those collected in Italy, show a stronger presence of subjective discourses. Attention is paid to a variegated range of demands, sometimes uncommon, while instrumental and economicist attitudes are rarer, contrary to the historical view of women's union commitment:

> Many women belong to the union, but most appear to have been concerned only with their wages and their domestic affairs, they simply paid their small subscription as a kind of insurance against the day when they might find themselves in dispute with the management. (Roberts, 1984, p. 147)

Most remarkably, in some interviews gender identity is put in the foreground. Many of the women are motivated primarily by a sense of discrimination at work: that is, they are motivated as *women* rather than as *workers* (a similar conclusion could be reached about some young activists in Piombino). The employer is then criticised in both class and gender terms.

> A CP [the lowest hierarchical level of technicians] made the gross mistake of giving birth. When she came back, they took off her CP overalls. They told her 'we know that now you won't be that available'. Fiat anyway is masculinist, very masculinist. [mc6]

The commitment takes then a much more personal dimension, where the affirmation of one's own identity is fundamental.

> Then I didn't like them to have won, and so I reacted in a certain way. Actually, I think I caused some turmoil in the personnel department, because they also knew me in Mirafiori, where some personalities seemingly asked for explanations from my supervisor as to my choice [of joining the union]. I hope, that they've really asked about it. [rf5]

Women activists are glad to be *women activists*, that is also in comparison with their male colleagues.

> There is a lot of interest among women. Maybe they see the problems more closely, with a freer eye than a man, who puts in first place various interests, that is if you're a member or not. If you're a member, 'OK, let's talk', otherwise you must first join the union. They are more direct, more determined on these matters. In contrast, we're sometimes less demanding, we consider relationships with people more important, understand people in order to... [rf6]

The female activist identity displays two sides, just like the worker movement: one made of weakness and domination, the other of potential revolt and subjectivity. These two sides are often interwoven.

> A united union is one that does the right things and where we're all equal, men and women, because in my opinion this difference exists... Above all in the factories because it's right that a woman has the same rights since by now we do the same jobs. But we see that the rights are only rights to work, because when there is overtime to do the woman is the first to be called. The man maybe because he has a second job refuses, women are more passive when they hear I put you here I put you there (...) The 4th qualification levels among women are extremely rare (...) After all it is a matter of principle, not of money: I do the same job, why do you get it and I don't? Like dent-removing, I asked to be trained, 'no, because you're a woman'. What's the difference, I can try, then maybe I can't do it but it's right to try. Women are much more combative because they are treated in a worse manner. OK, I'm much more feminist, but if they know they are right they impose their right. After all the man joins the union only when he sees that he's got some problem, possibly of health. For the woman the issue is maternity or the impositions from the foremen, like 'anyway you're a woman, we don't care about it, shut up', and this is wrong. [ri8]

The last extract introduces a point which might be seen as an extreme case of a new subjective way to join work and life-sphere experiences in trade union commitment. During the inquiry four women (three in Italy and one in Poland), from four different unions (Rivalta FIOM, Rivalta FIM, Mirafiori FIOM, Tychy *Sierpień 80*), were found to have started their union activity after the birth of their first child, and were motivated in the first place by the experience of maternity. This contrasts with the traditional view of women's attitudes to the unions, which see family roles and union roles as conflicting. Traditionally, and still in the 1970s in Italy, the common view was that if a woman ever became involved with a union, this was an unmarried woman; as soon as she had children (if not as soon as she got married), she would leave work, and if she didn't leave work, at least she would leave the union. A qualitative piece of research is unable to suggest what is the statistical relation between maternity and union commitment. However, it is able to show that a relation contrary to the one traditionally expected is *possible* and seen by the people concerned as *normal*. A family experience such as maternity may, instead of drawing the attention away from work, 'open the eyes' of the worker as to the nature of work relations.

Everything was fine, then I took maternity leave and when I came back, how to say it, the factory was overturned. It was like starting from the beginning again (...). You remain still maybe for the first few years. Then when I came back from maternity and I saw that they put me on the night shift although the child was little, they were not allowed but they did it, because of my ignorance I said OK, that is there wasn't a union in my place to help me, and they exploited it. When I came here to Rivalta [from Mirafiori] I said that's enough, now... that is, this helped me to grow up, at work if I know that I'm right I don't care (...).

While you're young, Fiat is happy, then when you're no longer necessary you're discarded. I've seen it after maternity: I was no longer necessary, and what does it mean? It's like saying you don't have the right to have children. I personally paid the cost of it, if I had a second child I would think about it, because it's not right that you come back after maternity and you lose your rights in the workplace. [ri8]

I started [to work for the union] because basically I felt really persecuted in the last few years. After coming back from the maternity leave I was penalised a lot because I didn't do overtime at work. According to my supervisor, I should have worked overtime in any case, remained in the evening and this kind of thing, and with an 18-months-old daughter it's clear that a woman can't (...). I joined the union because I felt discriminated against, a target. When there was some *cassa integrazione* [temporary unemployment] it was always for me. [rf5]

On these issues, work- and political sociology strongly need a contribution from gender studies and the sociology of the family. Only from that point of view is it possible to advance an interpretation of the increasingly 'chosen' rather than 'natural'(and thus increasingly *subjective*) character of family events. Subsequently, personal choices may favour forms of personal commitment. In fact, reflections on gender differences have already pointed to the subjective potentials of the maternity experience (Agacinski, 1998). It is simply the case that the sociology of work has remained unaware of it.

These points on the potential of female subjectivity for the unions do not imply that women automatically have on any issue a somehow more advanced orientation than men. On the contrary, I already recalled that most women display a very low solidarity towards other groups, starting with the foreign workers. In this regard any optimistic 'messianic' expectation from female activists should be avoided. In the past, messianic views already concerned the working class which was supposed, by breaking its chains, to break the chains of *every* domination. Similar messianic hopes were invested in colonised populations or, in the East, the dissidents (not to speak of the messianic halo which much less democratic movements attribute to themselves). In all these cases, such very high expectations were eventually disappointed, with the outcome of favouring counter-reactions (negative judgements on the unions often seem due to an unconscious comparison with labour movement iconography). In the case of women's commitment, radical accounts sometimes state, for instance, that women would:

> bring quite distinct modes of action and practice to trade unions, which have the potential of harnessing working women in support of the labor movement's version of an alternative, more human, post-Fordist future (...), [and] exemplify a new political style and a new organizational paradigm which emphasize workplace collectivity, political energy, a less bureaucratic, more 'dialogical' organizational style and a redefinition of the value of work itself. (Howell and Mahon, 1996, p. 506).

There is not (yet?) evidence of such an idyllic female pattern to union commitment. However, women are starting to bring their specific contribution to trade union agendas and bargaining platforms. Rivalta FIOM women, notably, are particularly active on the issue of working time organisation.[12] Potentially, this may bring about a reconsideration of the established 'protective boxes' of work regulation, and push the unions to repoliticisation and the elaboration of a new 'gender contract' (O' Reilly and Spee, 1998). We are not yet at this level, however. Currently, the positive and indispensable role of women in the trade unions is different, independent from the individual merits or faults of female activists. It lies in the fact that women, with their active presence, bring *diversity* into the union and stimulate *communication*. The link is indirect, but not less important for this. Similarly, life-sphere experiences are not automatically positive for the unions, the opposite being rather the case. But when these external factors eventually touch union commitment, they force the organisation to change, or at least to listen.

In this way, the presence of women in the unions at the Turin and Tychy Fiat factories, in contrast to the entirely male steelworks of Piombino and Warsaw, helps to explain the higher general openness of their unions.

How Polish Women Catch up with Those in the West, but in Their Own Way

The case of Polish working women requires a specific note, although unfortunately the female presence among the interviewees is too small for

258 Trade Union Activists, East and West

an empirical discussion. It must be recalled nonetheless that gender relations at work in the state socialist countries took a particular meaning.

In first place, those countries constructed a situation never achieved in capitalist countries in peace times: the full employment of women in the formal sector of the economy.[13] However, a high gender segregation endured (women were for instance almost completely absent from the party central committees) and an unequal division of housework persisted (Łobodzińska, 1995). As a result, contemporary surveys (notably, the 1994 ISSP module) reveal that in post-communist countries opinions about women's role are much more conservative than in the West, even in comparison with a relatively traditionalist and patriarchal country like Italy (Cichomski, Morawski and Zawadzki, 1996).

This point (like many others already discussed in the previous pages) can only partially be explained by the supposed 'backwardness' (or traditionalism) of post-communist societies, which would not yet have entered into modernity.[14] Actually, Eastern Europeans are not very traditionalist on another gender-related issue, that is sexual permissiveness. The same surveys show that the post-communist cluster (Russia, Poland, Bulgaria, Slovenia, Hungary, Czech Rep.) is much more liberal in the sexual sphere than the English-speaking cluster (USA, Ireland, Canada, Great Britain, New Zealand, Australia), which is by contrast liberal with respect to women's roles in the economy and in the home. This point remains valid, although less strongly, for Poland which is the least permissive in the post-communist group.

An alternative explanation, drawing on the interpretative schemes sketched in this book, requires attention to both opposition identities and subjective experiences. The main point is the fact that female employment in state socialist countries *was not chosen*, and was perceived as forced. For this reason, after the communist breakdown 'freedom' for working women also meant 'freedom to stay at home', at least in (rare) cases when the husband's income was sufficient.

Moreover, this kind of forced employment in societies which were in any case dominated by men, perpetuated 'micro' forms of segregation and domination which are evident in the workplace. In the Polish case, this is certainly reinforced by the Catholic culture, although the distinct influence of each of the two factors cannot be easily evaluated.

Nowadays, paternalistic attitudes towards women are frequent among the (male) Polish union activists.

A new problem is that the lightest posts, which are suitable for women, for older workers, for people with health problems, fall into the so-called *tercjaryzacja* [outsourcing]. At Fiat these posts have already become very scarce. There is a surplus of women (...) Many women work now for instance in the paint shop, the work conditions are such that they can't have children. [tp1]

Women themselves, somehow, often become accustomed to this attitude.

I don't know how it is now on the assembly line. I worked on the assembly line in the years 81-83, it was completely different. In particular, I was lucky to have the colleagues I did, there were few girls and the boys tried to help us. [ta4]

The tales from the Fiat plants introduce the issue of women's condition after communism. It is still disputable whether, and to what extent, women's conditions have worsened after 1989 (van der Lippe and Fodor, 1998; Titkow, 1998). As to blue-collar female workers in the factories, however, it is clear that working time organisation has worsened (with the subjection to shifting time) and that most women have been moved from indirectly to directly productive tasks. This situation is confirmed by other studies on Polish working women (Heinen, 1995).

In this situation Polish women, given the general identity of Polish workers described in the previous chapter, might become a sort of 'proletarians among the proletarians'. The potential for subjectivity found among the Italian women seems to be neutralised by the joint effect of poor mobilisation resources, the reaction to the former system of female full employment, and the Catholic culture. The outcome of this manifold situation has suggested to Polish sociologists to define working women as 'willing slaves,' with implicit very conservative consequences (Domański, 1999).

The situation is however not completely dark. Research carried out on a particularly disfavoured group of women (the unemployed) through sixty in-depth interviews in Łódź and Warsaw reveals a different reality (Heinen, 1995). According to this research, Polish women claim their professional activity as their own and attribute to it a decisive weight in the construction of their identity, far from defining themselves principally on the basis of their place in the family, as opinion polls would suggest. The active and positive attitude of Polish unemployed women, in comparison with unemployed men, is confirmed by other sources (Janowska, Martini-Fiwek and Góral, 1992).

Even in the more extreme case of Russia, where the situation both of the labour movement and women is incomparably worse than in Poland, some potential ground for women's participation has been detected (Bridger, Key and Pinnick, 1996). First of all, many Russian women (although there has unfortunately been the bias of concentrating on highly educated women), even while suffering the knocks of the process of change, are displaying levels of ingenuity, tenacity and adaptability which sit uneasily with the notion of 'victim' so often used. Furthermore, the success of the party 'Russia's Women' indicates that there is a possibility of reinterpreting, in a more subjective way, traditional gender ideology. 'Russia's Women', for instance, has gained substantial support by affirming that Russian women in politics and in economics are more trustworthy than the often heavy drinking men.

The interviews collected at Fiat Auto Poland do not constitute evidence in this sense. Two cases (an activist from *Metalowcy* and a newly arrived activist of *Sierpień 80*) show how Polish women can respectively start a personal career project in the union or take difficult subjective decisions about commitment (the second woman, a single mother, had recently quit *Metalowcy* and joined the militant *Sierpień 80*). The Danone case also revealed a multisided situation: women are marginalised by Solidarity in Warsaw, but they surprisingly make up the majority of the Solidarity plant executive in Bieruń Stary.

A Female Workers' Revolt: The Cotex Case

An even partial assessment of this issue required further research. For this reason a situation of important female-led industrial action was observed in Winter 1998-99. This also allowed us to check Kuroń's already mentioned opinion about the Polish female workers being typically directed by male activists. The case is that of Cotex, a textile factory employing 1,200 people of whom 1,000 are women in Płock (central Poland). The observation consisted in the collection of press and union materials, the interview of two Solidarity activists and of the Solidarity '80 leader, an afternoon's presence in the occupied factory, and the conversation with the inhabitants of the area.

Cotex, which previously produced for the Soviet Union market, fell into a deep crisis in the 1990s. Today, wages are at the minimum level allowed by the law, and rumours of imminent bankruptcy grow even louder. The militant National Solidarity 80 union, sometimes supported by the other three unions (OPZZ, Solidarity and a union of foremen) but often opposed by them, has been very active in the last few years. It has also organised very spectacular forms of protest like the blockade of the town bridge, a very important artery of the region. In Summer 1998, National

Solidarity 80 obtained the appointment of an agreed director. However, his activity very soon met the opposition of the other three unions, who asked for and obtained his removal by the voievod in November 1998. National Solidarity 80 refused to accept the director's removal and occupied the factory trying, without success, to maintain production. Actually, protesters rejected the term 'occupation' considering the director's removal illegitimate: in their opinion, they were working and the other unions were boycotting the factory. The action was ended by the intervention of the police the 12th of March 1999. The Solidarity 80-backed director was removed and production started again, but Solidarity 80 maintained its opposition role within the factory. Also thanks to the effective 'political bargaining' power acquired by the unions on the battlefield, there is today a strong interest of the public ownership in saving the company.

The Cotex case is extremely interesting for a number of reasons, like the nature of the conflict around restructuring and privatisation. However, what matters here is the gendered nature of the industrial action. Cotex represents a splendid case of women's self-organisation and mobilisation during work conflict. National Solidarity 80 is composed mainly of unskilled female workers and is led by a woman; among the founding members there was only one man. Hundreds of workers (about two thirds of the workforce), almost entirely women, occupied for four months (of winter) an almost unheated factory. All of the 'security service', involved in real battles with the non-occupying workforce and the police, were women. The self-organisation and resistance capacities were absolutely outstanding.

Their adversaries were the mostly male foremen, technicians and former directors, all charged with stealing the factory. As it often happens in Eastern Europe, a big state-owned company is invisibly privatised through the creation of small commercial and service firms. These are established by company employees and managers, who exploit the commercial links or the technical knowledge and machinery of the company. This is a continuation under new legal forms of the shadow economy practices of the last period of state socialism, and forces the 'mother' company to endure the competition of its own employees. At Cotex, these satellite/parasite firms were created by male technicians and managers, and the unions opposing National Solidarity 80 are also led by men. Moreover, the local inhabitants to whom I informally talked about the events at Cotex commented that the conflict had no solution because 'Polish *women* do not surrender'. The gender self-identity of the militants (the word is well-suited in this case) is explicit in the tales of the fights against the non-occupying workers or the police, when the general charge is 'they beat women'. By contrast, there is no sign of explicit ideological feminism as it is known in the West: Madonna images replace the Western protest iconography.

The heteronomy of which Kuroń spoke does exist, but only at the political level. National Solidarity 80, which split from Solidarity 80 in 1994, is also an extreme-right organisation led by Marian Jurczyk, one of the historical leaders of Solidarity, a Senator and (at the times of the events) Major of Stettin.[15] Jurczyk sent to Płock his closest collaborator (a man) as press-agent of the Cotex workers. However, the mobilisation was clearly led by the local female activists. Only, their action, alone, did not reach the political level without an external contribution. The work-level of the conflict was the most important: the protesting women did not claim wage increases but were only defending their jobs and their workplace, refusing any measure of 'assistance' from the state. In addition, while nationalism is the main feature of National Solidarity 80 at the political level, I was treated very kindly in spite of my foreign citizenship.

The sociological interpretation is not that easy. The events at Cotex might be seen as an extreme case of proletarian revolt, given the wages, the company situation, the peripheral position and, why not, the sex of the protagonists. It might also be seen, however, as proof of the reactive capacities of Polish women, not ashamed of using national and traditional identity resources, and of their attachment to a role at work.

Ten years after 1989, important events are confirming the potentialities of Polish working women for developing subjective action. I refer notably to three different, and apparently unrelated, events of summer 1999. The first is the strong and relatively successful nurses' movement, which differently than any other employees' mobilisation in Poland in the last years took a strong but independent political dimension (against the health-care reform) and received the sympathy of 80% of the population. This movement used an explicit gendered (female declination and conjugation) language, forgetting that there also are (rare) male nurses. The second fact was the opening, with many years of delay, of a participate debate on the role of women in Solidarity during the 1980s. This debate, which took place mainly in the pages of the newspaper *Gazeta Wyborcza*, revealed how women's social role has been occulted by the political and cultural elites before and after 1989. The last event was the protest campaign, launched by the women's magazine *Wysokie obcasy*, against the reform of the pension system. Buzek's reform, introducing the contributory system while maintaining an anticipated age of retirement for women (60 years instead of 65), under the appearances of 'protection' discriminates women, who eventually receive pensions about 33% lower for the same wage level. It is striking that in Italy, a country with important traditions of feminist mobilisation, a similar reform (Dini's reform in 1995) did not provoke reactions (although it has to be noted that Italian women, according to the Law n. 903 of 1977, can, if they want, continue to work after retirement age, maintaining the previous job security; Polish labour law is not as much definite on this point).

Seeking a Political Role for the Unions

The Decline of Class Politics

Some of the 'subjective' demands emerging from workers and activists are apt to motivate a re-politicisation of the unions. An example is that of working time reduction, which in both countries is first of all the object of a political, parliamentary debate. Pointing in the same direction are many elements of working class disintegration, which require a new 'social contract' and the necessarily political treatment of problems like social exclusion, unemployment, and welfare reform. In this situation of new political problems, the difficulties encountered during the plant-level comparison could be a manifestation of the need to change the level of analysis. If plant- and company-based models of unionism are fragile, the unions still face political problems at the central level in different ways according to national tradition. In spite of any decentralisation, therefore, the political level would be the only one on which an attentive comparison might be carried out.

This approach does not conflict with an investigation of the shop-floor level of action, which remains fundamental for union loyalty. What can be tried is a conjunction of the two levels, that is an investigation of how politics are understood by the rank-and-file members.

This piece of research, concentrated on personal experiences and on the plant, does not provide sufficient materials for assessing the differences between the political activities of the Italian and Polish unions. This is not only due to the fact that the political framework in Poland was still under construction at the time of the inquiry, and therefore unsuitable for precise comparative analysis. It also stems from the fact, which is an important finding itself, that union activists rarely speak *spontaneously* of politics when describe their experience. Moreover, they habitually repeat (in both countries) the commonplace that 'the trade union is the trade union, and politics is politics'.

There are of course exceptions, but as shown in chapter 3 they come in most cases from older activists linked to an older model of engagement. In the past, a class character allowed unionism to play an autonomous political role. Today, however, political identity is an obstacle rather than an aid to unions' participation in the political debate on new social issues. Rather than pushing towards the elaboration of a new social contract, this politically-based identity locks the unions into the defence of the old one. Using the definitions drafted above, it expresses the defensive and communitarian side of the working class rather than the subjective one.

The proof of a decay of class-based political unionism comes from the unions closest to working class consciousness, that is *Sierpień 80* and *Federacja*. If class was a suitable basis for political engagement, these should be the organisations with the clearest political awareness. In fact, the bewilderment there is particularly striking.

> Those from Solidarity say that on their side they will try to obtain something in the Sejm [lower chamber of the Polish parliament], in the parliamentary commission on privatisation, while we as a trade union have stayed in the queue for access to it. It's not politics, it's contacts with the politicians which is necessary, not the parliamentary elections like for Solidarity (...). In the mines, in the steelworks, people may fight, but this does not interest us so much, what happens there. We are interested first of all in what we do for ourselves, this is the most important thing, we don't care about politics. Maybe, if it is necessary to give support when some mine or foundry strikes, we'll do it, but first of all, there is the factory. [ta1]

> The union should be interested in politics, but when the laws are not good for the workers, I don't know whether they should vote for or against. [ta4]
> It's necessary to adjust certain things, it's very useful for the union to have somebody in parliament. [ta5]

> The union organises meetings with the local MPs, from different parties, it is the local representatives who matter (...). The unions cannot have an influence on the general situation, what can trade unions do with the economy? [ta6]
> The union should show interest in what happens in Poland, in some form of protest, go to Warsaw, blockades. Participation in politics is rather inconvenient (...). The union should not be in the Parliament because it is the protector of the worker, it can't vote laws, can it, which would damage that worker. [ta7]

> It should not be in politics, but have an influence on politics. There are trade union forms of influence, strikes, demonstrations, only these forms remain to us. [ta8]

I don't read newspapers. I read only the jobs ads., this interests me. [tz2]

This impression is confirmed at the central level, where *Sierpień 80* political activity is not very clear. Some leaders I met defined the union as 'left-wing', but the union organises demonstrations and appears to have good relations with the right-wing party KPN. In particular, *Sierpień 80* organised in Katowice (where it is strongest) two spectacular initiatives charged with not being democratic. During the electoral campaign of 1997 it walled up the doors of the Union of Freedom's offices. In December 1998 prevented the Solidarity delegation from participating in the commemorations of the bloody repression at the mine 'Wujek' in 1981. As a matter of fact, the political affiliates of *Sierpień 80* and Solidarity 80 in the last years have ranged from the extreme Right to the Peasants' Party and the Left. In January 2000, *Sierpień 80* stipulated an alliance, called 'National Popular Bloc', with the paysants' radical union 'Self-defence' and the authoritarianism-prone general Walicki. The workers' movement as link between the factory and society appears as disintegrated, leaving the space to any kind of political heteronomy. Therefore, a 'politics of the Subject' may emerge in the unions from below, from the concrete demands of the workers, more easily than from above, from neat ready-made political and ideological projects.

Seeking 'Encompassingness': The Forward and Backward Steps of Neocorporatism

In the period of change traversed by Italy and above all Poland, the dilemmas of politicisation are central with respect to two issues: the emerging of neo-corporatist arrangements and the role of the unions in the democratisation process.

The first issue was already discussed in chapter 3, with regard to the enduring feelings of opposition which impede a real 'social partnership'. After the discussion elaborated in this chapter, it may be added that in both countries corporatist solutions, especially if implemented only *from above*, risk being in conflict with the subjectivation process. In particular, there is a risk that the unions' monopoly of representation acted as a brake on the emergence of new demands and new, still underrepresented or marginal, groups. In Italy this risk has been clearly denounced by Bruno Trentin, CGIL leader until 1994.

When it is not the discovery of hot water, political exchange is a formula aiming at legitimising, in an elevated language, corporatist [the term is in

Italian negatively connoted] modes of arrangement characterised (...) by a process of exclusion and marginalisation of the unrepresented. (Trentin, 1994, p. 49)

In Poland, the problem has been involuntarily touched by the new Constitution, passed in 1997. Paragraph 59 reads: 'The freedom to *join* trade unions is guaranteed', forgetting the freedom to *constitute* trade unions.[16] This detail, although without any concrete relevance, betrays the tendency at the political system to consider the trade unions as *given* institutions (as prescribed by corporatist models), with little attention to change and innovation. In Poland, where the main trade unions Solidarity and OPZZ maintain strong political power, this is all the more evident. Schmitter himself (1981) acknowledges that the corporatist models possibly manifest a certain level of institutional sclerosis and a dubious capacity to answer to new political demands and to emerging identities.

While listening to the Italian and Polish workers even more might be said. Industrial workers have ceased to be central in political exchange, and have become themselves, both subjectively and according to the general social representation, a 'minority' like many others. Subsequently, workers' protest is no longer successfully restrained by neo-corporatism. This hypothesis contests the conclusions of cross-national analysis on political protest, according to which established neo-corporatist arrangements reduce the levels of political protest (e.g. Nollert, 1995). In-depth analysis allows us to distinguish between the *expression* of social protest and the subjective orientations of the actors, a distinction avoided by political scientists concentrating on 'macro' cross-national comparisons. It may be easily noted, in this way, that in Italy and Poland the major and maybe unique efforts made by successive governments since 1992 (with the notable exception of Berlusconi in Italy) have only marginally reduced feelings of opposition among workers. Certainly Italy and Poland do not represent the best cases of neo-corporatism implementation and consolidation. If one takes into account the general trends in class power relations, and the nature of the 'laboratories' of Italy and especially Poland in the last years, it may suggested that these countries are *anticipating* general trends, rather than catching up with them. In conclusion, when the neo-corporatist aim of shaping a more 'encompassing' representation becomes more topical, paradoxically its realisation gets more delicate and problematic.

Unions and Democracy: Promoters or Victims?

Just like theories on corporatism, theories on democratisation may also be assessed by a look 'from below'. The role of workers and trade unions in the process of democratisation had been conceived in very different ways. Classical theories, whether from the Right or from Marxist standpoints, tend to see democracy as the business of the bourgeoisie, or even to see workers as prone to authoritarianism (e.g. Lipset, 1959). More recently, the opposite thesis of the working class as the main promoter of democratisation has been advanced with a rich historical foundation (Rueschemeyer, Stephens and Stephens, 1992).

The cases of Italy in 1943-48 and Poland in the 1980s quite clearly support the second of these views. Moreover, the experience of direct, council democracy of the *rady robotnicze* in 1956-57 or of the *consigli di fabbrica* in 1968-70 had a meaning that went beyond the factory gates. The democratic orientations of the Polish workers in 1980-81 could not be stressed more than was done by Laba (1991) and Goodwyn (1991).

Yet today an answer to the problem of the relationship between workers, unions, and democracy requires further attention. The fears expressed by Ost (1994) about a non-democratic mobilisation of the suffering Polish working class have been confirmed neither by the interview materials presented here, nor by actual political developments. In other post-communist countries, however, there have been working-class mobilisations *against* democratisation (notably, Yugoslavia 1991 and Romania 1990-91). In Poland, the interviews show, rather than a rejection of democracy (which takes place only in very isolated cases like Ursus), a rapid disenchantment. Workers perceive that democracy, today, does not necessarily serve their interests, as was assumed by Rueschemeyer, Stephens and Stephens. More consistent seems the argument by Galin (1994), according to which the unions *weaken* after democratisation, rather than strengthening as it is usually expected. This is due to the loss of some important resources they have under undemocratic regimes: the unity due to the common enemy, international support, the mobilising myths. The experience of 'alternation' I described is particular strong in these regards.

This is only a part of the truth, however. Disenchantment with democracy is not specific to East Europeans. Western workers today also express increasing dissatisfaction with democracy, as is shown by their substantial support for parties like the *Front National*, the FPÖ, or the *Lega Nord* (and in the US for Pat Buchanan). The Italian union activists interviewed at Fiat, Lucchini and Danone, although far from being anti-democratic, are mostly very sceptical about the political role of the trade unions. Surveys suggest that in Poland, contrary to all the media-led anti-workers propaganda, the level of authoritarianism after 1989 has increased among the intelligentsia but declined among manual workers (Mach, 1998). Again, this confirms the usefulness of the idea of 'alternation' to understand changes in post-communist Europe.

What was described in the third chapter helps us to understand this situation. Both Italian and Polish trade unions are experiencing a parallel disintegration of working class consciousness. Therefore, the working class cannot any longer be a united political subject; in Touraine's terms, it is no longer a class. As a consequence, problems that were until now marginal in the Italian and Polish union movements, like the representation of minorities, the management of differences, the attention to individual professional paths and the international dialogue, require new ways of conceiving political engagement.

The history of Solidarity, shows that the defence of human prerogatives and culture may be a mobilisation resource for trade unions. Solidarity activists were fighting for the defence of the workers against exploitation, but also for the defence of the individual against standardisation. The sociologist Aris Accornero, pointing at the Italian Fiat workers, once commented 'of these men we have made machines for class struggle' (quoted in Lerner, 1988, p. 13). The Polish Fiat workers, in spite of all their proletarian reactions, have been less susceptible to be made class-machines. They may contribute to the elaboration of more 'laic' approaches to democracy.

Notes

1   According to a survey of Italian metalworkers, 67.8% identify the union in the shop steward (*delegato*), 12.3% in the full-time officer, 5.7% in the national leader, 3.8% in somebody else (Ires, 1995). Though the sample is not representative, the results seem quite telling.

2   I refer here to the 'vulgar' version of the classical theory of Milbrath (1965). Accordingly, party membership was rated very high, at the fifth level of a fourteen-level scale, above other indicators of 'sympathising'. In fact, this is true only for its vulgar version available in textbooks of political science and political sociology, since Milbrath more carefully spoke of '*active* party membership', and not of membership *tout court*.

3   The proposal came from the 'Congress of the Liberals' held in Gdańsk in December 1998. The 'Liberals' are active in both parties of the ruling coalition, i.e. the Union of Freedom and Solidarity Electoral Action.

4   Leader of the left-wing minority of the CGIL until 1994, and since then of *Rifondazione Comunista*, Fausto Bertinotti is considered one of the best Italian politicians for TV performances.
5   Left-wing film director. The quotation is from his film *'Aprile'*.
6   A Pensioners' Party has been active in Poland since 1995 (more than 5% at the 1997 elections if one also counts the votes for a second Pensioners' Party, created for disturbance purposes), but it defends mainly already retired people. Similar parties also exist in Italy, where in 1999 they gained a seat in the European Parliament.
7   The authors themselves acknowledge it: 'The interviewers have been obliged to adopt particular modes of approaching the bi-occupied, in order to overcome the widespread reluctance to discuss the research topic. This may have swelled the number of bi-occupied members of political parties' (Milanaccio, 1982, p. 302).
8   The *contratti di solidarietà*, envisaged by law 863 of 1984, consist in a reduction of working time whose costs are partially covered by the state, which refunds 50% of the working hours lost.
9   To give an example (although statistics, as already repeatedly observed, are often misleading in transitional economies), the ratio of wages of general managers to average wages has jumped between 1990 and 1994 from 2.5-3.5 to 2.8-7.5 in public enterprises, 11.3-22.6 in joint ventures, 4.7-11.3 in private enterprises. Even higher are the relative wages of the chiefs of foreign financial institutions: 64-86 times average salaries (Kabaj, 1998).
10   Regionally-based bargaining indeed has important potentialities (see e.g. Regalia, 1998), and may have different outcomes depending on the specific power relations between employers and unions (for instance in Germany it is the unions who mostly gain from regional bargaining). In any case the regulation of regional differences is everywhere a political problem for the unions, as German reunification has shown. In Eastern Germany, like in Southern Italy, a purely egalitarian policy without more focused developmental programs has failed, attesting the insufficiency of traditional Keynesian approaches for the growth of single regions integrated into wider markets.
11   There are however important differences among countries. Women and immigrants were segregated, in a way or in another, everywhere, but with respects to age and skills the European labour movements have been more integrative than the American one.
12   In 1996 they made three claims in the company-level bargaining forum: the possibility of benefiting from a part of the severance pay (*trattamento di fine rapporto*) for personal leave; the extension of part-time working; interrupted working time like for white-collar workers. None of these claims, however, was conceded, which points to the actual attitudes of employers and unions. A female activist comments: 'the union does not yet believe in these things' [rf7].
13   On this point Poland and Italy are very different. In 1994 28% of the Italian women and 53% of the Polish ones worked full time. The Polish rate, although is the lowest among the European post-communist countries, is higher than any other Western advanced country, included Scandinavia and North America (data: ISSP survey 1994 on 'Family and Changing Gender Role II).
14   The pre-modern or pre-industrial arguments are however valid for the Polish rural society. Polish surveys show the variable 'living in the countryside' to be an extremely strong determinant of people's answers.
15   The exact name of Jurczyk's organisation is '*National* Independent Self-Ruling Trade Union Solidarity 80' (*Krajowy Niezależny Samorządny Związek Zawodowy*

Solidarność 80), abbreviated *KNSZZ Solidarność 80*. Only the 'K' letter at the beginning differentiates it from the bigger organisation *NSZZ Solidarność 80*.

16   The corresponding paragraph of the Italian Constitution (n.39) states simply that 'trade unions' organisation is free'.

Conclusion

The Social Construction of Union Activism

We still know too little about the orientations of the trade unions' rank and file, paradoxically in a period when – as shown in Italy by the increasing number of workplace ballots in which unions' proposals are rejected – the tensions between ordinary members and the leaderships have become more problematic. There are, indeed, various forms of surveys, but these are still incapable, thirty years after Parkin's criticism, of discerning between 'dominant' and 'subordinate' systems of references: do workers say what they think, or just what they think they should think? Moreover, industrial relations studies still tend to treat trade unions as self-conscious, rational and strategically coherent interest associations. Consequently, the empiricist analysis of their *behaviour* is more than sufficient, because subjective meanings do not matter. However, can we really believe that if Italian workers massively vote for CGIL-CISL-UIL in RSU elections, this is because of their conviction concerning the strategic superiority of their national leaders' lines? Recent upheavals in Italian politics would recommend greater care. The problems are even more noticeable in the post-communist countries, where the meaning of the words themselves requires testing beforehand. As David Stark has proved, even a basic institution of capitalism like private property can take on disparate meanings in Eastern Europe. We will know little or nothing about post-communist workers' preferences as long as we continue to investigate them through the abstract notions of 'democracy', 'privatisation', or 'the free market'.

This book has provided several examples of incoherence between general ('dominant', in Parkin's terms) statements and everyday, individual orientations. Methodologically, it has moved tentatively towards a more interprétative approach. The complex, multifaced reality of workplace industrial relations requires prudence and further testing; moreover, such a reality implies that no approach can claim an explanatory monopoly. Nevertheless, the interpretative perspective used here has displayed specific potentialities. The typology of 'plant consciousnesses' described in the second chapter, for instance, although it does not correspond to any classical industrial relations indicator, accounts precisely for the most recent trends of the unions and their capacity to deal with the emerging issues of 'difference'. Culture and life-experiences do matter, and these explain differences within identical companies and between identical plants (like Mirafiori and Rivalta Fiat plants). In a period when new social movements often have a cultural or identity basis, we have to take into account the cultural and subjective factors even in the analysis of an *interest* organisation like the trade unions. Otherwise it would be difficult to assess issues like nationalism or gender policies in the unions.

This book has stressed the importance of reconstructing local experiences and cognitive frameworks for understanding social actors. The stress on experience and social construction must not, however, be read as a determination of consciousness by the circumstances. Social construction is not social determination, and the word 'constructing' itself implies a role for agency. Even the trade union most conditioned by its history and location among those studied in the book, the FIOM-CGIL from Piombino, is not socially determined. Even that model of unionism had been actively constructed by workers through their practice – and here one is tempted to give back to the term construction its practical, rather than theoretical or phenomenological meaning: Piombino workers *concretely* reconstructed, in a spontaneous move, their steelworks in 1945.

The usefulness of an approach should be evaluated first of all on the basis of its capacity to produce 'new' results, and additional knowledge on the topic. Therefore, in this conclusion, it is necessary to summarise and assess the main findings. In this book, they have been organised around three main statements.

The Deconstruction of Class

The first statement argues that in both Italy and Poland, on the two sides of the former iron curtain, a parallel process of 'class consciousness disintegration' is taking place. The social relations of production *in the workplace*, which are the basis of class consciousness, are no longer sufficient to explain trade unionism. The fact that Poles and Italians work for the same employers and in very similar workshops by no means makes them more alike. By contrast, a deep differentiation emerges: at Fiat and Lucchini ten different configurations of union consciousness were counted. Differences are entrenched not only between Italy and Poland, but also within the countries and even within the companies.

Indeed, working-class heterogeneity is not a novelty, especially in Italy where in social stratification terms, a homogeneous, large working class has never existed. Neither is the heterogeneity of working-class *consciousness* a novelty, as Marshall (1983) has illustrated at length well before the fall of the states claiming to be based on a working-class ideology. Nevertheless, an in-depth investigation allows us to go a step further than stating the presence of differences.

In both countries notably the same arguments and cognitive frameworks (called 'constants of disintegration') contrasting the current situation with the past have been found. Subjectively, if not objectively, the trade unionists studied indicate a process of social decline, egoistic withdrawal, generation fracture, organisational mistrust, and isolation. They express the same feelings of nostalgia for the former phase of the union movement. Nostalgia is by no means a congenital, unavoidable feature of workers' mentality: in-depth methods not limited to the question 'is it better now or before' actually detect that in many cases, on many issues, workers are able to appreciate change. However, in the current phase, as far as union activity is concerned, Polish and Italian activists have strikingly similar regrets. This is more than an anthropological tendency to remember the 'old good days': it is an inversion of references. When − as in Italy in 1995 on the pensions' reform − national union leadership can peacefully overlook the opinions of the large factories, we are witnessing a real departure from a model.

We cannot assert that the past was 'objectively' as they depict it, but the imagery inherited from that past, and now deconstructed, is the same in both countries. In spite of the 'nominal' antithesis in the ideological tradition (communist vs. anticommunist unionism), in the workplaces the historical evolution has been seen in similar ways. In the Polish car factories, in the eighties workers were fighting against piecework, a quintessential indicator of class opposition by all the sociology of work since Roy's (1952) fundamental studies. Still, today, occasionally, Polish activists refer to class arguments and make links between the current and past experience of work conflict. If one considers that Polish activists mostly share right-wing opinions, these elements of class consciousness cannot come from reading or from rhetoric − they must come from experience.

The current differences and divisions are perceived as problematic precisely because they diverge from the image of the past based on unity, strength, and social ascent. Once the 'class' icon has been breached, cultural, gender, professional identities start to be visible.

A Widening Divide

The second statement refers to the current differences between Italian and Polish workers, which are continuously socially constructed and reconstructed. There are basic distinguishing elements between the two nationalities: notably, the stronger 'monetary' orientations and the distinctive 'neo-proletarian' rhetoric of the Poles, versus 'resistance' attitudes in Italy. Moreover, in spite of European integration and the collapse of state socialism, the East-West distinction maintains a powerful meaning for the workers. We cannot be sure that Italians and Poles respectively represent Western and Eastern workers as a whole. However, the reciprocal difference is perceived by the workers themselves precisely in those terms: we are 'Western' and they are 'Eastern', and vice versa.

More complicated than the assertion of this difference has been its interpretation. The most commonplace explanations, based on the different level of institutionalisation or on standards of living, do not withstand close examination. Still less suitable, in this case, is 'path-dependency', although it provides explanations of the 'institutional' sides of industrial relations. Current differences in union activism are clearly not inherited from the past: twenty years ago, Italian trade unions were by no means 'conservative'; even less was Solidarity proletarian.

In particular, the findings contest the idea that the differences between East and West are due to the 'communist legacies' in which Eastern workers are locked. Polish unionists are often depicted as an obstacle to reforms. However, if one compares Polish activists not with ideal types, but with Westners in the flesh, they are very little conservative. They have even embraced many of the vales currently presented as 'modern' (flexibility, innovation, international adaptation, qualification, tertiarisation...). At the same time, they are aware of the new challenges and speak of deindustrialisation and internationalisation with greater ease than their Italian counterparts. In no way (apart from marginal exceptions) do they appear as 'backward'.

Through an interpretative approach, an alternative explanation has been suggested which gives a central role to the specific experience of regime change. The subjective experience of communist breakdown has been re-defined, drawing on Berger and Luckmann's, 'alternation', and abandoning the misleading concept of 'transition'. In essence, 'alternation' has promoted among Polish workers the positive value of change and the use of monetary evaluative references, but also a 'neo-proletarian' definition of identities. By contrast, the subjective Italian experience of slow change and crisis, defined as 'secondary socialisation', has the effect of pushing the Italian industrial unions towards (not necessarily unjustified) attitudes of 'resistance'. The legacies of the past are more visible in the West than in the East, where – as is clearly shown by the way itself people talk during the interviews – the experience of alternation induces a higher reflexivity, an important feature of both high modernity (according to Giddens) and new social movements (according to Touraine).

The forms of workers' consciousness are determined by social relations both *within* and *outside* the workplace. Which influence is more important depends on subjective experience. In post-communist countries, changes *outside* the workplace are more striking than the slower, more ambiguous changes *within* companies. This explains why unionists' consciousness is determined for the most part by societal experiences, and particularly by the systemic need for radical change. Since changes in the workplace are hardly discernible, while changes in the street are clearly positive (everybody likes to find consumer goods in the shops), attitudes towards change are altogether positive, and the class side is easily forgotten. Only when organisational changes dramatically reinforce Taylorist discipline and control – as in some workshops like the assembly line at Fiat in Tychy –, elements of the hibernated class consciousness are awakened by the shock. The radical union *Sierpień 80* demonstrates this exactly, although, no sooner does it develop a class reaction, than it starts to meet the same contradictions, isolation and political dilemmas of its Western comrades.

Timid Subjectivation

The third and last argument is about the ways trade union activists see the differences among workers: differences *among* nationalities and differences *within* the workplaces are perceived through a similar lens. They all challenge a mechanical form of solidarity, drawing attention to individual, subjective demands. As a result, the unions which are most internally differentiated and most open to these differences are also the ones that are most inclined to transnational dialogue and cooperation.

Interviews with activists show that this link between internal and external diversity is not an individual one: there is not, or at least not yet, a type of activist coherently well disposed to any kind of minority or different group. At this level, the research evidence rejects the hypothesis of an association. However, the link exists at the 'micro-social' level of workshop union organisation. The unions which are accustomed locally to listening to different people also listen more easily to foreign workers. This happens because both globalisation and internal differentiation raise, from different sides, the same problems of identity and solidarity redefinition. Just as it is impossible to satisfy everybody simply by claiming equal wages for workers of different qualifications, different ages, or different genders, so it is impossible to resolve the dilemmas of globalisation by demanding the same wages for Poles and Italians. In both cases an identity based on resemblance, like that inherent within class consciousness, is inadequate.

A more detailed analysis of subjective orientations at work and in the unions reveals, however, that not everything is sterile in the heritage of class consciousness. Besides the aspect of similarity and unity, class consciousness had – in Turin as well as in the Polish Solidarity – a 'subjective' side of 'voice', of opposition at work, involving a capacity to express human prerogatives and an autonomous point of view on working life. In certain cases, especially among youth and among women, this side has already merged with new, subjective forms of union commitment.

Within the process of subjectivation, the Italian unions have some comparative material advantages (money, time, and institutions) which help to add the life-sphere to workplace experience as an evaluative horizon. However, from the point of view of the activists, there are no major differences: subjectivity was found to be dominant in about one third of the activists in Poland as well as in Italy. Probably, the orientation to change and the lack of inertia among the Poles compensates for material disadvantage.

Scenarios for European Labour

This explanation is developed at a 'micro' level, but refer directly to the 'macro' level and merges with it. The differences between plants meant that it was necessary to search for the reason beyond the workplace. If we cannot extend the conclusions of limited case studies to large national societies, we can nonetheless understand better national societies if we become familiar with the way society members think about themselves. Indeed, similar arguments against the idea of Polish 'backwardness' may be proposed about Poland as a society. Some observers, like the economist, former-Solidarity advisor and politician Ryszard Bugaj (1999), are starting to argue that Poland is already more capitalist, and more 'American', than Western Europe. Examples of this are abundant: privatisation of the pension system; antiprogressive fiscal policies; deregulation of working time; social inequality in general (one could add, in foreign affairs, the staunch support for the US line). Such a rapid change would not have been possible if the Polish workers had been, as many still argue, conservative opponents of reform. Indeed, it is more frequent to hear Poland defined as 'nineteenth century capitalism'. However, this definition overlooks the analogies between the nineteenth and twenty-first centuries and hides the nature of Central-Eastern Europe (and especially Poland) as a pathfinder of the current global trend towards a resurgence of capitalism.

Interviews with union activists reveal that social needs are not forgotten in Poland: if the need were not there, workers would not willingly pay the costs of union commitment. However, Polish union members express these needs with a different language, and in consequence with different policies from their Italian colleagues. Ten years after 1989 the repression of social arguments implied by the logic of alternation is no longer so strong. The mobilisations and the protests around the health system reform reveal a revival of explicit social demands. This book accounts for the 1990s, that is the period of most radical rejection of the old, regime-based social paternalism, involving the neo-proletarian rhetoric and a strong orientation towards immediate monetary advantage which accompanied the 'primary accumulation'. This is not, however, condemned to last forever. As social demands come to be expressed more clearly, the space for the trade unions is also increasing. This space will be used in original forms marked by the alternation experience.

Some suggestions for today's trade unions can now be drawn. First of all, when dealing with Eastern Europe the trade unions should take into account the failure of 'evolutionary' approaches to the understanding of post-communism. Since the new Central and Eastern European democracies, following the drastic 'alternation' of priorities and references, try – though not always successfully – to embrace the newest and purest patterns of capitalism, the workplace reality is also sometimes more 'advanced' than in the West. So, for instance, Danone is experimenting with work councils in Eastern Europe before doing it in the West; subcontracting, internal mobility, and 'variable wages' are more 'highly' evolved in the Polish plants than in Italian ones; company bargaining is becoming increasingly important in Italy, to the point of threatening industry-level collective agreements, while in Poland it is 'already' the rule. The relations between Western and Eastern trade unions should no longer have the strongly 'asymmetric' nature which characterised the exchanges between CGIL-CISL-UIL (or the French CFDT) and Solidarity in the 1980s. Conversely, today the Western unions have much to learn from the Eastern ones.

A second lesson lies in the fact that by coming to terms with Eastern Europe the Western trade unions are forced to review their identities and basic values. Trade unions, especially where their 'encompassing' capacity is limited because, as in Italy and Poland, some sectors are underrepresented, risk forgetting the people who do not belong to the 'established' working class. Direct dialogue with Eastern Europe, just like openness to women, immigrants, or atypical workers, will certainly raise sensitive problems in the short run, in that it breaches established 'protective boxes'. Nevertheless, through the emergence of subjectivity analysed and defined in some workers' discourses, such dialogue is likely to open up new chances in the long run. The unions have to get used to difference, and international difference is both emblematic and instructive. The development of communication channels and shop-floor democracy, the elaboration of more operational conceptions of equity and solidarity and the attention to vocational courses (at a national as well as individual level) will contribute collectively to the better equipping of the union movement in the twenty-first century. On the other hans, Eastern trade unions, by virtue of strengthening interaction with their 'capitalist' counterparts, could avoid a direct consequence of alternation: the repudiation of alternatives. They could replace the 'transition' ideal types with real, practical examples and open up debate on concrete different choices – like between North American and Western European social models.

The study of two Italian and one French multinational companies reveals that ideological internationalism (like rhetorical egalitarianism) is backfiring rather. Moreover, there is no gain on the shop floor from international union contacts, when such contact only involves officers. Today, the views of Italian and Polish workers about each other are quite negative. What is required is the creation of 'global' experiences at a *Lebenswelt* level, capable of reducing the gap – created by globalisation – between borders of experience (and identities) and borders of interests. Therefore, a tighter link between institutions like the European Work Councils or the European Trade Union Confederation and shop-floor realities is necessary. Concrete exchange of information among plants, for example, has the immediate advantage of reducing the existing (more or less employer-led) misinformation on foreign realities, and a more long-term strength of redefining identities.

If communication is not achieved, the process of European integration, and of European Union enlargement in particular, risks to be far from peaceful. The reality of multinational companies shows an East-West divide in identities, involving reciprocal blame, that may quickly become much stronger than the existing divide between Southern and Northern Europe. Social dumping and national stereotypes might then impede any form of 'social Europe'. Polish trade union activists – in spite of their limitations and the mistakes made during the objective learning process – are neither 'conservative' nor 'nationalist reactionaries', but are often angry about injustice. Since they do not express this injustice in class terms, they might, if isolated, revert to the East-West category. Some smaller unions are already violently anti-European. However, pressured by the fact that inequality is more compelling in the East than in the West, post-communist union activists also might develop a deeper conception of equality.

The East-West divergent nascent trend risks ending in the construction of two opposed models of unionism, both equally inadequate: resistance unionism (in the West) and neo-proletarian unionism (in the East). The 'pride' and the 'proletarian' sides of the golden-era workers' movement tend to split geographically. But if unionism is to retain any kind of 'social movement' nature, albeit partial, these two sides have to be somehow reconnected. There is space for agency. The more East and West meet, the better it will be for both.

Annex

Information About the Interviews

Abbr.	Workshop	Age	Sex	Job	Function
bs1	Assembly	40	M	Supervisor	Member
bs2	Assembly	30	M	Skilled	Delegate
bs3	Toolroom	35	M	Skilled	Delegate
bs4	Assembly	45	M	Skilled	Delegate
bs5	Assembly	34	M	Unskilled	Delegate
bs6	Assembly	34	M	Unskilled	Member
bs7	Assembly	35	M	Skilled	Member
bs8	Assembly	40	M	Skilled	Member
bs9	Offices	55	M	Clerk	Member
tz1	Assembly	40	M	Unskilled	Member
tz2	Assembly	35	M	Unskilled	Member
tz3	Assembly	45	M	Unskilled	Member
ri1	Assembly	34	M	Unskilled	Delegate
ri2	Assembly	29	M	Unskilled	Delegate
ri3	Assembly	38	M	Unskilled	Delegate
ri4	Assembly	32	M	Unskilled	Member
ri5	Assembly	28	M	Unskilled	Delegate
ri6	Assembly	28	M	Unskilled	Delegate
ri7	Assembly	30	M	Unskilled	Member
ri8	Assembly	30	F	Unskilled	Member
ri9	Assembly	30	M	Unskilled	Delegate
rf1	Painting	47	M	Supervisor	Delegate
rf2	Painting	55	M	Unskilled	Member
rf3	Offices	48	M	Clerk	Delegate
rf4	Maintenance	46	M	Skilled	Delegate
rf5	Assembly	45	F	Clerk	Delegate
rf6	Assembly	35	F	Unskilled	Delegate
rf7	Welding	40	F	Unskilled	Delegate
rf8	Assembly	50	M	Unskilled	Delegate
hs1	Lamination	35	M	Unskilled	Delegate
hs2	Lamination	50	M	Unskilled	Delegate
hs3	Foundry	40	M	Unskilled	Delegate
hs4	Foundry	40	M	Unskilled	Delegate
hs5	Maintenance	35	M	Skilled	Delegate
hs6	Maintenance	43	M	Skilled	Delegate
hs7	Lamination	45	M	Superv.	Member

Abbr.	Workshop	Age	Sex	Job	Function
hs8	Foundry	40	M	Unskilled	Delegate
hm1	Foundry	45	M	Skilled	Delegate
hm2	Lamination	40	M	Skilled	Delegate
hm3	Maintenance	50	M	Skilled	Delegate
tm1	Maintenance	51	M	Unskilled	Member
tm2	Offices	40	F	Clerk	Delegate
tm3	Quality c.	38	F	Skilled	Delegate
pf1	Foundry	52	M	Skilled	Delegate
pf2	Transports	34	M	Skilled	Delegate
pf3	Foundry	45	M	Clerk	Delegate
pf4	Lamination	42	M	Unskilled	Delegate
pf5	Foundry	23	M	Unskilled	Member
pf6	Lamination	46	M	Unskilled	Delegate
pf7	Lamination	40	M	Unskilled	Delegate
pf8	Lamination	47	M	Unskilled	Delegate
pf9	Foundry	47	M	Unskilled	Member
pf10	Lamination	46	M	Unskilled	Delegate
pf11	Lamination	45	M	Unskilled	Member
pf12	Foundry	45	M	Unskilled	Delegate
pf13	Lamination	22	M	Unskilled	Member
pf14	Foundry	50	M	Skilled	Member
pf15	Transports	31	M	Unskilled	Member
tp1	Toolroom	40	M	Unskilled	Delegate
tp2	Maintenance	40	M	Skilled	Delegate
ta1	Painting	40	M	Skilled	Delegate
ta2	Welding	36	M	Skilled	Member
ta3	Assembly	33	M	Unskilled	Member
ta4	Assembly	35	F	Unskilled	Member
ta5	Assembly	23	M	Unskilled	Member
ta6	Assembly	25	M	Unskilled	Sympathiser
ta7	Assembly	50	M	Skilled	Member
ta8	Assembly	42	M	Skilled	Member
ta9	Presses	35	M	Unskilled	Member
ta10	Welding	45	M	Unskilled	Member
ta11	Assembly	40	M	Unskilled	Delegate
sf1	Maintenance	42	M	Unskilled	Delegate
sf2	Maintenance	30	M	Unskilled	Delegate
si1	Maintenance	25	M	Unskilled	Delegate
mf1	Presses	50	M	Unskilled	Delegate
mf2	Offices	48	M	Clerk	Delegate
mf3	Offices	45	M	Skilled	Delegate
mf4	Assembly	45	M	Unskilled	Delegate
mf5	Assembly	38	M	Unskilled	Delegate
mf6	Engine	50	M	Unskilled	Delegate
mf7	Offices	37	M	Unskilled	Delegate

Abbr.	Workshop	Age	Sex	Job	Function
mf8	Assembly	52	M	Unskilled	Delegate
mf9	Assembly	44	F	Unskilled	Member
ru1	Assembly	35	M	Unskilled	Delegate
mc1	Presses	28	M	Unskilled	Member
mc2	Assembly	57	M	Unskilled	Delegate
mc3	Assembly	35	M	Unskilled	Member
mc4	Maintenance	30	M	Unskilled	Member
mc5	Welding	31	M	Unskilled	Delegate
mc6	Assembly	34	F	Unskilled	Delegate
pc1	Welding	45	M	Unskilled	Delegate

Note

The abbreviations indicate the plant and the union. The first letter indicates the plant (b: Bielsko; t: Tychy; h: Huta Warszawa; p: Piombino; r: Rivalta; m: Mirafiori; s: Siderco). The second letter indicates the trade union (s: Solidarity; a: August 80 (*Sierpień 80*); m: *Metalowcy*, including *Hutnicy*; p: Popiełuszko; z: *Federacja*; f: FIOM; i: FIM; u: UILM; c: Cobas). The number indicates the order of observation.

The average length of the interviews was around one hour.

Bibliography

Abburrà, L. and Marcenaro, P. (1986), *Le ore e i giorni. L'orario di lavoro tra contrattazione e orientamento dei lavoratori. Un'indagine nel Gruppo Fiat*, Edizioni Lavoro, Rome.

Accornero, A. (1988), 'Torino da laboratorio a caso limite', *Politica ed Economia*, vol. 19, no. 1, pp. 14-16.

Accornero, A. (1992), *La parabola del sindacato*, Il Mulino, Bologna.

Accornero, A., Carmignani, F. and Magna, N. (1985), 'I tre "tipi" di operai Fiat', *Politica ed Economia*, vol. 16, no. 5, pp. 33-47.

Adamski, W. (1996), *Polacy 1981* (Poles 1981), IFiS PAN, Warsaw.

Adamski, W. (1998), *The Legacy of State Socialism as a Challenge to Systemic Transformation: Poland in Comparative Perspective*, WZB Paper P98-002, Berlin.

Adamski, W., Jasiewicz, K. and Rychard, A. (eds) (1986), *Polacy '84. Dynamika konfliktu i konsensusu* (Poles '84. The Dynamics of Conflict and Consensus), Uniwersytet Warszawski, Warsaw.

Agacinski, S. (1998), *Politique des sexes*, Seuil, Paris.

Aglieta, R., Bianchi, G., and Merli Brandini, P. (eds) (1970), *I delegati operai. Ricerca su nuove forme di rappresentanza operaia*, Coines, Rome.

Alasheev S. and Kiblitskaya M. (1996) 'How to survive on a Russian's wage', in S. Clarke (ed), *Labour Relations in Transition: Wages, Employment and Industrial Conflict in Russia*, Edward Elgar, Cheltenham, pp. 99-118.

Albert, M. (1991), *Capitalisme contre capitalisme*, Seuil, Paris.

Alvater, E. and Mahnkopf, B. (1995), 'Transmission Belts of Transnational Competition? Trade Unions and Collective Bargaining in the Context of European Integration', *European Journal of Industrial Relations*, vol. 1, no. 1, pp. 101-117.

Amatori, F. (1992), 'Cicli produttivi, tecnologie, organizzazione del lavoro. La siderurgia a ciclo integrale dal piano "autarchico" alla fondazione dell'Italsider (1937-1961)', *Ricerche Storiche*, vol. 3, pp. 557-612.

Amsden, A., Kochanowicz, J. and Taylor, L. (1994), *The Market Meets its Match: Restructuring the Economies of Eastern Europe*, Harvard University Press, Cambridge MA.

Anderson, L. and Trentin, B. (1996), *NordSud. Lavoro, diritti e sindacato nel mondo*, Ediesse, Rome.

Andreff, V. (1993), *La crise des économies socialistes: la rupture d'un système*, : Presses Universitaires de France, Paris.

Annibaldi, C. (1994), *Impresa, partecipazione, conflitto: considerazioni dall'esperienza FIAT. Dialogo con Giuseppe Berta*, Marsilio, Venice.

Arato, A. (1981), 'Civil Society Against the State: Poland 1980-81', *Telos*, no. 47, pp. 23-47.

Arnot, B. (1981) 'Soviet Labour Productivity and the Failure of the Shchekino Experiment', *Critique*, no. 15, pp. 31-56.

Arte, L. (1993), 'Azione sindacale e azione volontaria: la questione giovanile', in P. Giovannini (ed), *I rumori della crisi. Trasformazioni sociali e identità sindacali*, Angeli, Milan, pp. 57-80.

Ash, T.G. (1983), *The Polish Revolution: Solidarity 1980-82*, Jonathan Cape, London.

Automotive Department (1992), *Some Auto Capital Goes East: Challenges for Unions, Prospects for the Industry*, International Metalworkers Federation, Budapest.

Baccaro, L. and Locke, R. (1998) 'The End of Solidarity? The Decline of Egalitarian Wage Policies in Italy and Sweden', *European Journal of Industrial Relations*, vol. 4, no. 3, pp. 283-308.

Bacon, N. and Blyton, P. (1996), 'Re-Casting the Politics of Steel in Europe: The Impact on Trade Unions', *West European Politics*, vol. 19, no. 4, pp. 770-86.

Badora, B. and Starzyński, P. (1995), *Społeczne postrzeganie inwestycji kapitału zagranicznego w Polsce*, CBOS, Warsaw.

Bagnasco, A. (1986), *Torino. Un profilo sociologico*, Einaudi, Turin.

Bagnasco, A. (1990), *La città dopo Ford: il caso di Torino*, Bollati Berlinghieri, Turin.

Bakuniak, G. (1983a), 'Aktorzy działań - społeczności zakładowe' (The movement actors - the factory social groups), in G. Bakuniak, H. Banaszak, I. Krzemiński and A. Kruczowska, *Polacy. Jesień 80. Proces postawiania niezależnych związków zawodowych* (Poles. Autumn 1980. The emergence process of the independent trade unions). Uniwersytet Warszawski, Warsaw, pp. 42-84.

Bakuniak, G. (1983b), 'My Solidarność, nowy związek we własnych oczach' (We, Solidarity, new trade unions in its own eyes), in G. Bakuniak, H. Banaszak, I. Krzemiński and A. Kruczowska, *Polacy. Jesień 80. Proces postawiania niezależnych związków zawodowych* (Poles. Autumn 1980. The emergence process of the independent trade unions), Uniwersytet Warszawski, Warsaw, pp. 286-327.

Bakuniak, G., Banaszak, H., Krzemiński, I. and Kruczowska, A. (1983), *Polacy. Jesień 80. Proces postawiania niezależnych związków zawodowych* (Poles. Autumn 1980. The emergence process of the independent trade unions), Uniwersytet Warszawski, Warsaw.

Bakuniak, G. and Nowak, K. (1987), 'The Creation of a Collective Identity in a Social Movement: The Case of Solidarność in Poland', *Theory and Society*, vol. 16, no. 3, pp. 401-29.

Balcerowicz, L. (1995), *Socialism, Capitalism, Transformation*, Central European University Press, Budapest.

Baldissera, A. (1988), *La svolta dei quarantamila. Dai quadri Fiat ai Cobas*, Comunità, Milan.

Balibar, E. and Wallerstein, I. (1988), *Race, nation, classe. Les identités ambiguës*, La Découverte, Paris.

Banconi, P. (1979), *Il movimento operaio a Piombino*, La Nuova Italia, Florence.

Barbano, F. (1992), *Torino: una città incompleta*, Angeli, Milan.

Barnet, R. and Cavanagh, J. (1995), *Global Dreams. Imperial Corporations and the New World Order*, Touchstone, New York.

Bataille, P. (1997), *Le racisme au travail*, La Découverte, Paris.

Bate, P. and Child, J. (1987), *Organization of Innovation: East-West Perspectives*, De Gruyter, Berlin.

Beccalli, B. (1984), 'Italy', in A. Cook, V. Lorwin and A. Daniels (eds), *Women and Trade Unions in Eleven Industrialized Countries*, Temple University Press, Philadephia, pp. 184-214.

Beccalli, B. and Meardi, G. (2000), 'Women in Italian Trade Unions', in F. Colgan and S. Ledwith (eds), *Gender, Diversity and Trade Unions. International Perspectives*, Routledge, London.

Becchi Collidà, A. and Negrelli, S. (1986), *La transizione nell'industria e nelle relazioni industriali. L'auto e il caso Fiat*, Angeli, Milan.

Beissinger, M. (1989), *Scientific Management: Socialist Discipline and Soviet Power*, Harvard University Press, Cambridge MA.

Bélanger, J., Edwards, P.K. and Haiven, L. (eds) (1994a), *Workplace Industrial Relations and the Global Challenge*, ILR Press, Ithaca.

Bélanger, J., Edwards, P.K. and Haiven, L. (1994b), 'Globalisation, National Systems and the Future of Workplace Industrial Relations', in J. Bélanger, P.K. Edwards and L. Haiven (eds), *Workplace Industrial Relations and the Global Challenge*, ILR Press, Ithaca, pp. 275-84.

Beletsevkovsky, V. (1978), Workers' Struggles in the USSR in the Early Sixties, *Critique*, no. 10-11, pp. 37-50.

Bendix, R. (1956), *Work and Authority in Industry*, Harper and Row, New York.

Berelowitch, A. and Wieviorka, M. (1993), 'La formation d'acteurs sociaux, politiques, économiques et culturels en Russie post-communiste, *Cahiers internationaux de sociologie*, no. 95, pp. 237-54.

Berelowitch, A. and Wieviorka, M. (1996), *Les Russes d'en bas*, Seuil, Paris.

Berelson, B. (1952/1971), *Content Analysis*, Hafner Publ Co., New York.

Berger, P.L and Luckmann, T. (1967), *The Social Construction of Reality*, Penguin, London.

Berger, S. and Piore, M. (1980), *Dualism and Discontinuity in Industrial Societies*, Cambridge University Press, Cambridge.

Bernhard, M.H. (1992), 'Nowe spojrzenie na "Solidaność"' (A New Look at "Solidarity"), *Krytyka*, no. 38.

Bernhard, M.H. (1993), *The Origins of Democratisation in Poland: Workers, Intellectuals, and Oppositional Politics 1976-1980*, Columbia University Press, New York.

Berta, G. (1993), 'Conflitto industriale e sistema d'impresa. L'esperienza della Fiat, *Meridiana*, vol. 7, no. 16, pp. 157-78.

Berta, G. (1998a), *Mirafiori*, Il Mulino, Bologna.

Berta, G. (1998b), *Conflitto industriale e struttura d'impresa alla Fiat 1919-1979*, Il Mulino, Bologna.

Bertaux, D. (1980), 'L'approche biographique: sa validité méthodologique, ses potentialités', *Cahiers internationaux de sociologie*, no. 69, pp. 197-225.

Beynon, H. (1975), *Working for Ford*, EP Publishing, London.

Biagioni, E., Palmieri, S., and Pipan, T. (1980), *Indagine sul sindacato*, Esi, Rome.

Blackburn, R.M. and Mann, M. (1975), 'Ideology in the Non-Skilled Working Class', in M. Bulmer (ed), *Working-Class Images of Society*, Routledge and Kegan Paul, London, pp. 131-60.

Blanchet, A. (1987), 'Interviewer', in A. Blanchet, R. Ghiglione, J. Massonnat and A. Trognon, *Les techniques d'enquête en sciences sociales*, Dunod, Paris, pp. 81-126.

Blenchflower, P. and Freeman, R. (1994), *The Legacy of Communist Labor Relations*, National Bureau of Economic Research, Working Paper no. 4740.

Blenchflower, P. and Freeman, R. (1997), *The Attitudinal Legacy of Communist Labor Relations*, Industrial and Labor Relations Review, vol. 50, no. 3, pp. 438-59.

Bode, I. (1997), Le difficile altruisme des groupes d'intérêt, *Revue française de sociologie*, vol. 38, no. 2, pp. 269-300.

Boissonnat, J. (ed) (1995), *Le travail dans 20 ans*, Jacob, Paris.

Bologna, S. and Fumagalli, A. (eds) (1997), *Il lavoro autonomo di seconda generazione*, Feltrinelli, Milan.

Boltanski, L., and Thevenot, L. (1991), *De la justification. Les économies de la grandeur*, Gallimard, Paris.

Bonazzi, G. (1984), La lotta dei 35 giorni in FIAT: un'analisi sociologica, *Politica ed Economia*, vol. 15, no. 11, pp. 33-43.

Bonazzi, G. (1991), 'Qualità e consenso. L'evoluzione del lavoro operaio alla Fiat Mirafiori (1980-1990)', *Rassegna italiana di sociologia*, vol. 32, no. 1, pp. 3-25.

Bonazzi, G. (1993), *Il tubo di cristallo: modello giapponese e fabbrica integrata alla Fiat auto*, Il Mulino, Bologna.

Bonazzi, G. (1994) 'A Gentler Way to Total Quality? The Case of the 'Integrated Factory' at Fiat Auto', in T. Elger and C. Smith (eds), *Global Japanization?*, Routledge, London, pp. 266-96.

Bonazzi, G. (1997) 'Tra tamponamento delle emergenze e miglioramento continuo: capi UTE e tecnologi nella Fabbrica Integrata', *Quaderni di sociologia*, vol. 46, no. 15, pp. 117-37.

Bonazzi, G. (1998), 'La qualità come routine. Creazione di eventi e strategie cooperative alla Fiat Mirafiori', *Rassegna italiana di sociologia*, vol. 39, no. 2, pp. 181-201.

Bordogna, L. (1995), 'Tendenze recenti del conflitto industriale. Implicazioni per l'analisi e la regolazione', in A. Chiesi, I. Regalia and M. Regini (eds), *Lavoro e relazioni industriali in Europa*, NIS, Rome, pp. 159-84.

Bottighieri, B. and Ceri, P. (eds) (1987), *Le culture del lavoro. L'esperienza di Torino nel quadro europeo*, Il Mulino, Bologna.

Bourdieu, P. (1996), 'Understanding', *Theory, Culture & Society*, vol. 23, no. 2, pp. 17-37.

Boyer, R. (1993), *La place du système productif dans le passage au marché en Russie*, Cepremap, Paris.

Briante, G., Oddone, I. and Re, A. (1977), *Esperienza operaia, coscienza di classe e psicologia del lavoro*, Einaudi, Turin.

Bridger, S., Kay, R. and Pinnick, K. (1996), *No More Heroines? Russia, Women and the Market*, Routledge, London.

Brock, D. (1994), Über die Individualisierung der kulturellen Grundlagen der Arbeit, *Soziale Welt, Sonderband*, no. 9, pp. 257-68.

Bronzino, A., Germanetto, L. and Guidi, G. (1974), *Fiat. Struttura aziendale e organizzazione dello sfruttamento*, Mazzotta, Milan.

Bryman, A. (1988), *Quantity and Quality in Social Research*, Unwin Hyman, London.

Bugaj, R. (1999), 'Rygiel' (The bolt), *Rzeczpospolita*, 17-18 April, pp. 16-18.

Bujak, Z. (1991), *Przepraszam za Solidarność*, (I apologise for Solidarity), BGW, Warsaw.

Bulmer, M. (1975), 'Sociological Models of the Mining Community', *Sociological Review*, vol. 19, no. 1, pp. 61-92.

Burawoy, M. (1997), 'From Capitalism to Capitalism via Socialism: The Odyssey of a Marxist Ethnographer, 1975-1995', *International Labor and Working-Class History*, no. 50, pp. 77-99.

Burawoy, M. and Lukacs, J. (1985), 'Mythologies of Work', *American Sociological Review*, vol. 50, no. 6, pp. 723-37.

Burda, M. (1993), 'Labour Market in Eastern Europe', *Economic Policy*, vol. 16, pp. 101-28.

Campbell, B. (1982), 'Women: Not What They Bargained For', *Marxism Today*, no. 3.

Camuffo, A. and Volpato, G. (1995), 'Labor Relations Heritage and Lean Manufacturing at Fiat', *International Journal of Human Resource Management*, vol. 6, no. 4, pp. 795-824.

Camuffo, A. and Micelli, S. (1998) 'Les nouvelles formes d'organisation du travail chez Fiat', in J.P. Durand, P. Steuart and J.J. Castillo (eds), *L'avenir du travail à la chaîne*, La Découverte, Paris, pp. 199-215.

Candau, J. (1998), *Mémoire et identité*, Presses Universitaires de France, Paris.

Carbognin, M. and Paganelli, L. (1981), *Il sindacato come esperienza*, Edizioni Lavoro, Rome.

Carignani, N., Luchetti, R. and Poli, G. (1985), *La Camera del Lavoro di Piombino dalle origini agli anni Sessanta*, All'Insegna del Giglio, Florence.

Carrieri, M. *et al.* (1993), *Fiat. Punto e a capo*, Ediesse, Rome.

Casassus-Montero C. (1989), 'Les différentes approches dans les comparaisons internationales du travail industriel', *Sociologie du travail*, vol. 29, no. 2, pp. 153-62.

Castronovo, V. (1999), *Fiat 1989-1999. Un secolo di storia italiana*, Rizzoli, Milan.

CBOS (1992), *Mieszkańcy Tych o strajku w FSM* (Tychy inhabitants about the strike at FSM), Research report, Warsaw.

CBOS (1995), *Formy społecznego protestu. Analiza poziomu akceptacji i ocen skuteczności* (Forms of social protest. Analysis of the level of acceptance and of the judgements on efficacy), Research report, Warsaw.

CBOS (1999), *Opinie o związkach zawodowych* (Opinions on the trade unions), Research report, Warsaw.

Cella, G.P. (1999), *Il sindacato*, Laterza, Bari.

Cella, G.P. and Treu, T. (ed) (1998), *Le nuove relazioni industriali. L'esperienza italiana nella prospettiva europea*, Il Mulino, Bologna.

Cerruti, G. and Rieser, V. (1991), *Fiat: qualità totale e fabbrica integrata*, Ediesse, Rome.

Cerruti, G. and Rieser, V. (1993), 'Osservazioni sulle trasformazioni organizzative alla Fiat e sui problemi di setting', in M. Carrieri *et al., Fiat. Punto e a capo*, Ediesse, Rome, pp. 160-65.

Cerruti, G., and Rieser, V. (1994), 'La fabbrica integrata e il tempo. A proposito dell'accordo di Termoli', *Quaderni di ricerca Ires Lucia Morosini*, no. 15, pp. 17-22.

Cerruti, G. and Rieser, V. (1999), *Orari e qualità del lavoro*, IRES, Turin, mimeo.

Cersosimo, D. (1994), *Viaggio a Melfi: la Fiat oltre il fordismo*, Donzelli, Rome.

Chavance, B. (1995), 'Hierarchical Forms and Coordination Problems in Socialist Systems', *Industrial and Corporate Change*, vol. 4, no. 1, pp. 271-291.

Chauchat, H. and Durand-Delvigne, A. (1999), *De l'identité du Sujet au lien social*, Presses Universitaires de France, Paris.

Chinoy, E. (1955), *Automobile Workers and the American Dream*, University of Illinois Press, Chicago.

Chwalba, A. (1997), *Czasy Solidarności* (Solidarity's Times), Księgarnia Akademicka, Cracow.

Cichomski, B. and Morawski, W. (1988), 'Zróżnicowanie interesów pracowniczych i jego konsekwencje. Analiza porównawcza' (Differentiation of workers' interests and its consequences. A comparative analysis), *Studia socjologiczne*, no. 2, pp. 135-68.

Cichomski, B., Morawski, P. and Zawadzki, W. (1996), *Women's Role Ideology: Cultural Perspective in Cross-country Comparative Analysis*, ISS Working Paper, Warsaw.

Clarke, S. (1996a), 'Labour Relations and Class Formation', in S. Clarke (ed), *Labour Relations in Transition: Wages, Employment and Industrial Conflict in Russia*, Edward Elgar, Chaltenham, pp. 1-40.

Clarke, S. (1996b), 'Formal and Informal Relations in Soviet Industrial Production', in S. Clarke (ed), *Management and Industry in Russia*, Edward Elgar, Chaltenham, pp. 1-27.

Clegg, H. (1976), *Trade Unionism under Collective Bargaining*, Blackwell, Oxford.

CLES (1988), *Il mercato del lavoro: analisi delle tendenze*, Rome.

Cockburn, C. (1991), *In the Way of Women*, Macmillan, London.

Cohen J. and Rogers J. (1994), 'Solidarity, Democracy, Association', in W. Streeck (ed), *Staat und Verbände*, Westdeutscher Verlag, Opladen, pp. 136-59.

Colgan, F. and Ledwith, S. (eds) (2000), *Gender, Diversity and Trade Unions. International Perspectives*, Routledge, London.

Commons, J.R. (1909), 'American Shoemakers, 1648-1895: A Sketch of Industrial Evolution', *Quarterly Journal of Economics*, no. 19, pp. 1-32.

Comune di Piombino (1987), *Il comportamento elettorale a Piombino dal 1946 al 1987*, Bandecchi e Vivaldi, Pontedera.

Consoli, F., Ishikawa, A., Makó, R. and Martin, R. (eds) (1998), *Workers, Firms and Unions. Industrial Relations in Transition*, Peter Lang, Frankfurt a.M.

Corcuff, P. (1991), 'Eléments d'épistémologie ordinaire du syndicalisme', *Revue française de science politique*, vol. 41, no. 4, pp. 515-36.

Cosi, C. (1993), *Avvio o fine della Fabbrica Integrata? ovvero l'oscuramento del tubo di cristallo*, FIOM CGIL Piemonte, Turin.

Coulisk, J. (1996), 'Why Bounded Rationality?', *Journal of Economic Literature*, vol. 34, pp. 669-700.

Crespi, P. (1997), *La memoria operaia*, Edizioni Lavoro, Rome.

Cresti, C. and Orefice, G. (1990), 'La resistenza popolare e operaia a Piombino nel rapporto con lo sviluppo dell'industria siderurgica (1888-1939)', *Ricerche Storiche*, no. 1, pp. 201-40.

Crompton, R. and Sanderson, K. (1990), *Gendered Jobs and Social Change*, Unwin & Hyman, London.

Crouch, C. (1982), *Trade Unions: The Logic of Collective Action*, Fontana, London.

Crouch, C. (1993), *Industrial Relations and European State Traditions*, Oxford University Press, Oxford.

Crouch, C. (1998), 'Non amato ma inevitabile il ritorno al neo-corporatismo', *Giornale di diritto del lavoro e di relazioni industriali*, vol. 20, no. 1, pp. 155-80.

Crouch, C. (1999), *Social Change in Western Europe*, Oxford University Press, Oxford.

Crouch, C. (2000), 'National wage determination and European Monetary Union', in Crouch, C. (ed), *After the Euro: Shaping Institutions for Governance in the Wake for European Monetary Union*, Oxford University Press, Oxford.

Cunnison, S. and Stageman, J. (1995), *Feminising the Unions*, Avebury, Aldershot.

Czujka, Z. (1998), *Związki zawodowe wobec polityki płac w okresie transformacji* (The trade unions on the pay policy in the transformation period), IpiSS, Warsaw.

Dauderstädt, M. and Meyer-Stamer, J. (1995), 'Statt Sozialdumping: Eine Strategie für den "Standort Europa"', in W. Lecher and U. Optenhögel (eds), *Wirtschaft, Gesellschaft und Gewerkschaften in Mittel- und Osteuropa*, Bund, Köln, pp. 298-317.

Davies, N. (1981), *God's Playground. A History of Poland*, Oxford University Press, Oxford.

Davis, H.H. (1979), *Beyond Class Images*, Croom Helm, London.

Degiacomi, C. (ed) (1987), *Contrattare alla Fiat. Quindici anni di relazioni sindacali*, Edizioni Lavoro, Rome.

290   *Trade Union Activists, East and West*

Dejours, C. (1998), *Souffrance en France*, Seuil, Paris.
Della Porta, D. (1992), 'Life histories in the analysis of social movement activists', in M. Diani and R. Eyerman (eds), *Studying Collective Action*, Sage, London, pp. 168-93.
Della Rocca, G. (1994), 'Le relazioni sociali nella fabbrica automizzata', *Meridiana*, vol. 9, no. 21, pp. 69-101.
Delorme, R. (ed) (1996), *A l'Est du nouveau, changement institutionnel et transformations économiques*, L'Harmattan, Paris.
De Luca, M. (1992), 'La partecipazione nel settore siderurgico', in M. Ambrosini, M. Colasanto and L. Saba (eds), *Partecipazione e coinvolgimento nell'impresa degli anni '90*, Angeli, Milan, pp. 153-84.
Demazière, D. and Dubar, C. (1997), *Analyser les entretiens biographiques. L'exemple des récits d'insertion*, Nathan, Paris.
Dessewffy, T. (1992), *Communism as a Cultural System*, American Sociological Association Paper.
Di Siena, P. and Rieser, V. (eds) (1996), 'Inchiesta operaia alla Fiat di Melfi', *Finesecolo*, vol. 2, no. 3-4, pp. 11-151.
Domański, H. (1999), *Zadowolony niewolnik idzie do pracy. Postawy wobec aktywności zawodowej kobiet w 23 krajach* (The willing slave goes to work. Attitudes towards women's professional activity in 23 countries), IFiS PAN, Warsaw.
Drążkiewicz, J. and Rychard, A. (1990), 'Strajki w regionie warszawskim w lecie 1980' (The strikes in the Warsaw region in the summer 1980), in J. Kulpińska (ed), *Studia nad ruchami społecznymi, IV: Raport PTS - Strajki 1980: Mazowsze, Ursus, Żyrardów, Gdańsk, Szczecin, Wrocław* (Studies on social movements, IV: PTS Raport - Strikes 1980: Mazowsze, Ursus, Żyrardów, Gdańsk, Szczecin, Wrocław), Uniwersytet Warszawski - Instytut Socjologii - Polskie Towarzystwo Socjologiczne, Warsaw, pp. 7-36.
Dubar, C. (1992), 'Formes identitaires et socialisation professionnelle', *Revue française de sociologie*, vol. 33, no.4, pp. 505-29.
Dubet, F. (1994), *Sociologie de l'expérience*, Seuil, Paris.
Dubet, F. and Wieviorka, M. (1996), 'Touraine and the Method of Sociological Intervention', in J. Clark and M. Diani (eds), *Alain Touraine*, Falmer Press, London, pp. 55-75.
Dubois, P. (1981), *Les ouvriers divisés*, FNSP, Paris.
Dubost, N. (1979), *Flins sans fin*, Maspero, Paris.
Due, J., Jensen, C.S. and Madsen, J.S. (1995), 'A Role for a Pan-European Trade Union Movement? Possibilities in European Industrial Relations Regulation', *Industrial Relations Journal*, vol. 26, no. 1, pp. 4-18.
Durand, C. (1997), 'Le management occidental dans les pays de l'Est', in C. Durand (ed), *Management et rationalisation. Les multinationales occidentales en Europe de l'Est*, De Boeck, Brussels, pp. 325-37.
Durand, C. and Le Goff, J.L. (1996), 'Thomson en Pologne: le cas Polkolor', *Revue française de gestion*, no. 109, pp. 5-18.

Durand, C., Le Goff, J.L. and Tobera, P. (1997), 'Rationalisation et mobilisation, Thomson Polkolor', in C. Durand (ed), *Management et rationalisation. Les multinationales occidentales en Europe de l'Est*, De Boeck, Brussels, pp. 79-147.

Durkheim, E. (1893), *De la division du travail social*, Alcan, Paris.

Ebbinghaus, B. and Visser, J. (1994), 'Barrieren und Wege 'grenzloser' Solidarität: Gewerkschaften und Europäische Integration', in W. Streeck (ed), *Staat und Verbände*, Westdeutscher Verlag, Opladen, pp. 223-55.

Edwards, P.K. (1986), *Conflict at Work: A Materialist Analysis of Workplace Relations*, Blackwell, Oxford.

Edwards, P.K. (1992), 'La recherche comparative en relations industrielles: L'apport de la tradition ethnographique', *Relations industrielles/Industrial Relations*, vol. 47, no. 3, pp. 411-37.

Edwards, P.K. and Scullion, H. (1982), 'The Social Organization of Industrial Conflict: Control and Resistance in the Workplace', Blackwell, Oxford.

EIRR (1993), 'The Hoover Affair and Social Dumping', *European Industrial Relations Review*, no. 230, pp. 14-19.

Ekiert, G. and Kubik, J. (1995), *Rebellious Civil Society and the Consolidation of Democracy in Poland, 1989-1993*, Paper delivered at the 5th World Congress of Central and East European Studies, Warsaw.

Ernst, A-S., Klinger, G. and Timm, A. (1998), 'In Search of a Lost Working Class: Workers in the Soviet Occupation Zone/German Democratic Republic, 1946-1970', *International Labor and Working-Class History*, no. 54, pp. 135-38.

Fairris, D. (1997), *Shopfloor Matters: Labour-Management Relations in Twentieth-Century American Manufacturing*, Routledge, London.

Fantasia, R. (1988), *Cultures of Solidarity: Consciousness, Action and Contemporary American Workers*, University of California Press, Berkeley.

Favilli, P. (1974), *Capitalismo e classe operaia a Piombino 1861-1918*, Editori Riuniti, Rome.

Favilli, P. and Tognarini, I. (1994) 'L'organizzazione comunista di base in una città-fabbrica: il caso di Piombino', *Ricerche Storiche*, no.1, pp. 123-58.

Fiat Auto (1997), *Fabbrica Integrata*, Satiz, Turin.

Flanagan, R. (1998), 'Institutional Reformation in Eastern Europe', *Industrial Relations*, vol. 37, no. 3, pp. 337-57.

Florek, L. and Seweryński, M. (1996), 'Poland', in U. Carabelli and S. Sciarra (ed), *New Patterns of Collective Labour Law in Central Europe*, Giuffré, Milan, pp. 161-211.

Fofi, G. (1964/1975), *L'immigrazione meridionale a Torino*, Feltrinelli, Milan.

Fox, A. (1974), *Beyond Contract: Work, Power, and Trust Relations*, Faber and Faber, London.

Fraser, S. (1998), 'Is Democracy Good for Unions?', *Dissent*, no. 3, pp. 33-9.

Freeman, R.B. and Medoff, J.B. (1984), *What Do Unions Do?*, Basic Books, New York.

Frege, C. (1998), 'Institutional Transfer and Effectiveness of Employee Representation: Comparing Works Councils in East and West Germany', *Economic and Industrial Democracy*, vol. 19, no. 3, pp. 475-504.

Frege, C. and Tóth, A. (1999), 'Institutions Matter: Union Solidarity in Hungary and East Germany', *British Journal of Industrial Relations*, vol. 37, no. 1, pp. 117-40.

Frenkel, S. (1994), 'Patterns of Workplace Industrial Relations in the Global Corporation: Toward Convergence?', in J. Bélanger, P.K. Edwards and L. Haiven (eds), *Workplace Industrial Relations and the Global Challenge*, ILR Press, Ithaca, pp. 240-74.

Freyssinet, M. (1979), *Division du travail et mobilitation quotidienne de la main-d'oeuvre. Les cas Renault et FIAT*, Centre de sociologie européenne, Paris.

Friedrich Ebert Stiftung (1999), 'Gewerkschaften und Arbeitsmarkt in Ostmitteleuropa', *Politikinformation Osteuropa*, no. 77.

Frieske, K.W. (1997), *Institutional Pluralism or Personal Clout?*, Friedrich Ebert Stiftung, Warsaw.

Frieske, K.W. (1998), 'Modelowanie różnorodności: dynamika instytucjonalnej formuły stosunków pracy' (Modelling heterogeneity: the dynamics of the industrial relations' institutional formula), in J.P. Gieorgica (ed), *Związki zawodowe w okresie przeobrażeń politycznych i gospodarczych* (The trade unions during the political and economic transformations), CPS Dialog, Warsaw, pp. 97-122.

Frybes, M. (1993), 'Les nouveaux entrepreneurs d'Europe de l'Est', *L'Autre Europe*, no. 24-25, pp. 25-38.

Frybes, M. (1995), 'Syndicats et salariés dans les entreprises d'Europe Centrale en transition', *Revue de l'IRES*, no. 19, pp. 57-81.

Frybes, M. (1997), *Une expérience de dialogue Est-Ouest. Les dimensions de l'engagement de la CFDT en faveur du mouvement Solidarnosc*, CFDT-IRES, Paris.

Frybes, M. (1998), 'La mise en place de nouvelles régulations dans le domaine des relations du travail dans les sociétés de l'après-communisme. Expériences et tentative de bilan', *La revue de l'IRES*, no. 26, pp. 181-206.

Frybes, M. and Kuczyński, P. (1994), *W poszukiwaniu ruchu społecznego* (In the search of the social movement), Oficyna Naukowa, Warsaw.

Frybes, M. and Michel, P. (1996), *Après le communisme: mythes et légendes de la Pologne post-communiste*, Bayard, Paris.

Gąciarz, B. and Pańków, W. (1996a), 'Transformation of Enterprises: Social and Institutional Conditioning Factors', *Polish Sociological Review*, no. 3, pp. 231-51.

Gąciarz, B. and Pańków, W. (1996b), 'Fiat Auto Polen AG: Konflikte ohne Ende', in Deppe, R. and Tatur, M. (eds), *Ökonomische Transformation und gewerkschaftliche Politik: Umbruchprozesse in Polen und Ungarn auf Branchenebene*, Westfälisches Dampfboot, Münster, 136-70.

Gąciarz, B. and Pańków, W. (1997a), *Przekształcenia przedsiębiorstw przemysłowych: strategie, aktorzy, efekty* (Transformations of industrial enterprises: Strategies, actors, effects), Wydawnictwo Wyższej Szkoły Przedsiębiorczości i Zarządzania, Warsaw.

Gąciarz, B. and Pańków, W. (1997b), 'Evolution des relations industrielles dans la Pologne de l'après-guerre', *Revue de l'IRES*, no. 26, pp. 7-60.

Galin, A. (1994), 'Myth and Reality: Trade Unions and Industrial Relations in the Transition to Democracy', in R.D. Lansbury, J.R. Niland and C. Verevis, (eds), *The Future of Industrial Relations*, Sage, London, pp. 295-306.

Galli, P. and Pertegato, G. (1994), *Fiat 1980: sindrome della sconfitta*, Ediesse, Rome.

Gallie, D. (1978), *In Search of the New Working Class*, Cambridge University Press, Cambridge.

Gallie, D. (1983), *Social Inequality and Class Radicalism in France and Britain*, Cambridge University Press, Cambridge.

Gallie, D., Kostova, D. and Kuchar, P. (1999), 'Employment Experience and Organisational Commitment: An East-West European Comparison', *Work, Employment and Society*, vol. 13, no. 4, pp. 621-41.

Gallino, L. (ed) (1982), *Occupati e bioccupati. Il doppio lavoro nell'area torinese*, Il Mulino, Bologna.

Gallino, L. (ed) (1985), *Il lavoro e il suo doppio*, Il Mulino, Bologna.

Gallissot, R., Paris, R. and Weill, C. (ed) (1989), 'La désunion des prolétaires', *Le mouvement social*, no. 147.

Garavini, S. and Pugno, E. (1975), *Gli anni duri alla Fiat*, Einaudi, Turin.

Gardawski, J. (1996), *Poland's Industrial Workers on the Return to Democracy and Market Economy*, Friedrich Ebert Stiftung, Warsaw.

Gardawski, J. (1999), 'Zasięg związków zawodowych w wybranich działach przemysłu i sekcjach usług publicznych' (The scope of the trade unions in chosen secotrs of industry and public services), in J. Gardawski, B. Gąciarz, A. Mokrzyszewski and W. Pańków, *Rozpad bastionu? Związki zawodowe w gospodarce prywatyzowanej* (The fall of the bastion? Trade unions in the privatised economy), Instytut Spraw Publicznych, Warsaw, pp. 65-114.

Gardawski, J., Gąciarz, B., Mokrzyszewski, A. and Pańków, W. (1999), *Rozpad bastionu? Związki zawodowe w gospodarce prywatyzowanej* (The fall of the bastion? Trade unions in the privatised economy), Instytut Spraw Publicznych, Warsaw.

Gardawski, J., Gilejko, L. and Żukowski, T. (1994), *Związki zawodowe w przedsiębiorstwach przemysłowych* (The trade unions in industrial firms), Friedrich Ebert Stiftung, Warsaw.

Garfinkel, H. (1967), *Studies in Ethnomethodology*, Prenctice-Hall, Englewood Cliffs.

Garibaldo, F. (1993), 'Prime osservazioni a proposito di progettazione e participazione', in M. Carrieri *et al.*, *Fiat. Punto e a capo*, Ediesse, Rome, pp. 146-59.

Garrahan, P. and Stewart, P. (1995), 'Employee Responses to New Management Techniques in The Auto Industry', *Work, Employment and Society*, vol. 9, no. 3, pp. 517-36.

Ghiglione, R. and Blanchet, A. (1991), *Analyse de contenu et contenus d'analyses*, Dunod, Paris.

Gianotti, L. (1999), *Gli operai Fiat hanno cent'anni*, Editori Riuniti, Rome.

Giddens, A. (1973), *The Class Structure of the Advanced Societies*, Hutchinson, London.

Giddens, A. (1976), *New Rules of Sociological Method: A Positive Critique of Interpretative Sociologies*, Basic Books, New York.

Giddens, A. (1984), *The Constitution of Society*, Polity Press, Cambridge.

Giddens, A. (1991), *Modernity and Self-Identity. Self and Society in the Late Modernity Era*, Polity Press, Cambridge.

Gilbert, N. and Mulkay, M. (1983), 'In Search of the Action', in N. Gilbert and P. Abell (eds), *Accounts and Action*, Gower, Aldershot.

Gilejko, L. (1993), 'Społeczne ruchy i organizacje pracownicze' (Social movements and worker organisations), in L. Gilejko (ed), *Społeczne uwarunkowania przejścia do gospodarki rynkowej* (Social conditions of the transition to market economy), Szkoła Główna Handlowa, Warsaw, pp. 36-69.

Gilejko, L., Gieorgica, P. and Ruszkowski, P. (eds) (1997), *Społeczni aktorzy restrukturyzacji*. (The social actors of restructuration), Dialog, Warsaw.

Girardi, G. (ed) (1980), *Coscienza operaia oggi. I nuovi comportamenti operai in una ricerca gestita dai lavoratori*, De Donato, Bari.

Giugni, G. (1987), 'Il modello fantasma', *MicroMega*, no. 4, pp. 60-2.

Glaser, B.G. and Strauss, A.L. (1967), *The Discovery of Grounded Theory: Strategies for Qualitative Research*, Aldine, Chicago.

Glasman, M. (1994), 'The Great Deformation. Polanyi, Poland and the Terrors of Planned Spontaneity', *New Left Review*, no. 205, pp. 59-86.

Gobin, C. (1997), *L'Europe syndicale*, Éditions Labor, Brussels.

Goffman, E. (1967), *Interaction Ritual: Essays on Face-to-Face Behaviour*, Anchor Books, New York.

Golden, M. (1990), *A Rational Choice Analysis of Union Militancy with Application to the Cases of British Coal and Fiat*, Cornell University Press, Ithaca.

Goldfarb, J. (1989), *Beyond Glasnost: The Post-Totalitarian Mind*, Chicago University Press, Chicago.

Goldthorpe, J.H., Lockwood, D., Bechhofer, F. and Platt, J. (1969), *The Affluent Worker*, Cambridge University Press, Cambridge.

Golosenko, I.A. and Kirsanov, V.A. (1988), 'Sotsialnoe poznanie i mir povsednevnosti. Gorizonty i tupiki fenomenologicheskoy sotsiologii' (Social consciousness and the everyday world. Horizons and dead-ends in phenomenological sociology), *Sotsiologicheskie Issledovaniya*, vol. 15, no. 4, pp. 141-44.

Goodwyn, L. (1991), *Breaking the Barrier: the Rise of Solidarity in Poland*, Oxford University Press, New York.

Gordon, M. (1996), 'Ideology and Union Commitment', in P. Pasture, J. Verberckmoes and H. De Witte (eds), *The Lost Perspective?* Avebury, Aldershot, pp. 241-58.

Gorz, A. (1988), *Métamorphoses du travail, quête de sens. Critique de la raison économique*, Galilée, Paris.

Grancelli, B. (1995), 'Who Should Learn What?', in B. Grancelli (ed), *Social Change and Modernization. Lessons from Eastern Europe*, De Gruyter, New York, pp. 3-41.

Grémy J.-P. and Le Moan, M.-J. (1977), 'Analyse de la démarche de construction de typologies dans les sciences sociales', *Informatique et sciences humaines*, no. 35.

Grote, J. and Schmitter, P. (1997), *The Corporatist Sisyphus: Past, Present and Future*, EUI Working Paper SPS, 97/4.

Guarriello, F. and Jobert, A. (1992), *L'évolution des relations professionnelles dans les groupes multinationaux: vers un modèle européen?*, Centre d'Etudes de l'Emploi, Noisy Le Grand.

Haas, E. (1958), *The Uniting of Europe: Political, Social and Economic Forces 1950-1957*, Stevens, London.

Habermas, J. (1981), *Theorie des kommunikativen Handelns*, Suhrkamp, Frankfurt a.M.

Habermas, J. (1990), *Vergangenheit als Zukunft*, Pendo, Zurich.

Hammerslay, M. (1992), *What's Wrong with Ethnography: Methodological Explorations*, Routledge, London.

Haraszti, M. (1977), *A Worker in a Workers' State*, Penguin, Harmondsworth.

Hardy, J and Rainnie, A. (1995), 'Desperatly Seeking Capitalism: Solidarity and Polish Industrial Relations in the 1990s', *Industrial Relations Journal*, vol. 26, no. 4, pp. 267-79.

Hardy, J. *et al.* (1996), 'Restructuring Huta T. Sendzimira. From the Lenin Steelworks to Lean Production', *Communist Economies and Economic Transformation*, vol. 8, no. 2, pp. 237-49.

Hattam, V. (1993), *Labor Visions and State Power*, Princeton University Press, Princeton.

Hausner, J., Jessop, B. and Nielsen, K. (eds) (1995), *Strategic Choice and Path-Dependency in Post-Socialism*, Elgar, Aldershot.

Hausner, J., Pedersen, O.K. and Ronit K. (1995), *Evolution of Interest Representation and Development of the Labour Market in Post-Socialist Countries*, Cracow Academy of Economics, Cracow.

Heinen, J. (1995), *Chômage et devenir de la main-d'oeuvre en Pologne*, L'Harmattan, Paris.

Héthy, L. and Makó, C. (1974), 'Work Performance. Interests, Power and Environment. The Case of Cyclical Slowdowns in a Hungarian Factory', *European Economic Review*, no. 5, pp. 141-57.

Hirschman, A. 1982: *Shifting Involvements. Private interest and public action*, Princeton University Press, Princeton.

Hirszowicz, M. and Mailer, A. (1996), 'Trade Unions as an Active Factor in Economic Transformation', *Polish Sociological Review*, no. 3.

Hobsbawm, E.J. (1984), *Worlds of Labour*, Weidenfeld and Nicolson, London.

Hobsbawm, E.J. (1987), *The Age of Empire, 1875-1914*, Abacus, London.

Hoffman, R., Lind, J. and Waddington, J. (1998), 'Il sindacato europeo al bivio', *Il Progetto*, no. 21-22, pp. 60-87.

296   *Trade Union Activists, East and West*

Hoggart, R. (1957), *The Uses of Literacy. Changing Patterns in English Mass Culture*, Fair Lawn, New York.
Holzer, J. (1984), *Solidarność 1980-1981. Geneza i historia* (Solidarity 1980-1981. Genesis and history), Instytut Literacki, Paris.
Howard, A. (1995), 'Global Capital and Labor Internationalism in Comparative Historical Perspective', *Sociological Inquiry*, vol. 65, no. 3-4, pp. 365-394.
Howell, C. and Mahon, R. (1996), 'Strategies for Union Renewal: Women Wage Earners as the New Exemples? Editorial Introduction', *Economic and Industrial Democracy*, vol. 17, no. 4, pp. 499-509.
Hyman, R. (1975), *Industrial Relations. A Marxist Introduction*, Macmillan, London.
Hyman, R. (1989), *The Political Economy of Industrial Relations*, Macmillan, London.
Hyman, R. (1996a), 'Institutional Transfer: Industrial Relations in Eastern Germany', *Work, Employment and Society*, vol. 10, no. 4, pp. 601-40.
Hyman, R. (1996b), 'Union Identities and Ideologies in Europe, in P. Pasture, J. Verberckmoes and H. De Witte (eds), *The Lost Perspective?* Avebury, Aldershot, pp. 60-89.
Hyman, R. (1999), 'Imagined Solidarities: Can Trade Unions Resist Globalization?', in B. Leisink (ed), *Globalization and Labour Relations*, Elgar, Cheltenham, pp. 94-115.
Ingham, G.K. (1974), *Strikes and Industrial Conflict. Britain and Scandinavia*, MacMillan, London.
Ion, J. (1997), *La fin des militants*, Ed. de l'Atelier, Paris.
Ion, J. and Peroni, M. (eds) (1997), *Engagement public et exposition de la personne*, Ed. de l'Aube, La Tour d'Aigues.
Iref (1997), *La società civile in Italia*, Edizioni Lavoro, Rome.
Ires (1995), *I mutamenti del lavoro e dell'identità*, Ediesse, Rome.
Jacoby, O. (1996), 'European Monetary Union: A Quantum Leap?', *Transfer*, vol. 2, no. 2, pp. 233-44.
Jacoby, S.M. (1991), 'American Exceptionalism Revisited', in S.M. Jacoby (ed), *Masters to Managers*, Columbia University Press, New York.
Jacoby, S.M. (1995), 'Social Dimensions of Global Economic Integration', in S.M. Jacoby, *The Workers of Nations*, Oxford University Press, Oxford, pp. 3-29.
Janowska, Z., Martini-Fiwek, J., and Góral, Z. (1992), *Female Unemployment in Poland*, Friedrich Ebert Stiftung, Warsaw.
Jarosz, M. (ed.) (1996), *Kapitał zagraniczny w prywatyzacji* (Foreign capital in the privatization process), ISP PAN, Warsaw.
Jasińska-Kania, A. (ed) (1992), *Bliscy i dalecy* (Near and distant), Uniwersytet Warszawski - Instytut Socjologii, Warsaw.
Johnson, P. (1995), *Success While Others Fail: Social Movement Unionism and the Public Workplace*, ILR Press, New York.
Jonas, H. (1984), *Das Prinzip Verantwortung*, Suhrkamp, Frankfurt a.M.
Jürgens, U. (1995), *Implementing Lean Production in the German Industrial Relations Setting*, Paper for the IIRA 10th World Congress, Washington.

Kabaj, M. (1998), 'Searching for a New Results-oriented Wage Negotiation System in Poland', in D. Vaughan-Whitehead (ed), *Paying the Price: the Wage Crisis in Central and Eastern Europe*, Macmillan, Basigstoke, pp. 234-71.

Katnelson, I. and Zolberg, A. (1986), *Working-Class Formation: Ninetheenth-Century Patterns in Western Europe and the United States*, Princeton University Press, Princeton.

Katz, H. (1993), 'The Decentralization of Collective Bargaining: A Literature Review and Comparative Analysis', *Industrial and Labour Relations Review*, vol. 46, no. 1, pp. 3-22.

Kennedy, M.D. (1991), *Professionals, Power and Solidarity: a Critical Sociology of Soviet-Type Society*, Cambridge University Press, Cambridge, 1991.

Kerr, C. (1954), 'Industrial Conflict and its Mediation', *American Journal of Sociology*, vol. 49, no. 3, pp. 230-45.

Kerr, C. and Siegel, A. (1954), 'The Interindustry Propensity to Strike', in A. Kornhauser *et al.* (eds), *Industrial Conflict*, McGraw-Hill, New York, pp. 189-212.

Kirk, J. and Miller, M. (1986), *Reliability and Validity in Qualitative Research*, Sage, London.

Kitschelt, H. (1992), 'The Formation of Party Systems in East-Central Europe', *Politics and Society*, vol. 20, no. 1, pp. 7-50.

Kloc, K. (1993), 'Trade Unions and Economic Transformation in Poland', *Journal of Communist Studies*, vol. 9, no. 4, pp. 125-32.

Kloc, K. (1997), 'Konflikty przemysłowe, spory zbiorowe i mediacje' (Industrial conflicts, collective disputes, and mediations), in W. Kozek (ed), *Zbiorowe stosunki pracy w Polsce w perspektywie integracji europejskiej* (Industrial relations in Poland in the perspective of the European integration), Scholar, Warsaw, 115-38.

Knowles, K.G. (1952), *Strikes. A Study in Industrial Conflict*, Blackwell, Oxford.

Kochan, T., Locke, R. and Piore, M. (eds) (1995), *Employment Relations in a Changing World Economy*, MIT Press, Cambridge.

Kohn, M.L. and Słomczyński, K.M. (1988), *Sytuacja pracy i jej psychologiczne konsekwencje. Polsko-amerykanskie analizy porównawcze* (Work situation and its psychological consequences. Polish-American comparative analyses), Ossolineum, Wrocław.

Kolarska-Bobinska, L. (ed) (1993), *Ekonomiczny wymiar życia codziennego* (The economic dimension of everyday life), CBOS, Warsaw.

Konecki, K. and Kulpińska, J. (1995), 'Enterprise Transformation and the Redefinition of Organizational Realities in Poland', in E.J. Dittrich, G. Schmidt and R. Whitley (eds), *Industrial Transformation in Europe*, Sage, London, pp. 234-54.

Korporowicz, L. (1996), 'O międzykulturowych modelach zarządzania. Relacje między polskimi i zagranicznymi pracownikami firm' (About multicultural models of management. The relations between Polish and foreign employees), in Jarosz, M. (ed), *Kapitał zagraniczny w prywatyzacji* (Foreign capital in the privatisation process), ISP PAN, Warsaw, pp. 235-46.

Kowalik, T. (1994), 'A Reply to Maurice Glasman', *New Left Review*, no. 206, pp. 133-44.

Kowalski, S. (1990), *Krytyka solidarnościowego rozumu* (Critics of Solidarity's thinking), PEN, Warsaw.

Kozek, W. (1994), *Praca w warunkach zmian rynkowych* (Work under conditions of market changes), First Business College, Warsaw.

Kozek, W. (ed) (1997), *Zbiorowe stosunki pracy w Polsce w perspektywie integracji europejskiej* (Industrial relations in Poland in the European integration perspective), Scholar, Warsaw.

Kozek, W. (ed) (1999), *Społeczne organizacje biznesu w Polsce a stosunki pracy*, (Business Associations in Poland and Industrial Relations), CPS Dialog, Warsaw.

Kramer, M. (1995), 'Polish Workers and the Post-Communist Transition, 1989-1993', *Communist and Post-Communist Studies*, vol. 28, no. 1, pp. 71-114.

Kruczkowska, A. (1983), 'Proces tworzenia ruchu społecznego - Fragmenty wypowiedzi uczestników wydarzeń' (The social movement creation process - Talk fragments by the participants in the events), in G. Bakuniak, H. Banaszak, I. Krzemiński and A. Kruczowska, *Polacy. Jesień 80. Proces postawiania niezależnych związków zawodowych* (Poles. Autumn 1980. The emergence process of the independent trade unions), Uniwersytet Warszawski, Warsaw, 561-611.

Krzaklewski, M. (1998), 'Będę stał na straży' (I shall vigilate), *Rzeczpospolita*, 24 September, p. 3.

Krzemiński, I. (1989), *Solidarność 1980*, Wola, Warsaw.

Krzemiński, I. (1997), *Solidarność. Projekt polskiej demokracji*, (Solidarity. The project of Polish democracy), Oficyna Naukowa, Warsaw.

Kubik, J. (1994a), 'Who Done It, Workers, Intellectuals or Some One Else: A Controversy over Solidarity's Origins and Social Composition', *Theory and Society*, vol. 23, no. 3, pp. 441-66.

Kubik, J. (1994b), *The Power of Symbols against the Symbols of Power*, Pennsylvania State University Press, University Park.

Kubik, W. (1991), 'Praca a probem tożsamości jednostki' (Work and the problem of the individual's identity), in W. Jecher (ed), *Analiza struktur i zachowań w przedsiębiorstwie* (Analysis of the structures and behaviours in the enterprise), Uniwersytet Śląski, Katowice, pp. 49-59.

Kulpińska, J. (ed) (1990), *Studia nad ruchami społecznymi, IV: Raport PTS - Strajki 1980: Mazowsze, Ursus, Żyrardów, Gdańsk, Szczecin, Wrocław* (Studies on social movements, IV: PTS Raport - Strikes 1980: Mazowsze, Ursus, Żyrardów, Gdańsk, Szczecin, Wrocław), Uniwersytet Warszawski - Instytut Socjologii - Polskie Towarzystwo Socjologiczne, Warsaw.

Kulpińska, J. (1993), *Changes in Power Structure in the Polish Enterprises and the Process of Transformation toward Market Economy*, Paper presented at the International Workshop on Market Economy and Social Justice, Tokyo.

Kulpińska, J. (1995), 'La classe ouvrière en Pologne', in J. Denoit and C. Dutheil (eds), *Méthamorphoses ouvrières*. L'Harmattan, Paris, pp. 165-69.

Kurczewki, J. (1981), 'Solidarność od wewnątrz' (Solidarity from inside), in OBS, *Niepodległość pracy* (Work independence), NSZZ Solidarność Region Mazowsze, pp. 35-62.

Kuroń, J. (1993), *Maintenant ou jamais*, Fayard, Paris.

Laba, R. (1991), *The Roots of Solidarity*, Princeton University Press, Princeton.

Lane, A. (1974), *The Union Makes Us Strong*, Arrow, London.

Lane, C. (1989), *Management and Labor in Europa*, Edward Elgar, Cheltenham.

Lane, D. (1987), *Soviet Labour and the Ethic of Communism*, Wheatsheaf Books, Brighton.

Latoszek, M. (ed) (1991), *Sierpień '80 we wspomnieniach. Relacje z wybrzeża* (August '80 in memory. Accounts from the littoral), Wydawnictwo Morskie, Gdańsk.

Latoszek, M. (1994), 'Drogi życiowe i tożsamość robotników' (Life-courses and workers' identity), *Studia socjologiczne*, no. 1, pp. 107-24.

Lattard, A. (1995), 'Le syndicalisme allemand face à la crise: une lente érosion', *Allemagne d'aujourd'hui*, no. 131, pp. 21-43.

Lebel, Y., Oberti, M. and Reillier, F. (1996), 'Classe sociale: un terme fourre-tout?' *Revue française de sociologie*, vol. 37, no. 2, pp. 195-207.

Lecher, W. (ed) (1994), *Trade Unions in European Union*, Lawrence and Wishart, London.

Lecher, W. (1998), 'European Works Councils: Experiences and Perspectives', in W. Lecher and H.W. Platzer (eds), *European Union - European Industrial Relations?*, Routledge, London, pp. 234-51.

Le Goff, J.L. (1997), 'Management et gestion de la main-d'oeuvre dans les pays de l'Est', in C. Durand (ed), *Management et rationalisation. Les multinationales occidentales en Europe de l'Est*, De Boeck, Brussels, pp. 301-23.

Lepenies, W. (1996), 'Le nationalisme allemand n'est selon moi, qu'un phénomène superficiel' *Le monde*, 1 Octobre, p. 14.

Lerner, G. (1988), *Operai. Viaggio all'interno della Fiat*, Feltrinelli, Milan.

Levada, Y. (1993), *Entre le passé et l'avenir. L'homme soviétique ordinaire*, Presses de la FNSP, Paris.

Lévi-Strauss, C. (1964), *Mythologies. Vol.1, Le cru et le cuit*, Plon, Paris.

Levy, M.A. (1993), 'East-West Environmental Politics after 1989: The Case of Air Pollution', in R.O. Koehane, J.S. Nye and S. Hoffmann (eds), *After the Cold War*, Harvard University Press, Cambridge, pp. 310-41.

Linhart, R. (1978), *L'établi*, Minuit, Paris.

Lipset, M. (1959), 'Some social requisites of democracy: economic development and political legitimacy', *American Political Science Review*, no. 53.

Łobodzińska, B. (1995), 'The Family and Working Women during and after Socialist Industrialization and Ideology', in B. Łobodzińska (ed), *Family, Women, and Employment in Central-Eastern Europe*, Greenwood Press, London, pp. 3-46.

Locke, R.M. (1992), *Industrial Restructuring and Industrial Relations in the Italian automobile Industry*, in M. Golden and J. Pontusson (eds), *Bargaining for Change*, Cornell University Press, Ithaca, pp. 247-76.

Locke, R.M. and Negrelli, S. (1989), 'Il caso FIAT Auto', in M. Regini and C. Sabel (eds), *Strategie di riaggiustamento industriale*, Il Mulino, Bologna, pp. 61-94.

Lockwood, D. (1958), *The Blackcoated Worker*, George Allen and Unwin, London.

Lockwood, D. (1966), 'Sources of Variation in Working-Class Images of Society', *Sociological Review*, vol. 10, no. 14, pp. 249-67.

Lockwood, D., (1981), 'The Weakest Link in the Chain? Some Comments on the Marxist Theory of Action', in G. Simpson and I. Simpson (eds), *Research in the Sociology of Work*, Jai Press, Greenwich.

Long, K. (1996), *We All Fought for Freedom: Women in Poland's Solidarity Movement*, Westview Press, Boulder.

Luckmann, T. and Schutz, A. (1989), *The Structures of Life World*, Northwestern, Evanston.

Lukács, G. (1923/1971), *History and Class Consciousness*, Merlin Press, London.

MacDuffie, J.P. and Pil, F.K. (1997), 'Changes in Auto Industry Emplyment Practices: An International Overview', in T. Kochan, R. Lansbury and J. MacDuffie (eds), *After Lean Production. Evolving Employment Practices in the World Auto Industry*, ILR Press, London, pp. 9-42.

Mach, B. (1998), *Transformacja ustrojowa a mentalne dziedzictwo socjalizmu* (System transformation and the mental legacy of socialism), ISP PAN, Warsaw.

Makó, C. and Novoszáth, P. (1995), 'Employment Relations in Multinational Companies: the Hungarian Case', in E. Dittrich, G. Schmidt and R. Whitley (eds), *Industrial Transformation in Europe*, Sage, London, pp. 255-76.

Makó, C. and Simonyi, A. (1995), 'Participation at the Firm Level in the Transformation Process', in B. Grancelli (ed), *Social Change and Modernization. Lessons from Eastern Europe*, De Gruyter, New York, pp. 181-95.

Mahnkopf, B. (1985), *Verbürgerlichung. Die Legende vom Ende des Proletariats*, Campus, Frankfurt.

Manghi, B. (1987), 'Sindacalismo torinese: vivere dopo la leggenda', *Prospettiva sindacale*, no. 64, pp. 83-91.

Mann, M. (1973), *Consciousness and Action among the Western Working Class*, Macmillan, London.

Marciniak, P. (1990), 'Horyzont programowy strajków 1980r.' (The program horizon of 1980 strikes), in P. Marciniak and W. Modzelewski (eds), *Studia nad ruchami społecznymi, II.* (Studies on social movements, II), Uniwersytet Warszawski - Instytut Socjologii, Warsaw, pp. 131-200.

Marcinowski, A. (1998), 'Praktyka socjalizacji i kultura organizacyjna w firmach prywatnych' (Socialization practice and organisational culture in private firms), in W. Kozek and J. Kulpińska (eds), *Zbiorowe stosunki pracy w Polsce. Obraz zmian* (Industrial relations in Poland. A picture of changes), Scholar, Warsaw, pp. 91-108.

Marginson, P. *et al.* (1988), *Beyond the Workplace: Managing Industrial Relations in Multi-Establishments Enterprises*, Blackwell, Oxford.

Marini, D. (ed) (1997), *I lavoratori dipendenti in Italia: opinioni e orientamenti*, Fondazione Corazzin, Venice.

Marschall, G. (1983), 'Some Remarks on the Study of Working-Class Consciousness', *Politics and Society*, no. 3, pp. 263-301.

Martell, L. and Stammers, N. (1996), 'The Study of Solidarity and the Social Theory of Alain Touraine', in J. Clark and M. Diani (eds), *Alain Touraine*, Falmer Press, London, pp. 127-43.

Martin, R. (1987), *Langage et croyance. Les univers de croyance dans la théorie sémantique*, P. Mardaga, Brussels.

Martinet, G. (1979), *Sept syndicalismes*, Seuil Paris.

Marx, K. (1847), *Misère de la philosophie*, Paris-Bruxelles.

Marx, K. (1852), 'Der Achzehnte Brumaire von Louis Bonaparte', *Die Revolution*, no. 1.

Marx, K. and Engels, F. (1845-1846/1932), *Die deutsche Ideologie*, Berlin.

Marx, K. and Engels, F. (1848), *Manifest der Kommunistischen Partei*, London.

Maslow, A. (1954), *Motivation and Personality*, Harper and Row, New York.

Meardi, G. (1993), *L'inserimento lavorativo dei disabili psichici. Due progetti mirati nelle municipalizzate milanesi*, Tesi di laurea in Scienze Politiche, Università degli Studi di Milano, Milan.

Meardi, G. (1996), 'Trade Union Consciousness, East and West: A Comparison of Fiat Factories in Poland and Italy', *European Journal of Industrial Relations*, vol. 2, no. 3, pp. 275-302.

Meardi, G. (1998), 'Stosunki przemysłowe w polskich zakładach firm międzynarodowych' (Industrial relations in the Polish plants of multinational companies), in W. Kozek and J. Kulpińska (eds), *Zbiorowe stosunki pracy w Polsce. Obraz zmian* (Industrial relations in Poland. A picture of changes), Scholar, Warsaw, pp. 26-40.

Méda, D. (1995), *Le travail: une valeur en voie de disparition*, Aubier, Paris.

Mehl, R. (1993), *Fiat Auto. Struktur schlägt Strategie. Aufstieg und Fall eines autoritär geführten Unternehmens*, Sigma, Berlin.

Merton, R.K. (1966), *Social Theory and Social Structure*, Free Press, New York.

Michnik, A. (1990), *La deuxième révolution*, La Découverte, Paris.

Milanaccio, A. (1982), 'Gli orientamenti politico-sindacali dei bioccupati', in L. Gallino (ed), *Occupati e bioccupati. Il doppio lavoro nell'area torinese*, Il Mulino, Bologna, pp. 297-323.

Milbrath, L.W. (1965), *Political Partecipation*, Rand McNally, Chicago.

Milic-Czerniak, R. (ed) (1998), *Gospodarstwa domowe w krajach Europy Środkowej. Skutki przemian 1990-95* (Households in the Central European Countries. The effects of changes 1990-1995), IFiS PAN, Warsaw.

Milkman, R. (1997), *Farewell to the Factory. Auto Workers in the Late Twentieth Century*, University of California Press, Los Angeles.

Milkman, R. (1998), 'The New American Workplace: High Road or Low Road?', in P. Thompson and C. Warhust (eds), *Workplaces of the Future*, Macmillan, London, pp. 25-39

Misztal, B. and Wasilewski, J. (1986) 'Les vainqueurs et les vaincus: la Pologne après décembre 1981', *Life Stories/Récits de vie*, no. 2, pp. 21-33.

Mitchell, J.C. (1983), 'Cases and Situation Analysis', *Sociological Review*, vol. 27, no. 2, pp. 187-211.

Mucchielli, A. (1991), *Les méthodes qualitatives*, Presses Universitaires de France, Paris.

Müller, F. and Purcell, J. (1992), 'The Europeanisation of Manufacturing and the Decentralisation of Bargaining', *International Journal of Human Resource Management*, vol. 3, no. 1, pp. 15-34.

Musso, S. (1995), 'Production Methods and Industrial Relations at Fiat (1930-1990)', in H. Shiomi and K. Wada (eds), *Fordism Transformed. The Development of Production Methods in the Automobile Industry*, Oxford University Press, Oxford, pp. 243-68.

Musso, S. (1999), 'Le relazioni industriali alla Fiat', in C. Annibaldi and G. Berta (eds), *Fabrica e grande impresa. Studi per il centenario della Fiat*, Il Mulino, Bologna.

Negri, T. (1997), 'La banlieu postmoderna', *DeriveApprodi*, no. 14, p. 12.

Nollert, M. (1995), 'Neocorporatism and Political Protest in the Western Democracies: A Cross-National Analysis', in J.C. Jenkins and B. Klandermand (ed), *The Politics of Social Protest*, University of Minnesota Press, Minneapolis, pp. 138-64.

Nowak, S. (1979), 'System wartości społeczeństwa polskiego' (The values system of Polish society), *Studia socjologiczne*, no. 4, pp. 155-73.

Oakeley, A. (1981), 'Interviewing Women: a Contradiction in Terms', in H. Roberts (ed), *Doing Feminist Research*, Routledge, London.

Offe, C. (1972), *Strukturprobleme des kapitalistischen Staates*, Suhrkamp, Frankfurt a.M..

Offe, C. (1985), *Disorganized Capitalism: Contemporary Transformation of Work and Politics*, Polity Press, Cambridge.

Offe, C. (1994), *Der Tunnel am Ende des Lichtes. Erkundungen der politischen Transformationen im Neuen Osten*, Campus, Frankfurt a.M./New York.

Offe, C. and Wiesenthal, H. (1980), 'Two Logics of Collective Action: Theoretical Notes on Social Class and Organisational Form', *Political Power and Social Theory*, no. 1, pp. 67-115.

Ogien, A. (1987), *Le parler frais d'Erving Goffman*, Minuit, Paris.

Ollivier, B. (1996), *L'acteur et le sujet*, Desclée de Brouwer, Paris.

Olmo, C. (ed) (1997), *Mirafiori 1936-1962*, Allemandi, Turin.

Olson, M. (1982), *The Rise and Decline of Nations*, Yale University Press, London.

O' Reilly, J. and Spee, C. (1998), 'The Future of Regulation of Work and Welfare: Time for a Revised Social and Gender Contract?', *European Journal of Industrial Relations*, vol. 4, no. 3, pp. 259-81.

Osa, M. (1997), 'Creating Solidarity: The Religious Foundations of the Polish Social Movement', *East European Politics and Societies*, vol. 11, no. 2, 339-65.

Ost, D. (1990), *Solidarity and the Politics of Anti-Politics*, Temple University Press, Philadephia.

Ost, D. (1994), 'Class and the Organisation of Anger in Post-Communist Poland', *EMERGO*, vol. 1, no. 2, pp. 116-29.

Ost, D. (1995), 'Labor, Class and Democracy: Shaping Political Antagonism in Post-Communist Societies', in B. Crawford, *Markets, States and Democracy*, Westview Press, Boulder, pp. 177-203.

Ost, D. (1996), 'Polish Labor before and after Solidarity', *International Labor and Working-Class History*, no. 50, pp. 29-43.

Ost, D. and Weinstein, M. (1999), 'Unionists Against Unions: Towards Hierarchical Management in Post-Communist Poland', *East European Politics and Societies*, vol. 13, no. 1, pp. 1-33.

Pakulski, J. (1993), 'Mass Social Movements and Social Class', *International Sociology*, vol. 8, no. 2, pp. 131-58.

Pańków, W. (1990), 'L'entreprise polonaise collectivisée. Diagnostic et éléments de prévision', in CNRS-IRESCO, *Modernisation des entreprises en France et en Pologne dans les années 1980*, Travaux Sociologiques du LSCI, Paris.

Pańków, W. (1993), *Work Institutions in Transformation. The Case of Poland 1990-92*, Friedrich Ebert Stiftung, Warsaw.

Pańków, W. (1999), 'Funkcje związków zawodowych w zakładach pracy' (The functions of trade unions in the workplaces), in J. Gardawski, B. Gąciarz, A. Mokrzyszewski and W. Pańków, *Rozpad bastionu? Związki zawodowe w gospodarce prywatyzowanej* (The fall of the bastion? Trade unions in the privatised economy), Instytut Spraw Publicznych, Warsaw, pp. 163-208.

Parkin, F. (1971/1973), *Class Inequality and Political Order*, MacGibbon and Kee Ltd., London.

Parkin, F. (1980), 'Reply to Giddens', *Theory and Society*, vol. 9, no. 6, pp. 891-94.

Passerini, L. (1984), *Torino operaia e fascismo. Una storia orale*, Laterza, Bari.

Passerini, L. (1988), *Storia e soggettività*, La Nuova Italia, Firenze.

Pasture, P. and Verberckmoes, J. (eds) (1998), *Working-Class Internationalism and the Appeal of National Identity*, Berg, Oxford.

Penn, S. (1994), 'The National Secret', *Journal of Women's History*, vol. 5, no. 3, pp. 55-69.

Perdue, W. (1995), *Paradox of Change. The Rise and the Fall of Solidarity in the New Poland*, Praeger, Westport.

Perna, T. (1997), 'Albania. Una moderna economia di rapina', *Il manifesto*, 11 February, p. 19.

Perna, T. (1998), 'Un camino para Tirana', *Cuadernos Africa América Latina*, no. 30.

Pero, L. (1998), 'The case of Fiat-Sata at Melfi', in MIP, *Participation and Joint Training in European Automotive Industry: Trade Union-Enterprise Committees*, Litogì, Milan, pp. 189-208.

Perotti, P. and Revelli, M. (1987), *Fiat autunno '80. Per non dimenticare*, Cric, Turin.

304   *Trade Union Activists, East and West*

Pessa, P. (2000), 'La "Terziarizzazione" in FIAT', *L'Unità*, 15 February.
Pessa, P. and Sartirano, L. (eds) (1993), *FIAT Auto. Ricerca sull'innovazione dei modelli organizzativi*, FIOM CGIL Piemonte, Turin.
Pharo, P. (1985), 'Problèmes empiriques de la sociologie compréhensive', *Revue française de sociologie*, vol. 26, no.1, pp. 120-49.
Pickels, J. and Smith, A. (eds) (1998), *Theorising Transition: The Political Economy of Post-Communist Transformation*, Routledge, London.
Pimenta, M.S. (1996), *Le tournant de la Fiat Mineira; travail, imaginaire et citoyenneté dans l'expérience des travailleurs*, Thèse de doctorat, Paris I, Paris.
Piontkowski, U., Öhlschlegel-Hanbrock, S. and Hölker, P. (1997), 'Annäherung oder Abgrenzung? Ergebnisse einer Längschnittstudie zur Wirksamkeit der Ost-West Kategorie', *Zeitschrift für Soziologie*, vol. 26, no. 2, pp. 128-38.
Pirdas, J. (1997), 'Le sujet au travail et dans l'entreprise, in G. Bajoit and E. Belin, *Contributions à une sociologie du sujet*, L'Harmattan, Paris, pp. 227-44.
Pizzorno, A. (1966), 'Introduzione allo studio della partecipazione politica', *Quaderni di sociologia*, vol. 10, no. 3-4, pp. 235-87.
Pizzorno, A., Regalia, I., Regini, M. and Reyneri, E. (1978), *Lotte operaie e sindacato in Italia: 1968-1972*, Il Mulino, Bologna.
Pizzorno, A. (1985), 'On the Rationality of Democratic Choice', *Telos*, no. 63, pp. 41-69.
Ploszajki, P. (1995), 'Polish Reform: the Fine Art of Learning and Forgetting', in B. Grancelli (ed), *Social Change and Modernization*, De Gruyter, New York, pp. 197-211.
Pochet, P. (1998), 'Les pactes sociaux en Europe dans les années 1990', *Sociologie du travail*, vol. 38, no. 2, pp. 173-90.
Polanyi, K. (1944), *The Great Transformation*, Beacon P, Boston.
Pollert, A. (1999), *Transformation at Work*, Sage, London.
Polo, G. (1989), *I tamburi di Mirafiori. Testimonianze operaie attorno all'autunno caldo alla Fiat*, Cric, Turin.
Poprzęcki, D. (1999), *Stanowiska europejskich związków zawodowych wobec swobodniego przepływu osób* (Opinions of the European trade unions on the free people movement), Instytut Spraw Publicznych, Warsaw.
Poznański, K. (1996), *Poland's Protracted Transition. Institutional Change and Economic Growth, 1970-1994*, Cambridge University Press, Cambridge.
Price, R. (1983), 'The Labour Process and Labour History', *Social History*, no. 8, pp. 57-75.
Przeworski, A. (1985), *Capitalism and Social Democracy*, Cambridge University Press, Cambridge.
Radźko, A. (1981), 'Członkowie 'Solidarności' o związku i sprawach kraju' (Solidarity members on the union and the country), in OBS, *Niepodległość pracy* (Work independence), NSZZ Solidarność Region Mazowsze, Warsaw, pp. 136-47.
Raymond, H. (1968), 'Analyse de contenu et entretien non directif: application au symbolisme de l'habitat', *Revue Française de sociologie*, vol. 9, no. 2, pp. 167-79.

Reading, A. (1992), *Polish Women, Solidarity and Feminism*, Macmillan, London.

Rebughini, P. (1998), 'La comparazione qualitativa di oggetti complessi e gli effetti della riflessività', in A. Melucci (ed), *Verso una sociologia riflessiva*, Il Mulino, Bologna, pp. 219-41.

Regalia, I. (1984), *Eletti e abbandonati. Modelli e stili di rappresentanza in fabbrica*, Il Mulino, Bologna.

Regalia, I. (ed) (1998), *Regioni e relazioni industriali in Europa*, Angeli, Milan.

Regalia, I. and Regini, M. (1997), 'Employers, Unions and the State: The Resurgence of Concertation in Italy?', *West European Politics*, vol. 20, no. 1, pp. 210-30.

Regalia, I. and Regini, M. (1998), 'Italy: The Dual Character of Industrial Relations', in A. Ferner and R. Hyman (eds), *Changing Industrial Relations in Europe*, Blackwell, Oxford, 459-503.

Regini, M. (1981), *I dilemmi del sindacato*, Il Mulino, Bologna.

Regini, M. (1997), 'Still Engaging in Corporatism? Recent Italian Experience in Comparative Perspective', *European Journal of Industrial Relations*, vol. 3, no. 3, pp. 259-78.

Reutter, W. (1996), 'Trade Unions and Politics in Eastern and Central Europe: Tripartism without Corporatism', in P. Pasture, J. Verberckmoes and H. De Witte (eds), *The Lost Perspective?*, Avebury, Aldershot, Vol.2, pp. 137-57.

Revelli, M. (1989), *Lavorare in Fiat. Da Valletta ad Agnelli a Romiti: operai, sindacati, robot*, Garzanti, Milan.

Revelli, M. (1996), 'Worker Identity in the Factory Desert', in M. Hardt and P. Virno (eds), *Radical Thought in Italy. A Potential Politics*, University of Minnesota Press, Minneapolis, pp. 114-19.

Rieser, V. (1992), 'La FIAT e la nuova fase della razionalizzazione', *Quaderni di sociologia*, vol. 36, no. 3, pp. 35-62.

Rieser, V. (1996), 'La fabbrica integrata "realizzata"', *Finesecolo*, vol. 2, no. 3-4, pp. 27-99.

Rieser, V. (1997), *Lavorare a Melfi*, Calice Editori, Rionero.

Rifkin, J. (1995), *The End of Work*. Putnam, New York.

Roberts, E. (1984), *A Woman's Place. An Oral History of Working-Class Women 1890-1940*, Blackwell, Oxford.

Robinson, W.S. (1951), 'The Logical Structure of Analytical Induction', *American Sociological Review*, vol. 16, pp. 812-18.

Rogers, C. (1945), 'The Non-Directive Method as a Technique of Social Research', *American Journal of Sociology*, vol. 51, no. 4, pp. 279-83.

Roll, Z. (1988), 'Přístupy ke zkoumami jazika v tzv. Interpretativni sociologii', (Approaches to language research in so-called interpretative sociology), *Sociologický Časopis*, vol. 25, no. 5, pp. 518-28.

Rolle, P. (1995), 'Trois entreprises dans la Province Russe', *Le travail à l'Est*, no. 2.

Rolle, P. (1998), *Le travail dans les révolutions russes*. Page deux, Lausanne.

Rollier, M. (1986), 'Changes of industrial relations at Fiat', in O. Jacobi, B. Jessop, H. Kastendiek and M. Regini (eds), *Technological change, rationalisation and industrial relations*, Croom Helm, London, pp. 116-34.

Romano, O. (1997), 'La demodernizzazione. Un'indagine sul mutamento socio-culturale dell'Albania', *Rassegna italiana di sociologia*, vol. 38, no. 3, pp. 313-42.

Rosanvallon, P. (1988), *La question syndicale*, Hachette, Paris.

Rose, M. (1987), 'Economic Nationalism Versus Class Solidarity: The Perspective of Active Trade Union Members', in G. Spyropoulos (ed), *Trade Unions Today and Tomorrow. Vol I: Trade Unions in a Changing Europe*, Presses Universitaires Europeéennes, Maastricht, pp. 179-98.

Ross, R. and Trachte, K. (1990), *Global Capitalism: The New Leviathan*, State University of New York Press, Albany.

Roy, D. (1952), 'Quota Restriction and Goldbricking in a Machine Shop', *American Journal of Sociology*, vol. 57, pp. 427-42.

Rubery, J. and Fagan, C. (1995), 'Comparative Industrial Relations: Towards Reversing the Gender Bias', *British Journal of Industrial Relations*, vol. 33, no. 2, pp. 209-36.

Rueschemeyer, D., Stephens, E.H. and Stephens, J.D. (1992), *Capitalist Development & Democracy*, Polity Press, Cambridge.

Ruszkowski, P. (1991), *Struktury organizacyjne ruchu samorządów pracowniczych w latach 1981-1990* (Organisational structures of the worker self-government movement in the years 1981-1990), Instytut badawczy samorządu załogi, Warsaw.

Rutkevitch, E.D. (1990), 'Fenomenologicheskaya sotsiologiya P. Bergera', (The phenomenological sociology of Peter Berger), *Sotsiologicheskie Issledovanija*, vol. 17, no. 7, pp. 119-27.

Rychard, A. (1988), 'Pouvoir et économie: trois perspectives théoriques', in Adamski, W. *et al.* (eds), *La Pologne en temps de crise*, Méridiens Klincksieck, Paris.

Sabel, C. (1982), *Work and Politics. The Division of Labour in Industry*, Cambridge University Press, Cambridge.

Sachs, J. (1994), *Poland's Jump to the Market Economy*, MIT Press, Cambridge.

Sainsaulieu, R. (1990), *L'entreprise, une affaire de société*, Presses de la FNSP, Paris.

Santielli, G. (1987), 'L'évolution des relations industrielles chez Fiat: 1969-1985', *Travail et emploi*, no. 31, pp. 27-36.

Schienstock, G. and Traxler, F. (1993), 'Von der stalinistischen zur marktvermittelten Konvergenz? Zur Transformation der Struktur und Politik der Gewerkschaften in Osteuropa', *Kölner Zeitschrift für Soziologie und Sozialpsychologie*, vol. 45, no. 3, pp. 484-506.

Schmitter, P. (1974), 'Still the Century of Corporatism?', *The Review of Politics*, vol. 36, no. 1, pp. 85-131.

Schmitter, P. (1981), 'Interest Intermediation and Regime Governability in Contemporary Western Europe and North America', in S. Berger (ed),

Organizing Interests in Western Europe, Cambridge University Press, Cambridge, pp. 287-330.

Schulten, T. (1996), 'European Works Councils: Prospects for a New System of European Industrial Relations', *European Journal of Industrial Relations*, vol. 2, no. 3, pp. 303-24.

Scott, A. (1991), 'Action, Movement and Intervention: Reflection on the Sociology of Alain Touraine', *Canadian Review of Sociology and Anthropology*, vol. 28, no. 1, pp. 30-45.

Seideneck, P. (1993), 'Vertiefung oder Erweiterung? Zur aktuellen Problemen der Europäischen Gewerkschaftspolitik', *Gewerkschaftliche Monatshefte*, no. 9, pp. 543-52.

Shorter, E. and Tilly, C. (1974), *Strikes in France, 1830-1968*, Cambridge University Press, Cambridge.

Silverman, D. (1993), *Interpreting Qualitative Data*, Sage, London.

Simmel, G. (1908), *Soziologie*, Duncker & Humblot, Berlin.

Simpson, H. (1989), 'The Sociology of Work: Where Have the Workers Gone?' *Social Forces*, vol. 67, no.3, pp. 563-81.

Soufflet, G. (1998), *De l'autogestion au libéralisme. Trajets d'entreprises, en Pologne, à la fin du communisme*, Mémoire de D.E.A. en sociologie, E.H.E.S.S., Paris.

Staniszkis, J. (1984), *Poland's Self-Governing Revolution*, Princeton University Press, Princeton.

Staniszkis, J. (1989), *Ontologia socjalizmu* (Socialism's ontology), In Plus, Warsaw.

Staniszkis, J. (1991), *The Dynamics of Breakthrough in Eastern Europe. The Polish Experience*, University of California Press, Los Angeles.

Stanojevic. M. (1999), *Successful Immaturity: Communist Legacies in the Market Context. Comparing Industrial Relations in Slovenia and Hungary*, Paper presented at the international conference 'David or Goliath: Trade unions and the workers' movement in East-central Europe after communism', Warsaw, May 27-29.

Stark, D. (1992), 'From System Identity to Organizational Diversity: Analyzing Social Change in Eastern Europe', *Sisyphus*, vol. 8, no. 1, pp. 77-86.

Stark, D. (1996), 'Recombinant Property in East European Capitalism', *American Journal of Sociology*, vol. 102, no. 4, pp. 993-1027.

Stepan-Norris, J. and Zeitlin, M. (1996), *Talking Union*, University of Illinois Press, Urbana.

Steeck, W. (1998), 'The Internationalization of Industrial Relations in Europe: Prospects and Problems', *Politics & Societies*, vol. 26, no. 4, pp. 429-59.

Strauss, K.M. (1997), *Factory and Community in Stalin's Russia. The Making of an Industrial Working-Class*, University of Pittsbourgh Press, Pittsbourgh.

Supiot, A. (ed) (1999), *Au-delà de l'emploi*, Flammarion, Paris.

Sylos Labini, P. (1975), *Saggio sulle classi sociali in Italia*, Laterza, Bari.

Szakolczai, A. (1996), *In a Permanent State of Transition: Theorising the East European Condition*, EUI Working Paper SPS, 96/9.

Szczepański, M.S. (1993), 'A New "Socialist City" in the Upper Silesian Industrial Region', in M.S. Szczepański (ed), *Dilemmas of Regionalism and the Region of Dilemmas. The Case of Upper Silesia*, Uniwersytet Śląski, Katowice, pp. 142-61.

Szelényi, I., Fodor, É. and Harley, E. (1997), 'Left Turn in Postcommunist Politics: Bringing Class Back in?', *East European Politics and Societies*, vol. 11, no. 1, pp. 190-224.

Sztompka, P. (1993), 'Civilizational Incompetence: The Trap of Post-Communist Societies', *Zeitschrift für Soziologie*, vol. 22, no. 2, 85-95.

Tannenbaum, F. (1951), *A Philosophy of Labor*, Alfred Knopf, New York.

Tarrow, S. (1994), *Social Movements in Europe: Movement Society or Europeanization of Conflict?*, EUI Working Paper RSC, 94/8.

Tatò, S. (ed) (1981), *A voi cari compagni. La militanza sindacale ieri e oggi. La parole ai protagonisti*, De Donato, Bari.

Tatur, M. (1989), *Solidarność als Modernisierungsbewegung: Sozialstruktur und Konflikt in Polen*, Campus, Frankfurt a.M.

Tatur, M. (1995), 'Towards Corporatism? The Transformation of Interest Policy and Interest Regulation in Eastern Europe', in E.J. Dittrich, G. Schmidt and R. Whitley (eds), *Industrial Transformation in Europe*, Sage, London, pp. 163-84.

Therborn, G. (1995), *European Modernity and Beyond. The Trajectory of European Societies 1945-2000*, Sage, London.

Thomas, W. and Znaniecki, F. (1927), *The Polish Peasant in Europe and America*, Alfred Knopf, New York.

Thompson, E.P. (1963), *The Making of the English Working Class*, Gollancz, London.

Thompson, E.P. (1978), *Poverty of Theory*, Martin, London.

Thompson, P. and Traxler, F. (1997), 'The Transformation of Industrial Relations in Post-socialist Economies', in G. Schienstock, P. Thompson and F. Traxler (eds), *Industrial Relations Between Command and Market*, Nova Science Publisher Inc., New York, pp. 291-314.

Thuderoz, C. (1995), 'Du lien social dans l'entreprise', *Revue Française de Sociologie*, vol. 36, no. 2, pp. 325-54.

Tilly, C. (1995), 'Globalization Threatens Labor's Rights', *International Labor and Working Class History*, no. 47, pp. 1-23.

Timko, C. (1996), *The 1992-93 strike wave and the disorganization of worker interests in Poland*, Paper presented at the 1996 annual meeting of the American political association.

Tischner, J. (1984), *The Spirit of Solidarity*, Harper and Row, London.

Tischner, J. (1992), *Etyka solidarności oraz Homo Sovieticus* (The Ethics of Solidarity and the Homo Sovieticus), Znak, Cracow.

Tismaneanu, V. (1996), 'The Leninist Debris or Waiting for Peron', *East European Politics and Societies*, vol. 10, no. 3, pp. 504-35.

Titkow, A. (1998), 'Polish Women in Politics', in M. Rueschemeyer (ed), *Women in the Politics of Postcommunist Eastern Europe*, M.E. Sharpe, London, pp. 24-32.

Tixier, P.E. (1992), *Déclin ou mutation du syndicalisme? Le cas de la CFDT*, Presses Universitaires de France, Paris.

Tobiasz, A. (1999), 'Kobiety w Solidarności' (Women in Solidarity), *Biuletin Ośka*, no. 3.

Tóth, A. (1996a), 'Suzuki in Ungarn: Depression statt Kompromissuche', in R. Deppe and M. Tatur (eds), *Ökonomische Transformation und gewerkschaftliche Politik: Umbruchprozesse in Polen und Ungarn auf Branchenebene*, Westfälisches Dampfboot, Münster, pp. 171-207.

Tóth, A. (1996b), 'GM-Hungary: Eine Gewerkschaft in der Zwickmuehle zwischen Management und Betriebsrat', in R. Deppe and M. Tatur (eds), *Ökonomische Transformation und gewerkschaftliche Politik: Umbruchprozesse in Polen und Ungarn auf Branchenebene*, Westfälisches Dampfboot, Münster, pp. 208-41.

Touraine, A. (1966), *La conscience ouvrière*, Seuil, Paris.

Touraine, A. (1977), *The Self-Production of Society*, Chicago University Press, Chicago.

Touraine, A. (1981), *The Voice and the Eye: An Analysis of Social Movements*, Cambridge University Press, Cambridge.

Touraine, A. (1995), *Critique of Modernity*, Blackwell, Oxford.

Touraine, A. (1996), 'Passato e futuro della sociologia del lavoro', *Sociologia del lavoro*, no. 61, pp. 91-104.

Touraine, A. (1997), *Pourrons-nous vivre ensemble? Egaux et différents*, Fayard, Paris.

Touraine, A., Dubet, F., Wieviorka, M. and Strzelecki, J. (1983), *Solidarity*, Cambridge University Press, Cambridge.

Touraine, A., Dubet, F. and Wieviorka, M. (1987), *The Workers' Movement*, Cambridge University Press, Cambridge.

Trentin, B. (1994), *Lavoro e libertà*, Donzelli, Rome.

Turner, L. (1996), 'The Europeanization of Labour: Structure before Action'. *European Journal of Industrial Relations*, vol. 2, no. 3, pp. 325-44.

Tymowski, A. (1991), 'Workers vs. Intellectuals in Solidarnosc', *Telos*, no. 90, pp. 165-66.

Valkenburg, B. (1996), 'Individualization and Solidarity: the Challenge of Modernization', in P. Leisink, J. Van Leemput and J. Vilrokx (eds), *The Challenges to Trade Unions in Europe. Innovation or Adaptation*, Elgar, Cheltenham, pp. 89-104.

van der Lippe, T. and Fodor, E. (1998), 'Changes in Gender Inequalities in Six Eastern European Countries', *Acta Sociologica*, vol. 17, no. 2, pp. 131-49.

Vaughan-Whitehead, D. (ed) (1998), *Paying the Price: the Wage Crisis in Central and Eastern Europe*, Macmillan, Basigstoke.

Viacelli, L. (1994), *La mobilità ideale. Gervais Danone italiana: un caso di outplacement*, Edizioni Lavoro, Rome.

Visser, J. (1995), 'Trade Unions from a Comparative Perspective', in R. Huiskamp, J. Van Hoeh and J. Van Ruysseveldt, *Comparative Industrial and Employment Relations*, Sage, London, pp. 37-67.

Volpato, G. (1996), *Il caso Fiat. Una strategia di riorganizzazione e di rilancio*, Isedi, Turin.

Von Hirschhausen, C. (1996), *Du combinat socialiste à l'entreprise capitaliste, une analyse des réformes industrielles en Europe de l'Est*, L'Harmattan, Paris.

Voß, G. (1994), 'Das Ende der Teilung von "Arbeit und Leben"? An der Schwelle zu einem neuen gesellschaftlichen Verhältnis von Betriebs- und Lebensführung', in N. Beckenbach and W. van Treeck (eds), *Umbrüche gesellschaftlicher Arbeit*, Soziale Welt, Sonderband 9, Göttingen.

Wałęsa, L. (1987), *Un chemin d'espoir*, Fayard, Paris.

Weller, J.M. (1994), 'Le mensonge d'Ernest Cigare. Problèmes épistémologiques et méthodologiques à propos de l'identité au travail', *Sociologie du travail*, vol. 34, no. 1, pp. 25-42.

Wiaderny, J. (1999), 'Temu rządowi nie odpuścimy' (We do not forgive this government), *Trybuna*, 25 May, p. 10.

Wieviorka, M. (1984), *Les Juifs en Pologne et Solidarité*, Denöel, Paris.

Wieviorka, M. (1988), *Société et terrorisme*, Fayard, Paris.

Wieviorka, M. (1992), 'Analyse sociologique et historique de l'antisémitisme en Pologne', *Cahiers Internationaux de Sociologie*, no. 93, pp. 237-49.

Wieviorka, M. (1995), *The Arena of Racism*, Sage, London.

Wieviorka, M. (1998), 'Actualité et futur de l'engagement', in M. Wieviorka (ed), *Raison et conviction: l'engagement*, Textuel, Paris, 9-49.

Williams, C.L. (1989), *Gender Differences at Work*, University of California Press, Berkeley.

Willis, P. (1977), *Learning to Labour. How Working Class Kids Get Working Class Jobs*, Columbia University Press, New York.

Winiecki, J. (1998), *Institutional Barriers to Economic Development: Poland's Incomplete Transition*, Routledge, London.

Wittel, A. (1998), 'Gruppenarbeit und Arbeitshabitus', *Zeitschrift für Soziologie*, vol. 27, no. 3, pp. 178-92.

Womack, J.P., Jones, D.T. and Roos, D. (1990), *The Machine that Changed the World*, Macmillan, New York.

Wright, E.O. (1976), 'Class Boundaries in Advanced Capitalist Societies', *New Left Review*, no. 98, pp. 3-42.

Yow, V. (1994), *Recording Oral History: A Practical Guide for Social Scientists*, Sage, London.

Zaslavskij, V. (1995), 'Contemporary Russian Society and its Soviet Legacy: the Problem of State-Dependent Workers', in B. Grancelli (ed), *Social Change and Modernization*, De Gruyter, New York, pp. 45-62.

Żbikowska, M. and van Kooten, G. (1990), 'Strajki w Ursusie w latach 1976-1980', (Strikes in Ursus in the 1976-1980 years), in J. Kulpińska (ed), *Studia nad ruchami społecznymi, IV: Raport PTS - Strajki 1980: Mazowsze, Ursus, Żyrardów, Gdańsk, Szczecin, Wrocław* (Studies on social movements, IV: PTS Raport - Strikes 1980: Mazowsze, Ursus, Żyrardów, Gdańsk, Szczecin, Wrocław), Uniwersytet Warszawski - Instytut Socjologii - Polskie Towarzystwo Socjologiczne, Warsaw, pp. 37-52.

Zoll, R. (1978), *Der Doppelcharakter der Gewerkschaften*, Suhrkamp Verlag, Frankfurt a.M.
Zoll, R. (1992), *Nouvel individualisme et solidarité quotidienne*, Kimé, Paris.

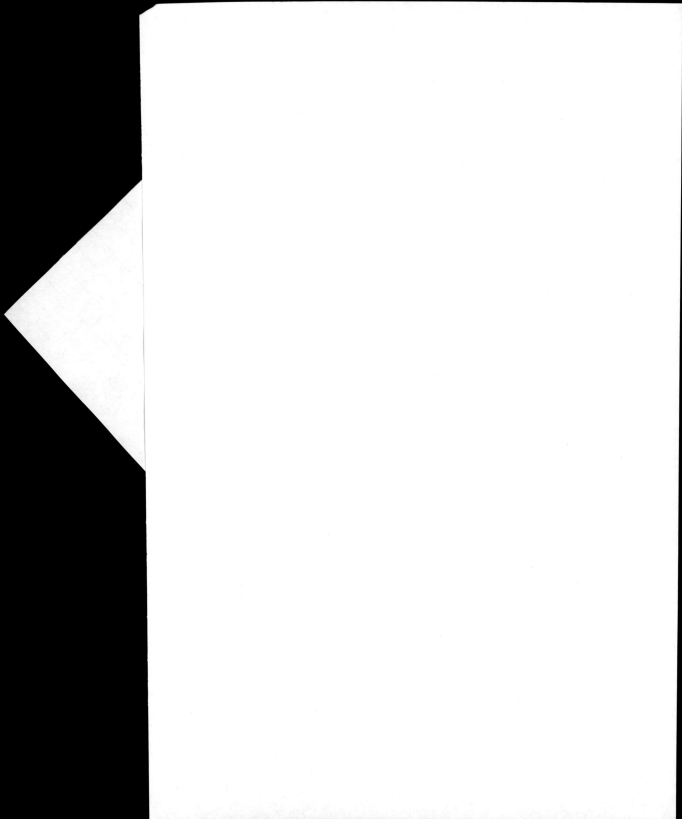

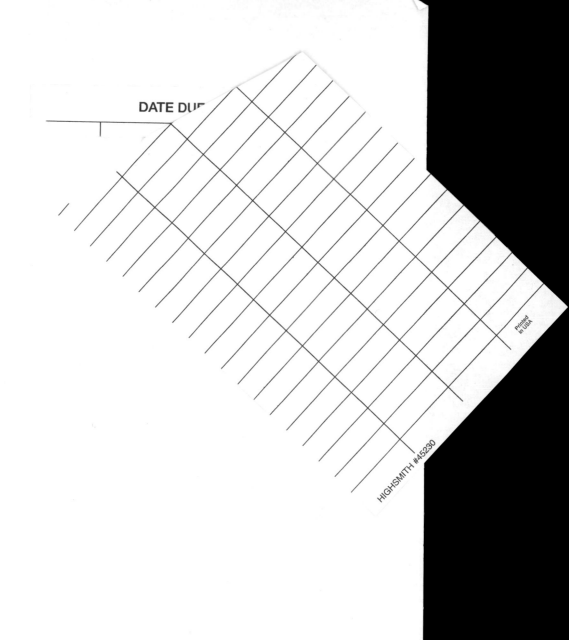

DATE DUE

HIGHSMITH #45230

Printed in USA